WHAT THEY BELIEVE

Dr. Harold J. Berry

Former Professor of Bible & Greek

Grace University

Omaha, Nebraska

What They Believe
Published by Back to the Bible
1987, 1988, 1989, 1990, 1992, 1997, 2006 by Harold J. Berry

Unless otherwise noted, all Scripture is taken from the New King James Version®. Copyright © 1982 by Thomas Nelson, Inc. Used by permission. All rights reserved.

Project editor: Rachel Derowitsch
Cover and interior design: Laura Poe
Cover photo: shutterstock.com

ISBN-10: 0-578-47409-3
ISBN-13: 978-0-578-47409-0

Printed in the United States of America.

To the students, alumni, faculty and staff
of Grace University,
whose friendship has greatly enriched my life.

Contents

Acknowledgments

More than 40 years ago I joined Back to the Bible's editorial staff, after spending two years in the organization's counseling department answering letters from listeners. Ernest E. Lott (1907–2001) was the associate editor of the *Good News Broadcaster* then. He had long wanted a series published on counterfeit religious groups and asked if I would write one. So began my long-standing interest in researching and writing about these various groups.

In those days I was fresh out of seminary and just beginning my professional ministry. Many young people do not have the opportunity to write for such a prestigious organization, nor someone like Mr. Lott—as I called him in those days—to believe in their ability to do so. I will always be indebted to Ernest Lott, who was the age of my father and who saw potential in my researching and writing abilities.

Also, Rachel Derowitsch is gratefully acknowledged for her editing skills and the good working relationship we had as we communicated in the process of revising and enlarging *What They Believe*.

Special thanks go to my wife of more than 50 years, Donna, who kept things running at home while I spent so much time researching and writing. She deserves far more credit than these simple lines can convey, not only for what she does but for who she is. She is an excellent example of a loving, godly wife, mother and grandmother.

Finally, special thanks to those friends who expressed concern and support and prayed for the completion of this important project.

May God be pleased to use *What They Believe* to warn readers not to become a part of these groups and to help believers answer the counterfeits.

—Harold J. Berry
Lincoln, Nebraska

What's New in This Edition

Each chapter in *What They Believe* has been revised by

- updating statistics where possible
- updating credentials of sources where possible
- researching sources published since 1997 to see if anything of significance concerning a group should be included
- adding sources in Recommended Reading

What They Believe has been enlarged by adding the following chapters:

- Muslims—chapter 6
- Roman Catholics—chapter 8
- Seventh-day Adventists—chapter 11

Introduction

Know what your neighbor believes; know what you believe. There is probably no greater need for the believer in the 21st century. Counterfeit religious groups are multiplying. Believers today must be alert for those who twist the truth of biblical Christianity. Even in the first century, Christians were commanded, "Do not believe every spirit" (1 John 4:1). That admonition is just as important for us today, for false systems of belief seem to be harder to discern because their differences from Christianity, and from each other, are more subtle.

To find out what your neighbor believes—whether that neighbor lives next door, sits at the next desk at the office or is in the next room in the college dorm—you need to know what questions to ask to get at the heart of his or her belief system. For this reason, this book follows a similar pattern for each group it evaluates. After giving a brief history about the group under discussion, I focus on the doctrinal beliefs of the group: the source of authority, God (especially Jesus Christ), sin, salvation and the future life. The emphasis of each of these topics varies somewhat with the particular group under discussion.

Although the background and characteristics of people in a religious group might be intriguing to consider, they do not in and of themselves make that group a spiritual counterfeit. Instead, it is the doctrinal beliefs that determine whether a group deviates from biblical Christianity.

Consider what this book is not saying: it is not suggesting that those who believe differently are not lovely people. We probably all have friends who believe something other than biblical Christianity, yet we consider them nice people whose friendships we enjoy.

Neither is this book suggesting that these groups do not do good for mankind. Some groups are aggressive in caring for the physical needs and self-improvement of others. *What They Believe*, however, is concerned about helping people for eternity, not just for time.

Neither is *What They Believe* distinguishing between differences among evangelical beliefs. The issue under consideration in this book is not whether one is premillennial or amillennial, dispensational or covenant in theology, for example, but whether one holds

What They Believe

to the basic beliefs of orthodoxy, emphasized in the subheadings in each chapter.

In the process of researching and writing, I sought to follow three guidelines:

1) as much as possible research the primary resources of the group; that is, those materials written by the leaders of the group for adherents to the group.

2) emphasize salvation by grace alone through faith alone in the Lord Jesus Christ alone, apart from works.

3) distinguish what an individual in the group believes from what the official teaching of the group is.

Some readers have charged that previous editions of *What They Believe* have not told the truth about what their particular group believes. This accusation may result from the followers not knowing the official teachings of their leaders. Just as some evangelical Christians are not knowledgeable about what biblical Christianity teaches, so some adherents to counterfeit Christianity groups do not know the official teachings of their groups.

This also explains why my main approach in evaluating the groups discussed in *What They Believe* was not to interview adherents of the groups but to research the writings of the leaders. Furthermore, I relied on printed material rather than spoken or taped messages because, for the most part, materials in print have been more carefully thought through and edited; therefore, they are considered more reliable in reflecting the author's precise meaning.

You will also notice one word missing from comments about groups in *What They Believe* (unless found in quotations from others). It is the word *cult*. This word has such varied meanings in the minds of readers that it is avoided in this book.

Someone may ask, "What is the common denominator in deciding which groups to include among those in *What They Believe*?" The answer is, "Any group whose *official* teaching will not lead a person to heaven." Such groups have twisted the truth by deviating from what the Bible teaches concerning Christ's deity and the way of salvation.

The material in *What They Believe* has grown out of writings that were originally produced to answer questions sent to Back to the Bible by its friends and radio listeners. At first the articles were made

12

available only in separate booklet form; then after a revision they were combined and published in 1977 in a volume entitled *Examining the Cults*. In yet a later revision they were put in a series and published in 1989 under the title *What They Believe*, and still later under the title *The Truth Twisters* (1992) and then simply as *Truth Twisters* (1997). The volume is once again being revised and enlarged and is renamed *What They Believe*.

There is nothing more heart-wrenching than talking with members of one of these counterfeit religious groups and having them respond as if you're talking about the same thing, or to look at you blankly as if they have never heard of evangelical Christianity. After saying all there is to be said, you know they reject the message that could give forgiveness of sin and eternal life. But praise the Lord there are exceptions.

On one occasion a father brought his teenage son to visit me in the office. The son was involved in The Way International. Rather than coming down hard on his beliefs, I sought to treat him with respect. I assured him that he was free to believe whatever he wanted to, even if he chose to believe Jesus Christ is not God. I reminded him that his belief would not affect me personally because I would have to stand before God to answer for myself. But I urged him to think it through carefully because I was convinced his eternal destiny was at stake. That day as he left with his father I prayed for him and wondered if I would ever hear from him again. What a relief it was later to hear that the son had trusted Christ as his Savior.

At the end of each chapter is a list of books and other resources called Recommended Reading. Most of these books are currently in print and can be found in Christian bookstores, or ordered through any bookstore. Regrettably, many excellent books on these groups are no longer in print. In your search for source materials, be sure to make use of public libraries that can locate books for you through Inter-Library Loan.

My prayer is that *What They Believe* will be of significant help as you "sanctify the Lord God in your hearts, and always be ready to give a defense to everyone who asks you a reason for the hope that is in you, with meekness and fear" (1 Pet. 3:15).

—Harold J. Berry
March 2019

CHAPTER ONE

Biblical Christianity

The World Almanac and Book of Facts reports that there are more than two billion Christians in the world.[1] But how are we to understand the word *Christians*?

A politician spoke, a woman prayed, a minister preached—they all had something in common: they used the name "God." But what did that mean? Was it spiritually significant or not? What did each individual mean by a reference to God?

Even more specific than a reference to God, what if someone says he believes in Christ—and perhaps adds that Christ is "in him"? Is the individual to be accepted as a fellow believer?

Some people might even say that Jesus Christ is the greatest teacher who ever lived. Does such a statement indicate the person is a believer in biblical Christianity?

We should not be suspicious and disbelieving of every statement another person makes, but neither should we be naive and gullible. Far too many people—even from Bible-teaching churches—jump to the wrong conclusions when someone uses such terms as *Christian, born again, God* and *Christ.*

Too many people think, for instance, that when they hear the name "God," that others are referring to the God of the Bible. But not necessarily so. The Masonic Lodge, for example, requires a person to acknowledge a belief in God before he can become a Mason. That statement sounds so good that it's hard to find fault with it. But which God is being referred to? Is it the god of the Hindus, the god of Islam, the god of Christian Science, the God of the Bible—or another God? A study of the sources published by the leaders of

What They Believe

Freemasonry reveals that it is not necessary to define which "God" one believes in as long as allegiance is pledged to the Masonic Lodge. (See the chapter on Masons.)

What about those who refer to "Christ"? The Bible is the source of authority concerning who the Lord Jesus Christ is, but some people use the name "Christ" to refer to something entirely different. Groups such as Christian Science, New Age and Unity School of Christianity do not view Christ as a person with intellect, emotions and will. They use the name to refer only to a "principle" that they say exists within all creation. So those who speak of "Christ within" may mean only that everyone has the Christic principle within them.

Other people view Jesus Christ as a person, but they believe He was only a man, not God. Groups such as the Jehovah's Witnesses, Unification Church, Unitarian Universalists and The Way International believe that Jesus Christ was a great man and a great teacher. They refuse to believe, however, that He was and is God.

WHO IS RIGHT? HOW DOES A PERSON DECIDE WHAT TO ACCEPT AS BIBLICAL CHRISTIANITY?

Who is right? And how does a person decide what is to be accepted as biblical Christianity?

The term *Christianity* has been used in widely differing ways. It was first used in the city of Antioch, the third-largest city in the Roman Empire during the first century (Acts 11:26). The word referred to one who belonged to Christ, or was His follower. The term also appears in Acts 26:28 and 1 Peter 4:16.

Still today, many people use the word *Christian* in a variety of ways. You might discover this when you ask someone, "Are you a Christian?" His response might be, "Of course I am. Do you think I'm a Buddhist?" Such a person would be using the term to distinguish Christianity from other world religions, such as Buddhism, Hinduism, Islam, Judaism or Shintoism.

Used in this broad sense, there are more than two billion Christians in the world. Many within these groups, however, do not adhere to what will later be described as biblical Christianity. The following chart compares the growth of groups within Christianity, as the term is used in the broadest sense.[2]

Adherents (in millions)			
GROUP	1995	2000	2005
Roman Catholics	1,042	1,026	1,092.80
Protestants	382	316	364
Eastern Orthodox	62.6	163	218
Anglicans	173	213	217
Others	195	NA	406

The term *Christianity* is also used in a more narrow sense to distinguish evangelical and biblical Christians from non-evangelical and non-biblical ones. Although there are various ways to define who evangelicals are, Richard V. Pierard, professor emeritus of history at Indiana State University (Terre Haute), says that in general the following can be considered true about the evangelical movement: "A modern Christian movement which transcends confessional and denominational boundaries to emphasize conformity to the basic principles of the Christian faith and a missionary outreach of compassion and urgency."[3]

Concerning the beliefs of evangelicalism, Pierard says, "An evangelical is one who believes and proclaims the gospel of Jesus Christ, the message that Christ died for human sins, was buried, and rose again on the third day in fulfillment of the prophetic Scriptures, thereby providing the means of redemption for sinful humanity (1 Cor. 15:1–4)."[4]

George Barna, directing leader of The Barna Group, defines biblical, or evangelical, Christians this way on his Web site:

> We categorize an "evangelical" based upon their answers to nine questions about faith matters. Those included in this segment meet the criteria for being born again; say their faith is very important in their life today; believe they have a personal responsibility to share their religious beliefs about Christ with non-Christians; believe that Satan exists; believe

that eternal salvation is possible only through grace, not works; believe that Jesus Christ lived a sinless life on earth; and describe God as the all-knowing, all-powerful, perfect deity who created the universe and still rules it today.[5]

Defining biblical Christianity in this manner, Barna's research indicates that evangelicals account for 7 percent of the U.S. population. That includes 14–16 million evangelical adults.[6]

For the purposes of this book, "biblical Christianity" will be defined as it is explained in this chapter under the headings of source of authority, God, the Trinity, Jesus Christ, the Holy Spirit, sin, salvation and future life.

Christianity, as its name implies, centers on Christ, or as He is more formally called, the Lord Jesus Christ. To understand Christianity, however—just as with other religions—it is necessary to understand its background.

BACKGROUND

The Old Testament, which contains 39 books, provides the background for Christianity. It records how God prepared the way for the coming of Christ. The first 11 chapters of Genesis refer to the way God worked with the world in general. He brought the world and mankind into existence (ch. 1–2). But man turned away from God and experienced death (ch. 3). This death was both spiritual (Eph. 2:1) and physical (Rom. 5:12). God saw that mankind's heart was evil continually, so He sent a flood and destroyed everything except Noah and his immediate family and what they took on the ark (Gen. 6–8).

After showing how God worked with the world in general, Genesis records how He began to work with and through one man. God called Abraham (also known as Abram) out of Ur of the Chaldees, a city in the ancient region of Sumer, now southeastern Iraq. God gave him specific promises, found in Genesis 12:1–3. He promised Abraham and his descendants a land (v. 1); a seed, or descendants (v. 2); and a blessing (vv. 2–3). This is commonly referred to as the Abrahamic Covenant.

Throughout the Old Testament, God used human authors to record His revelation concerning how He would provide salvation for the descendants of Abraham in particular and for the world in general.

The promised Redeemer was to come from the physical descendants of Abraham, known as "Hebrews" in the Old Testament (Gen. 14:13; 40:15). Abraham's grandson, Jacob, had his name changed to "Israel." As a result, Jacob's 12 sons and their descendants were commonly known by such expressions as "the children of Israel" or "Israelites." One of Jacob's sons was Judah, whose descendants were known as "Jews." (A descendant of Judah was not only a Jew but was also an Israelite and a Hebrew, because he was also a descendant of Jacob and Abraham, respectively.)

"In you," God promised Abraham, "all the families of the earth shall be blessed." The New Covenant, which further detailed the blessing aspect of the Abrahamic Covenant, promised the Israelites salvation. "They all shall know Me," said the LORD, "from the least of them to the greatest of them. For I will forgive their iniquity, and their sin I will remember no more" (Jer. 31:34). The Bible later reveals that salvation for the Jewish nation—and for all families of the earth—was possible because the Lord Jesus Christ entered the world through the physical seed of Abraham. This is why Jesus could tell the Samaritan woman who had come to draw water at Jacob's well, "Salvation is of the Jews" (John 4:22).

When He died on the cross to provide salvation for the Jewish nation, Jesus Christ also provided it for the entire world. "He Himself is the propitiation [satisfaction] for our sins," wrote the apostle John, "and not for ours only but also for the whole world" (1 John 2:2).

While the Old Testament provides the background for Christianity, the 27 books of the New Testament record its beginning and development. The New Testament tells of Jesus' birth, life, death and resurrection. Once again God used human authors to record His story. They tell how Christ fulfilled the prophecies of the Old Testament by providing salvation for the world. And they provide firsthand accounts of how Christ's followers told people everywhere how they could be saved by faith in Christ.

Having overviewed the background and beginning of historical Christianity, let us now focus on its doctrinal beliefs.

BELIEFS

During the time of the apostles—the chosen representatives of the Lord Jesus Christ—God gave revelation directly to them. In turn, they communicated these truths to the next generation. Before long, however, disputes arose as to what the Bible actually taught concerning itself, God, Jesus Christ, the Holy Spirit, sin and salvation. The following are commonly held beliefs of biblical Christianity in regard to these key doctrines.

SOURCE OF AUTHORITY

Biblical Christianity accepts the Bible—and the Bible alone—as its final source of authority. It is the standard by which all doctrines and practices are judged. The 39 books of the Old Testament and the 27 books of the New Testament are held to be inspired by God in the original manuscripts (Matt. 5:18; 2 Tim. 3:16; 2 Pet. 1:21). The Old Testament was written in Hebrew, the language of the Jewish people (with some portions in Aramaic). The New Testament was written in Greek, the universal language during Jesus' life on earth.

Some clarification is needed concerning what biblical Christianity does not claim to be inspired. It does not consider the human authors God used to write the Scriptures to be inspired. Being a God of miracles, God was able to guide fallible men in such a way that He produced an infallible record without destroying their personalities. Also, inspiration is not claimed for copies or translations made from the original manuscripts. Although the original manuscripts do not now exist, sufficient copies are available to reliably reconstruct the originals. This would be comparable today to dictating a letter to several others for them to copy and then losing the original letter. By collecting and comparing the available copies, one could quite accurately reconstruct what was in the original. Neither is one person's interpretation—or one church group's interpretation—considered to be the final authority. If that were the case, the interpretation and not the Bible would be the source of authority. Such a position is rejected by biblical Christianity. This is an important consideration when viewing various religious groups. In several of the groups studied in this book, it seems that the leaders' interpretation of Scripture is regarded as greater authority than what Scripture itself teaches.

Concerning which books should be accepted as authoritative Scripture, early believers generally recognized which ones met the standards and should be accepted into what was called the "canon" (referring to a "measuring rod") of Scriptures. This was not necessarily a simple or easy process. Difficult questions were asked and had to be answered. For instance, New Testament books were considered authoritative if they were written by an apostle or his associate. If that was not easily determined, the book needed to be in line with what the apostles wrote. Some books claimed inspiration for themselves, but this in itself would not qualify them for inclusion. Church historian Earle Cairns comments, "The development of the

MANY PEOPLE DO NOT CONSIDER GOD TO BE A PERSON.

canon was a slow process substantially completed by A.D. 175, except for a few books whose authorship was disputed."[7] By A.D. 367, however, church leaders generally agreed that 66 books were inspired by God as authoritative Scripture. These same books are what we find in our Bibles today. People who now reject any of these, or their supreme authority, are not in agreement with biblical Christianity.

Since the time of the Reformation, which began in 1517 when Martin Luther challenged the sale of indulgences, the Roman Catholic Church has accepted other books, known as the Apocrypha, as authoritative. These extra books had not been previously considered on the same authoritative level as the 66. With the Reformers attacking such teachings as purgatory, however, the Roman Catholic Church accepted these books as canonical at the Council of Trent in A.D. 1548. Anyone who disputed this claim of the authority of the Apocrypha was anathematized (ecclesiastically banned or excommunicated) by the Roman Catholic Church.[8]

GOD

Many people outside of historical Christianity with different worldviews do not consider God to be a person. Others who do consider Him to be a person do not believe He is a trinity. Let us now examine what the Bible says about the nature of God.

What They Believe

When most people in the Western world hear that an individual believes in God, they probably think of the God of the Bible. This God is a person with intellect, emotions and will. But not everyone is referring to Him when they talk about God. Hinduism, for example, considers God to be only an impersonal, philosophical absolute. That belief system does not view God as a person with intellect, emotions and will.[9] Many religious groups in America seem to have been affected by the Hindu view, such as Christian Science, the New Age Movement, Transcendental Meditation and Unity School of Christianity. God's personhood has been accepted without question by biblical Christianity. His acts clearly show that the God of the Bible is a person with intellect, emotions and will. The language of the Bible is meaningless if God is not a person.

Those who deny the personhood of God are not within the scope of biblical Christianity. Although God's personhood has not been questioned, there has been a debate about the relationship of the Persons within the Godhead.

THE TRINITY

"Hear, O Israel: The LORD our God, the Lord is one!" says Deuteronomy 6:4.

How then do we explain the relationship of the three Persons—Father, Son and Holy Spirit? Is only one of the Persons God while the others are less than God? In the early centuries of church history, differences arose concerning the relationship of the Father, the Son and the Holy Spirit.

The word *Trinity* came to be used to summarize the belief that the three Persons are one, though distinct. "It signifies," says G. W. Bromiley, "that within the one essence of the Godhead we have to distinguish three 'persons' who are neither three gods on the one side, nor three parts or modes of God on the other, but coequally and coeternally God."[10]

Trinitarian statements are found in the Apostles' Creed, one of the oldest creeds in existence. It was used as early as A.D. 150.[11] Used by both Roman Catholics and Protestants, the Apostles' Creed "has maintained in modern times its distinction as the most widely accepted and used creed among Christians."[12]

"This creed, which is definitely Trinitarian," says historian Cairns, "gives attention to the person and work of each of the three persons of the Trinity."[13]

Several present-day groups deny the Trinitarian nature of God, such as the Jehovah's Witnesses, Unitarian Universalists and The Way International. These groups, with their denials of the Trinity, are outside the mainstream of biblical Christianity.

JESUS CHRIST

Just as some groups deny the personhood of God, so some deny the personhood of Jesus Christ. They say that Christ was only a principle, not a person, so they do not believe that He is God. What does biblical Christianity believe?

Some people make a distinction between the names *Jesus* and *Christ*. The name *Jesus*, they say, refers to Jesus the man, and *Christ* refers to the Christic principle that is within every person. This is the belief of the Rosicrucians. Christian Science says *Christ* refers to the "divine idea." Unity School of Christianity says *Christ* refers to the "divine Mind." Such views have never been held by biblical Christianity; rather, the debate has been whether or not the Person of the Lord Jesus Christ is God.

In the early centuries of church history, theologians debated the deity of Christ. Was He really God, or only a man? A man named Arius (c. A.D. 250—c. 336) "began to disseminate the view that Jesus, though the Son of God, could not be coeternal with His Father; and that He must be regarded as external to the divine essence, and only a creature."[14]

Church historian Cairns says, "The method adopted by the church to resolve the vital differences of opinion concerning the teachings of the Scriptures was the ecumenical or universal council, usually called and presided over by the Roman emperor. There were seven councils that were representative of the whole Christian church."[15]

The first ecumenical council was called by Constantine. It met in Nicea in Bithynia (now Isnik, Turkey) in A.D. 325 to consider the controversy raised by Arius. The Council of Nicea condemned Arius's view as heresy. Although his view continued to flourish for a while, by A.D. 381 "the question was officially settled by the church."[16]

A debate also arose about how the two natures of Christ were to be understood. Some emphasized His deity at the expense of His humanity; others, His humanity at the expense of His deity. The Council of Chalcedon (A.D. 451) declared Him to be "true God and true man."

Biblical Christianity accepts the teaching that Jesus Christ is God. John 1:1 says, "In the beginning was the Word, and the Word was with God, and the Word was God."

The rest of the chapter, especially verse 14, makes it clear that "the Word" refers to Christ. The Jews of Christ's day clearly understood that when He referred to God as His Father, He was "making Himself equal with God" (John 5:18). That is why Jesus could say, "I and My Father are one" (John 10:30).

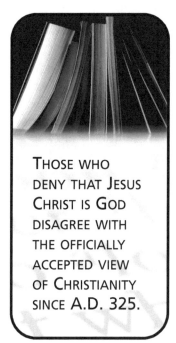

THOSE WHO DENY THAT JESUS CHRIST IS GOD DISAGREE WITH THE OFFICIALLY ACCEPTED VIEW OF CHRISTIANITY SINCE A.D. 325.

Those who deny that Jesus Christ is God disagree with the officially accepted view of Christianity since A.D. 325. This also reveals that doctrinal deviations are not new. Groups such as Jehovah's Witnesses and The Way International, who teach that Jesus Christ is not God, are merely espousing the Arian view, which was condemned as heresy at the Council of Nicea. It was decided then, and should be remembered now, that if Jesus Christ was less than God, He could not save mankind.

THE HOLY SPIRIT

Some groups today teach that the Holy Spirit is not a person. Just as man has a spirit, they say, so God has a spirit. Because God is holy, they reason, He has a holy spirit. Such logic denies the personhood of the Holy Spirit, but this doctrinal position is not new. Arius had also taught that the Holy Spirit was not a person.

Macedonius, bishop of Constantinople from A.D. 341 to 360, denied the deity of the Holy Spirit (although he did not seem to deny His personhood). At the ecumenical council in Constantinople in 381, Macedonius's view was condemned. Biblical Christianity believes in both the personhood and the deity of the Holy Spirit.

The Bible refers to the Holy Spirit as a person. He does things only a person can do. He convicts, guides, discloses things to come and glorifies Christ (John 16:7–15). He searches the depths of God and knows His thoughts (1 Cor. 2:10–11). It is also possible for the Holy Spirit to be grieved (Eph. 4:30). In addition, the Holy Spirit is called "God" (Acts 5:3–4). What He does, only God can do. Those who deny the personhood or the deity of the Holy Spirit do not align themselves with what is taught in the Bible nor with what is accepted by biblical Christianity.

Sin

Does mankind need redemption? Does sin exist? What is sin?

Theologian Millard J. Erickson defines sin as, "Any act, attitude, or disposition which fails to completely fulfill or measure up to the standards of God's righteousness. It may involve an actual transgression of God's law or failure to live up to his norms."[17]

Such groups as Christian Science, Masons, Unity School of Christianity and the more recent New Age Movement reject the biblical view of sin. Any "weaknesses" or "mistakes" can be overcome, they claim, through wisdom and right thinking ("enlightenment") rather than by a personal relationship with Jesus Christ.

In the fifth century, a British monk named Pelagius claimed that man had the capacity to do what was right on his own because he was created as free as Adam, uncontaminated by Adam's sin. Church leader Augustine argued against this position. He claimed that "sin incapacitates man from doing the good, and because we are born as sinners we lack the power to do the good. Yet because we willfully choose the bad over the good, we must be held accountable for our sin."[18] Augustine believed "that all inherit sin through Adam and that no one, therefore, can escape original sin."[19]

Although Augustine's views were not entirely accepted, Pelagius's view was condemned at the Council of Ephesus in A.D. 431. Biblical Christianity holds that man is a sinner in need of God's grace for salvation. On his own, man does not have the capacity to overcome his sin.

The Bible clearly states, "All have sinned and fall short of the glory of God" (Rom. 3:23). This is because sin has been passed down to us from Adam. "Just as through one man sin entered the world, and death through sin, and thus death spread to all men, because all sinned" (Rom. 5:12). We are not only sinners by nature, we are also sinners by action. All of us need forgiveness of sin and eternal life.

SALVATION

Nothing is more important than how a person can have his sins forgiven and therefore be right with God. If a group does not accept the biblical truth that all are sinners, it will not see the need for salvation. Historical Christianity agrees that all people are sinners; it disagrees, however, on how one becomes right with God. It was over this issue, during the Reformation, that Roman Catholicism and Protestantism took different theological paths.

During the 1500s, Martin Luther became spiritually troubled about the works-righteousness taught by the Roman Catholic Church, in which he was a priest. The Church taught that a person could become right with God if he performed certain "works," or deeds. Such a view was seen when 60 million Roman Catholics visited Rome in 2000. Reporting on an outreach planned for that year, *The Church around the World* said, "Many Catholics believe that by walking through a special 'holy door' in St. Peter's Basilica during the year of Jubilee, they gain forgiveness of past sins."[20]

Luther became more disturbed as he concentrated on the books of Romans and Galatians in his studies. In particular, he was gripped by the tremendous truth of the Scriptures: "The just shall live by faith" (Rom. 1:17; Gal. 3:11).

In addition, Luther was incensed by the Roman Catholic Church's sale of indulgences through Tetzel, a German teacher and preacher of the Dominican Order. Tetzel "gave the impression that it would not only remit the guilt and penalties of even the most serious sins, but that its benefits could be applied to the dead in purgatory."[21] The Church taught that every person who qualified for heaven had to spend some time after death in a place called purgatory in order to atone for his sins. An indulgence was a document that could be purchased to free a person from the penalty of sin. "It was believed that Christ and the saints had achieved so much merit during their earthly lives that the excess merit was laid up in a heavenly treasury of merit on which the pope could draw on behalf of the living faithful."[22]

Luther maintained that the believer had forgiveness of sin without indulgences, and he challenged the pope's authority over purgatory. In 1517, when Luther nailed his ninety-five theses to the Catholic church door in Wittenberg, the Reformation began. The three great Reformation principles became: "1) man is justified by faith alone; 2) every believer has direct access to God; and 3) the Bible is the sole source of authority for faith and life."[23]

These positions were in contrast to the Roman Catholic teaching that 1) a person could be saved only through the Church; 2) a person had to come through a Catholic priest to obtain forgiveness of sin; and 3) tradition and the word of the pope were as authoritative as the Bible. (See the chapter on Roman Catholics.)

Four years after the Reformation began, Luther was excommunicated by the Roman Catholic Church.

Since the Reformation, one of the distinctives of evangelical Christianity is its emphasis on justification by faith. In other words, evangelicals believe that a person becomes right with God through faith in Jesus Christ alone. This stands in contrast to those groups or branches of Christianity that require certain works, in addition to faith, to earn salvation.

That man is justified by faith alone is seen from such Scripture passages as Romans 4:5: "But to him who does not work but believes on Him who justifies the ungodly, his faith is accounted for righteousness"; and Ephesians 2:8–9: "For by grace you have been saved through faith, and that not of yourselves; it is the gift of God, not of works, lest anyone should boast."

That every believer has direct access to God through Jesus Christ is seen from such passages as 1 Timothy 2:5: "For there is one God and one Mediator between God and men, the Man Christ Jesus."

That the Bible alone is authoritative is seen from various passages.

What They Believe

Matthew 4:4 records Jesus' words, "It is written, 'Man shall not live by bread alone, but by every word that proceeds from the mouth of God.'" Jesus also said, "For assuredly, I say to you, till heaven and earth pass away, one jot or one tittle will by no means pass from the law till all is fulfilled" (Matt. 5:18). Such commands and promises have never been made for the words of a human or for the human hierarchy of any church body.

FUTURE LIFE

Biblical Christianity teaches that all who have died will be resurrected. It believes that all who accept God's gift of salvation will enjoy eternal bliss, but that all who reject the salvation God offers will suffer eternal judgment.

Although Eastern religions believe in reincarnation—and some Western religions have adopted it—biblical Christianity rejects such teaching. If the Bible is accepted as the final authority, we must accept such statements as Hebrews 9:27: "And as it is appointed for men to die once, but after this the judgment." Once a person dies, he has no second chance for salvation.

All who believe in Jesus Christ for salvation will have forgiveness of sins and eternal life. The Bible says, "He who believes in Him is not condemned; but he who does not believe is condemned already, because he has not believed in the name of the only begotten Son of God" (John 3:18).

Those who reject God's offer of salvation in Jesus Christ will experience eternal condemnation. Matthew 25:46 speaks of unbelievers as going away "into everlasting punishment, but the righteous into eternal life." Revelation 20:15 says, "Anyone not found written in the Book of Life was cast into the lake of fire."

But no one will experience this awful judgment if he trusts Jesus Christ as his personal Savior.

CONCLUSION

When we hear such terms as *Christian, born again, God* and *Christ,* we need to realize that many people do not use these terms to refer to truths accepted by biblical Christianity. It is important to determine what each speaker or writer means by these terms.

In determining whether or not a person or group believes in biblical Christianity, we need to examine what the individual or group says about its source of authority, God, Jesus Christ, the Holy Spirit, sin, salvation and the future life. The Bible defines what is meant by each and we need to believe its truths.

Those who reject the absolutes of the Bible would have us live by their manmade absolutes. We need to be on guard toward those who would twist the truth. And we need to choose carefully what absolutes we accept. Our eternal destiny depends on it.

ENDNOTES

[1] *The World Almanac and Book of Facts 2005* (New York: World Almanac Education Group, Inc., 2005), 731.

[2] *The World Almanac and Book of Facts 1995, 2000, 2005* (New York: World Almanac Education Group, Inc.).

[3] Richard V. Pierard, "Evangelicalism," *New 20th-Century Encyclopedia of Religious Knowledge*, ed. J. D. Douglas (Grand Rapids, Mich.: Baker Book House, 1991), 311.

[4] Ibid.

[5] "Evangelical Christians," The Barna Group, www.barna.org, Oct. 24, 2005.

[6] Ibid.

[7] Earle Cairns, *Christianity through the Centuries* (Grand Rapids, Mich.: Zondervan Publishing House, 1954, 1981), 118.

[8] D. H. Wallace, "Apocrypha, Old Testament," *Evangelical Dictionary of Theology*, ed. Walter A. Elwell (Grand Rapids, Mich.: Baker Book House, 1984), 66.

[9] For information about Hinduism, see *Dictionary of Cults, Sects, Religions and the Occult*, by George A. Mather and Larry A. Nichols (Grand Rapids, Mich.: Zondervan Publishing House, 1993).

[10] G. W. Bromiley, "Trinity," in *Evangelical Dictionary of Theology*, 1,112.

[11] Fulton J. Sheen and Mervin Monroe Deems, in "Apostles' Creed," in *The World Book Encyclopedia*, Vol. 1 (Chicago: World Book, Inc., 1986), 530.

[12] O. G. Oliver, Jr., "Apostles' Creed," in *Evangelical Dictionary of Theology*, 73.

[13] Cairns, *Christianity through the Centuries*, 117.

[14] Elgin Moyer, "Arius," *The Wycliffe Biographical Dictionary of the Church*, revised and enlarged by Earle E. Cairns (Chicago: Moody Press, 1982), 17.

[15] Cairns, *Christianity through the Centuries*, 133.

[16] Moyer, "Arius," *The Wycliffe Biographical Dictionary of the Church*, 17.

[17] Erickson, Millard J. *Concise Dictionary of Christian Theology* (Grand Rapids, Mich.: Baker Book House, 1986), 152.

[18] D. G. Bloesch, "Sin, Historical Controversy over Sin," *Evangelical Dictionary of Theology*, 1,013.

What They Believe

[19] Cairns, *Christianity through the Centuries*, 138.

[20] "Rome Outreach Planned for 2000," *The Church around the World*, 1997.

[21] R. W. Heinze, "Ninety-five Theses, The," *Evangelical Dictionary of Theology*, 778.

[22] Cairns, *Christianity through the Centuries*, 282.

[23] Moyer, "Luther, Martin," *The Wycliffe Biographical Dictionary of the Church*, 251.

CHAPTER TWO

Christian Scientists

A bad fall on the ice on February 1, 1866, became the turning point in the life of 44-year-old Mary Baker Patterson, later known as Mary Baker Eddy. Her injuries were so severe that the doctors had given up all hope for recovery. Three days later she turned to the account of the healing of the palsied man in Matthew 9, and supposedly, by reading this passage she was healed.

This experience caused her to study more carefully the records of healing in the Scriptures. From her study she discovered the principles that she called Divine, or Christ, Science. This became the foundation for the movement known as Christian Science.

According to the official Web site of The First Church of Christ, Scientist, "Before Mrs. Eddy died in 1910, the religion she established had spread around much of the world, and she had become one of the most recognized public figures in America. In 1995, she was elected to the National Women's Hall of Fame as the only American woman to found a worldwide religion."[1]

Her fall was only one of many circumstances that caused Mrs. Patterson, as she was known then, to search for relief from suffering and grief. These experiences played a significant role in the formation of her unusual beliefs. In order to understand the doctrines of the Christian Scientists, it is important to look at the life of their founder and spiritual leader, Mary Baker Eddy.

BACKGROUND

Mary Ann Baker was born in Bow, New Hampshire, on July 16, 1821. Her parents, Mark and Abigail Baker, were strict Congregationalists. As a child and young woman she suffered from a spinal weakness that affected her mentally and physically. In December

1843, at the age of 22, she married Col. George Washington Glover. Seven months later he died from yellow fever in Wilmington, South Carolina. The shock of his death further weakened her physical and mental condition.

On June 21, 1853, Mrs. Glover married Dr. Daniel M. Patterson, an itinerant dentist. It was an unhappy marriage and they were separated in the summer of 1866. She did not divorce him until seven years later, however, claiming that he had abandoned her.

While she was married to Dr. Patterson, she visited Phineas P. Quimby (1802–1866), a famous drugless healer who practiced a type of mind-cure that included dipping his hands in water and then rubbing the patient's head. "He told her that her ailments—and all diseases—were traceable to causes in the invisible world of mind; that mental factors produced powerful changes in the fluids and processes of the body; and that he was able by some sort of electrical transference, to take his patient's ills upon himself and destroy them. While at this period he did not consider himself a mesmerist (hypnotist), the methods he used would today be considered a form of mental suggestion."[2]

Mrs. Patterson became a devoted follower of Quimby after this initial visit in 1862, in which he supposedly healed her of a back injury. She began teaching small groups in Massachusetts from Quimby's writings. After Quimby's death and her alleged healing in 1866 from her fall on the ice, she "reached the scientific certainty that all causation rests with Mind, and that every effect is a mental phenomenon."[3]

Even in their own literature, the Christian Scientists cite German church historian Karl Holl to show similarities as well as differences between Eddy and Quimby. As to a similarity, Holl said, "That which connected her with Quimby was her conviction that all disease in the last analysis has its roots in the mind, and that healing therefore must be effected through mental influence."[4]

Eddy took Quimby's teachings one step further, however, teaching that sickness, death and even our bodies do not exist—they are only imagined. Based on this belief, she began formulating her unique interpretations of Scripture. These, along with many of the teachings of Quimby and others, were incorporated into her book *Science and Health with Key to the Scriptures*, which was published in 1875.

In 1877, at the age of 56, Mrs. Patterson married Asa Gilbert Eddy, one of her followers. He was the first to advertise himself publicly as a Christian Science practitioner and was also the first to conduct a Christian Science Sunday school. Six years following their marriage, Mr. Eddy died of a heart attack. Mary Baker Eddy contested the autopsy report, finding another doctor to support her claim that her husband's death was due to "arsenic poisoning mentally administered." An inquiry was later made into the credentials of this doctor. He was exposed as a fraud and sentenced to prison for running an illegal hospital.

Commenting on this incident, the late Walter Martin, a foremost authority on counterfeit religious groups and founder of Christian Research Institute, wrote: "Mrs. Eddy's letter to the *Boston Post* dated

EDDY [TAUGHT] THAT SICKNESS, DEATH AND EVEN OUR BODIES DO NOT EXIST—THEY ARE ONLY IMAGINED.

June 5, 1882, in which she accused some of her former students of mentally poisoning Asa Eddy with malicious mesmerism in the form of arsenic mentally administered, is of the most pathetic examples of Mrs. Eddy's mental state ever recorded and one which the Christian Science Church would like to forget she ever wrote."[5]

In 1879 Mary Baker Eddy organized the Church of Christ Scientist in Charlestown, Massachusetts. Thirteen years later the name of this church was changed to the First Church of Christ, Scientist. Today it is known as the Mother Church, and other Christian Science churches throughout the world are members of this Mother Church. Following her death in 1910, control of the church was given to a self-perpetuating board of five people, who run the church according to Mary Baker Eddy's *Church Manual*.

Exact membership figures from the group are not available, since the Church Manual forbids reporting of such figures.[6] But *The World Almanac and Book of Facts 2005* mentions 2,000 churches and 880,000 members.[7]

BELIEFS

In order to understand many of the doctrines and interpretations of Christian Science, it is necessary to look briefly at the teachings of New Thought. Like Mary Baker Eddy, Julius Dresser—the father of New Thought—was a student of Phineas Quimby and adapted many of Quimby's teachings on mind healing to his religion. Charles and Myrtle Fillmore, the founders of Unity School of Christianity, were also greatly influenced by Quimby and Dresser.

What is New Thought? Theologian John H. Gerstner described it this way: "New Thought is a modified pantheism. Eastern religions, Theosophy, and Christian Science identify or tend to identify, metaphysically, the individual with the whole."[8] The term *pantheism* is derived from the Greek words *pan* (all) and *Theos* (God); hence, it is the belief that all—or everything—is God. God is not only the Creator; He is also the creation. *Metaphysics* has to do with that which is after (*meta*) or beyond the realm of the physical.

These religious groups teach that mankind and matter are part of divine essence. Christian Science differs from the others in that it denies the existence of matter altogether.

At the heart of New Thought and Christian Science is non-biblical teaching prevalent even in New Testament times—a dualism that considered matter evil and spirit good. This leads Christian Science to conclude, therefore, that the only reality is the mind. This emphasis on dualism between flesh and spirit is the most fundamental difference between Christianity and Christian Science.[9]

Their view of God and of the existence of mankind affects the Christian Scientists' interpretation of every part of Scripture. It is important that we look at the beliefs and claims of this group and see how they differ from the teachings of the Word of God.

SOURCE OF AUTHORITY

The Christian Scientists have maintained through the years that the Bible is basic to their teachings. Mary Baker Eddy wrote, "In following these leadings of scientific revelation, the Bible was my only textbook." She later added, "The Bible has been my only authority. I have had no other guide in 'the straight and narrow way' of Truth."[10]

However, the Christian Scientists' view of the Bible reveals that they do not consider it to be as trustworthy as Eddy's teachings. Their writings clearly show that they do not believe in the absolute inspiration or inerrancy of the Bible. Eddy claimed that the versions of the Bible had thousands of errors: "The manifest mistakes in the ancient versions; the thirty thousand different readings in the Old Testament, and the three hundred thousand in the New—these facts show how a mortal and material sense stole into the divine record."[11]

It is an irresponsible and misleading statement—and it only impresses the uninformed—to refer to "manifest mistakes in ancient versions." This phrase could refer to a few mistakes or to hundreds of them. And what is a "mistake"? It is common knowledge among those who work with ancient versions that there are different readings because of the development in languages, such as the difference in the English words "publickly" (Acts 18:28, KJV) and "publicly" in modern translations; or the difference between "Saviour" (Titus 2:13, KJV) and "Savior." Unintentional errors also occurred when others copied what a reader recited, such as errors of faulty hearing (mistaking vowels that sound alike but are written differently). When copying from a manuscript, errors of faulty eyesight sometimes occurred (picking up at the wrong line when two lines end the same, or copying twice what should have been copied only once). But these kinds of problems are not errors of substance, and hundreds of such differences would also be seen in the transmission of *Science and Health with a Key to the Scriptures*, which was first published in 1875 but is now available in contemporary American English more than 130 years later. Would Eddy say these are mistakes? Surely not, since her book was considered "final revelation."

Sometimes, admittedly, an overzealous scribe may have made a change to "help clarify" a Scripture reading, but this was detectable by comparing manuscripts.

And what does Eddy want us to understand by her statement that there are "thirty thousand different readings in the Old Testament, and the three hundred thousand in the New"? Certainly different readings would creep in as manuscripts were copied by hand, as they would today if even three people copied by hand the Book of Titus, which has only three chapters. There would be differences in spelling, and an occasional word or even perhaps an occasional line would be left out. But by comparing the three copies it would be relatively easy to reconstruct the text being copied.

Bruce M. Metzger is a long-time respected authority in analyzing Bible manuscripts and how they have been transmitted. Metzger tells of Johann Bengel (1687–1752), who was greatly disturbed "by the 30,000 variants which had recently been published in Mill's edition of the Greek Testament, and he resolved to devote himself to the study of the transmission of the text."[12] After using all manuscripts available to him, Bengel "came to the conclusion that the variant readings were fewer in number than might have been expected, and that they did not shake any article of evangelic doctrine."[13]

Eddy's statement seems to be an obvious attempt to disparage the Bible and to focus attention on the authority of her own words. Such a statement was not well-informed then, and is definitely not supported today by those who study the various texts as practice of the science known as textual criticism.

Likewise, the importance of the Bible as the rule of faith and practice is downplayed by the Christian Scientists: "The material record of the Bible . . . is no more important to our well-being than the history of Europe and America."[14]

> EDDY'S TEACHINGS ARE CONSIDERED TO BE DIVINELY INSPIRED BY GOD AND THE "FINAL REVELATION" TO MANKIND.

On the other hand, Eddy's teachings are considered to be divinely inspired by God and the "final revelation" to mankind. In writing about the principles of Divine Science that she "discovered" in 1866, Eddy stated, "God had been graciously preparing me during many years for the reception of this final revelation of the absolute divine Principle of scientific mental healing."[15]

Eddy not only claimed that she had received a new and final revelation from God, but it is also clear that she considered her writings to be divinely inspired as well. In commenting about *Science and Health*, the Christian Scientists' main source of teaching, she stated, "I should blush to write of *Science and Health with Key to the Scriptures* as I have, were it of human origin and I apart from God its author, but as I was only a scribe echoing the harmonies of Heaven in divine metaphysics, I cannot be super-modest of the Christian Science Textbook."[16] In the book itself she boldly proclaimed: "No human pen nor tongue taught me the Science contained in this book, SCIENCE AND HEALTH; and neither tongue nor pen can overthrow it"[17] (emphasis hers).

This leaves little doubt that the followers of Mary Baker Eddy consider her writings to be more authoritative than the Bible. The Bible is interpreted by her writings; it is not allowed to sit in judgment on her views—no matter how much they contradict God's Word.

Evidence clearly indicates that her teachings were of human origin. Walter Martin gives numerous examples of how she plagiarized from the works of Phineas Quimby, Francis Lieber and others.[18] Georgine Milmine, who published an extensive biography of Eddy's life, also confirmed these plagiarisms when she wrote in 1909: "The basic ideas of the book and much of the terminology were, of course, borrowed from the Quimby papers which Mrs. Glover had carried reverently about with her since 1864, and from which she had taught his doctrines. But in the elaboration and amplification of the Quimby theory, Mrs. Glover introduced some totally new propositions and added many as an ingenious ornament."[19]

In the revised edition of Walter Martin's *The Kingdom of the Cults*, under the supervision of general editor Ravi Zacharias, the chapter on Christian Science was updated by Dan Schlesinger. In this chapter, Schlesinger cites the July 10, 1904, edition of *The New York Times* that printed in parallel columns Eddy's and Quimby's writings "proving Quimby to have been at least a partial source of her 'revelation' of *Science and Health*.[20] Schlesinger does the same with another source as an "example of the contemporary consensus of opinion in Eddy's day that her writings were not original."[21]

Even the title, *Science and Health*, was apparently "an adaptation of Quimby's name for his healing system, 'The Science of Health.'"[22] The followers of Christian Science later denied any similarity between the teachings of Eddy and Quimby, but the parallel passages are too many to deny. Eddy not only borrowed freely from the work of others for her "inspired" book, but various revisions of the original manuscript have been made both by Eddy and others.

The Language Problem

Probably the greatest barrier to understanding the teachings of Christian Science is its use of language. The basis for interpreting any language or terminology is the principle that words are understood as they are normally and customarily used. Of course, this allows for metaphors and other figures of speech, but even they must be defined on the basis of normal use.

For example, when John the Baptist referred to Jesus Christ as the "Lamb of God" (John 1:29), he did not mean that Jesus was actually a lamb. It was a figure of speech based on the customary use of the word *lamb* in the Old Testament. The lamb was a sacrificial animal offered for the sins of the people. Thus, John was announcing that Jesus had come to offer Himself as the final sacrifice for sin. So John's figure of speech would have been understood in the way the word was normally used.

Christian Scientists, however, have ignored all rules of grammar and usage. The meanings they have assigned to various words have nothing to do with their normal sense. This becomes glaringly evident when you glance at the glossary in *Science and Health*. Referring to the chapter containing the glossary, Eddy wrote, "It contains the metaphysical interpretation of Bible terms, giving their spiritual sense, which is also their original meaning."[23] But who becomes the authority in deciding the "original meaning"? Would another person come up with the same metaphysical meaning? In this regard, the imagination of Eddy became the source of authority rather than the normal use of language in the Bible.

Note some sample entries in the glossary of *Science and Health*: "Gihon (river). The rights of woman acknowledged morally, civilly, and socially." "Hiddekel (river). Divine Science understood and acknowledged."[24] How does someone derive such unusual meanings from the names of two rivers?

Biblical terms lose all historical significance with such an allegorical, metaphysical approach. Everything is spiritualized to the point that the physical no longer exists. Thus, for example, Adam was not an actual person who was created by God and fell into sin. According to Christian Scientists, *Adam* means "error; a falsity; the belief in 'original sin,' sickness, and death; evil; the opposite of good."[25] By denying the existence of the person Adam, Christian Science negates the need for Christ to pay the penalty for sin, which is the only way men and women might find their way back to God.

THE TRINITY

Like many other groups, the Christian Scientists deny the biblical view of the Trinity. Mary Baker Eddy wrote, "The theory of three persons in one God (that is, a personal Trinity or Tri-unity) suggests polytheism, rather than the one ever-present I Am."[26]

Christian Scientists have taken this erroneous belief one step further than most groups by even denying that God is a person. Note Eddy's metaphysical interpretation of the Trinity: "Life, Truth, and Love constitute the triune Person called God—that is, the triply divine Principle, Love."[27] Thus, the Christian Scientists view God as an impersonal idea—He is merely the "divine Principle." The personhood of Jesus Christ and of the Holy Spirit is also denied: "God the Father-Mother; Christ the spiritual idea of sonship; divine Science or the Holy Comforter."[28]

Biblical Christianity, on the other hand, believes that God is a trinity. There is one God who exists in three Persons—Father, Son and Holy Spirit. Throughout the Bible, we find plural pronouns used in referring to God. In Genesis 1:26 God stated, "Let us make man in our image, after our likeness" (see also 11:7). These passages show that Jesus Christ and the Holy Spirit were with God from the beginning and were one with Him. The New Testament states clearly that Jesus Christ is God (John 1:1–3; 8:58; 10:30; Phil. 2:5–11; Col. 2:9).

In addition, the Bible contains indisputable evidence of the personhood of God, Jesus Christ and the Holy Spirit. The attributes of God reveal that He is a person and not merely a divine principle of love. He sees (Gen. 6:5), hears (Ex. 2:24) and speaks (3:4–6; Matt. 3:17). He has a mind and a will. He thinks, remembers and knows everything (Jer. 29:11; 2 Tim. 2:19; 1 John 3:20).

Likewise, the Holy Spirit is more than the idea of "divine Science." He has a mind, emotions and will, just like a person. He reproves the world (John 16:8), He teaches (14:26), He regenerates (3:6), He baptizes (1 Cor. 12:13) and He can be grieved (Eph. 4:30).

JESUS CHRIST

As we have seen, the Bible clearly teaches that Jesus Christ is God, the second Person of the Trinity. However, Christian Scientists use Christ's title as the "Son of God" in a literal sense. Mary Baker Eddy wrote, "The Christian who believes in the First Commandment is a monotheist. Thus he virtually unites with the Jew's belief in one God, and recognizes that Jesus Christ is not God, as Jesus himself declared, but is the Son of God."[29]

Not only do Christian Scientists deny that Jesus Christ and God are one, but they also teach that the names *Jesus* and *Christ* do not refer to the same person. "Jesus," Eddy wrote, "is the name of the man who, more than all other men, has presented Christ, the true idea of God. . . . Jesus is the human man, and Christ is the divine idea; hence the duality of Jesus the Christ."[30]

As mentioned earlier, in the systems of New Thought, Unity School of Christianity and Christian Science, dualism is a key concept. They teach that only the immaterial—or spirit—is good and that anything material should be denied or overcome. Because they believe that all matter is evil, or nonexistent, they reason that the spiritual cannot live in the material. Thus, Christ, "the true idea of God," could not have lived in a man's body. Likewise, they teach that God cannot indwell man: "God is indivisible. A portion of God could not enter man; neither could God's fulness [sic] be reflected by a single man, else God would . . . become less than God."[31]

Rather than describing two separate beings, however, the names given to Jesus indicated the various aspects of His character and ministry. The name *Jesus* (Greek, *Iesous*) was a personal name that designated Him as Savior. "You shall call His name Jesus," the angel told Joseph, "for He will save His people from their sins" (Matt. 1:21). The name *Christ* (Greek, *Christos*) was His official title, which designated Him as the "anointed one," or Messiah (John 1:41).

Not only do Christian Scientists deny the personhood and oneness of Jesus Christ, they also reject the vital aspects of His work in our behalf. Because she denied the reality of sin, Eddy saw little significance in the biblical record of the death of Jesus Christ for sin. "One sacrifice, however great, is insufficient to pay the debt of sin. The atonement requires constant self-immolation on the sinner's part. That God's wrath should be vented upon His beloved Son, is divinely unnatural. Such a theory is man-made. The atonement is a hard problem in theology, but its scientific explanation is, that suffering is an error of sinful sense which Truth destroys, and that eventually both sin and suffering will fall at the feet of everlasting Love."[32]

BECAUSE SHE DENIED THE REALITY OF SIN, EDDY SAW LITTLE SIGNIFICANCE IN THE BIBLICAL RECORD OF THE DEATH OF JESUS CHRIST FOR SIN.

Although Eddy said that the Bible was her "only authority," she did not teach biblical truth about the atonement. The Bible teaches that the Heavenly Father placed the sins of the human race on His Son when He died for us (Isa. 53:6; 2 Cor. 5:21). The truth that God's Son suffered the wrath of the Father in our place is not a man-made theory. God's Word tells us that Jesus Christ is "the propitiation [satisfaction] for our sins, and not for ours only but also for the whole world" (1 John 2:2). Those who trust in Jesus Christ for salvation pass from death to everlasting life (John 5:24).

Christian Science also teaches that Jesus Christ did not die on the cross but that He remained alive while in the tomb. Eddy stated, "His disciples believed Jesus to be dead while he was hidden in the sepulchre, whereas he was alive, demonstrating within the narrow tomb the power of Spirit to overrule mortal, material sense."[33]

The Bible, however, gives abundant testimony to the fact that Christ died on the cross (John 19:33; Rom. 5:6,8,10). Jesus Christ not only died and rose again, but His death also erased the guilt of our sins: "Christ died for our sins according to the Scriptures" (1 Cor. 15:3).

What They Believe

Sin

The Christian Scientists' views of Jesus Christ and the atonement are the result of their beliefs about man and sin. Because they deny the existence of the physical aspects of mankind, they also deny the reality of sin: "Man is not matter; he is not made up of brain, blood, bones, and other material elements. . . . Man is spiritual and perfect. . . . Man is incapable of sin, sickness, and death. The real man cannot depart from holiness, nor can God, by whom man is evolved, engender the capacity or freedom to sin."[34]

In order to deal with the sin that exists in the world, Christian Scientists have endeavored to explain it away by saying that man's problem is not sin but the *belief* of sin. Eddy wrote, "The only reality of sin, sickness, or death, is the awful fact that unrealities seem real to human, erring belief, until God strips off their disguise. They are not true, because they are not of God." She added, "Sin, sickness, and death are to be classified as effects of error. Christ came to destroy the belief of sin."[35] (This exposes another inconsistency in her teaching: How could "Christ," an idea and not a person, according to Eddy, "come to destroy" anything?)

The Bible teaches, however, that sin is real and that death is the result of sin. The fact that Christian Scientists experience physical death, just as every person does, should be proof enough to them of the reality of sin. "Therefore, just as through one man sin entered the world, and death through sin, and thus death spread to all men, because all sinned" (Rom. 5:12).

Salvation

Since they believe that Adam was not an actual person who sinned and that sin is only a figment of man's mind, Christian Scientists see no need for salvation provided by Jesus Christ. Eddy boldly claimed, "Final deliverance from error, whereby we rejoice in immortality, boundless freedom, and sinless sense, is not reached through paths of flowers nor by pinning one's faith without works to another's vicarious effort."[36]

Yet despite the fact that they deny the existence of sin, sickness and death, Christian Scientists still teach that people earn their salvation through victory over suffering and temptation: "Waking to

Christ's demand, mortals experience suffering. This causes them, even as drowning men, to make vigorous efforts to save themselves; and through Christ's precious love these efforts are crowned with success. 'Work out your own salvation,' is the demand of Life and Love, for to this end God worketh with you. . . . When the smoke of battle clears away, you will discern the good you have done, and receive according to your deserving. Love is not hasty to deliver us from temptation, for Love means that we shall be tried and purified."[37]

The Christian Scientists' view of salvation by works is not only inconsistent with their teachings (there is no need of salvation if there is no sin), but also directly contradicts the Scriptures. God's Word clearly states the only way we can be saved: "For by grace you have been saved through faith, and that not of yourselves; it is the gift of God, not of works, lest anyone should boast" (Eph. 2:8–9). While trials and temptations are part of the Christian life, no amount of suffering can earn God's salvation. Only the suffering and death of Christ was sufficient to save us.

Hell

Jesus taught that hell was an actual place that we should avoid at all costs. "If your eye causes you to sin, pluck it out," He said. "It is better for you to enter the kingdom of God with one eye, rather than having two eyes, to be cast into hell fire where 'their worm does not die, and the fire is not quenched'" (Mark 9:47–48). Jesus also said, "Do not fear those who kill the body but cannot kill the soul. But rather fear Him who is able to destroy both soul and body in hell" (Matt. 10:28).

Once again, Christian Scientists have reinterpreted Christ's clear teachings, denying the existence of hell and eternal punishment by giving them a metaphysical connotation. The glossary of *Science and Health* defines hell as "mortal belief; error; lust; remorse; hatred; revenge; sin; sickness; death; suffering and self-destruction; self-imposed agony; effects of sin; that which 'worketh abomination or maketh a lie.'"[38]

According to Christian Scientists, hell is merely a state of mind in which we torment ourselves with the guilt of our imagined sin. Eddy stated, "The olden opinion that hell is fire and brimstone, has yielded somewhat to the metaphysical fact that suffering is a thing of mortal mind instead of body; so, in place of material flames and odor, mental anguish is generally accepted as the penalty for sin."[39] Thus, Christian Science does not agree with the teachings of Jesus Christ about hell.

DISEASE AND DEATH

The foundation of the teachings of Christian Science is its doctrine of Divine Science. Eddy claimed that she had discovered and reinstated Christ's principles of divine healing found in the Scriptures. But do her teachings and practices match the record of Christ's miraculous healings?

According to Eddy, organic disease does not exist: "The cause of all so-called disease is mental."[40] Of course, medical science is now discovering that a person's mental outlook does affect him physically. Psychosomatic illness (disease that is brought on by a person's mindset) does exist. The Bible taught this truth a thousand years before Christ. Solomon wrote: "A merry heart does good, like medicine, but a broken spirit dries the bones" (Prov. 17:22).

But this is not what Eddy meant. She denied the existence of matter and everything associated with the physical body. Thus, since our bodies do not exist, disease is only an illusion. She said the same of death, defining it as "an illusion, the lie of life in matter; the unreal and untrue; the opposite of Life."[41]

Christian Science teaches that the cause of all sickness and death is the *belief* in it. Therefore, the healing they claim to perform involves helping the person to deny the reality of his illness. Failure to heal is due to the person's inability to overcome his belief. But is this how Jesus healed? Nowhere in the Gospels do we find Jesus denying the reality of a person's illness. Instead, He provided visible physical healing.

Eddy claimed to have healed hundreds of people using Divine Science, but her claims have been strongly challenged.[42] The fact that she obtained medical attention on a number of occasions following her "discovery" in 1866 proves that she did not truly believe what she taught and that she did not possess the ability to heal herself, let alone others.

Of course, the greatest proof of her erroneous teachings is the fact that, after a lifetime of teaching and writing about the nonexistence of sin, disease and death, Mary Baker Eddy died on December 3, 1910.

CONCLUSION

As we have seen, the teachings of Christian Science are contradictory and far removed from the doctrines of the Scriptures. The followers of Mary Baker Eddy emphasize "Truth," but in reality, the truth is not in them. By denying the existence of sin, they have deceived themselves and made God a liar: "If we say that we have no sin, we deceive ourselves, and the truth is not in us. . . . If we say that we have not sinned, we make Him a liar, and His word is not in us" (1 John 1:8,10).

Christian Science cannot be considered a movement that is based on God's Word. As Mather and Nichols write, "Christian Science . . . bears little resemblance to Christianity. Each is built on wholly different foundations: the former on the fundamentals of Greek and Cartesian dualism; the latter on a Hebraistic worldview and a biblical monotheism."[43]

As an expert observer of counterfeit religions, J. K. Van Baalen rightly concluded about Christian Science: "Most assuredly, the apostles would not have approved, and the Early Church would not have tolerated, a 'religion' that, in veiled language and much double talk, teaches that Jesus was laid down, as a result of an apparent death, into a fictitious tomb, in an unreal body, to make an unnecessary atonement for sins that had never been a reality and had been committed in an imaginary body, and that He saves from non-existing evil those headed toward an imaginary hell, the false fancy of erroneous Mortal Mind."[44]

Summary

Name:	The Church of Christ, Scientist
Also Known As:	Christian Scientists
Founder:	Mary Baker Eddy (1821–1910)
Headquarters:	Boston, Massachusetts
Membership (2005):	2,000 churches and 880,000 members
Web Site:	www.tfccs.com
Publications:	*The Christian Science Journal*
	Christian Science Sentinel
	The Herald of Christian Science
	Christian Science Quarterly Weekly Bible Lessons
	The Christian Science Monitor

What They Believe

Christian Scientists: **Biblical Christians:**

Source of Authority

Mary Baker Eddy claimed the Bible was the only textbook for her teachings. Her followers say the Bible has "manifest mistakes"—30,000 "different readings" in the Old Testament and 300,000 in the New Testament. Eddy's discovery of Divine Science is the "final revelation" from God.

The Bible alone is the final source of authority for beliefs and practices. The original manuscripts of the Bible were inspired of God and without error and that variant readings of copies do not effect basic doctrines. There is no claim for inspired revelation to any person after inspiration of 66 books of the Old and New Testaments.

The Trinity

Deny biblical doctrine of Trinity. Interpret the Trinity metaphysically, saying it is "Life, Truth, and Love."

Accept Trinitarian view of Godhead expressed in the Apostles' Creed, used as early as A.D. 150. The three Persons of the Godhead are one, yet distinct—with each being "coequally and coeternally God."

Jesus Christ

"Jesus" is the human man and "Christ" is the divine idea. Jesus was not dead in the tomb.

The name the "Lord Jesus Christ" refers to the same Person, who was both human and divine. Jesus died, was buried and rose on the third day.

Sin

Man is "incapable of sin, sickness, and death." Deny reality of sin, saying man's problem is the belief of sin.

Believe "all have sinned and fall short of the glory of God" (Rom. 3:23). From Adam all inherit sin and that death is the result of sin (Rom. 5:12).

Salvation

Sin is not real; therefore, there is no need for salvation in Jesus. Salvation is based on works.

All people need salvation through Christ. Salvation is by faith alone in Christ alone.

Hell

Deny existence of hell and eternal punishment. Hell is "mortal belief, error, lust, remorse, hatred, revenge, sin, sickness, death."

Believe in Jesus' warnings about the reality of hell. Hell is a place where "their worm does not die, and the fire is not quenched" (Mark 9:48).

Disease and Death

"The cause of all so-called disease is mental." Death is "an illusion, the lie of life in matter; the unreal and untrue; the opposite of Life."

Because of a sin nature all mankind eventually dies (Rom. 5:12). Physical death is the separation of soul and body, and spiritual death is the separation of soul from God.

Recommended Reading

Boa, Kenneth. *Cults, World Religions & the Occult.* Wheaton, Ill.: Victor Books, 1990.

Braswell, George W., Jr. *Understanding Sectarian Groups in America.* Nashville, Tenn.: Broadman & Holman Publishers, 1994.

Ehrenborg, Todd. *Mind Sciences: Christian Science, Religious Science, Unity School of Christianity.* Grand Rapids, Mich.: Zondervan Publishing House, 1995.

Martin, Walter R. *The Kingdom of the Cults.* Ravi Zacharias, gen. ed. Minneapolis: Bethany House Publishers, 2003.

Mather, George A., and Nichols, Larry A. *Dictionary of Cults, Sects, Religions and the Occult.* Grand Rapids, Mich.: Zondervan Publishing House, 1993.

McDowell, Josh, and Stewart, Don. *Handbook of Today's Religions.* San

What They Believe

Bernardino, Calif.: Here's Life Publishers, Inc., 1983.

Robertson, Irvine. *What the Cults Believe*. Chicago: Moody Press, 1991.

ENDNOTES

[1] www.tfccs.com, June 6, 1997.

[2] John DeWitt, *The Christian Science Way of Life* (Englewood Cliffs, N.J.: Prentice-Hall, 1962), 142–143.

[3] Ibid., 148.

[4] Christian Science: *A Sourcebook of Contemporary Materials* (Boston: The Christian Science Publishing Society, 1990), 265.

[5] Walter R. Martin, *The Kingdom of the Cults* (Minneapolis: Bethany House Publishers, 1985), 127.

[6] Mary Baker Eddy, *Church Manual*, 1924 ed. (Boston: Published by the Trustees under the Will of Mary Baker G. Eddy, 1895), 48.

[7] *The World Almanac and Book of Facts 2005* (New York: World Almanac Books, 2005), 731.

[8] John H. Gerstner, *The Theology of the Major Sects* (Grand Rapids, Mich.: Baker Book House, 1960), 63.

[9] George A. Mather and Larry A. Nichols, *Dictionary of Cults, Sects, Religions and the Occult* (Grand Rapids, Mich.: Zondervan Publishing House, 1993), 74.

[10] Mary Baker Eddy, *Science and Health with Key to the Scriptures* (Boston: The First Church of Christ, Scientist, 1994), 110, 126.

[11] Ibid., 139.

[12] Bruce M. Metzger, *The Text of the New Testament* (New York: Oxford University Press, 1968), 112.

[13] Ibid.

[14] Eddy, *Miscellaneous Writings*, 1883–1896 (Boston: Published by the Trustees under the Will of Mary Baker G. Eddy, 1896), 170.

[15] Eddy, *Science and Health*, 107.

[16] *Christian Science Journal*, January 1901, cited by Josh McDowell and Don Stewart, *Handbook of Today's Religions* (San Bernardino, Calif.: Here's Life Publishers, Inc., 1983), 123.

[17] Eddy, *Science and Health*, 110.

[18] Martin, *Kingdom of the Cults*, 128–133.

[19] Georgine Milmine, *The Life of Mary Baker G. Eddy and the History of Christian Science* (Grand Rapids, Mich.: Baker Book House, reprinted 1971), 178–179.

[20] Walter Martin, *The Kingdom of the Cults*. Ravi Zacharias, gen. ed. (Minneapolis: Bethany House Publishers, 2003), 152–153.

[21] Ibid., 155–156.

[22] Milmine, 178.

[23] Ibid., 579.

[24] Ibid., 587–588.

[25] Ibid., 579.

[26] Ibid., 256.

[27] Ibid., 331.

[28] Ibid.

[29] Ibid., 361.

[30] Ibid., 473.

[31] Ibid., 336.

[32] Ibid., 23.

[33] Ibid., 44.

[34] Ibid., 475.

[35] Ibid., 472–473.

[36] Ibid., 22.

[37] Ibid.

[38] Ibid., 588.

[39] Eddy, *Miscellaneous Writings*, 237 (cited in Martin, *Kingdom of the Cults*, 140).

[40] Eddy, *Science and Health*, 377.

[41] Ibid., 584.

[42] Martin, *Kingdom of the Cults*, 160–162.

[43] Mather and Nichols, *Dictionary of Cults, Sects, Religions and the Occult*, 74.

[44] J. K. Van Baalen, *Chaos of the Cults*, 4th rev. ed. (Grand Rapids, Mich.: Wm. B. Eerdmans Publishing Company, 1962), 97.

CHAPTER THREE

Jehovah's Witnesses

Few people in the United States have not been called on at least once by the Jehovah's Witnesses. These door-to-door evangelists are members of one of the most aggressive religious groups in the world. And their evangelism is paying off. In 2005 followers numbered an estimated 1,022,397 in 11,876 congregations in the United States, up from 945,990 in 1996.[1] Worldwide their membership was estimated at 2.2 million in 1986;[2] in 2004 it was estimated to be 6.5 million.[3]

Despite the lack of welcome they receive in many homes, the Jehovah's Witnesses single-mindedly march on to the next house. Many people who talk with the Jehovah's Witnesses soon realize that their beliefs differ greatly from those of historical Christianity. What causes this group to be so aggressive in its witnessing? And where did its unusual beliefs originate?

BACKGROUND

The first recognized leader—and first president—of the group now known as the Jehovah's Witnesses was Charles Taze Russell. Born in Pittsburgh, Pennsylvania, on February 16, 1852, Russell had a Presbyterian and Congregational upbringing. However, he became opposed to organized religion and to many of the teachings of historical Christianity. "By his own admission, it was the Adventists who delivered Russell from his early skepticism," Anthony Hoekema wrote. "From the Adventists Russell obviously borrowed such doctrines as the extinction of the soul at death, the annihilation of the wicked, the denial of hell, and a modified form of the investigative judgment."[4]

Many Jehovah's Witnesses and Seventh-day Adventists have denied this association with the teachings of Adventism. However, J. K. Van Baalen, a counter-cult specialist of a past generation, wrote: "The origin of the Russell-Rutherford-Knorr theology, especially of its eschatology, lies in Seventh-day Adventism. This was asserted in *The Chaos of Cults* in 1929, hotly disclaimed by LeRoy E. Froom, and has since been reaffirmed by Lehman Strauss, F. E. Mayer, and E. C. Gruss."[5] ("Russell-Rutherford-Knorr" refers to the first three presidents of the group.)

When only 18 years old (1870), Russell organized a Bible class in Pittsburgh. This group met regularly to study the Scriptures about Jehovah's Kingdom and the Second Coming of Christ. Even though Russell had no formal theological training, he became the undisputed leader of the group.

> CHALLENGING THE WATCHTOWER IS CONSIDERED AN INTOLERABLE OFFENSE.

Undisputed is a key word when talking about leadership of the Jehovah's Witnesses. Even today, "Jehovah's Witnesses are instructed that unquestioned obedience to Watchtower doctrines is expected of them. If someone questions or rejects a particular Watchtower doctrine, he can be 'disfellowshipped'—or kicked out of the organization,"[6] says Ron Rhodes, watcher of counterfeit religious groups and former associate editor of the *Christian Research Journal*. (He is now president of Reasoning from the Scripture Ministries.) He adds, "To question the authority of the Watchtower Society essentially amounts to questioning God's authority. Hence, challenging the Watchtower is considered an intolerable offense."[7]

This opinion is shared by Irving Hexham, professor of religious studies at the University of Calgary, who says, "The spiritual obedience demanded by the leadership of the Witnesses is like the Roman Catholic understanding of the pope's ability to speak *ex cathedra*."[8] Careful readers of the literature produced by the Jehovah's Witnesses will see that this has been true since the beginning.

In 1879 Russell began publishing a magazine entitled *Zion's Watch*

Tower and Herald of Christ's Presence, since renamed *The Watchtower Announcing Jehovah's Kingdom*. It is commonly known as *The Watchtower*, or more simply *Watchtower*. This magazine is the group's main source of authoritative teaching. Since its inception, the publication has grown tremendously and is distributed by the millions each month.

The Jehovah's Witnesses was incorporated in Pennsylvania in 1884 under the name Zion's Watch Tower Tract Society. Russell was a prolific writer. In addition to many other works, he produced six volumes of *Studies in the Scriptures*. In 1907 a person could purchase all "six volumes of over 3,000 pages for $2.25."[9]

One of Russell's special emphases was prophecy. He fully expected the Times of the Gentiles (referred to in such passages as Luke 21:24) to end in 1914. The Witnesses acknowledge, "C. T. Russell had been critical of those who had set various dates for the Lord's return, such as William Miller and some Second Adventist groups. Yet, from the time of his early association with Nelson Barbour, he was convinced that there was an accurate chronology, based on the Bible, and that it pointed to 1914 as the end of the Gentile Times."[10]

World War I had begun that summer, and on October 2, 1914, at the Brooklyn headquarters, Russell triumphantly remarked, "The Gentile Times have ended; their kings have had their day!"[11]

Not to be defeated, the Jehovah's Witnesses now say, "No, the Bible Students were not 'taken home' to heaven in October 1914. Nevertheless, the Gentile Times did end that year."[12] This is the Watchtower's typical response to prophecies unfulfilled by its "prophets." The organization keeps going as if it were of no consequence that an authoritative teaching failed to be true. Yet if followers question the authority of the Watchtower Society, they are in danger of being disfellowshipped.

For years it was binding teaching that the generation that was alive in 1914 would live to see Armageddon and Christ's earthly return. (Those who were born in 1914 would be 91 years old at the time of this publishing.) In 1996 a news item in *Christianity Today* entitled "Sect Postpones Armageddon" reported, "In November, the religious group's magazines, *Awake!* and *Watchtower*, both retreated from the 1914 timeline as the start of the end."[13] Again, the authoritative prediction that failed to come true is shrugged off by the current leaders of the Jehovah's Witnesses. Their media spokesperson says the new view resulted from reexamining the Scripture. "It doesn't change our belief," he said, "that we are living in the time of the end."[14]

After Russell's death in 1916 (two years after the declared date when Christ would return to establish His kingdom), a seventh volume was published in the series *Studies in the Scriptures,* which resulted in a division among his followers. In the seventh volume, Russell was described as the "faithful and wise servant" of Matthew 24:45. The organization now claims that such a title was never applied to Russell, but the evidence indicates otherwise.[15] The position now is that this verse applies to a class of persons. It is interesting to note that the Scripture index in the 804-page *Pastor Russell's Sermons* does not list a single reference to Matthew 24:45.

To this day, however, the followers of Russell have a high view of his position in church history. A year after his death, the publishers of *Pastor Russell's Sermons* wrote: "When the history of the Church of Christ is fully written, it will be found that the place next to St. Paul in the gallery of fame as an expounder of the Gospel of the great Master will be occupied by CHARLES TAZE RUSSELL"[16] (emphasis theirs). If that leaves any doubt as to their reverence for Russell, the following statement should remove it: "In the first three chapters of Revelation we are informed that to the Gospel Church have been sent seven special Messengers. Of these St. Paul was the first, and Pastor Russell the last."[17]

Russell was involved in many conflicts during his life. The integrity and stability of his life were less than admirable. In 1913 the courts granted his wife a divorce, and he was charged with fraud and perjury. Walter Martin has reproduced many of these records in his outstanding work, *The Kingdom of the Cults.*[18] Concerning this first leader of the Jehovah's Witnesses, Martin summarized, "As a speaker, Russell swayed many; as a theologian, he impressed no one competent; as a man, he failed before the true God."[19]

After Russell's death in 1916, Joseph F. Rutherford, who had been the society's legal counselor since 1907, succeeded him to the presidency. Some of Russell's followers separated from the main group and formed the Dawn Bible Students Association and other splinter groups, but most accepted Rutherford's leadership.

Although the loosely associated groups were known earlier as Russellites, Millennial Dawn People and International Bible Students,[20] it was during Rutherford's presidency in 1931—15 years after Russell's death—that the group officially adopted the name Jehovah's Witnesses. This name is derived from the American Standard Version translation of Isaiah 43:12: "Ye are my witnesses, saith Jehovah, and I am God."

Rutherford was also a prolific writer and ruled the group with an iron fist. Mather and Nichols point out that during Rutherford's presidency, "The Brooklyn office became the Watchtower version of the Vatican."[21] Under his leadership, the Jehovah's Witnesses began their strong emphasis on door-to-door visitation and literature distribution.

Upon Rutherford's death in 1942, he was succeeded by Nathan H. Knorr. Since 1942, the organization has grown at a phenomenal rate. Knorr was responsible for improving the group's training program and for producing a vast amount of literature. *Awake!*, another authoritative magazine of the Jehovah's Witnesses, was begun by Knorr and is published in more than 80 languages each month.

During Knorr's presidency, the Watchtower Bible and Tract Society published the Jehovah's Witnesses "official" version of the Bible, the *New World Translation of the Holy Scriptures*. This differs from other translations inasmuch as the non-traditional Christian theology of the Jehovah's Witnesses is woven into the translation of the Scriptures.

Frederick W. Franz succeeded Knorr to the presidency in 1977. He served as a member of the Governing Body until his death on December 22, 1992, at 99 years of age. Key publications during his lifetime included the revised edition of the *New World Translation* (1984); a commentary on every verse of Revelation, *Revelation—Its Grand Climax At Hand* (1988); a two-volume Bible encyclopedia, *Insight on the Scriptures* (1988); and a study of the life and teachings of Jesus Christ, *The Greatest Man Who Ever Lived* (1991).[22] Another important book produced under Franz's leadership is *Reasoning from the Scriptures*, first published in 1985 and revised in 1989. This is a tool provided for the Witnesses to know how to begin conversations at your door and how to answer your objections, such as what they might answer if you ask the Jehovah's Witnesses if they are "born again."

What They Believe

The current president is Don A. Adams. Born around 1925, he had been secretary to Nathan H. Knorr, the third president of the organization.[23] The most important matter for our consideration, however, is the theological beliefs of the Jehovah's Witnesses.

BELIEFS

The Jehovah's Witnesses are probably best known for some of their practices, such as not celebrating Christmas, birthdays and other holidays because they believe these are forms of idolatry. They refuse to serve in the military or to salute their country's flag. They will not accept blood transfusions for themselves or members of their family because they think this violates the Old Testament prohibition against "eating" blood.

Even more important than their practices are the doctrines the Jehovah's Witnesses believe and teach. Crucial to any belief system is the source of authority the group follows.

SOURCE OF AUTHORITY

The Jehovah's Witnesses claim the Bible is their final authority. In their book *Let God Be True* they state, "To let God be found true means to let God have the say as to what is the truth that sets men free. It means to accept his Word, the Bible, as the truth. . . . Our obligation is to back up what is said herein by quotations from the Bible for proof of truthfulness and reliability."[24] But do they follow this claim?

When talking with the Jehovah's Witnesses, one soon learns that the interpretations of their leaders are considered to be the final authority, not the Bible itself. In *The Watchtower*, Russell stated, "If the six volumes of 'Scripture Studies' are practically the Bible, topically arranged with Bible proof texts given, we might not improperly name the volumes 'The Bible in an Arranged Form.' That is to say, they are not mere comments on the Bible, but they are practically the Bible itself. Furthermore, not only do we find that people cannot see the divine plan in studying the Bible by itself, but we see, also, that if anyone lays the 'Scripture Studies' aside, even after he has used them, . . . and goes to the Bible alone, though he has understood his Bible for ten years, our experience shows that within two years, he goes into darkness. On the other hand, if he had merely read the 'Scripture Studies' with their references and had not read a page of the Bible as such, he would be in the light at the end of two years, because he would have the light of the Scriptures."[25]

Thus, the Jehovah's Witnesses believe that the writings of Russell and succeeding presidents take precedence over the Bible. God's Word is allowed to have more authority, however, now that the Jehovah's Witnesses have their own version. First published in 1950, the New World Translation contains many changes in the wording of key passages that reflect the binding interpretations of the group's leaders.

THE TRINITY

The biblical teachings concerning the Trinity are vital in understanding the doctrinal errors of the Jehovah's Witnesses. The Witnesses emphatically deny the Trinitarian view of God. They believe that God is only the "Jehovah God" referred to in the Old Testament; they deny the concept of one God who exists in three distinct Persons—Father, Son and Spirit—which the Bible teaches. The Jehovah's Witnesses claim that trinitarianism is a belief in three gods, which is polytheism.

The Jehovah's Witnesses and others who deny that God is a trinity frequently cite Deuteronomy 6:4 as proof of their views. This verse says, "Hear, O Israel: The LORD our God, the LORD is one!" However, the Hebrew word translated "one" in this passage does not refer to an absolute unity but to a composite unity. This is the same word used in Genesis 2:24 to describe the marriage relationship. Here the husband and wife are said to be "one flesh." Therefore, Deuteronomy 6:4 in no way excludes the Trinity. The plural pronouns used for God also give evidence of the Trinity (Gen. 1:26; 11:7).

> THE WITNESSES EM-PHATICALLY DENY THE TRINITARIAN VIEW OF GOD.

The word *trinity* is not used in the Bible, so the Witnesses say it is not a biblical teaching. But neither are the words *theocracy* or *theo-*

cratic used in the Scripture, which the Jehovah's Witnesses use frequently. A concept can be taught in the Scripture without using a specific English word.

The existence of the Trinity is revealed in the Bible; however, our limited minds often find this doctrine difficult to comprehend. The term "signifies that within the one essence of the Godhead we have to distinguish three 'persons' who are neither three gods on the one side, nor three parts or modes of God on the other, but coequally and coeternally God."[26]

The Jehovah's Witnesses denial of the Trinity is essentially Arianism. In the fourth century, Arius "began to disseminate the view that Jesus, though the Son of God, could not be coeternal with His Father; and that He must be regarded as external to the divine essence, and only a creature."[27] The Council of Nicea, in A.D. 325, condemned his belief as heresy. In rejecting the Trinity, the Jehovah's Witnesses de-emphasize the Person of Christ by denying His deity.

JESUS CHRIST

Because they deny the doctrine of the Trinity, the Jehovah's Witnesses—like The Way International, Latter-Day Saints (Mormons) and Unitarian-Universalists—do not believe that Jesus Christ is God. As a result, the Jehovah's Witnesses add this view to their translation of the Bible wherever they are able to fit it in. Commenting on Colossians 1:15, they say of Christ, "Thus he is ranked with God's creation, being first among them and also most beloved and most favored among them. He is not the author of the creation of God; but, after God had created him as his firstborn Son, then God used him as his working Partner in the creating of all the rest of creation. It is so stated at Colossians 1:16–18 and at John 1:1–3, NW."[28]

The Jehovah's Witnesses frequently cite passages from Colossians and the Gospel of John to prove that Jesus Christ is not God. In examining their teachings, it is important to note how the *New World Translation* renders these vital passages.

Colossians 1:16–17 states in the *New World Translation*, "Because by means of him all [other] things were created in the heavens and upon the earth, the things visible and the things invisible, no matter whether they are thrones or lordships or governments or authorities.

All [other] things have been created through him and for him. Also he is before all [other] things and by means of him all [other] things were made to exist."[29]

These verses serve as a key example of the extent to which the Jehovah's Witnesses will go to support their belief that Jesus Christ is not God: they have even changed the translation of the Bible. The Greek text contains no word that could be translated "other" in this passage, yet they have added the word four times in these two verses. The original version of the *New World Translation* did not contain the brackets around the word *other* to show that it was not part of the Greek text. The Jehovah's Witnesses have since added the brackets with this explanation: "Brackets . . . enclose words inserted to complete the sense in the English text."[30]

There is no basis, however, for the assumption that the word *other* is needed to complete the sense in this passage. They have inserted this word to prevent the text from saying that Jesus Christ created all things. To allow the Bible to say that Jesus created all things would destroy their teaching that Christ was created by Jehovah. Thus, He could create only "other" things.

Although the Jehovah's Witnesses insert the word *other* into the *New World Translation*, their own *Emphatic Diaglott*—a Greek-English interlinear version—does not include the word *other* in the Greek text or in the English translation of this passage.[31] Clearly, the *New World Translation's* interpretation is not based on the original language of the New Testament. The Greek text of Colossians 1:16–17—including the *Emphatic Diaglott* of the Jehovah's Witnesses—states that Jesus Christ created all things, serving as indisputable proof that He is God.

Jehovah's Witnesses are also fond of taking advantage of people's ignorance of the original language of the New Testament in their reference to John 1:1. The *New World Translation* renders this verse: "In [the] beginning the Word was, and the Word was with God, and the Word was a god." The Witnesses have added the word *a* in front of *god* in order to support their belief that Jesus Christ is not Jehovah God.

The Greek language has only the definite article (the), not the indefinite article (a). When no article appears, one must decide whether or not to supply the indefinite article for the sake of smoothness in an English translation. The Jehovah's Witnesses, however, have gone beyond the rules of Greek grammar to support their theology. The elementary Greek grammar book, *Essentials of New Testament Greek, Revised*, states, "Greek writers usually included the article when they wanted to identify and specify, and did not include it when the emphasis was quality or essence."[32] Therefore, in terms of quality, the Word was God; that is, Jesus Christ is deity.

The debated phrase in John 1:1 has two nouns—*God* and *Word*. According to the rules of Greek grammar, when only one noun has the definite article in this kind of construction, it is the subject of the sentence. The noun without the article is the predicate (it makes a statement about the subject). Thus, the proper translation of this verse is "The Word was God."

The Jehovah's Witnesses are not intellectually honest in their handling of the Greek New Testament. They are quick to supply the indefinite article (a) in John 1:1 to back up their teaching that Jesus is not God. But in verses 6, 12, 13 and 18 of the same chapter, the word *God* is not preceded by an article, yet they do not supply the indefinite article in these passages. Only where the reader might think Jesus is God do they think it is necessary to place an *a* before the Greek word for God.

The Jehovah's Witnesses are also inconsistent regarding their own teachings. They claim to worship only one God, while accusing Trinitarians of being polytheistic. Yet by insisting that John 1:1 should be translated "The Word was a god," they are in fact guilty of polytheism—they consider Jesus Christ to be one of the gods. And further, since they believe Jesus Christ was created by God, they are guilty of believing that the first act of Jehovah was to create another god!

New Testament Greek students could give other examples of how the Jehovah's Witnesses have misused the Greek language. The heart of the issue, however, is not their misuse of Greek but the fact that they are adding their own interpretations to the Bible in order to support their faulty theology. But the Christian can be assured that every argument of the Jehovah's Witnesses from the Greek text can be answered by those believers who know Greek well. The false doctrines of this cult cannot stand in the light of the Scriptures.

USE OF THE NAME "JEHOVAH"

The Jehovah's Witnesses try so hard to distinguish between Jesus and Jehovah that they do not notice how their own translation reveals that Jesus is Jehovah. Isaiah 40:3 says, "The voice of one crying in the wilderness: 'Prepare the way of the LORD; make straight in the desert a highway for our God.'" The Hebrew word translated "LORD" in this verse is the one from which *Jehovah* is derived, and is translated "Jehovah" in the *New World Translation*. This verse is a commonly accepted prophecy about the first coming of the Lord Jesus Christ, as announced by John the Baptist.

All four Gospel accounts allude to the fact that Jesus is the fulfillment of Isaiah 40:3. Notice how the New World Translation renders the various verses: "This, in fact, is the one spoken of through Isaiah the prophet in these words: 'Listen! Someone is crying out in the wilderness, "Prepare the way of Jehovah, people! Make his roads straight"'" (Matt. 3:3).

Mark 1:1–3 especially pinpoints Jesus Christ as the fulfillment of Isaiah's prophecy. The *New World Translation* says, "[The] beginning of the good news about Jesus Christ: Just as it is written in Isaiah the prophet: '(Look! I am sending forth my messenger before your face, who will prepare your way;) listen! someone is crying out in the wilderness, "Prepare the way of Jehovah, YOU people, make his roads straight"'" (emphasis theirs).

Luke 3:4 and John 1:23 contain similar statements, showing that Jesus indeed is the fulfillment of Isaiah's prophecy. Thus, when John the Baptist was preparing the way for Jesus Christ, he was in reality preparing for the arrival of Jehovah on earth. Once again the Witnesses' own translation contradicts their teaching that Jesus Christ is not God.

Ron Carlson, the president of Christian Ministries International, is an effective witness to the Jehovah's Witnesses. He has spoken in 79 countries on six continents. He likes to ask Jehovah's Witnesses to help him understand three verses. First, he turns to Revelation 1:8 and asks them who is the "Alpha and Omega" that is referred to in the verse. They are pleased to tell him that it is Jehovah God. Then he goes to Revelation 21:5–7 and asks them who is the "Alpha and Omega" in verse 6. Again they're quick to say it is the Jehovah God.

What They Believe

Then Carlson turns to Revelation 1:17, which says, "And when I saw Him, I fell at His feet as dead. But He laid His right hand on me, saying to me, 'Do not be afraid; I am the First and the Last.'" Carlson asks the Jehovah's Witnesses to tell him who is the "First and the Last." Again, they respond it refers to Jehovah God. Then he urges them to read the next verse, "I am He who lives, and was dead, and behold, I am alive forevermore. Amen. And I have the keys of Hades and of Death" (v. 18). Then Carlson asks, "When did Jehovah die? When did God die?" They have no answer because they cannot admit that Jesus is Jehovah.[33]

THE RESURRECTION OF CHRIST

In addition to holding erroneous views about the Person of Christ, the Jehovah's Witnesses also teach false doctrine concerning His resurrection. In *Let God Be True*, they state, "God did not purpose for Jesus to be humiliated thus forever by being a fleshly man forever. No, but after he had sacrificed his perfect manhood, God raised him to deathless life as a glorious spirit creature. He exalted him above all angels and other parts of God's universal organization, to be next-highest to himself, the Most High God."[34] Notice their claim that Jesus was raised from the dead as a "glorious spirit creature."

This is not what the Bible teaches. After the resurrection of Christ, the Scriptures record that Mary Magdalene mistakenly thought He was the gardener (John 20:15). The Lord Jesus Christ also invited Thomas to feel the wounds in His side and hands (v. 27). These and other passages show that the resurrected Christ had a physical body.

The Jehovah's Witnesses explain all of this by saying that Jesus "materialized" at various times so He could be seen alive, even though He did not have a physical body. Such a view distorts the normal sense of the Scriptures. It is another evidence that the Jehovah's Witnesses follow their leaders' interpretations more than they do the teachings of the Bible. The main point of 1 Corinthians 15—a central passage on the resurrection—is that the physical resurrection of Christ assures believers of a physical resurrection for themselves one day.

THE HOLY SPIRIT

Since the Jehovah's Witnesses deny the Trinity and the deity of

Christ, it is no surprise that they reject the deity of the Holy Spirit as well. Concerning the Holy Spirit, they wrote, "No, the holy spirit is not a person and it is not part of a Trinity. The holy spirit is God's active force that he uses to accomplish his will. It is not equal to God but is always at his disposition and subordinate to him."[35] Not only do the Jehovah's Witnesses deny that the Holy Spirit is God, but they also do not believe He is a person.

The Scriptures teach, however, that the Holy Spirit is not a "force"; He is a person who possesses intellect, emotions and will. He does things only a person can do—and some only God can do. He re-proves the world of sin, of righteousness and of judgment (John 16:8); He teaches (14:26); He regenerates (3:6); He baptizes (1 Cor. 12:13); and He can be grieved (Eph. 4:30).

SALVATION

According to the Jehovah's Witnesses, salvation is a reward for good works. In *Let God Be True* they express this belief: "All who by reason of faith in Jehovah God and in Christ Jesus dedicate themselves to do God's will and then faithfully carry out their dedication

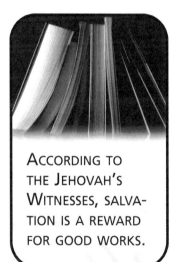

ACCORDING TO THE JEHOVAH'S WITNESSES, SALVATION IS A REWARD FOR GOOD WORKS.

will be rewarded with everlasting life (Romans 6:23). However, that life will not be the same for all. The Bible plainly shows that some of these, that is, 144,000, will share in heavenly glory with Christ Jesus, while the others will enjoy the blessings of life down here on earth (Revelation 14:1,3; Micah 4:1–5)."[36]

The Watchtower indicates that salvation is determined not by faith in Christ, but by loyalty to the Jehovah's Witness leaders: "Your attitude toward the wheatlike anointed 'brothers' of Christ . . . will be the determining factor as to whether you go into 'everlasting cutting off' or receive 'everlasting life.'"[37] This helps explain why the Jehovah's Witnesses evidence such great zeal in spreading their teaching from house to house—they are doing it to earn salvation. They teach a salvation by works, not by faith.

Once again the Jehovah's Witnesses have departed from biblical Christianity in their doctrines regarding the means of salvation. They see works as being part of the requirements for obtaining salvation rather than being a result of salvation. The Bible clearly states the means of salvation in Ephesians 2:8–9. Even the *New World Translation* renders these two verses so clearly that Witnesses would change their theology if they took them seriously: "By this undeserved kindness, indeed, YOU have been saved through faith; and this not owing to YOU, it is God's gift. No, it is not owing to works, in order that no man should have ground for boasting" (emphasis theirs).

When Jesus Christ shed His blood on the cross, He propitiated (satisfied) God's demand for righteousness. As a result, all who place their faith in Him have the benefits of His death applied to them. They are justified, or declared righteous, before God.

Because Jehovah's Witnesses believe that a person is "rewarded with everlasting life," they teach that a person does not know until death whether or not he has done enough to be rewarded with everlasting life. How many good works and door-to-door contacts does it take for a person to merit God's favor? According to the Bible, a believer can know for sure he has everlasting life from the moment of his salvation. This is made clear even in the Jehovah's Witnesses' own translation: "And this is the witness given, that God gave us everlasting life, and this life is in his Son. He that has the Son has this life; he that does not have the Son of God does not have this life. I write YOU these things that YOU may know that YOU have everlasting life, YOU who put YOUR faith in the name of the Son of God" (1 John 5:11–13, NWT, emphasis theirs).

The Jehovah's Witnesses use salvation terminology but twist the normal meaning. For example, Jesus' told Nicodemus, "You must be born again" (John 3:7). The field manual issued to the Witnesses, *Reasoning from the Scriptures*, instructs a Jehovah's Witness how he might answer if someone asks, "Are you born again?" "You could say," the manual teaches, 'You want to know whether I have accepted Jesus as my Savior and have received the holy spirit, is that right? May I assure you that the answer is Yes; otherwise I would not be talking to you about Jesus.'"[38] Such a statement is misleading considering the Jehovah's Witness do not believe Jesus is God or that the Holy Spirit is even a person. Truth twisting is accomplished by first twisting the meanings of the terms.

SOUL SLEEP

The Jehovah's Witnesses—along with the Seventh-day Adventists—teach that when a believer dies, he remains in an unconscious state of existence in the grave until he is resurrected by God. The Jehovah's Witnesses do not believe the soul of a person is a separate entity that has consciousness.

The Bible teaches, however, that a person has both a material and immaterial part, each separate from the other. When the body dies, the soul and spirit do not cease to exist but are merely separated from the body. Matthew 10:28 says, "And do not fear those who kill the body but cannot kill the soul. But rather fear Him who is able to destroy both soul and body in hell."

Luke 16:19–31 offers proof of a conscious existence after death. This account tells of a rich man and a beggar named Lazarus. Because Lazarus had believed in God during his lifetime, he was in a conscious state of bliss after physical death. The rich man, on the other hand, had rejected God and thus was in a conscious state of torment. The rich man not only was conscious, but he also retained his memory of his life on earth. He remembered his five brothers and wanted Abraham to send Lazarus to warn them about the place of torment. Thus, we see from this passage that both the saved and unsaved are in a conscious state after physical death.

While the Jehovah's Witnesses often point to a number of Old Testament passages to substantiate their teachings regarding soul sleep, nowhere in the Bible do we find this idea expressed. The apostle Paul recognized no middle ground between this life and the next. He knew that at the moment of death, he would immediately be with the Lord Jesus: "We are confident, yes, well pleased rather to be absent from the body and to be present with the Lord" (2 Cor. 5:8).

First Thessalonians 4:14 states conclusively that believers are not in an unconscious state in the grave while they are waiting for the resurrection. This is seen even in the *New World Translation*: "For if our faith is that Jesus died and rose again, so, too, those who have fallen asleep [in death] through Jesus God will bring with him." Notice where the believers are. Even though their bodies are in the grave, the real persons—the souls and spirits of departed believers—are with Christ and come back with Him at His appearance. When Christ returns, the bodies of believers will be resurrected from the grave and united with their souls and spirits. If believers were in an unconscious state in the grave, it would be impossible for God to bring them back with Him.

The Scriptures teach that even though the believer's body remains in the grave at death, his soul and spirit go directly to be with Christ. On the other hand, the soul and spirit of the unbeliever experience torment after death.

ANNIHILATION OF THE WICKED

Like many counterfeit religious groups, the Jehovah's Witnesses also teach that the wicked will not be punished forever but will be annihilated.

According to the Witnesses, "The doctrine of a burning hell where the wicked are tortured eternally after death cannot be true, mainly for four reasons: (1) It is wholly unscriptural; (2) it is unreasonable; (3) it is contrary to God's love; and (4) it is repugnant to justice."[39]

The doctrine of a burning hell is not unscriptural or unreasonable unless a person reads the Bible with his conclusions already drawn regarding what is reasonable. Actually, it is more unreasonable to think that God would extend His grace and forgiveness to sinners who trust in Jesus Christ for salvation, but the Bible reveals that He does.

An eternal hell is not contrary to God's love. Instead, its existence helps explain why God exercised His love by sending His Son to die on the cross so people might receive Him as Savior and escape the burning hell. If the doctrine of hell is unreasonable, why then don't the Jehovah's Witnesses say it is contrary to God's love to require His Son to suffer agony and death on the cross for sin?

Likewise, the doctrine of a burning hell is not repugnant to justice. God has given man his choice either to believe in Christ by faith for the forgiveness of sin, or to refuse to trust in Christ and spend eternity in hell. We choose the judgment we will receive. What could be more just?

According to the Bible, a person cannot claim everlasting life for the believer unless he claims everlasting punishment for the unbeliever. In referring to those whom the Lord will judge when He returns to earth, Matthew 25:46 concludes, "And these will go away into everlasting punishment, but the righteous into eternal life."

The Jehovah's Witnesses and others who believe in the annihilation of the wicked have tried to make a distinction between the words *everlasting* and *eternal* in this passage. They teach that the "everlasting punishment" refers to the fact that the wicked will be cut off from God forever; however, they will not endure eternal torment but will instead be immediately annihilated. But this supposition is not supported in the original language. These words are merely two translations of the same Greek word—their meaning is the same. Once again, the Jehovah's Witnesses have attempted to distort the normal sense of the Scriptures in order to support their faulty theology.

A comparison of two verses in the Book of the Revelation sheds additional light on the eternal state of unbelievers. At the end of the Tribulation, two individuals known as "the beast" and "the false prophet" will be "cast alive into the lake of fire burning with brimstone" (19:20).

Following this event, Christ will reign on earth for 1,000 years (20:1–6). During a "little season" at the end of this 1,000-year period, Satan will be loosed from the bondage he was in during the Millennium and will gather a group to fight against God and His armies (vv. 7–9). Satan and his forces will be defeated at that time. Then, according to Revelation 20:10, "The devil, who deceived them, was cast into the lake of fire and brimstone where the beast and the false prophet are. And they will be tormented day and night forever and ever." Although 1,000 years will have passed, the beast and the false prophet will still be in the lake of fire. They will not have been annihilated.

PROPHECY

The Watchtower Bible and Tract Society is a date-setting organization. It believes that God still makes new revelations through "prophets" today. In the eyes of the Jehovah's Witnesses, a false prophet is a person who prophesies something that does not occur. By this definition, they are guilty of being false prophets many times over!

However, while they have frequently given false predictions of events, they have later managed to explain away the false prophecies by fanciful spiritualizing. Some of these attempts to set dates (and later to reinterpret them when they didn't occur) include:

- the invisible Second Coming of Jesus in 1874

- the end of the world in 1914 and again in 1975

- the prediction that all members of the Body of Christ would be changed to heavenly glory in 1925

- that World War II was Armageddon[40]

After examining the above predictions from the Watchtower Society, Duane Magnani—who was a Jehovah's Witness for 18 years—said, "The record clearly destroys any claims to the prophetic authority of the Watchtower Bible and Tract Society."[41]

> LIKE THE JEWS OF PAUL'S DAY, THE JEHOVAH'S WITNESSES "HAVE A ZEAL OF GOD, BUT NOT ACCORDING TO KNOWLEDGE" (ROM. 10:2).

Ed Gruss, also a former Jehovah's Witness, examined predictions of the Watchtower Society back to 1877. He concluded, "When I looked at the many events the Jehovah's Witnesses had predicted and the specific dates they had set, I found that in *every case* the prediction had proved to be false" (emphasis his).[42]

Even though their predictions that the world would end in 1914 and again in 1975 were erroneous, the Jehovah's Witnesses still have not given up their date-setting practices. They again predicted that the world would end in 1984. Gary and Heather Botting have exposed the group's false prophecies in their book, *The Orwellian World of Jehovah's Witnesses* (University of Toronto Press).[43]

Raymond Franz is a former member of the Governing Body of Jehovah's Witnesses. To retrace his break with the Witnesses, Franz wrote *Crisis of Conscience: The Struggle Between Loyalty to God and*

Loyalty to One's Religion. He explains that what he went through was similar to that experienced by Hans Küng (Roman Catholic), Desmond Ford (Seventh-day Adventist) and Edward Dunlap (Jehovah's Witnesses) when each disagreed with the official teachings of the group in which he had been involved.[44]

CONCLUSION

As we have seen from this brief study, the Jehovah's Witnesses deny many fundamentals of the Christian faith, including the deity of the Lord Jesus Christ. A closer look at their doctrines reveals many other areas in which they have departed from the Bible's teachings. For this reason, they cannot be considered "Christians" in the scriptural sense of the word. While we may admire their dedication and enthusiasm toward their beliefs, their zeal and sincerity are not acceptable before God as substitutes for doing His will and teaching His truth. Like the Jews of Paul's day, the Jehovah's Witnesses "have a zeal of God, but not according to knowledge" (Rom. 10:2).

Summary

Name:	Watchtower Bible and Tract Society
Also Known As:	Jehovah's Witnesses
Founder:	Charles Taze Russell (1852–1916)
U.S. Headquarters:	Brooklyn, New York
Membership (2004–05):	U.S.: 1,022,397; Worldwide: 6.5 million
Publications:	*The Watchtower*
	Awake!

What They Believe

Jehovah's Witnesses:	Biblical Christians:

Source of Authority

Claim the Bible is their final authority. The Watchtower is a main source of authority, and interpretations of leaders are final authority.

Accept the Bible alone as their final authority. No commentary or comments of leaders are accepted as "official" interpretations of the Bible.

The Trinity

Do not believe God is a trinity, and consider such a belief to be polytheism.

The three Persons of the Godhead are one, yet distinct, with each being co-equally and coeternally God.

Jesus Christ

Jesus is "son of God" but not God. Translate John 1:1 to make Jesus Christ "a god," thus being guilty of polytheism. Christ was resurrected as a "glorious spirit creature" and did not have a physical body.

Jesus is God. Believe John 1:1 should be translated, "The Word was God." Believe in the bodily resurrection of Christ after three days in the grave.

Holy Spirit

Deny the Holy Spirit is the third Person of the Trinity; He is only an "active force."

The Holy Spirit is not only a person but also God, the third Person of the Trinity.

Salvation

Everlasting life is a reward for doing the will of God and carrying out one's dedication.

Salvation is by grace alone through faith in Christ alone.

Soul Sleep

At death, a righteous person remains in an unconscious state in the grave waiting for the resurrection.

At death, the soul and spirit of the believer in Christ go immediately into the presence of Christ.

Destiny of the Wicked

At death, the wicked will cease to exist and will not suffer everlasting punishment.

Those who reject the salvation provided by God will suffer everlasting punishment.

Recommended Reading

Ankerberg, John, and Weldon, John. *Encyclopedia of Cults and New Religions*. Eugene, Ore.: Harvest House Publishers, 1999.

Braswell, George W., Jr. *Understanding Sectarian Groups in America*. Nashville: Broadman & Holman Publishers, 1994.

Enroth, Ronald, & Others. *A Guide to Cults & New Religions*. Downers Grove, Ill.: InterVarsity Press, 1983.

Franz, Raymond. *Crisis of Conscience: The Struggle Between Loyalty to God and Loyalty to One's Religion*. Atlanta: Commentary Press, 1983.

Geisler, Norman L., and Rhodes, Ron. *Correcting the Cults*. Grand Rapids, Mich.: Baker Books, 1997.

Gruss, Edmond C. *Cults and the Occult*. Phillipsburg, N.J.: P&R Publishing, 1994.

Magnani, Duane, and Barrett, Arthur. *The Watchtower Files: Dialogue with a Jehovah's Witness*. Minneapolis: Bethany House Publishers, 1985.

Martin, Walter. *The Kingdom of the Cults*. Ravi Zacharias, gen. ed. Minneapolis: Bethany House Publishers, 2003.

Mather, George A., and Nichols, Larry A. *Dictionary of Cults, Sects, Religions and the Occult*. Grand Rapids, Mich.: Zondervan Publishing House, 1993.

McDowell, Josh, and Stewart, Don. *Handbook of Today's Religions*. San Bernardino, Calif: Here's Life Publishers, Inc., 1983.

Reed, David A. *Jehovah's Witnesses Answered Verse by Verse*. Grand Rapids, Mich.: Baker Book House, 1986.

Rhodes, Ron. *Reasoning from the Scriptures with the Jehovah's Witnesses*. Eugene, Ore.: Harvest House Publishers, 1993.

Robertson, Irvine. *What the Cults Believe*. Chicago: Moody Press, 1991.

ENDNOTES

[1] *The World Almanac and Book of Facts 1997* (Mahwah, N.J.: K-111 Reference Corporation), 644, and *The World Almanac and Book of Facts 2005* (New York: World Almanac Books, 2005), 731.

[2] *The World Book Encyclopedia*, 1986, Vol. 11, 70.

[3] "Membership and Publishing Statistics," www.jw-media.org/people/statistics.htm, Oct. 24, 2005.

[4] Anthony Hoekema, *The Four Major Cults* (Grand Rapids, Mich.: Wm. B. Eerdmans Publishing Company, 1963), 224.

What They Believe

[5] J. K. Van Baalen, *The Chaos of the Cults*, 4th rev. ed. (Grand Rapids, Mich.: Wm. B. Eerdmans Publishing Company, 1962), 257.

[6] Ron Rhodes, *Reasoning from the Scriptures with the Jehovah's Witnesses* (Eugene, Ore.: Harvest House Publishers, 1993), 15.

[7] Ibid.

[8] Hexham, "Jehovah's Witnesses," in *Dictionary of Christianity in America*, 591.

[9] *Studies in the Scriptures, Series VI* (Allegheny, Pa.: Watchtower Bible Tract Society, 1907), 10.

[10] *Jehovah's Witnesses—Proclaimers of God's Kingdom* (Allegheny, Pa.: Watchtower Bible and Tract Society of Pennsylvania, 1993), 60.

[11] Ibid., 61.

[12] Ibid., 62.

[13] *Christianity Today*, Feb. 5, 1996, 106.

[14] Ibid.

[15] See Duane Magnani and Arthur Barrett, *The WatchTower Files* (Minneapolis: Bethany House Publishers, 1985), 25–26.

[16] *Pastor Russell's Sermons* (Brooklyn, N.Y.: Peoples Pulpit Association, 1917), 3.

[17] Ibid.

[18] Walter Martin, *Kingdom of the Cults* (Minneapolis: Bethany House Publishers, 1985), 39–45.

[19] Ibid., 45.

[20] Frank S. Mead, rev. by Samuel S. Hill, *Handbook of Denominations in the United States* (Nashville: Abingdon Press, 1995), 154.

[21] Mather and Nichols, *Dictionary of Cults, Sects, Religions and the Occult*, 149.

[22] *Jehovah's Witnesses—Proclaimers of God's Kingdom*, 111.

[23] http://en.wikipedia.org/wiki/Don_A._Adams, Oct. 24, 1005.

[24] *Let God Be True*, 2nd ed. (Brooklyn: Watchtower Bible and Tract Society, 1952), 9.

[25] *The Watchtower*, Sept. 15, 1910, 298, cited by Walter Martin, *The Kingdom of the Cults*, 46, and by Anthony Hoekema, *Four Major Cults*, 227.

[26] G. W. Bromiley, "Trinity," in *Evangelical Dictionary of Theology*, ed. by Walter A. Elwell (Grand Rapids, Mich.: Baker Book House, 1984), 1,112.

[27] Elgin Moyer, "Arius," in *The Wycliffe Biographical Dictionary of the Church*, revised and enlarged by Earle E. Cairns (Chicago: Moody Press, 1982), 17.

[28] *Let God Be True*, 33.

[29] *New World Translation of the Holy Scriptures* (Brooklyn: Watchtower Bible and Tract Society, 1984).

[30] Ibid., 6.

[31] *The Emphatic Diaglott*, rev. ed. (Brooklyn: International Bible Students Association Watchtower Bible and Tract Society, n.d.).

[32] Ray Summers, revised by Thomas Sawyer, *Essentials of New Testament Greek, Revised* (Nashville: Broadman and Holman Publishers, 1995), 153.

[33] Ron Carlson & Ed Decker, *Fast Facts on False Teachings* (Eugene, Ore.: Harvest House Publishers, 1994), 129–131.

[34] *Let God Be True*, 41.

[35] *Should You Believe in the Trinity?* (Brooklyn: Watchtower Bible and Tract Society, 1989), 23.

[36] *Let God Be True*, 298.

[37] *The Watchtower*, Aug. 1, 1981, cited by Mariasusai Dhavamony in "Salvation Offered by Sects," *Studia Missionalia*, Vol. 41, 331.

[38] *Reasoning from the Scriptures* (Brooklyn: Watchtower Bible and Tract Society, 1989), 79.

[39] *Let God Be True*, 99.

[40] For documentation of the Jehovah's Witnesses' claims, see Duane Magnani, *The Watchtower Files*, rev. ed. (Minneapolis: Bethany House Publishers, 1985), 63–99.

[41] Ibid., 67.

[42] Dave Hunt, *The Cult Explosion* (Eugene, Ore.: Harvest House Publishers, 1980), 208.

[43] Religious News Service, "Do Jehovah's Witnesses Still Hold to Their 1984 Doomsday Deadline?" *Christianity Today*, Sept. 21, 1984, 66–67.

[44] Raymond Franz, *Crisis of Conscience: The Struggle Between Loyalty to God and Loyalty to One's Religion* (Atlanta: Commentary Press, 1983), 4–5.

CHAPTER FOUR

Masons

Masons seem to be everywhere, although there are only about 1.7 million in the United States.[1] They appear at public functions, such as the dedications of buildings, and seem to be involved in all aspects of life, up to and including the funeral service for their "Brothers." Besides being involved in many other organizations, Masons are found in churches of most denominations. In churches with liberal theology, one would not expect concern over theological differences; but in the theologically conservative Southern Baptist Convention, at one time 14 percent of pastors and 18 percent of deacon board chairs were Masons.[2]

Although only men can be Masons, related organizations are available for their relatives. The Order of the Eastern Star can include both men and women. DeMolay is for young men, and Rainbow Girls and Job's Daughters are for young women.

Many other secret societies seem to be patterned after the Masons. L. James Rongstad says, "[Freemasonry] is the 'Granddaddy' of all lodges. Its teachings, rituals, customs, and practices, and its secrecy have had an inspirational effect on other similar groups such as the Moose, Eagles, Elks, and the National Grange."[3]

William J. Whalen, author of *Handbook of Secret Organizations*, refers to other groups influenced by the Masons—including college fraternities. Whalen quotes William H. Shideler, founder of Phi Kappa Tau and a Mason himself, who stated, "Most of the rituals of college fraternities are based more or less directly upon the . . . Masonic ritual."[4]

Some people even think that the symbols on the back of the U.S. dollar bill have their origin in—or at least relate to—Freemasonry. The pyramid, the all-seeing eye, the number of feathers on the eagle's spread wings, the stars above the eagle's head in the shape of the Star of David, and the mottoes *e pluribus unum* (out of many one) and *novus ordo seclorum* (a new order of the ages)—are believed to have obvious connections to Freemasonry.[5] This is difficult to prove, however.

The Masons are involved in many worthy causes. The public is perhaps most aware of the Shriners because of their entertaining and colorful involvement in parades. The most distinctive symbol of the Shriner is his red fez hat with the black tassel. To be a Shriner, a person must be a 32nd Degree Scottish Rite Mason or its equivalent in the York Rite (Knights Templar).

Shriners Hospitals for Crippled Children in the United States, Canada and Mexico have been of enormous help to many families.

CAN A KNOWLEDGEABLE AND COMMITTED MASON BE A KNOWLEDGEABLE AND COMMITTED CHRISTIAN?

These orthopedic and burn hospitals are free to those 18 and under who might not otherwise be able to obtain treatment. While I was attending Dallas Theological Seminary, my wife worked as a registered nurse in the Texas Scottish Rite Hospital for Crippled Children in Dallas. She was highly impressed with the quality of care and concern given to children by that orthopedic hospital.

According to their own testimony: "Masons practice charity and benevolence and strive to promote human welfare. All over the world Masons care for their indigent Brethren, widows and orphans; maintain homes; support their mother countries in great wars; aid medical research, gerontology, blood banks, youth programs, military rehabilitation; contribute scholarships and practice character building."[6]

"What," you ask, "can possibly be wrong with an organization that does all of that?" People differ on their answers to that question.

Some think Freemasonry is only a fraternal or social organization. As such, they see no problem with a Christian being a Mason. Others are greatly concerned about the beliefs of Freemasonry and maintain that its views are in open conflict with biblical Christianity.

Local churches can face difficult decisions when receiving new members or considering members for leadership positions. How significant is it to the church that a person is a Mason?

It is important to compare the teachings of Masonry with the Bible, the written revelation of God. For only then can the question be answered: Can a knowledgeable and committed Mason be a knowledgeable and committed Christian?

There is no intent to reveal in these pages any "secrets" of the Masonic Lodge. If such is done, it will be unintentional—and unnecessary. If the published literature of the Masons clearly shows that their teachings are contrary to the teaching of the Bible, it does not matter what the secrets are.

BACKGROUND

Some Masons trace the origin of their organization back to the beginning of time, but most modern Masons are more moderate in their claims. Although much of their teaching is tied to Solomon's temple, which was erected during Old Testament times, modern Masonry dates only to 1717. It was in that year that four lodges in Great Britain formed the first Grand Lodge of England, which became known as the Premier Grand Lodge of the world.

The terminology and symbolism of Masonry seem to come mostly from the actual craft of stonemasonry during the Middle Ages. Stonemasons gathered as a union to develop their craft and keep secrets from others. It is uncertain where the *free* is derived from in the word *Freemasonry*. Some think it was used because masons worked with freestones, or stones that could be cut without splitting. "Such workmen were first called masons of free stone, then, free stone masons, and finally freemasons."[7] The term *free* in Masonry is also taught to mean "free-born"; that is, never having been a slave.

Those actually working with stone were known as "operative" masons. Later, when non-stone workers joined the group, they were referred to as "speculative" Masons. "Speculative Freemasonry is also called symbolic Freemasonry, since the working tools of operative

Masonry are used as symbols to teach moral and philosophical lessons."[8] These non-operative Masons were also referred to as "Accepted."

Stonemasons had three classifications for workers practicing their craft: Apprentice, Fellow Craft and Master Mason. This is also the terminology used for the first three degrees in Freemasonry.

Masons of the first three degrees form the Blue Lodge of Masonry. Blue apparently is symbolic of the sky, and so the Blue Lodge relates to universal Masonry. A man is not considered a full-fledged Mason until he has reached the Third Degree—Master Mason. In a sense, he can never be a higher Mason than he is after having received this Third Degree, even if he goes on to other degrees.

Once a man has become a Master Mason, he need not go any further; and apparently most do not. But those who wish to pursue more of the mysteries of Masonry—to search for greater light—can become a part of the Scottish Rite or the York Rite. The Scottish Rite offers degrees 4 through 32 (the 33rd Degree is honorary). The York Rite has fewer titles, but they are equivalent to various degrees of the Scottish Rite. For example, as mentioned previously, The Order of the Knights Templar of the York Rite is equivalent to the 32nd Degree of the Scottish Rite.

Masons claim they never invite anyone to join their membership—that it is necessary for an interested person to ask to become a member. There is a thin line, however, between merely telling a person the advantages of being a Mason and implying that he should become one. But Masonry says, "All you have to do is ask"—even using the passage from the Bible: "Ask, and it will be given you; seek, and you will find; knock, and it will be opened to you" (Matt. 7:7). A person must "ask" to be a candidate; then "knock, and it will be opened to you" is a prompt for the candidate to knock and gain admission to the lodge room.

Many allegories and symbols are used in Masonry. It is common for Masonic writers to refer to an ancient definition of their ancient craft: "Freemasonry is a system of morality, veiled in allegory, and illustrated by symbols."

To construct an adequate allegory or symbol, a person must have precisely in mind what he is endeavoring to allegorize or symbolize.

But the Masonic "authorities" do not agree about what their allegories and symbols refer to. Carl Claudy, author of many books on Freemasonry, explains, "A symbol may have many meanings, all of them right, so long as they are not self-contradictory."[9] Symbols can be made to mean almost anything a person chooses to make them mean.

While it is interesting to know how the Masonic Lodge got started, our chief concern should be the beliefs of Freemasonry. Do those beliefs conflict with biblical Christianity?

BELIEFS

Masonry is not just a social fellowship—it has a system of beliefs about cardinal doctrines of Christianity, including the source of authority, God, Jesus Christ, sin, salvation and the future life. It is apparent that Freemasonry is actually a religion.

As Elliot Miller, specialist in New Age beliefs, pointed out, "The U.S. Supreme Court has ruled that a primary characteristic of a religion is that it adheres to and promotes 'underlying theories' concerning such 'ultimate' realities as man's nature and his place in the universe."[10] This is certainly true not only of the New Age Movement but also of Freemasonry.

Though many Masons are unaware that Freemasonry is a religion, consider what some of their leaders say. Joseph Fort Newton (1880–1950), an Episcopal minister and recognized authority in the Masonic world, said, "Masonry is not a religion but Religion—not a church but a worship, in which men of all religions may unite."[11] Newton seemed to detract somewhat from his former statement when he later said, "Masonry is not a religion, but it is religious."[12]

Newton also wrote: "Religion, then, is the bond that binds us, first, to God, Whose [sic] is 'the something universal' *which unites all things into one whole*, and gives to the universe meaning and beauty. Second, it is the tie by which we are united to our fellow men in the service of duty, the sanctity of love, and the *spirit of fraternal righteousness*"[13] (emphasis mine).

The teaching that everything is of one essence is known as monism, from the Greek word for "one." This is the view of Hinduism, which has influenced so many religious groups in North

What They Believe

America—such as Christian Science, Unity School of Christianity, Rosicrucianism and the New Age Movement. Also, righteousness—contrary to Newton's comments—is not obtained by fraternal relationships but by a relationship with a personal God (Rom. 3:22).

Henry Wilson Coil, born in 1885, was the author of the encyclopedia that many lodges now accept as their authoritative source. When John Ankerberg, host of the nationally televised "John Ankerberg Show," polled the Grand Lodges (there is one Grand Lodge in each state), 44 percent of those who responded recommended *Coil's Masonic Encyclopedia* as their authoritative source.[14]

Coil rejects any statement that says Masonry is not a religion, only religious. "It would be as sensible to say that man had no intellect but was intellectual or that he had no honor but was honorable."[15] Coil further comments, "If Freemasonry were not religion, what would have to be done to make it such? Nothing would be necessary or at least nothing but to add more of the same. That brings us to the real crux of the matter; the difference between a lodge and a church is one of degree and not of kind."[16]

Coil adds, "Freemasonry has a religious service to commit the body of a deceased brother to the dust whence it came and to speed the liberated spirit back to the Great Source of Light. Many Freemasons make this flight with no other guarantee of a safe landing than their belief in the religion of Freemasonry. If that is a false hope, the Fraternity should abandon funeral services and devote its attention to activities where it is sure of its ground and its authority."[17] These comments clearly show that Freemasonry is considered by some of its significant leaders to be a religion.

Freemasonry considers Christianity to be only one religion among many others, such as Judaism, Islam and Buddhism. Freemasonry also considers itself to be above these, for it supposedly holds the tenets to which most all religions subscribe—the Fatherhood of God, the brotherhood of man and the immortality of the soul. But is this biblical Christianity?

The answer is found as we examine the beliefs of Freemasonry concerning the source of authority, God, Jesus Christ, sin, salvation and the future life.

SOURCE OF AUTHORITY

In Freemasonry the Bible is called the "Volume of the Sacred Law" (sometimes abbreviated V.S.L.). The V.S.L. is an indispensable part of what is called "the furniture" in a Masonic Lodge.

North Americans are more impressed than they should be about the Lodge's use of the Bible. If they joined the Lodge in some other parts of the world, the V.S.L. would be something other than the Bible.

No better authority can be cited to confirm this than Albert Pike (1809–1901), who was responsible for virtually rewriting the Scottish Rite degrees into their present form. Pike said, "The Bible is an indispensable part of the furniture of a Christian Lodge, only because it is the sacred book of the Christian religion. The Hebrew Pentateuch in a Hebrew Lodge, and the Koran in a Mohammedan one, belong on the Altar; and one of these, and the Square and Compass, properly understood, are the Great Lights by which a Mason must walk and work."[18] Notice that the "Great Lights" include the Mason's tools of the square and compass as well as the Bible. No claim is made for the sole authority of the Bible as the only Great Light.

Knowledgeable Masons know how the Bible is viewed by Freemasonry. Carl Claudy agrees with Pike when he tells the Entered Apprentice, or one who has achieved the first degree, that the Bible is always referred to as "The Great Light" in this country, but "the practice may be and often is different in other lands. What is vital and unchangeable, a Landmark of the Order is that a *Volume of the Sacred Law be open upon the Masonic altar whenever the lodge is open.* A lodge wholly Jewish may prefer to use only the Old Testament; in Turkey and Persia the Koran would be used as the V.S.L. of the Mohammedan; Brahmins would use the Vedas"[19] (emphasis his). Where many races and creeds exist, as in the Far East, Claudy explains that some lodges provide several holy books for the initiate to make his choice.[20] It appears that Masonry does not care what book a person considers sacred or uses in his search for the light. Masonry's only concern is that each person must swear by the most holy book he knows that he will keep the oaths of Freemasonry.

In their excellent book *The Deadly Deception*, Jim Shaw and Tom

McKenney expose Freemasonry for what it really is. Shaw was a 33rd Degree Scottish Rite Mason before he saw the darkness of Freemasonry and turned to the light by trusting the Lord Jesus Christ as his Savior. "Masonry, contrary to popular belief," Shaw says, "is NOT based upon the Bible. Masonry is actually based on the Kabala (Cabala), a medieval book of magic and mysticism"[21] (emphasis his).

According to *Coil's Masonic Encyclopedia*, the Kabala "contains the mystic lore of the Jews. . . . It contains both Babylonian mythological and Zoroastrian theological concepts."[22] Coil claims no relationship of the Kabala to Freemasonry "except that the originators of the Hauts Grades on the Continent of Europe resorted to it in search of ritualistic lore and the consequences will be observed in some of the mystical and philosophical degrees."[23]

Newton acknowledged that the "Square, Rule, Plumb-line, the perfect Ashlar, the two Pillars, the Circle within the parallel lines, the Point within the Circle, the Compasses, the Winding Staircase, the numbers Three, Five, Seven, Nine, the double Triangle—these and other such symbols were used alike by Hebrew Kabbalists and Rosicrucian Mystics."[24] Newton, however, did not believe Freemasonry borrowed these symbols from others; he claimed the others borrowed them from Freemasonry.[25]

Pike, however, was more emphatic than Coil and Newton about the importance of the Kabala. In explaining the Hebrew letter Yod (written like the English apostrophe) enclosed in a triangle, a symbol used in Masonic lodges, Pike said, "Yod is, in the Kabalah, the symbol of Unity, of the Supreme Deity, the first letter of the Holy Name; and also a symbol of the Great Kabalistic Triads. To understand its mystic meanings, you must open the pages of . . . kabalistic books, and ponder deeply on their meaning."[26]

In explaining another symbol, Pike told the Entered Apprentice, "That meaning is not for the Apprentice. The adept [the one in possession of the secrets] may find it in the Kabalah."[27] Pike left no doubt about his belief that the Kabalah was the ultimate source of Masonic beliefs. He said, "Masonry is a search after Light. That search leads us directly back, as you see, to the Kabalah."[28]

Masons who think the Bible is taken seriously by Freemasonry as a guide of faith and practice do not know what their own leaders have written. Furthermore, the Freemasons' failure to accept the Bible as the only source of authority is seen in what they believe about God.

GOD

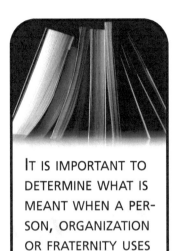

IT IS IMPORTANT TO DETERMINE WHAT IS MEANT WHEN A PERSON, ORGANIZATION OR FRATERNITY USES THE WORD *GOD.*

In today's theologically confused world, it is important to determine what is meant when a person, organization or fraternity uses the word *God.* Some groups, such as Christian Science, Unity School of Christianity and the Rosicrucians, perceive God to be a principle rather than a person with intellect, emotions and will. Transcendental Meditation and the New Age Movement—true to their Hindu origin—believe God to be an impersonal being or essence of the universe. What do the Masons believe about God?

This answer is especially important since no one can become a Mason unless he believes in God. Claudy emphasizes, "The petitioner knows it before he signs his application. He must answer 'Do you believe in God?' before his petition can be accepted. He must declare his faith in a Supreme Being before he may be initiated."[29]

This may impress many people that Freemasonry is biblical, but consider Claudy's following comments: "But note that he is not required to say, then or ever, *what* God. He may name Him as he will, think of Him as he pleases; . . . Freemasonry cares not"[30] (emphasis his).

Rather than even using the word *God,* the Masons more commonly refer to their deity by another expression—Great Architect of the Universe—usually abbreviated G.A.O.T.U.[31] In the Fellow Craft, or Second Degree, deity is further explained as "God, Great Architect of the Universe, Grand Artificer, Grand Master of the Grand Lodge Above, Jehovah, Allah, Buddha, Brahma, Vishnu, Shiva, or Great Geometer[;] a symbol of the conception shines in the East of every

American Masonic lodge, as in the center of the canopy of every English lodge."[32]

Many people see the Masonic ring, with its emblem of a compass and a square with the letter "G" in the center, and presume that the "G" refers to God. Although that is one of its symbolic meanings, the "G" can also refer to geometry, the science of the stonemason. Claudy quotes Plato, who said, "God is always geometrizing." Then Claudy adds, "It is merely an accident of the English language that geometry and God begin with the same letter."[33]

The Masons are fond of speaking of the Fatherhood of God, as in the expression, "There is one God, the Father of all men." In the sense that God created mankind, it is true that He is the Father of us all. But the Bible clearly distinguishes between those who have come into a right relationship with the Father and those who have not. Those outside of that relationship are not considered the children of God. Instead, they are known as the children of the Devil. Jesus told some unbelievers, "You are of your father the devil, and the desires of your father you want to do" (John 8:44). The Lord Jesus Christ never spoke of the Fatherhood of God in the sense in which the Masons use the expression. But notice what the Masons believe about Jesus.

Jesus Christ

Those who claim no conflict exists between the beliefs of Freemasonry and Christianity need to look more carefully at what some of the Masonic leaders have written. Historical Christianity believes that Jesus Christ is a triune member of the one Godhead, and as such He is God. The Lord Jesus Christ became a man that He might die for the sins of the world. Had He not become man, He could not have died for our sins. Had He not been God, His death could not have provided salvation for all who trust Him as Savior. But what does Freemasonry say about all of this?

It is interesting—and significant—to note that Joseph Fort Newton's book, *The Builders*, has no entry in the index for "Jesus" or "Christ." *Coil's Masonic Encyclopedia* has no such separate entry either, although he groups many elements under "Religion." Neither does Holman's Masonic Edition of the Holy Bible include an entry of either "Jesus" or "Christ" in its "One Hundred and Sixty Questions and Answers," which was compiled from the works of Albert Mackey and other eminent Masonic authorities in 1935. The closest this index comes to a direct reference to Jesus Christ is what is said under the entry "Lost Word." Mansonry claims that the actual name for "God" has been lost. Under this entry is posed the question: "What is the true meaning of the Lost Word?" The answer given is: "The true meaning of the Lost Word is Divine Truth, symbolically speaking. This is what the old writers claim and has reference to the Ineffable name. St. John 1:1."[34]

John 1:1 says, "In the beginning was the Word, and the Word was with God, and the Word was God." Masonry seems to believe that the reference to *Word* in this verse has to do with the lost word of God's "ineffable" name. But verse 14 explains what the "Word" of verse 1 refers to: "And the Word became flesh and dwelt among us, and we beheld His glory, the glory as of the only begotten of the Father, full of grace and truth." The "Word" clearly refers to the Lord Jesus Christ. But, of course, the Masons cannot acknowledge this, or it would offend the Jews, Muslims and members of other non-Christian religions who are allowed to be part of Freemasonry.

The Gospel of John records the words of Jesus, "I am the way, the truth, and the life. No one comes to the Father except through Me" (14:6). No one who is knowledgeable of and committed to Masonry can agree with Jesus' words. Freemasonry does not believe that Jesus Christ is God nor that salvation is available only through Him.

Freemasonry is a search for light. The Masons acknowledge that "light is a symbol of knowledge. It is the ultimate desire of every Mason to be well informed on Masonry, and may every Mason strive constantly for light, and especially for light eternal."[35] But the Lord Jesus Christ said, "I am the light of the world. He who follows Me shall not walk in darkness, but have the light of life" (John 8:12).

Many references in the four Gospels speak of light as referring to the Lord Jesus Christ. John 1:1–18 sufficiently shows that any use of language that shows the light to be something other than the Lord Jesus Christ is a use of language that allows man to make up any meaning he wants.

Referring to the Hindu teaching of reincarnation and the Hebrew concept of the afterlife—which he thinks is founded on the same teaching—George H. Steinmetz reveals how Masonic thinking conflicts with biblical teaching: "Neither philosophy has ever taught of the coming of an INDIVIDUAL who would be the 'Savior,' the 'Messiah' or 'Redeemer.' When properly understood these great philosophies teach that through many incarnations and the slow process of evolution the ENTIRE HUMAN RACE is rising toward perfection. The Messiah, then, will be the final achievement of that 'plan' of the Supreme Architect—NOT AN INDIVIDUAL, but—THE PERFECTION OF THE RACE!"[36] (emphasis his).

Steinmetz adds, "It is not our intention to review the endless arguments as to the divinity of either Krishna or Jesus. Regardless of whether or not they were mystically conceived, there is little room for argument that the stories told about them and their legendary background partake of the incidents and are of the essence of the legend of the 'Dying God,' and it has been determined that the origin of that legend is the journey of the sun through the zodiacal signs of the heavens."[37]

When comparing the various religions and legends, Steinmetz sees little that is distinctive about Christianity. "Thus we discover that most of the events, the allegories and symbolism of the various 'Messiahs,' seemingly have their origin in that most ancient of religious beliefs—Solar Worship."[38]

Does Steinmetz think Solar Worship is also the origin of the teachings of Freemasonry? For instance, the legend of Hiram Abiff (whom Masons regard as the chief architect of Solomon's temple) is a major part of Masonry. What is its source? "There is a similarity between the Hiramic legend and these other legends," Steinmetz acknowledges, "but our ignorance of the origin of the former does not permit the categorical statement that it is taken from them; it may have its own particular line of descent directly from the Solar Myths."[39]

Although Steinmetz admits that the Hiramic legend is derived from Solar Myths, it is significant that he wishes to claim more distinctiveness for the Hiramic legend than for the beliefs of other world religions.

Former 33rd Degree Mason Jim Shaw says of Hiram Abiff: "It is the consensus of opinion among Masonic authorities, philosophers and writers of doctrine that the legend of Hiram Abiff is merely the Masonic version of a much older legend, that of Isis and Osiris, basis of the Egyptian Mysteries."[40]

When the Bible is used in Freemasonry, the references to Jesus Christ are omitted, lest other religions be offended. For instance, when 1 Peter 2:5 is used in a Masonic lodge, it is quoted as: "Ye also, as lively stones, are built up a spiritual house, an holy priesthood, to offer up spiritual sacrifices, acceptable to God" (KJV). But Masons deliberately omit the last three words of the verse: "by Jesus Christ." This shows the true attitude of the Lodge toward Christianity.

Also, although prayer pervades all the rituals of Masonry, they are Christless prayers. A well-ordered lodge never allows prayer to be offered in the name of Jesus Christ.

The Entered Apprentice is told: "In his private devotions a man may petition God or Jehovah, Allah or Buddha, Mohammed or Jesus; he may call upon the God of Israel or the Great First Cause. In the Masonic Lodge he hears humble petition to the Great Architect of the Universe, finding his own deity under that name. A hundred paths may wind upward around a mountain; at the top they meet."[41]

Freemasonry does not adjust its beliefs to fit the Bible; the Bible is adjusted to fit the beliefs of Freemasonry.

Sin

One must search hard to find references to sin in the writings of the Masonic leaders. It is only mentioned in passing as they discuss other topics. Masons are like Christian Scientists, the New Age Movement and Unity School of Christianity in this regard: They deny the reality of sin as mentioned in the Bible. They think that any shortcomings can be overcome by greater enlightenment. When the Masons refer to sin, their comments are far from the biblical teaching on the subject.

The Bible clearly talks about the reality of sin and the penalty it carries with it. Romans 3:23 says, "All have sinned and fall short of the glory of God." Romans 5:12 says, "Just as through one man sin entered the world, and death through sin, and thus death spread to all men, because all sinned." Romans 6:23 says, "For the wages of sin is death," and the Bible teaches that both physical and spiritual death result from sin.

In answer to the question, "What is the symbolism of a Master Mason, and how is it represented?" the notes in the Holman Masonic Edition of the Bible say in part: "By its legend and all its ritual, it is implied that we have been redeemed from the death of sin and the sepulchre of pollution."[42]

BECAUSE MASONS DO NOT RECOGNIZE THE SINFULNESS OF HUMANITY, THEY SEE NO NEED FOR SALVATION IN THE BIBLICAL SENSE.

SALVATION AND FUTURE LIFE

If sin and its penalty do not exist, we have nothing to be saved from. But if that were the case, Jesus would not have left His position with the Father to take upon Himself human form so that He could redeem mankind, as recorded in Philippians 2. Of course, for Masons this isn't a conflict since they don't believe in Jesus Christ of the Bible anyway.

All are guilty of sin; but fortunately, 1 John 2:1–2 says, "If anyone sins, we have an Advocate with the Father, Jesus Christ the righteous. And He Himself is the propitiation [satisfaction] for our sins, and not for ours only but also for the whole world." Any person may receive eternal life and forgiveness of sin by receiving Jesus Christ as Savior (John 1:12; Rom. 6:23). But what do the Masons propose as the means of salvation?

"What then is this thing called 'SALVATION'?" asks Steinmetz in *The Lost Word*.[43] He answers his own question: "It is but to be brought from the material to the spiritual; . . . man must return to his forgotten inherent spirituality"[44] (emphasis his).

Referring to the Sublime Degree of Master Mason, Claudy comments: "The degree delves into the deepest recesses of a man's nature. While it leads the initiate into the Sanctum Sanctorum [Holy of Holies] of the Temple, it probes into the Holy of Holies of his heart.

"As a whole the degree is symbolical of that old age by the wisdom of which 'we may enjoy the happy reflection consequent on a well-spent life, and die in the hope of a glorious immortality.'"[45]

Notes in the Holman Masonic Bible say of the Master Mason, "The conclusion we arrive at is, that youth, properly directed, leads us to honorable and virtuous maturity, and that the life of man, regulated by morality, faith, and justice, will be rewarded at its closing hour, by the prospect of eternal bliss."[46] This is clearly a salvation by works, or character development—not a salvation by faith in Christ alone, who has paid the penalty for our sins.

Because Masons do not recognize the sinfulness of humanity, they see no need for salvation in the biblical sense. Former Mason Jim Shaw says of the Masonic doctrine of redemption: "Faith in the atonement of Jesus has nothing to do with it; it is rather a matter of enlightenment, step by step, which comes with initiation into the Masonic degrees and their mysteries."[47]

One of Shaw's great disillusionments with Masonry, however, was that when he got to the top as a serious seeker, he still did not find the Light he was looking for. When he took the 32nd Degree, he was told, "You have reached the mountain peak of Masonic instruction, a peak covered by a mist, which YOU in search for further light can penetrate only by your own efforts"[48] (emphasis his).

Biblical Christianity teaches that redemption is available only through the saving grace of the Lord Jesus Christ. "Nor is there salvation in any other, for there is no other name under heaven given among men by which we must be saved" (Acts 4:12).

Although any salvation of the Masons is sought through self-reformation, the Bible says, "By grace you have been saved through faith, and that not of yourselves; it is the gift of God, not of works, lest anyone should boast" (Eph. 2:8–9).

D. W. Kerr summarizes the Bible's teaching about the future life: "Immortality in the biblical sense is a condition in which the individual is not subject to death or to any influence which might lead to death."[49] He adds, "Immortality, for the Christian, involves the resurrection and may be fully attained only after it."[50]

The Masons speak of their three great beliefs: the Fatherhood of God, the brotherhood of man and the immortality of the soul. But what do they mean by the "immortality of the soul"? Masonry has little to say directly about immortality except through veiled references to it in other comments. And because Masons see immortality as a reward for character development, it is always uncertain whether they will receive the reward of immortality; or, if all are to receive the reward, what kind of a reward is it?

CONCLUSION

Serious conflict exists between biblical Christianity and Freemasonry. From the testimony of many of the leaders in Freemasonry about the spiritual views of Masons, there seems to be no way a man can be both a knowledgeable and committed Mason and knowledgeable and committed Christian.

It is not surprising that churches with liberal theology see no conflict between Christianity and Freemasonry. If a church does not believe that the Bible is God's written revelation or that Jesus is God (a triune member of the one Godhead), or that salvation is available only through Him, it will see little apparent conflict with Masonry.

But it was a surprise to many evangelicals in June 1993 when delegates at the Southern Baptist Convention, after reading a seven-page report from its Home Mission Board, passed a resolution that "membership in a Masonic order [should] be a matter of personal conscience."[51]

If you are a Mason who endeavors to take your Christianity seriously, you've probably been surprised at the things you've read in this chapter. Perhaps you're thinking, *That's not what Masons believe.*

Don't take my word for it. Check the endnotes for references, and examine the Masonic sources for yourself. If you genuinely have the desire to find the true Light, you will be led to it. Ask the superiors at your lodge about the use of the Koran, the Vedas—and other holy books—as the Volume of the Sacred Law in non-Christian countries. Ask if the lodge is serious about following the specific teachings of the Bible or if it is only using it as a symbol. Ask your lodge leaders if they believe Jesus Christ is the only way of salvation.

What should a Bible-believing church do about admitting Masons to its membership and to leadership positions? Such a church should want only members and leaders who are believers and who are committed to following the Lord Jesus Christ.

In interviews for church membership and leadership, it is usually better to let the interviewee say what he believes rather than simply answering yes or no to a carefully worded doctrinal statement. For instance, rather than asking, "Do you believe that Jesus Christ is God and that salvation is available only through Him because of what He accomplished on the cross?" it is better to say, "Tell us what you believe about who Jesus Christ is and how a person can have forgiveness of sins and eternal life." Do not expect polished statements, of course, from a person without much theological background. But a Christian should be able to express the basics of what he believes.

Since Freemasonry sees itself as superseding and unifying all religions, a Mason may believe what he wants as long as he does not try to impose his views on others. This means that those who believe what a Bible-believing church teaches would be accepted as Masons as long as they do not insist their views are the only right ones.

Although it is better to let the interviewee respond in his or her own words, here are some suggested questions designed for yes-or-no answers that you might ask those who see no conflict between Freemasonry and Christianity:

1. Do you think that the Bible is God's written revelation to mankind and that it is the only such revelation?

2. Do you believe that Jesus Christ is God?

3. Do you believe that only the Bible explains how we can be saved from eternal condemnation?

4. Do you believe that trusting in Jesus Christ as Savior is the only way to obtain salvation?

5. Do you believe that Jesus Christ is the Light of the world and that all who do not follow Him walk in darkness, as John 8:12 says?

A knowledgeable and committed Mason would have to answer no to all of these questions if he is truthful. Freemasonry claims that nothing in it would offend the Christian, the Jew, the Muslim or the Brahmin—which means it cannot believe biblical truths about Jesus Christ. And because Freemasonry believes that only Masons are in the light and that all non-Masons are in darkness, no good Mason could say yes to the last question.

What They Believe

Be sure when dealing with a Mason—as with others—that you ask him to define his terms. What does he mean by such words as *God, Christ, light, Fatherhood of God* and *salvation*? Freemasonry's mystical and metaphysical expressions are not easily understood, even by its own followers.

Perhaps the most significant issue for the person joining your church is that of authority. Matthew 6:24 says, "No one can serve two masters; for either he will hate the one and love the other; or else he will be loyal to the one and despise the other. You cannot serve God and mammon."

A Bible-teaching church needs to determine if an individual is giving total allegiance to Jesus Christ or to something else. A Mason has sworn allegiance to the religion of Freemasonry. Claiming that Christ is his Lord clearly presents a conflict with his Masonic beliefs.

While researching the beliefs of the Masons, I came into contact with an Air Force officer who had been a fourth-generation Mason. By the age of 23, he was a 32nd Degree Scottish Rite Prince of the Royal Secret, a York Rite Knight Templar, the Senior Deacon of a Blue Lodge that he attended and the unofficial Tyler of another lodge he frequently attended. He had been to lodges in New Hampshire, Arkansas, Oklahoma, Maine, Nebraska—even Japan and the Philippines. He not only attended but was active in most of these lodges. Of his own free will and accord he came to see that Jesus Christ was the true Light and the chief cornerstone that the builders had rejected (1 Pet. 2:6–7).

When he became a Master Mason, he was given a Masonic edition of the Bible. When he opened it, his eyes fell on Matthew 6:24, where he read that it is impossible to serve two masters. This caused him to think seriously about the conflicts that he knew existed between Freemasonry and Christianity. He eventually realized he had to forsake Masonry—which he had given allegiance to as his master—and follow only the Lord Jesus Christ. A well-read student of both Freemasonry and Christianity, he believes there is no possibility that a knowledgeable and committed Christian can also be a Mason.

Those faced with trying to assess to what extent Freemasonry conflicts with biblical Christianity should acquire books written by former Masons, such as those by Jim Shaw and Dale Byers (see Recommended Reading). These books, by those who have been there, reveal the darkness of Masonry.

Those who think the Bible and its teachings are taken seriously by Freemasonry need to be reminded of the words of Masonic authority Henry Wilson Coil: "The prevailing Masonic opinion is that the Bible is only a symbol of Divine Will, Law, or Revelation, and not that its contents are Divine Law, inspired, or revealed. So far, no responsible authority has held that a Freemason must believe the Bible or any part of it."[52]

Summary

Name: Freemasonry
Also Known As: Masons, Masonic Lodge
U.S. Headquarters: Alexandria, Virginia
Membership (2004): U.S.: About 1.7 million

What They Believe

Masons: **Biblical Christians:**

Source of Authority

Use the Bible only in a "Christian" lodge; the Hebrew Pentateuch in a Hebrew lodge; the Koran in a Muslim lodge; the Vedas in a Brahmin lodge. Pike said the Masonic search after light leads directly back to the Kabala.

Claim the Bible as the sole authority for beliefs and practices. Jesus Christ is the only true Light.

God

Masonic candidate is never required to say what God he believes in, for "Freemasonry cares not." Explain deity as Grand Artificer, Grand Master of the Grand Lodge Above, Jehovah, Allah, Buddha, Brahma, Vishnu, Shiva or Great Geometer.

Define God in terms and descriptions found in the Bible. God shares His glory with none other.

What They Believe

Jesus Christ

Omit references to Jesus Christ when quoting from the Bible. Do not care whether a person privately petitions God or Jehovah, Allah or Buddha, Mohammed or Jesus, the God of Israel or the Great First Cause; but in the lodge they petition only the Great Architect of the Universe.

The death, burial and resurrection of Jesus Christ is the special focus of Christianity. All access to God is through the Lord Jesus Christ because of His finished work on the cross.

Sin

Deny the reality of sin in the biblical sense. Any shortcomings can be overcome by greater enlightenment.

Sin is any act or character that fails to measure up to God's standard. All have sinned and come short of God's glory.

Salvation

Salvation is by works or character development.

Salvation is by grace through faith in the finished work of the Lord Jesus Christ, apart from works.

Recommended Reading

Ankerberg, John, and Weldon, John. *The Facts on the Masonic Lodge*. Eugene, Ore: Harvest House, 1988.

_____. *The Secret Teachings of the Masonic Lodge*. Chicago: Moody Press, 1990.

Byers, Dale. *I Left the Lodge*. Schaumburg, Ill.: Regular Baptist Press, 1989.

Mather, George A., and Nichols, Larry A. *Masonic Lodge*. Grand Rapids, Mich.: Zondervan Publishing House, 1995.

McClain, Alva J. *Freemasonry and Christianity*. Winona Lake, Ind.: BMH Books, 1979.

Rongstad, L. James. *The Lodge*, rev. ed. St. Louis: Concordia Publishing House, 1995.

Shaw, Jim, and McKenney, Tom. *The Deadly Deception: Freemasonry Exposed ... by One of Its Top Leaders*. Lafayette, La.: Huntington House, Inc. 1988.

ENDNOTES

[1] "Masonic Statistics," www.bessel.org/masstats.htm, Oct. 24, 2005.

[2] *Christianity Today*, May 17, 1993, 81.

[3] L. James Rongstad, *How to Respond to . . . the Lodge* (St. Louis: Concordia Publishing House, 1977), 10.

[4] William J. Whalen, *Handbook of Secret Organizations* (Milwaukee: The Bruce Publishing Company, 1966), 43–44.

[5] Dale A. Byers, *I Left the Lodge: A Former Mason Tells Why* (Schaumburg, Ill.: Regular Baptist Press, 1988), 17–18.

[6] Henry C. Clausen, 33rd Degree, *To a Non-Mason: You Must Seek Masonic Membership!* (Washington, D.C.: The Supreme Council, 33rd Degree, Mother Council of the World, Ancient and Accepted Scottish Rite of Freemasonry, Southern Jurisdiction, U.S.A., report, 1984), 4.

[7] Henry Wilson Coil, 33rd Degree, *Coil's Masonic Encyclopedia* (New York: Macoy Publishing & Masonic Supply Company, 1961), 266.

[8] Ibid., 631.

[9] Carl H. Claudy, *Introduction to Freemasonry*, Vol. II (Washington, D.C.: The Temple Publishers, 1943), 55–56.

[10] Elliott Miller, "Saying No to the New Age," *Moody Monthly,* February 1985, 25.

[11] Joseph Fort Newton, *The Religion of Masonry: An Interpretation* (Richmond, Va.: Macoy Publishing and Masonic Supply Company, Inc., 1969), 11.

[12] Ibid., 12.

[13] Ibid., 34

[14] Ankerberg and Weldon, *The Facts on the Masonic Lodge: Does Masonry Conflict With the Christian Faith?* (Eugene, Ore.: Harvest House Publishers, Inc., 1989), 8–9.

[15] Coil, *Coil's Masonic Encyclopedia*, 512.

[16] Ibid.

[17] Ibid.

[18] Albert Pike, *Morals and Dogma of the Ancient and Accepted Scottish Rite of Freemasonry* (Charleston, S.C.: Supreme Council of the Thirty-Third Degree, 1905), 11.

[19] Claudy, *Introduction to Freemasonry*, Vol. I, 37.

[20] Ibid.

[21] Jim Shaw and Tom McKenney, *The Deadly Deception: Freemasonry Exposed . . . by One of Its Top Leaders* (Lafayette, La.: Huntington House, Inc., 1988), 128.

[22] Coil, *Coil's Masonic Encyclopedia*, 111.

[23] Ibid.

[24] Joseph Fort Newton, *The Builders: A Story and Study of Freemasonry* (Richmond, Va.: Macoy Publishing and Masonic Supply Company, Inc., 1979), 146.

[25] Ibid., 147.

[26] Pike, *Morals and Dogma*, 15.

[27] Ibid., 17.

[28] Ibid., 741.

[29] Claudy, *Introduction to Freemasonry*, Vol. II, 109–110.

[30] Ibid., 110.

What They Believe

31 Ibid.

32 Ibid.

33 Ibid., 109.

34 Holy Bible: Masonic Edition (Philadelphia: A. J. Holman Company, 1951), 21.

35 Ibid., 20.

36 George H. Steinmetz, *The Lost Word: Its Hidden Meaning* (Richmond, Va.: Macoy Publishing and Masonic Supply Company, 1953), 135–136.

37 Ibid, 136.

38 Ibid., 155.

39 Ibid.

40 Shaw and McKenney, *The Deadly Deception*, 152.

41 Claudy, *Introduction to Freemasonry*, Vol. I, 38.

42 Holy Bible: Masonic Edition, 22.

43 Steinmetz, *The Lost Word,* 156.

44 Ibid., 157.

45 Claudy, *Introduction to Freemasonry*, Vol. III, 125.

46 Holy Bible: Masonic Edition, 22.

47 Shaw and McKenney, *The Deadly Deception*, 132.

48 Ibid., 157.

49 D. W. Kerr, "Immortality" in *Evangelical Dictionary of Theology*, Walter A. Elwell, ed. (Grand Rapids, Mich.: Baker Book House, 1984), 551–552.

50 Ibid., 552.

51 Timothy C. Morgan, in *Christianity Today*, July 19, 1993, 54.

52 Coil, *Coil's Masonic Encyclopedia*, 520.

CHAPTER FIVE

Mormons

"I asked the Personages who stood above me in the light, which of all the sects was right—and which I should join. I was answered that I must join none of them, for they were all wrong."[1]

So begins the account of the history of one of the largest religious groups in the world today—the Church of Jesus Christ of Latter-day Saints, more commonly known as LDS or Mormons. According to Joseph Smith, the founder and "prophet," when he was only 14 years old he received this vision while praying for wisdom in the woods of upstate New York in 1820. Having been "called" by God to form His "only true church," Smith reportedly was directed by an angel to a set of golden plates containing God's true revelation, which he translated with the help of two magical stones. This translation—known as the *Book of Mormon*—along with many subsequent "revelations" given to Smith, became the basis for many of the beliefs still taught by the Mormons today. Even current president Gordon Hinckley said, "[D]octrines won't change," as he was installed as the LDS president on March 18, 1995.[2] Yet, as we will see later, Mormon doctrines (teachings) have changed over the years, even though they are supposedly received as revelation from God, who does not change (Heb. 6:17–18).

Mormonism is one of the fastest-growing religions in the world. According to their Web site, worldwide membership is now more than 12 million, including about 5.6 million in the U.S.[3]

Much of this tremendous growth can be attributed to the church's aggressive missionary outreach. Mormon young men, mostly 19 through 25 years of age, are expected to dedicate two years of missionary service on a self-supporting basis. Young women also do this but not nearly in the numbers of the men. Currently the group has about 56,000.[4]

This growth, coupled with its requirement that each member tithe 10 percent of his income, has made the church one of the wealthiest organizations in the United States. Reporting for *Time*, S. C. Gwynne and Richard Ostling pointed out that in 1996 the LDS had an estimated annual income of $5.9 billion, of which $5.3 billion was from tithes and offerings, and assets worth $30 billion.[5] Gwynne and Ostling concluded, "If it were a corporation, its estimated $5.9 billion in annual gross income would place it midway through the Fortune 500.[6]

In addition, the Mormons wield a great deal of social and political influence. A number of key business and political leaders are Mormons, as well as several popular entertainers and athletes. In contrast to the Jehovah's Witnesses, who refuse to salute the flag or serve in the military, there are many Mormons among military personnel.

BACKGROUND

To understand Mormonism, we must first look at the life of the founder, Joseph Smith Jr., for he is at the center of Mormon theology. The Mormons believe that Smith was God's prophet. Their faith is based on the revelations he supposedly received from the Lord. Yet there is even debate about what the Mormons call the First Vision that he received, referred to at the beginning of this chapter. Former Mormon Janis Hutchinson points out there are three versions of the First Vision: "1832 account—Jesus only; 1835–36 diary—Angels only; 1838 account—God the Father and Jesus."[7] Hutchinson concludes, "Smith just couldn't keep his stories straight. To make matters worse, Mormon leaders insist that 'during Joseph Smith's lifetime, he told but one story.'"[8]

The importance Mormons place on Joseph Smith is clearly seen in statements they have made about him. For instance, Brigham Young, the second president of the church, wrote of Smith: "Whosoever confesseth that Joseph Smith was sent of God . . . that spirit is of God; and every spirit that does not confess that God has sent Joseph Smith, and revealed the everlasting Gospel to and through him, is of Antichrist."[9] Such a statement is highly significant when we realize that a president of the church is considered the prophet who speaks for God. The LDS Web site stated, "Divine revelation for the direction of the entire Church comes from God to the President of the Church. The Presidents of the Church down through the years since it was restored in 1830 have been and are viewed by Latter-day Saints as prophets in the same sense as are Abraham, Moses, Peter, and other such biblical leaders."[10]

Through the years the Mormons have maintained that Smith possessed a flawless character. Brigham Young boasted, "Examine the character of the Savior, and . . . of those who have written the Old and New Testament; and then compare them with the character of Joseph Smith, the founder of this work . . . and you will find that his character stands as fair as that of any man's mentioned in the Bible. We can find no person who presents a better character to the world when the facts are known than Joseph Smith, Jun., the prophet, and his brother Hyrum Smith, who was murdered with him."[11] When the facts are known about Joseph Smith, however, we see that his character and life were far from perfect.

THROUGH THE YEARS THE MORMONS HAVE MAINTAINED THAT SMITH POSSESSED A FLAWLESS CHARACTER.

Joseph Smith was born into poverty in Sharon, Vermont, on December 23, 1805. When Joseph was 10, the family moved to Palmyra, New York. Smith's father "was a mystic, a man who spent most of his time digging for imaginary buried treasure (he was particularly addicted to Captain Kidd's legendary hoard)."[12] At that time, treasure hunting was a common pastime. Frequently, money diggers would use "peep stones" or "seer stones" to search for buried treasure. According to former Mormons Jerald and Sandra Tanner, "These stones were sometimes placed in a hat and used to locate buried treasure."[13]

Joseph often joined his father and brother Hyrum in searching for buried treasure. In fact, it appears that his interest in money digging was even greater than that of his father. The evidence also indicates that he made frequent use of seer stones and other occult articles in searching for treasures for himself and for others. The Tanners cite a number of examples of Smith's money-digging activities. Their book also includes a photograph of a court document that "proves that Joseph Smith was a 'glass looker' and that he was arrested, tried and found guilty by a justice of the peace in Bainbridge, New York, in 1826."[14] Fawn M. Brodie also reproduced this and other records in her revealing biography of Joseph Smith.[15]

According to Mormon records, Joseph Smith's revelations and visions began at an early age. When he was 14, Smith reportedly became concerned about which denomination he should join. (He had been impressed with Methodism, but later his family converted to Presbyterianism.) After reading James 1:5, instructing any who lack wisdom to ask God for it, the future prophet went to the woods to pray. As he prayed, he was supposedly overcome by an enemy spirit. Suddenly two "personages" appeared, causing the enemy spirit to flee. One of the personages addressed Smith and—pointing to the other personage—said, *"This is My Beloved Son. Hear Him!"*[16] (emphasis his). The personages then proceeded to tell Smith that all of the churches were wrong and that he should not join any of them. Thus, Mormons would have us believe that, with one vision given to a 14-year-old boy, God wiped out 18 centuries of historical Christianity.

Three years later, at the age of 17, Smith supposedly received the extraordinary revelation that became the basis for Mormonism. As he lay in bed praying, the angel Moroni reportedly appeared to him and told him where to find some buried golden plates that contained the history of ancient America. The heavenly messenger added that on the plates was written "the fulness of the everlasting Gospel, . . . as delivered by the Savior to the ancient inhabitants."[17]

Since these plates were supposedly written in "reformed-Egyptian characters" (a nonexistent language), the angel told Smith that he would also find a pair of transparent stones set in silver bows (like spectacles) to use in translating the plates. When Smith found the plates, however, he was not allowed to take them but was told to wait four more years. Finally, in 1827, after the angel had made several more appearances, Smith was allowed to take the plates with strict instructions to keep them hidden.

In 1829 a teacher named Oliver Cowdery visited Smith and was soon converted to the new religion. Cowdery then became Smith's scribe. As Smith gazed through the stones (known as the Urim and Thummim), the reformed-Egyptian hieroglyphics would appear to him in English. He would then read the translation to Cowdery, who would record it. Cowdery and the other helpers never saw the plates, however, for the helpers were always separated from Smith by a screen or curtain.

About a month after Smith and Cowdery started the translation, they were supposedly visited by John the Baptist, who told them to baptize and lay hands on each other, thus ordaining themselves into the Aaronic priesthood. Later, Peter, James and John appeared and ordained them to the Melchizedekian priesthood.

In 1830 the translation, called the *Book of Mormon*, was published. On April 6 of that year, 24-year-old Joseph Smith and five other men officially organized what would later be named the Church of Jesus Christ of Latter-day Saints.

Shortly after this first official meeting, Smith and his followers moved west and settled in Kirtland, Ohio. In Kirtland the first quorum of 12 apostles was chosen, with Smith as the president. In June 1831, God supposedly commanded the followers of Smith to settle in Missouri, the "land of Zion." (The LDS own thousands of acres in Jackson County, Missouri, where Jesus supposedly will return to set up His kingdom.[18]) A number of Mormons moved to Missouri, while the rest remained in Ohio. Smith went from one locality to another because he was accused of many misdeeds, including immorality.[19] It seems that Brigham Young and others had a higher view of the character of the first president than did some Mormons of Smith's day.

During the next few years, the followers in both locations, now numbering several thousand, were at odds with the non-Mormons. In Missouri, after several clashes, the Mormons were finally forced to flee the state in 1838. They had also been driven out of Ohio. Smith eventually led the majority of the group to Commerce, Illinois, which he renamed Nauvoo. Smith was Nauvoo's mayor. It was here that he joined the Masonic Lodge, explaining many similarities between Mormon and Masonic rituals.[20] The Tanners conclude, "Although Mormon apologists would have us believe that Joseph Smith received the temple ceremony by revelation from God, the evidence is against it and clearly shows that he borrowed heavily from Masonry.[21]

Persecution from non-Mormons and unrest within the church continued to hound Smith, largely due to the "revelation" that the prophet received in 1831 establishing the practice of polygamy. Sources differ on how many wives Smith had. In his book, *In Sacred Loneliness: The Plural Wives of Joseph Smith* (Signature Books, 1997), Mormon biographer Todd Compton says that Smith had 33 wives ranging in age from 14 to 58 (11,15–16).

In 1844 Smith entered national politics by becoming a candidate for president of the United States. A newspaper started by some excommunicated Mormons, *The Nauvoo Expositor*, exposed the Mormons' polygamous practices and criticized Smith's political aspirations. In essence, the paper put Smith on trial in the eyes of his followers. A group of Smith's followers broke into the newspaper office, destroyed the press and burned copies of the paper. Joseph and Hyrum were arrested and placed in a jail in Carthage, Illinois, to await trial. However, three days later (June 27, 1844), a mob stormed the jail and killed both Joseph and Hyrum.

After the death of Joseph Smith, a struggle ensued among his followers regarding who would succeed him. Brigham Young, president of the Twelve Apostles, managed to keep the majority under his leadership, but several splinter groups developed. Even today there are various groups among the Latter-day Saints. According to the *Handbook of Denominations in the United States*, there are Latter-day Saints (Mormon), Church of Christ (Temple Lot), Church of Jesus Christ (Bickertonites), Church of Jesus Christ of Latter-day Saints (Strangite) and the Reorganized Church of Latter-day Saints.[22]

Brigham Young eventually led the largest group of the Latter-day Saints westward to the valley of the Great Salt Lake in what would later be known as Utah, arriving in 1847. In 1997 the Mormons commemorated the 150th anniversary of those who trudged the Mormon Trail with a wagon train reenactment of the trek from Omaha to Salt Lake City. But the Mormons in 1847 did not receive the positive press that accompanied the 150th anniversary celebration. In those days they were actually trying to get outside of the United States. Utah was not a state then and it wasn't allowed to become one until the Mormons officially renounced their practice of polygamy. In 1890, 59 years after the first president/prophet received the revelation authorizing polygamy, another president/prophet—Wilford Woodruff—rescinded it. Six years later, Utah became a state.

The second-largest group of Joseph Smith's followers settled in Independence, Missouri, and called themselves the Reorganized Church of Jesus Christ of Latter-day Saints (RLDS). In contrast to the 5.6 million followers of LDS in the United States, there are fewer than 145,000 of the RLDS.[23] The church in Missouri chose a son of Joseph Smith for their leader. They were referred to as Josephites, because they believed a descendant of Joseph Smith should be the head of the church. Those who followed Brigham Young were referred to as Brighamites.

The RLDS does not want to be confused with the LDS; that is, the Missouri followers of Joseph Smith are adamant about not wanting to be identified with his Utah followers. They do not use the name "Mormon" and differ with the Mormons on several issues. In addition to disagreeing over prophetic succession, the Reorganized Church rejects the historical practice of polygamy. Specifically, they do not believe that Joseph Smith practiced it, which is difficult to maintain in the light of evidence presented by the Utah Mormons and by a number of other historical documents and books. Both groups follow the *Book of Mormon* and the other writings of Smith in addition to the Bible. Both believe in continuing revelation. Both also regard the teachings of "Prophet" Joseph Smith to be divinely inspired and to be the foundation of their beliefs.

Much more could be written about both groups and about the specific beliefs of the Missouri followers, but this discussion of beliefs will be limited to the Latter-day Saints (Mormons).

BELIEFS

The beliefs and practices of the Mormon church bear little resemblance to the teachings in God's Word or to the practices of the early church. The LDS Web site said, "The Church is Christian but is neither Catholic nor Protestant. Rather, it is a restoration of the Church of Jesus Christ as originally established by the Savior."[24]

Mormons added the phrase "Latter-day Saints" to their name to indicate their belief that they are a latter-day restoration of the church that

Jesus Christ personally established while He was on earth. They teach that, after Christ ascended, He visited the American continent and preached the Gospel to the ancient inhabitants. He then instituted the doctrines and practices of His "true church," which were duly recorded on the golden plates. However, the people were destroyed before they could establish the new order, so the world had to wait 1,400 years for this restoration to take place.

Mormons believe their mission is "proclaiming a new dispensation, the restoration of the priesthood and rituals of the 'true church,' and the eligibility for the attainment of deity by all Mormons."[25]

SOURCE OF AUTHORITY

IN ADDITION TO THE BIBLE, THE MORMONS HAVE THREE OTHER VOLUMES THAT THEY BELIEVE ALSO CONTAIN REVELATIONS FROM GOD.

In addition to the Bible, the Mormons have three other volumes that they believe also contain revelations from God—the *Book of Mormon, Doctrine and Covenants* and the *Pearl of Great Price.* The Mormon scriptures are held in higher esteem than the Bible, for Mormons follow these three books even if the teachings in them contradict the Bible. And there are many contradictions.[26]

The Mormon church says, "*The Book of Mormon: Another Testament of Jesus Christ* is divinely inspired scripture, as is the Holy Bible."[27]

The Bible is placed in a weakened position among Mormon scriptures by their eighth Article of Faith, which states, "We believe the Bible to be the word of God as far as it is translated correctly; we also believe the Book of Mormon to be the word of God." To say the Bible is the word of God "as it is translated correctly" allows Mormon leaders to reject the Bible whenever they wish.

The main story in the *Book of Mormon* covers a period of 1,000 years—from 600 B.C. to A.D. 400. The Introduction to the *Book of*

Mormon says, "The book was written by many ancient prophets by the spirit of prophecy and revelation. Their words, written on gold plates, were quoted and abridged by a prophet-historian named Mormon. The record gives an account of two great civilizations. One came from Jerusalem in 600 B.C., and afterward separated into two nations, known as the Nephites and the Lamanites. The other came much earlier when the Lord confounded the tongues at the Tower of Babel. This group is known as the Jaredites. After thousands of years, all were destroyed except the Lamanites, and they are the principal ancestors of the American Indians."[28]

This introduction to the *Book of Mormon* also quotes Joseph Smith's words: "I told the brethren that the Book of Mormon was the most correct of any book on earth, and the keystone of our religion, and a man would get nearer to God by abiding by its precepts, than by any other book."[29] But notice what the publishers are forced to admit in the comments about this same edition of the *Book of Mormon*: "Some minor errors in the text have been perpetuated in past editions of the Book of Mormon."[30]

Think about it. Even the Mormons admit that errors have been perpetuated in the *Book of Mormon*! And how interesting that the publisher calls them "minor errors." With the claims the Mormons make for the writings of Joseph Smith, there are no such things as minor errors. An error is an error. Yet the Mormons don't even cite an example of these "minor errors."

Regarding this note in the 1981 edition of the *Book of Mormon* about corrections, Kurt Van Gorden says in *Kingdom of the Cults*, "Without blushing, the Mormon Church boldly asserts the unfounded claim that the prepublication manuscripts agree with their most recent changes. Our access to the handwritten copies of the original *Book of Mormon* deny such a claim and proves once again that the Mormon Church will sacrifice truth for the sake of public relations."[31]

Kingdom of the Cults gives various examples of the Mormons correcting contradictions, such as:

> The Roman Catholic Church should be delighted with page 25 of the original edition of *The Book of Mormon*, which confirms one of their dogmas, namely, that Mary is the Mother of God. "Behold, the virgin which thou seest, is the mother

of God." Noting this unfortunate lapse into Romanistic theology, Joseph Smith and his considerate editors changed 1 Nephi 11:18 (as well as 1 Nephi 11:21, 32; 13:40), so that it now reads: "Behold, the virgin whom thou seest, is the mother of the Son of God."[32]

The historical accuracy of the *Book of Mormon* presents an interesting problem. The Mormons claim the *Book of Mormon* is a history of ancient America, but non-Mormon archaeologists find no support for such a claim. Letters from qualified sources make such statements as "The book [*Book of Mormon*] is untrue Biblically, historically and scientifically," and "The Smithsonian Institution has never used the *Book of Mormon* in any way as a scientific guide. Smithsonian archeologists see no direct connection between the archeology of the New World and the subject matter of the book."[33]

The *Book of Mormon* has not been found accurate in its historical comments either as a guide to exploration or in agreeing with known history. If a book is to guide us in truths about the world we have not yet seen, then surely it should be accurate when it speaks about the world we have seen. By contrast, the Bible has been used as such a guide in archaeological exploration in the Middle East, particularly in Palestine. The Bible has been found to be geographically and historically accurate. It is expected, of course, that those who refuse to accept the Bible as final authority would also seek to discredit archeological discoveries that confirm its truths.

In the 2003 edition of the late Walter Martin's classic work, *Kingdom of the Cults*, Kurt Van Gorden revised and updated the chapter on the Mormons. (This edition retains Martin's comments and indicates additions by those who later revised and updated.) Concerning genetics research, Martin wrote:

> A thorough study of anthropology and such writers as W. C. Boyd (*The Contributions of Genetics to Anthropology*) and Bentley Glass, the gifted geneticist of Johns Hopkins University, reveals that Mormon findings based upon *The Book of Mormon* are out of harmony with the findings of geneticists and anthropologists. There is simply no foundation for the postulation that the Native American (Lamanites, according to Mormons) is in any way related to the race to which Nephi (a Semite) allegedly belonged.[34]

In the online edition of *Christianity Today*, John Kennedy writes that scientist Simon G. Southerton of Australia cites 7,500 DNA tests that show there is no link between American Indians and ancient Israel. This article discusses Southerton's book, *Losing a Lost Tribe: Native Americans, DNA, and the Mormon Church* (Signature Books).[35]

Another difference between the Bible and the *Book of Mormon* is the original language. The inspired text of the Bible was given by God to the authors in the common language of the people, whereas the *Book of Mormon* was supposedly translated from Egyptian hieroglyphics. It seems strange, therefore, that many passages in the *Book of Mormon* are exactly as stated in the King James Version of the Bible published in 1611. Martin documented some of these passages.[36] According to him, the *Book of Mormon* contains at least 25,000 words from the King James Bible.

Many people believe that the actual basis of the *Book of Mormon* was a book written by Solomon Spaulding (also spelled "Spalding") entitled *Manuscript Found*, rather than a supernatural revelation as the Mormons claim. This is the belief of the three authors of *Who Really Wrote the Book of Mormon?* Their evidence includes testimonies, handwriting analyses and statements from Smith and Spaulding and their relatives.[37]

Another important debate is over the "Book of Abraham," which is a part of the *Pearl of Great Price*, accepted by the Mormons as scripture. The "Book of Abraham," supposedly written by Abraham himself, gave the Mormon church its anti-black doctrine. (The church taught until 1978 that black people were under a curse and could not serve in the priesthood.) It has now been established—although understandably not accepted by the LDS—that the "Book of Abraham" was not written by Abraham himself. Even the Reorganized Church of Latter-day Saints (RLDS) seems to accept this, but not the Utah Mormons.[38]

The Tanners, former Mormons themselves, say, "We feel that if any person will honestly examine this matter he will see that the evidence to disprove the 'Book of Abraham' is conclusive. We have shown that the original papyrus fragment Joseph Smith used as the basis for the 'Book of Abraham' has been identified and that this fragment is in reality a part of the Egyptian 'Book of Breathings.' It is a pagan text and contains absolutely nothing concerning Abraham or his religion."[39]

For a church whose presidents/prophets still receive revelation from God, who does not change, it is interesting that a "new" revelation was received in 1978 reversing the previous revelation about blacks being cursed and not worthy of priesthood privileges. Although the church has been evasive about how the new revelation was received, it did reverse the previous revelation.[40]

The Mormons place all of their scriptures (including not only the *Book of Mormon* but also *Doctrine and Covenants* and the *Pearl of Great Price*) above the Bible in authority. Wallace Bennett has said, "We recognize the Bible's limitations as well as its value. We do not ascribe final authority to any of its statements because we believe that God has reestablished the authority to speak in His name, and has given it again to righteous men. Obviously, we do not accept the idea that with the adoption of the present contents of the Bible the whole canon of scriptures was closed for all time."[41]

Writing from the viewpoint of the Latter-day Saints, Steven Shields says, "One of the most important doctrines for both the RLDS church and LDS church is that the canon of scripture is not full— that God continues to direct the church through revelation to the prophet."[42]

By placing their presidents/prophets as the source of authority in directing the church, the Mormons thus reject the Bible as final authority and as such are not in line with biblical Christianity.

GOD

The Mormons hold many doctrines that are contrary to the Word of God. Their beliefs about the Person of God are at great variance with what God has revealed about Himself in the Bible. The Bible teaches that God is one, yet He exists in three Persons—Father, Son and Holy Spirit. According to Walter Martin, "Mormon theology . . . is polytheistic, teaching in effect that the universe is inhabited by different gods who procreate spirit children which are in turn clothed with bodies on different planets, 'Elohim' being the god of this planet (Brigham's teaching that Adam is our heavenly Father is now officially denied by Mormon authorities, but they hold firm to the belief that our God is a resurrected, glorified man)."[43]

Regarding the Father, the Bible says that He is spirit; therefore, He does not have a physical body. Jesus told the Samaritan woman, "God is Spirit, and those who worship Him must worship in spirit and truth" (John 4:24). The Mormon scriptures say, however, "The Father has a body of flesh and bones as tangible as man's."[44] Joseph Smith believed that God "was once as we are now, and is an exalted man."[45] He taught that God had once dwelt on a planet as a man and that through self-effort He eventually became God. This led Smith to teach that all good Mormons could become gods: "You have got to learn how to be Gods yourselves; to be kings and priests to God, the same as all Gods have done."[46]

When current president/prophet Gordon Hinckley was asked by *Time* reporters Gwynne and Ostling about the Mormon doctrine of man becoming gods, Hinckley "seemed to qualify the idea that men could become gods, suggesting that 'it's of course an ideal. It's a hope for a wishful thing,' but later affirmed that 'yes, of course they can.'"[47] How could the president/prophet, who is supposed to speak with the certain voice of God, be so uncertain?

Nor did Hinckley appear definitive when asked about the Mormon teaching that God was once a man. "I don't know that we teach it," he responded. "I don't know that we emphasize it . . . I understand the philosophical background behind it, but I don't know a lot about it, and I don't think others know a lot about it."[48] This side-stepping answer doesn't sound like one who is supposed to speak for God in articulating the doctrines of the church.

Mormon theology humanizes God and deifies man. Orson Hyde, a contemporary of Joseph Smith who was also a theologian recognized by the Mormon church, said, "Remember that God, our heavenly Father, was perhaps once a child, and mortal like we ourselves, and rose step by step in the scale of progress, in the school of advancement; has moved forward and overcome, until He has arrived at the point where He now is."[49]

Such views reveal that the Mormon scriptures not only add to the Bible, but they also often contradict what the Bible clearly teaches.

CHRIST

Regarding the deity of Christ, the Mormons are far from being in agreement with what the Scriptures teach. Mormons teach that all men existed in eternity as spirit beings before they were given physical bodies. They believe Christ was simply a spirit being like the rest of us before He came to the earth. On the one hand, the Mormons ascribe deity to Christ; on the other hand, they bring Him down to a human level. Mankind is placed on the same level as Christ. According to *Doctrine and Covenants*, Jesus said, "I was in the beginning with the Father, and am the Firstborn. . . . Ye were also in the beginning with the Father."[50] The Mormons believe Christ was created in the same sense that we were created; in fact, they believe Lucifer (the Devil) was a "son of God" even as Jesus was a "son of God."

The Bible, however, teaches that mankind did not exist in eternity past. Man did not exist until he was created by God (Gen. 1:26–27). By contrast, Christ was not created; He did exist in eternity (John 1:1, 14).

Mormons are also unscriptural in their view of the virgin birth of Christ. Brigham Young stated, "He [Christ] was not begotten by the Holy Ghost. . . . Jesus, our elder brother, was begotten in the flesh by the same character that was in the garden of Eden, and who is our Father in Heaven."[51] Walter Martin therefore concludes that the Mormons believe the "Savior was produced, not by a direct act of the Holy Spirit but by actual sexual relations between 'an immortal or resurrected and glorified Father,' and Mary. . . . There can be no mistaking the fact that the Adam-god doctrine is meant here, no matter how vehemently the Mormon apologists of today may deny that it was ever taught."[52]

David Reed and former Mormon John Farkas comment about the Mormons' Adam-God: "Joseph Smith's successor, Brigham Young, taught that Adam (Eve's husband) is God—the only God worshiped by the Mormons. The LDS Church leadership today publicly repudiates this doctrine, and most Mormons are unaware that Brigham Young actually taught it throughout his presidency."[53]

The Mormons do not believe in the virgin birth of Christ. Ed Decker, a Latter-day Saint for 20 years who is now seeking to reach Mormons with the gospel, says of the god of the Mormons: "He is said to physically live with His many wives near the star Kolob, where he procreates spirit children with his wives through natural means. Mormonism teaches that this god came down to earth in the flesh and was the physical father of Jesus."[54] This teaching opposes the scriptural teaching that Jesus was conceived by a direct act of the Holy Spirit (Matt. 1:18, 20; Luke 1:35).

The Mormons, in keeping with their doctrine of "plural marriage," or polygamy, believe that Jesus Christ was a polygamist. In the Mormon scriptures, it is "revealed" that unmarried people, and couples whose marriages are not sealed by the temple endowments, can become only "angels in heaven."[55] If their marriages are sealed, "Then shall they be gods."[56]

If, therefore, Christ had not married in this life, He would not have been able to rise above the position of an angel in the next life. Brigham Young believed that Jesus Christ was a polygamist. He believed that Mary and Martha (the sisters of Lazarus) and Mary Magdalene were the wives of Christ. Young also taught that the bridal feast in Cana of Galilee was the occasion of one of Christ's own marriages. And remember, Prophets Smith and Young were "prophets in the same sense as are Abraham, Moses, Peter, and other such biblical leaders."[57]

ALTHOUGH SOME MEN IN BIBLE TIMES HAD MANY WIVES, THIS WAS NOT GOD'S WILL.

Once again the teachings of the Mormons stand in sharp contrast to what is taught in the Bible. Nowhere does the Bible teach polygamy. Although some men in Bible times had many wives, this was not God's will, according to Deuteronomy 17:14–18. Instead of polygamy, the Bible teaches the sacredness of the commitment of one man and one woman to each other until death separates them (1 Cor. 7; 1 Tim. 3:2; Titus 1:5–6). It is interesting that some Mormons now deny that their church ever taught this doctrine.

Also, nowhere in the Bible do we find any evidence to support the idea that Christ was married—let alone that He had more than one wife. It is obvious that the Mormons have rewritten the Bible to match their theology rather than taking their theology from the Bible.

SALVATION

The crucial doctrines of any religious group are what they teach about the Person of Christ and about salvation. What they teach in these two areas reveals whether or not they are following the Bible. Concerning salvation, the Bible says, "For by grace you have been saved through faith, and that not of yourselves; it is the gift of God, not of works, lest anyone should boast" (Eph. 2:8–9). John 1:12 tells us that we become the children of God by receiving Christ as Savior by faith. Obedience and good works are evidence that a person has trusted Christ for salvation, but they are not a means of salvation. Because salvation is a gift, it cannot be earned.

Mormonism, however, teaches that—in addition to necessary faith—salvation is earned by works. The LDS third article of faith states, "We believe that through the Atonement of Christ, all mankind may be saved, by obedience to the laws and ordinances of the Gospel."[58]

For the Mormons, salvation depends on their works. This is evident from their doctrine of baptismal regeneration—the teaching that a person cannot be saved without being baptized with water. They say, "As stated by Joseph Smith, the first principles and ordinances of the gospel of Jesus Christ are, 'first, Faith in the Lord Jesus Christ; second, Repentance; third, Baptism by immersion for the remission of sins; fourth, Laying on of hands for the gift of the Holy Ghost' (Articles of Faith 1:4)."[59]

The Mormons even teach that salvation will be available in the next world to those who have not become Mormons in this life. Because they teach that water baptism is necessary for salvation, however, they also teach that those who are alive should be baptized for the dead so that those who have believed after death can become Mormons. This means that a Mormon would be baptized for his own salvation and again for someone deceased.

A verse the Mormon church uses concerning its belief in baptism for the dead is 1 Corinthians 15:29: "Otherwise, what will they do who are baptized for the dead, if the dead do not rise at all? Why then are they baptized for the dead?" There are several possible interpretations of what this verse means. The most likely one that fits the context—and harmonizes with the rest of the Bible—is that new believers were being baptized and were taking the place of older believers who had died. All of this would be meaningless if there were no resurrection of the dead.

To insist, however, that this baptism has merit for those who have died would contradict the clear teaching of the rest of the Bible. A person should not build a doctrine on one verse—and certainly not on one that could just as easily have another interpretation.

The Bible does not support the Mormon doctrine of salvation after death. Hebrews 9:27 says, "It is appointed for men to die once, but after this the judgment." Our only opportunity to trust Christ as Savior is while we are alive. Neither does the Bible support the idea that we must be baptized in order to be saved. We are saved by means of the death of Christ; He paid the penalty for our sins. Nothing can be added to what Christ has accomplished for us.

HEAVEN AND HELL

The Mormons teach that heaven is comprised of three levels and that individuals will be graded as to what category of heaven they will enter. Section 76 of *Doctrine and Covenants* teaches that there is the celestial kingdom, the highest level, which is prepared for the righteous who have been faithful in keeping the commandments of the Lord and who have been cleansed of all their sins. Only Mormons will enter this kingdom, which is subdivided into three levels. Only those Mormons whose marriage has been sealed by the temple endowments will reach the highest level, where they eventually achieve godhood.

Then there is the terrestrial kingdom. Those who go there have lived clean lives but were not willing to receive the Mormon gospel or were not valiant in the faith. Also in this kingdom are those who refused to receive the gospel on earth but who accepted the testimony of Jesus in the spirit world.

The third division is the telestial kingdom, into which will go all those who have been unclean in their earthly lives. These subjects are placed in the telestial kingdom after they have been punished for a time for their sins.

Regarding hell, Joseph Smith essentially adopted the teaching of the Universalists—that all mankind will eventually be saved. The official Mormon position now seems to be that hell is the place for those who cannot be redeemed, who are called "sons of perdition." This group, however, is "but a small portion of the human race."[60] Because only a "small portion" is excluded from salvation, Anthony Hoekema rightly observes, "One could . . . call Mormons virtual Universalists since, according to their teaching, the vast majority of the human race will attain to some kind of salvation."[61]

The Mormons do not teach biblical truths regarding heaven or hell. The Bible nowhere teaches that heaven contains various levels or that all mankind will be saved. Instead, the Bible teaches that our eternal destiny is determined in this life by whether we accept or reject Christ's death and resurrection on our behalf. Those who accept the gospel message go to heaven, while those who reject it go to hell.

In their attempt to prove that heaven has three levels, Mormons cite 1 Corinthians 15:40: "There are also celestial bodies and terrestrial bodies; but the glory of the celestial is one, and the glory of the terrestrial is another." But the context of this verse makes it clear that the apostle Paul was comparing the resurrection body we will receive with the earthly body we have now. He was not talking about two (and certainly not three) levels of heaven.

CONCLUSION

The Mormons follow the teachings of Joseph Smith and Brigham Young rather than the Bible. When Joseph Smith became a polygamist, he received a new "revelation" to replace his former revelation that had condemned polygamy. He also became a Mason and integrated much of the Masonic ritual into his temple ceremony, which contradicted his former condemnation of secret societies. What started out to be a "latter-day restoration" of Christ's "true church" has become latter-day confusion.

The Mormons have added many of their own doctrines to what is taught in the Bible, claiming that God did not close the canon of Scripture when the Bible was completed. God has a severe warning, however, to those who would add anything to His Word: "If anyone adds to these things, God will add to him the plagues that are written in this book" (Rev. 22:18).

Mormons clearly are not followers of the Christ of the Bible. The revelations they claim God has given them contradict what the Bible teaches about God, Christ, salvation, heaven and hell. If Mormons were Christians in the New Testament sense of the word, they would accept what Jesus Christ says about Himself and what He says about mankind. They would accept the fact that all of us have sinned and come short of the glory of God and that the only way to obtain salvation is by personally receiving Jesus Christ as Savior (Rom. 3:23; Acts 16:31).

The Mormons say of themselves, "The Church is Christian but is neither Catholic nor Protestant." Because they reject the teachings of biblical Christianity, to be intellectually honest the Mormons ought also to say that their church is not Christian.

Summary

Name:	The Church of Jesus Christ of Latter-day Saints
Also Known As:	Mormons, LDS
Founder:	Joseph Smith Jr. (1805–1844)
U.S. Headquarters:	Salt Lake City, Utah
Membership (2004):	U.S.: 5.6 million; Worldwide: 12 million
Web Site:	www.lds.org

What They Believe

Mormons:	Biblical Christians:

Source of Authority

The Book of Mormon, Doctrine and Covenants and the *Pearl of Great Price* contain God's revelations just as the Bible does. Believe in continuing revelation; the canon of Scripture was not closed when the Bible was completed. The Mormon presidents are prophets in the same sense as were Abraham, Moses, Peter and other such biblical leaders.	The Bible alone is final authority. The canon of Scripture was closed when the 66 books of the Bible were completed. No one today is like the Old Testament prophets, who received direct revelation from God.

God

He was once a man who, through self-effort, became God. Good Mormons become gods.	God has existed in eternity past, although the second Person of the Trinity became incarnate to die for the sins of mankind. Man can never become God.

Christ

Deny His deity by teaching that He was simply a spirit being before coming to earth. Deny the virgin birth by claiming Jesus was conceived when Adam-God had sexual relations with Mary. Jesus was a polygamist.	Jesus Christ is God, the second Person of the Trinity. Jesus was supernaturally conceived by Mary through the Holy Spirit. Jesus was never married.

Salvation

Salvation is earned by works in addition to faith. One cannot be saved unless he is baptized with water for the remission of sins. Practice baptizing for the dead so that those who have believed after death can become Mormons.	Salvation is granted only by grace through faith alone in the Lord Jesus Christ. Baptism is a public witness of salvation, not a requirement to be saved. There is no other chance for salvation after death.

Heaven and Hell

There are three levels of heaven: Celestial, where good Mormons enter and achieve godhood; Terrestrial, where those who enter are good people who do not comply with teachings of Mormonism; and Telestial, where those who enter have lived unclean earthly lives. The vast majority of mankind will be saved—virtual universal salvation.

Hell is the future place of punishment for those who reject salvation through Christ. Although there may be different degrees of punishment, all will be punished for rejecting Christ.

Salvation is only for those who trust in Christ; all who reject Him go to an eternal hell.

Recommended Reading

Decker, Ed. *Decker's Complete Handbook on Mormonism*. Eugene, Ore.: Harvest House Publishers, 1995.

Enroth, Ronald, and others. *A Guide to Cults and New Religions*. Downers Grove, Ill.: InterVarsity Press, 1983.

Fraser, Gordon H. *Is Mormonism Christian?* Chicago: Moody Press, 1977.

Hutchinson, Janis. *The Mormon Missionaries: An Inside Look at Their Real Message and Methods*. Grand Rapids, Mich.: Kregel Resources, 1995.

Martin, Walter R. *The Kingdom of the Cults*. Minneapolis: Bethany House Publishers, 1985.

Mather, George A., and Nichols, Larry A. *Dictionary of Cults, Religions and the Occult*. Grand Rapids, Mich.: Zondervan Publishing House, 1993.

McDowell, Josh, and Stewart, Don. *Handbook of Today's Religions*. San Bernardino, Calif.: Here's Life Publishers, Inc., 1983.

Reed, David A., and Farkas, John R. *Mormons Answered Verse by Verse*. Grand Rapids, Mich.: Baker Book House, 1992.

Robertson, Irvine. *What the Cults Believe*. Chicago: Moody Press, 1991.

Scott, Latayne C. *Why We Left Mormonism: Eight People Tell Their Stories*. Grand Rapids, Mich.: Baker Book House, 1990.

Tanner, Jerald, and Tanner, Sandra. *The Changing World of Mormonism: A Behind-the-Scenes Look at Changes in Mormon Doctrine & Practice*. Chicago: Moody Press, 1980.

Van Gorden, Kurt. *Mormonism*. Grand Rapids, Mich.: Zondervan Publishing House, 1995.

What They Believe

White, James R. *Letters to a Mormon Elder: Eye-Opening Information for Mormons and Christians Who Talk With Them*. Minneapolis: Bethany House Publishers, 1993.

ENDNOTES

[1] "Writings of Joseph Smith," 2:18–19 in *Pearl of Great Price* (Salt Lake City: The Church of Jesus Christ of Latter-day Saints, 1968), 48.

[2] *Christianity Today*, April 24, 1995, 45.

[3] "Key Facts and Figures," www.lds.org./newsroom, Oct. 24, 2005.

[4] "The Missionary Program," www.lds.org./newsroom, Oct. 24, 2005.

[5] S. C. Gwynne and Richard Ostling, *Time*, Aug. 4, 1997, 54.

[6] Ibid., 52.

[7] Janis Hutchinson, *The Mormon Missionaries: An Inside Look at Their Real Message and Methods* (Grand Rapids, Mich.: Kregel Resources, 1995), 100.

[8] Ibid.

[9] Brigham Young, *Journal of Discourses*, Vol. 8, 176, cited by Jerald and Sandra Tanner, *The Changing World of Mormonism* (Chicago: Moody Press, 1980), 448.

[10] "Continuing Revelation," www.lds.org/Global_Media_Guide/Core_Beliefs_and_-Doctrines.html, Aug 5, 1997.

[11] Brigham Young, *Journal of Discourses*, Vol. 14, 203, cited by Tanner and Tanner, *The Changing World of Mormonism*, 448.

[12] Walter R. Martin, *The Kingdom of the Cults*, 3rd rev. ed. (Minneapolis: Bethany House Publishers, 1985), 169.

[13] Tanner and Tanner, *The Changing World of Mormonism*, 78.

[14] Ibid., 67–68.

[15] Fawn M. Brodie, *No Man Knows My History: The Life of Joseph Smith* (New York: Alfred A. Knopf, 1985), 20–21, 427–429.

[16] "Writings of Joseph Smith" 2:17, in *Pearl of Great Price*, 48.

[17] Ibid., 2:34, 51.

[18] Gwynne and Ostling, *Time*, Aug. 4, 1997, 55.

[19] see comments by Walter Martin, *Kingdom of the Cults*, 174.

[20] Tanner and Tanner, *The Changing World of Mormonism*, 534–547.

[22] Ibid., 547.

[23] *The World Almanac and Book of Facts 2005* (New York: World Almanac Education Group, Inc., 2005), 731.

[24] www.lds.org/Global_Media_Guide/Core_Beliefs_and_Doctrines.html, Aug. 5, 1997.

[25] "Mormon," *The New Encyclopaedia Britannica, Micropaedia/ Ready Reference*, Vol. 8, 15th ed. (Chicago: Encyclopaedia Britannica, Inc., 1987), 328.

[26] For documentation see Einar Anderson, *The Inside Story of Mormonism* (Grand

Rapids, Mich.: Kregel Publications, 1973), 150–158.

[27] www.lds.org/Global_Media_Guide/Core_Beliefs_and_Doctrines.html, July 1997.

[28] "Introduction" in *The Book of Mormon* (Salt Lake City: 1981).

[29] Ibid.

[30] Ibid., "A Brief Explanation about The Book of Mormon."

[31] Walter Martin, *The Kingdom of the Cults*. Ravi Zacharias, gen. ed. (Minneapolis: Bethany House Publishers, 2003), 217.

[32] Ibid., 218

[33] Cited by Martin, *The Kingdom of the Cults*, 184.

[34] Ibid., 217.

[35] www.christianitytoday.com/ct/2004/010/8.20.html, Sept. 30, 2005.

[36] Ibid., 187.

[37] Wayne L. Cowdrey, Howard A. Davis and Donald R. Scales, *Who Really Wrote the Book of Mormon?* (Santa Ana, Calif.: Vision House Publishers, 1980).

[38] Tanner and Tanner, "Fall of the Book of Abraham" in *The Changing World of Mormonism*, 329–363.

[39] Ibid., 363.

[40] Tanner and Tanner, "Changing the Anti-Black Doctrine" in *The Changing World of Mormonism*, 291–328.

[41] Bennett, *Why I Am a Mormon*, 159.

[42] Steven L. Shields, *Latter Day Saint Beliefs: A Comparison Between the RLDS Church and the LDS Church* (Independence, Mo.: Herald Publishing House, 1986), 22.

[43] Martin, *The Kingdom of the Cults*, 204.

[44] *Doctrine and Covenants*, 130:22.

[45] *Teachings of the Prophet Joseph Smith*, 345, cited by Martin, *The Kingdom of the Cults*, 202.

[46] *Times and Seasons*, Aug. 15, 1844, 613–614, cited by Martin, *The Kingdom of the Cults*, 204.

[47] Gwynne and Ostling, *Time*, Aug. 4, 1997, 56.

[48] Ibid.

[49] Orson Hyde, *Journal of Discourses*, Vol. 1, 123, cited by Martin, *The Kingdom of the Cults*, 203.

[50] *Doctrine and Covenants*, 93:21, 23.

[51] Brigham Young, *Journal of Discourses*, Vol. 1, 50–51, cited by Martin, *The Kingdom of the Cults*, 213.

[52] Martin, *The Kingdom of the Cults*, 213.

[53] David A. Reed and John R. Farkas, *Mormons Answered Verse by Verse* (Grand Rapids, Mich.: Baker Book House, 1992), 22.

[54] Ed Decker, *Decker's Complete Handbook on Mormonism*, 417.

[55] *Doctrine and Covenants*, 132:15–16.

[56] Ibid., 132:20.

[57] www.lds.org/Global_Media_Guide/Core_Beliefs_and_Doctrines.html, Aug. 1997.

[58] Article 3 of "The Articles of Faith of The Church of Jesus Christ of the Latter-day Saints," *Pearl of Great Price*, 60.

[59] www.lds.org/Global_Media_Guide/Core_Beliefs_and_Doctrines.html, Aug. 1997.

[60] Hyrum Smith and Janne Sjodahl, *The Doctrine and Covenants Commentary*, 453, cited by Anthony Hoekema, *Four Major Cults* (Grand Rapids, Mich.: Wm. B. Eerdmans Publishing Company, 1963), 72.

[61] Anthony Hoekema, *Four Major Cults*, 74.

CHAPTER SIX

Muslims

The date September 11, 2001, is burned into most people's memories. When four planes piloted by terrorists slammed into the World Trade Center, the Pentagon and a field in Pennsylvania, life in the United States—and the world—was forever changed.

Since that date, in an endeavor to calm the spirits of troubled Americans, many in the news media have been promoting that Christians and Muslims worship the same God and that Islam is a religion of peace.

For instance, a conservative newspaper in the midlands, the *Omaha World-Herald*, printed a story entitled "Fasting for God." It was about a Muslim boy observing Ramadan while attending a public school in Omaha, Nebraska.[1] I wrote to the editors of the Public Pulse, the opinion page of the *World-Herald*, to ask why they used the name "God" in the headline, and throughout the article, without once using the name "Allah." I concluded my remarks by saying, "This perpetuates the myth that the God of Islam and the God of Christianity are the same. Nothing could be further from the truth. Islam denies that Jesus Christ was crucified and rose from the dead. If there is no resurrection there is no forgiveness of sins, no salvation—and no hope."[2]

My letter was never printed.

This is an example of how frequently only one side of a debate or issue is presented in the media.

After more correspondence, the editor of the Public Pulse, Jim Anderson, wrote back and said he had talked to the writer of the story. Anderson mentioned such things as the Arabic translation of the word *God* being "Allah," that even Arab Christians use the name "Allah" for God, and that Muslims believe the God of Islam and the

God of Christianity (as well as the God of Judaism) is the same God.[3]

There was no need for our interchange to continue. In my final note, I commented to the editor that it is correct that the Arabic word for *God* is "Allah." (The editor didn't seem to understand that this logic argued for using "Allah" throughout the piece; instead it was not once used.) I finished my last e-mail to him by saying, "If the God of Islam and the God of Christianity are the same, why in Muslim countries do they persecute and even seek to kill those who turn from the God of Islam to the God of Christianity?"[4]

Those who are critical of Islam are sometimes painted with a broad brush as themselves being "terrorists." Some people even consider a critical evaluation of Islam to be "hate speech," not understanding the difference between debate and hate. The question remains, What do orthodox Islam and orthodox Christianity teach? And most significantly, is Muhammad superior to Jesus Christ?

Many people say that most adherents to the Islamic faith are "moderate" Muslims. Muslim clerics who would be representative of "moderate Muslims," however, have been slow to speak out to condemn the acts of the radical or extreme Muslims. In addition, there is little difference in the beliefs of the moderates and radicals. Bernard Lewis, a leading historian of the Middle East and a professor emeritus of Near Eastern Studies at Princeton University, states:

> The Muslim fundamentalists, unlike the Protestant groups whose name was transferred to them, do not differ from the mainstream on questions of theology and the interpretation of scripture. Their main critique is, in the broadest sense, societal. The Islamic world, in their view, has taken a wrong turning.[5]

This is seen in a report from the Associated Press about the attack in Riyadh, Saudi Arabia: "Saudis blamed al-Qaida on Sunday [Nov. 9, 2003] for the suicide car bombing of a Riyadh housing complex that killed 17 people, declaring it proof of the terror network's willingness to shed Muslim blood in its zeal to bring down the U.S.-linked Saudi monarchy."[6]

This is a "religion of peace"? Muslims kill fellow Muslims during the holy month of Ramadan.

Even though there may be more moderate Muslims than orthodox ones, asking a moderate Muslim about Islam would be similar to asking a liberal theologian about Christianity. One would learn opinions but little about the true teachings of the religion by those who take it seriously. So this work will focus on the teachings of "orthodox" Islam.

Before going further, it is important to understand what certain terms mean.

Allah. The God of Islam that some think is the same as the God of Christianity.

Islam. The religion founded by Muhammad, although Muslims believe Islam has always existed. "Islam" means "submission" to the will of Allah.

Muhammad (or Mohammed). The Prophet of Islam. He was born in Mecca, in what is now Saudi Arabia, in A.D. 570. He died in 632 and his remains are in the Prophet's Tomb in Medina.

> ALLAH—THE GOD OF ISLAM THAT SOME THINK IS THE SAME AS THE GOD OF CHRISTIANITY.

Muslim (or Moslem). A follower of Islam and someone who is submitted to Allah's will.

Quran (or Qur'an or Koran). The book that the Muslims believe was revealed to Muhammad by the angel Gabriel beginning in A.D. 610.

THE FIVE PILLARS

Muslims adhere to what is commonly called "The Five Pillars." These pillars are the recital of the creed, prayer, fasting, almsgiving and pilgrimage.

The Creed. Describing how to become a Muslim, Seyyed Hossein Nasr, professor of Islamic studies at George Washington University in Washington, D.C., says, "It is sufficient to bear testimony before two Muslim witnesses that 'There is no god but God' and that 'Muhammad is the Messenger of God'" [Arabic expressions omitted].[7]

What They Believe

Brothers Ergun Mehmet Caner and Emir Fethi Caner are former Muslims who are now believers in the Lord Jesus Christ and evangelical Christian theologians. They tell of a custom in Islam when, even at birth, a father whispers into a son's ears, "There is no god but Allah. Muhammad is the messenger of Allah." The Caners add:

> What seems like a simple statement is actually comprehensive in its scope. The admission of Muhammad as the final messenger of Allah places the believer within the prophet's belief system. Therefore, the Muslim maintains what the prophet believed, including that the Qur'an is the final and perfect revelation of Allah, that prophets are messengers to all people groups, and that angels do the will of Allah.[8]

But one doesn't have to accept just what former Muslims say. An Islamic Web site for those interested in becoming Muslims states, "If anyone has a real desire to be a Muslim and has full conviction and strong belief that Islam is the true religion ordained by Allah for all human-beings, then, one should pronounce the 'Shahada,' the testimony of faith, **without further delay**"[9] (emphasis theirs).

And in case one wonders what Islam thinks about other religions, the same Web site says, "In another verse of the Holy Qur'an, Allah states, *'If unyone* [sic] *desires a religion other than Islam (Submission to Allah), Never will it be accepted of him; and in the Hereafter he will be in the ranks of those who have lost (their selves* [sic] *in the hell fire)'* (Qur'an 3:85)"[10] (emphasis theirs).

Whenever believers of biblical Christianity claim that faith in Jesus Christ is the only way of salvation, the news media show alarm at such "narrow thinking." The same media, however, seem to turn a deaf ear to the claims of Islam to be the only true religion and that all other members of other faiths will spend eternity in hell.

Prayer. Those submitted to Allah offer prayer five times a day while facing Mecca. This prayer is not "petition," as is commonly thought of in Christianity. The Caners say, "Even during the prayer time (*rakats*), no Muslim truly makes supplication. It is the repetition of the first surah (chapter) of the Qur'an that takes up most of the prayer time in each of the five positions of prayer. This repetition is a type of mantra, invoking the power of Allah, but does not request anything."[11]

Fasting. Muslims fast from sunrise to sunset during the month of Ramadan, the month when Gabriel supposedly began delivering the Quran to Muhammad.

Almsgiving. Muslims are to give to charity at least two and a half percent of their annual net income.

Pilgrimage. At least once in his lifetime, every Muslim who is "mentally, financially and physically fit" has the obligation to make a pilgrimage to Mecca.

MUSLIMS IN AMERICA

It is estimated that there are more than one billion Muslims in the world, or about one out of every six people. What is less known is what is pointed out by *WORLD Magazine*, a weekly publication analyzing the news from a "perspective committed to the Bible as the inerrant Word of God." *WORLD* published a special issue on "Islam and Terrorism," in which it stated that only about 15 percent of Muslims are Arabs.[12] In fact, the four nations with the highest number of Muslims—Indonesia, Pakistan, India and Bangladesh—do not have Arabic as their first language. This point is significant when one realizes that these Muslims in non-Arabic speaking countries must worship Allah with memorized Arabic phrases they don't understand.

Reporting in 2002, *WORLD Magazine* said, "Perhaps five million Muslims now live in the United States, up from about 800,000 three decades ago."[13] The 2005 *World Almanac and Book of Facts* estimates the total a little less, at 4.6 million.[14]

One example of the inroads Islam has made in the United States can be found on the Web site of the Islamic Society of North America (ISNA), regarding Muslim-type meals on university campuses:

> By introducing on-campus halal meals, Virginia Tech University has joined the company of Harvard and Syracuse universities, where Muslim students are served meat-based foods that Muslim students can enjoy. The University of Maryland at College Park offers halal meals on a limited basis. Virginia Tech was adamant at first. However, things changed quickly when the dietary issue was brought to the notice of President Dr. Paul Torgersen.[15]

In an item about a Muslim student in a university, the same Web site reports:

> Saousan Kiwan, a student at Washtenaw Community College, won her rights after CAIR [Council on American-Islamic Relations] told President Larry L. Whitworth that an instructor had warned her against repeating the common Islamic phrase: "In the name of God, most merciful, most gracious," before her presentations. He had claimed that it was "inappropriate and unacceptable in an American classroom" and violated the separation of church and state.[16]

If that incident involved an evangelical Christian, one can imagine how quickly the American Civil Liberties Union (ACLU) would be running to the courts to stop the practice.

And what do you think would happen if a group of evangelical believers demonstrated in a Muslim-controlled country to have non-Muslim-type meals? There is no religious freedom in a Muslim country. Muslims come to America and other non-Muslim countries and demand freedoms they would never grant Christians in their own countries.

> MUSLIMS COME TO AMERICA AND OTHER NON-MUSLIM COUNTRIES AND DEMAND FREEDOMS THEY WOULD NEVER GRANT CHRISTIANS IN THEIR OWN COUNTRIES.

BACKGROUND

What is the background of this fast-growing religion? Who or what is responsible for having taken a billion people worldwide into the fold of Islam?

The most prominent person in regard to Islam is Muhammad. The Muslims are offended, however, if they are referred to as "Muhammadans." This gives the impression, they believe, that they worship Muhammad, whereas they emphasize that they worship none but Allah.

Muslims believe that Islam is a universal religion; that is, they think it has always existed, even before Muhammad. With this in mind, they don't refer to Muhammad as having "founded" Islam, but only of his having restored it.[17]

Muhammad was born in Mecca in A.D. 570. His father died just before Muhammad was born and his mother died when he was only six. Muhammad was actually named by his grandfather, 'Abdu'l-Muttalib. On hearing of his son's death, he went to his daughter-in-law's house, took the baby in his arms and called him "Muhammad," which means "The Praised One."

Nothing seems extraordinary about Muhammad's boyhood and early youth, according to the standards of the sixth century. Occasionally he traveled with his uncle to Damascus and other cities. Muhammad became proficient enough at the trading business in these caravans that at 25 he entered into the service of a rich widow, Khadijah, who lived in Mecca.

Impressed with his service—and although he was 15 years younger than she—Khadijah offered to marry Muhammad. He accepted and was deeply devoted to her, as evidenced by the fact that as long as Khadijah lived Muhammad did not take another wife.

After Khadijah's death, Muhammad took other wives. There is some uncertainty about how many wives he had eventually, even though the Quran permits only four (4:3). The controversy in the press since 9/11 has been over how young one of his wives was. In this age of pedophiles, it is not popular to report that his youngest wife, Aishah (also spelled 'Ayisha), was either nine or ten years old. This does not appear to be contrary to the facts, however. Those who have been reared in the Muslim tradition before trusting in Christ as Savior confirm that Aishah was only nine or ten.[18]

Muslims explain these marriages as being partly for political reasons and partly out of pity for the wives whose husbands had been killed in battle defending the Islamic community.

Some of the chroniclers of Muhammad's life point out that many things troubled the future prophet. He had experienced some tragic circumstances early in his life, and the death of his sons had left him without an heir (by the standards of that day). In addition, other burdens were weighing him down. Throughout Mecca in the bazaars and shrines, the ancient virtues of honor and generosity were declining.

Muhammad was an introspective man. While living in Mecca he withdrew each year to a cave on Mount Hira in the nearby desert. There he meditated and prayed for several days. During the month of Ramadan (the ninth month of the Islamic calendar), as Muhammad was meditating in a cave, a voice called out to him, "Recite!" At first he was frightened. He did not understand what he was to recite. Then the voice said, "In the name of thy Lord the Creator, who created mankind from a clot of blood, recite!"

Muhammad was extremely disturbed as he went home to his wife. He was afraid that an evil spirit possessed him. Khadijah consoled him and then called for her cousin, an elderly convert to Christianity. He assured Muhammad that he was not crazy but that he had experienced a true revelation like those God had allowed Moses and the prophets. Khadijah said that Muhammad must submit to this revelation.

The counsel from this elderly man significantly affected Muhammad's understanding of God and religion. Just as other converts have not necessarily had a clear grasp of biblical Christianity, so was the case with Khadijah's cousin. He had been largely influenced by a Nestorian view of Christianity, especially concerning Jesus Christ. (I will explain the beliefs of Nestorius later.)

The revelations continued for Muhammad, and they were later recorded in what is called the Quran, which means "recite."

Muhammad never claimed that he was proclaiming a new religion. He believed that what had been revealed to him was the same religion revealed to other prophets, such as Abraham, Moses, Solomon, Jonah and Jesus. And Muslims believe that even those prophets taught Islam. Muhammad thought, however, that the religion revealed to the earlier prophets had become corrupted and that he was now restoring it to its original purity.

Muhammad emphasized monotheism, the belief in one God. This brought him into conflict with his fellow Meccans, who believed in polytheism (many gods). In particular, the cubed stone building known as the *Ka'aba* had 360 idols of the local Arab tribes. It also had a black stone supposedly given to Adam and later found by

Abraham to specify the place of the worship of Allah.

Because the Arabs trace their lineage through Abraham's son Ishmael, they also associate Ishmael with the *Ka'aba*. They believe that Abraham and his son Ishmael built the *Ka'aba* for worship of the one true God.

Muslims also believe that it was Ishmael, not Isaac, who was to have been sacrificed by Abraham, although the Quran does not specify that. One of their reasons for believing this is that the son is referred to as an "only" son (Gen. 22:2). Isaac was not born until Ishmael was 14, so they reason that the "only" son had to be Ishmael. This disregards the fact that Hebrews 11:17 refers to Isaac as Abraham's "only begotten" son. The Greek word translated "only begotten" does not refer to birth but to a unique relationship. So even though Abraham had two sons, Isaac could be referred to as an "only" son in this distinct sense.

Muhammad's anti-idolatry message in Mecca made him an enemy of the city. Opposition to his views continued to escalate until finally, in 622, he was forced to flee to Medina (then known as Yathrib), about 250 miles north of Mecca. His flight was known as the "*Hegira*" (also spelled *Hejira*). The name of the city was later changed to Medina, which means "City of the Prophet."

Islam shifted at this point from a monotheistic *religion* to a monotheistic *philosophy* of religion, politics and daily life. Muhammad was offered leadership in Yathrib, and he took it.

So significant was Muhammad's flight to Medina that the year (622) became the first year in the Islamic calendar. Dates are noted as A.H.—after *Hegira*.

At first, Muhammad apparently expected the Jews and Christians to accept him as a prophet. He even originally chose Jerusalem as the direction to be faced during prayer. But when the Jews of Medina aligned with his enemies in Mecca, Muhammad drove them from the city and organized a purely Muslim society. He commanded Muslims to face Mecca, instead of Jerusalem, when praying.

Muhammad gathered forces together that enabled him to conquer Mecca in 630. He destroyed the idols in the *Ka'aba* and proclaimed it a "mosque." Two years later Muhammad died, and his tomb is in the Prophet's Mosque in Medina.

What They Believe

Church history reveals that the greatest gains of this new, dynamic faith took place between 632 and 732. By 640, Syria and Palestine were conquered, and the Mosque of Omar was soon erected in Jerusalem.

Although Muslims consider it a weakness of Christianity that there are so many different groups within it, there are also many sects within Islam—some say more than 150. The largest sects in Islam are the Sunnis and the Shi'ites. About 90 percent of all Muslims are Sunnis, who trace their heritage to Muhammad's first four spiritual and political successors.

The Shi'ites are the next largest sect of Islam. They insist that the true line from Muhammad came through his son-in-law, Ali. (Muhammad's daughter Fatima had married Ali, the son of Abu Talib.)

Some of the other sects in Islam are the Sufis, Alawites, Takfirs and the Wahhabis. The Wahhabis are found primarily in Saudi Arabia and have been in the news since September 11, 2001. Their most notable member, no doubt, is Osama bin Laden.

BELIEFS

Although the background of a religious group may be interesting, that which matters most is their beliefs. If people are to be helped not only for the present but also for eternity, it is essential that they believe the truth revealed by God concerning Himself and the salvation He offers. So the important question is, What are the beliefs of Islam?

SOURCE OF AUTHORITY

Biblical Christianity adheres to only one source of authority—the Bible and the Bible alone. It is necessary to make an important distinction in this regard, however. It is not a person's interpretation, nor a church's interpretation of the Bible, but the Bible and the Bible alone that is that sole authority of biblical Christianity.

Written by about 40 authors inspired by God during a period of more than 1,500 years, the Bible is God's written revelation to mankind. As such, it is often referred to as the "Word of God." The 39 books of the Old Testament were written in Hebrew (with small portions in Aramaic), and the 27 books of the New Testament were written in Greek.

The Bible claims for itself, "All scripture is given by inspiration of God, and is profitable for doctrine, for reproof, for correction, for instruction in righteousness" (2 Tim. 3:16). This verse presents the *fact* of inspiration.

Jesus' words about the authority of the written Word are recorded in Matthew 5:18, "Till heaven and earth pass away, one jot or one tittle will by no means pass from the law till all is fulfilled." A "jot" is a reference to the smallest letter of the Hebrew alphabet, in which the Old Testament was written. This letter (*yodh*) was written above the line and looks like the English apostrophe mark. A "tittle" refers to the distinguishing characteristics on the Hebrew letters, similar to the difference in an English O and Q. This verse presents the *extent* of inspiration.

Writing by inspiration about the way the Word of God has come down to us, the apostle Peter penned, "For prophecy never came by the will of man, but holy men of God spoke as they were moved by the Holy Spirit" (2 Pet. 1:21). This verse presents the *method* of inspiration.

In contrast to a single source of authority for biblical Christianity, Islam has several. It has the Quran, the "exemplary life" of Muhammad, the Hadith, the past decisions by the community of Islamic scholars and the history of Islam.

Quran. Nasr, referred to above and called by his publisher "The World's Leading Islamicist," says, "All Muslims agree that the Quran is the verbatim revelation of God. They also agree about its text and content; that is, no variant texts are found among any of the schools, although the exegetical meaning can, of course, differ from one school to another."[19]

To the claim of the Muslims that the Quran is "perfect," Ravi Zacharias, a Christian apologist who was born in India and has lectured in several of the world's most prominent universities, refers to the comments of a Muslim scholar:

> Ali Dashti, an Iranian author and a committed Muslim, commented that the errors in the Koran were so many that the grammatical rules had to be altered in order to fit the

claim that the Koran was flawless. He gives numerous examples of these in his book *Twenty Three Years: The Life of the Prophet Mohammed*. (The only precaution he took before publishing this book was to direct that it be published posthumously.)[20]

It is especially significant to note the words, "All Muslims agree that the Quran is the verbatim revelation of God." Muhammad was illiterate, so he was unable to write anything Allah supposedly revealed to him. Others, they say, memorized these words to produce the Quran.

To say "no variant texts are found among any of the schools" reveals the viewpoint that not a single copy was made of the Arabic manuscripts first produced by Muhammad's followers. If so, why did an "official" copy of the Quran need to be produced by Uthman, the third Caliph (A.D. 644–656)? This contradiction is clearly presented by James R. White, Christian apologist, debater of counterfeit religious groups and director of Alpha and Omega Ministry.[21] After pointing this out, White adds an endnote, "The fact that Uthman had to undertake such a revision should indicate to the open-minded investigator that a *need* existed for the work, which immediately causes one to wonder why one should accept the final decision of Uthman"[22] (emphasis his).

And what have you learned about trusting someone's memory? If the copied or printed page can be faulty, memory is even worse. You have probably had the experience of someone telling you something that was so vivid in his mind but later you discovered that he was confused about the details.

A Muslim, of course, could never raise such questions about the Quran. In the 21st Century Edition of *Operation World*, the definitive prayer guide to the nations, peoples and cities of the world, there is a sobering statement about Pakistan. Under "Challenges for Prayer" for September 5, the statement is made: "*Shari'a law* [legislation derived from the Quran and Hadith] has only been partially implemented, but its effects for minorities are dire. There is a mandatory death sentence for 'disrespect to the Prophet' and a life sentence for desecration of the Qur'an."[23]

In contrast to the Christian Bible that was written over a period of 1,400 years, Muslims believe the Archangel Gabriel first appeared to

Muhammad in 610 and that Allah revealed the Quran to Muhammad over the next 23 years.

The Quran is given the highest reverence by the Muslims. Anish A. Shorrosh is a former Muslim and now a believer in Christ and preacher of the Gospel. He writes, "They dare not touch it without first being washed and purified. They read it with the greatest care and respect, never holding it below their waist."[24]

The Quran is a little smaller in size than the Christian New Testament. It is divided into Surahs, or chapters, which grow progressively shorter from beginning to end, except for the first one that serves as an introductory prayer. Those at the end are the first revelations Muhammad received, so chronological development is seen as one reads the Quran from the back to the front.

Muslims consider the Quran to be a "perfect" revelation from Allah and a faithful reproduction of an original that was engraved on a tablet in heaven, which has existed for all eternity.

In a debate with Islamic scholar Ahmad Deedat, former Muslim Shorrosh dared, "Let me challenge you! Seventy-five percent of the glorious Quran in my expressive language of Arabic is from the Holy Bible. I would urge you with all my might to look into the Bible and find the main sources of the Quran."[25]

> MUSLIMS CONSIDER THE QURAN TO BE A "PERFECT" REVELATION FROM ALLAH.

The "exemplary life" of Muhammad. The Muslims consider that all that Muhammad did and said were to be taken as examples of what Muslims should do. Whereas Christians have popularized the initials WWJD (What Would Jesus Do?), faithful Muslims would follow—although they would never express it as such—WWMD (What Would Muhammad Do?).

The Hadith. Although not seen fit to be a part of the Quran, the Hadith are the collected "reputed" sayings and actions of Muhammad that might have value. These consist of many volumes of collected sayings that vary in the extent of their acceptability by Islamic scholars.

The past decisions by the community of Islamic scholars. The studied opinions of these scholars are used as a basis for action.

The history of Islam. This history reveals the way in which the Islamic movement made decisions and how history unfolded. The rulers of the Islamic world had the power to do certain things; therefore, it was Allah's will.[26]

TRINITY

Muslims are repelled by the thought of a "Trinity"; that is, that God is a tri-unity. They consider such a belief to be polytheism, the belief in many gods. Muslims, as do the Jews, believe God is an absolute rather than a composite unity. Perhaps this is why Muhammad at first did not expect opposition from the Jews. Most probably, however, Muhammad's views of Christianity first came from those who denied the Trinity.

Muslims never refer to Allah as "Father." To do so, they reason, would be to imply they are His children, or even equal with God. For this reason they also avoid expressions such as "sons of God" and "children of God." God would need a wife, they reason, in order for Him to have children. Rather than viewing themselves in a father-son relationship, Muslims view their relationship with God as a master-slave relationship.

Biblical Christianity accepts the teaching that God is a Trinity. The three Persons of the Godhead are one, though distinct. The Father, Son and Holy Spirit comprise a composite unity. G. W. Bromiley, writing in *Evangelical Dictionary of Theology*, says, "Within the one essence of the Godhead we have to distinguish three 'persons' who are neither three gods on the one side, nor three parts or modes of God on the other, but coequally and coeternally God."[27]

In the Old Testament, the plural pronouns used for God indicate the three Persons of the one Godhead (Gen. 1:26; 11:7). A careful examination of the Christian Scriptures reveals that each of the three Persons of the one Godhead possesses divine attributes. Each is omnipresent, omnipotent and omniscient; each also receives worship, which only God is allowed to do.

The distinctiveness of the three Persons in the one Godhead is seen in Matthew 28:19, where "name" is singular, although the three Persons—Father, Son and Holy Spirit—are mentioned.

Trinitarian statements about the Godhead are found in the Apostles' Creed, one of the oldest creeds in existence. It was used as early as A.D. 150, more than 400 years before Muhammad was born.[28]

Because Islam rejects a Trinity that orthodox Christianity accepts, this shows they do not have the same God.

ALLAH

The Arabic name for "God" is loaded with meaning. The generic term may refer to almost anything, so one must ask, Who or what is the God of Islam?

Some confusion—perhaps much confusion—has been generated because in the Arabic Bible "Allah" is used to translate the word *God*. This leads some to think that the God of Islam is referred to in the Bible. Not so.

Robert Morey, executive director of the Research and Education Foundation that investigates topics that affect Western culture and values, explains how this confusion began. He points out that the Bible was not translated into Arabic until the ninth century (Muhammad died in the seventh century). Morey writes:

> By the ninth century, Islam was the dominant political force in Arab lands and the men who translated the Bible into Arabic faced a difficult political situation. If they did not use 'Allah' as the name for God, they might suffer at the hands of fanatical Muslims who, as part of their religion, believed that Allah of the Quran was the God of the Bible.

> Since 'Allah' was by this time the common name for 'God' because of the dominance of Islam, translators bowed to the political and religious pressures and put 'Allah' into the Arabic Bible.[29]

The Christian Information Foundation has produced an excellent brochure titled *Fundamentalism: Contrasting Christianity and Islam*.

Concerning the name "Allah," the publication says:

> There is substantial evidence that Allah has roots in pre-Is-
> lamic paganism. There were 360 idols (gods) worshipped in
> Mecca at the time of Muhammad. The supreme god of the
> Quraish tribe (from which Muhammad came) was Allah.
> Muhammad's father's name was Abd-Allah, which means
> "slave of Allah." This supports the notion that the concept of
> Allah has its roots in pagan gods.[30]

We must consider more than the word *Allah* when thinking about
the God of the Quran. His characteristics are in great contrast to the
God of the Bible. For example, the God of the Bible loves all
mankind and sent His Son to provide salvation for all (John 3:16),
although only those who place faith in Him will receive forgiveness
of sin and eternal life (John 1:12; 3:18). The God of the Bible is
grieved when unbelievers do not trust in Him. The apostle Peter was
inspired to write that God "is longsuffering toward us, not willing
that any should perish but that all should come to repentance" (2
Pet. 3:9). On the other hand, Allah loves only those who love him.
Former Muslims Ergun and Emir Caner write:

> Allah's heart is set against the infidel (*kafir*). He has no love
> for the unbeliever, nor is it the task of the Muslim to 'evan-
> gelize' the unbelieving world. Allah is to be worshipped,
> period. Any who will not do so must be defeated, silenced,
> or expelled. The theme is conquest, not conversion, of the
> unbelieving world.[31]

The God of Quran and the God of the Bible are not the same.

The specific, personal name for the God of the Bible is "Jehovah,"
from the four-letter (tetragrammaton) Hebrew word YHWH, pronounced *Yahweh*. This word is commonly translated in English
Bibles as "LORD" or "Jehovah." Insight is given into its meaning in
Exodus 3:13–15. The background of these verses is that God was
calling Moses to return to Egypt to lead the descendants of Jacob to
the Promised Land. Moses thought no one would believe him, so he
asked God, "Indeed, when I come to the children of Israel and say
to them, 'The God of your fathers has sent me to you,' and they say
to me, 'What is His name?' what shall I say to them?" (v. 13).

Moses was probably inquiring about more than just God's name;

he also needed to know His character. Verse 14 says, "And God said to Moses, 'I AM WHO I AM.' And He said, 'Thus you shall say to the children of Israel, "I AM has sent me to you."'" The words I AM are related to the word YHWH or *Jehovah*, which emphasizes that God is the ever-existing one—past, present and future.

The differences between Allah of the Quran and Jehovah of the Bible show that the two groups do not have the same God.

JESUS CHRIST

Jehovah also can be thought of as the God of Christianity because the Lord Jesus Christ applied this word to Himself in such passages as John 8:58, "Jesus said to them, 'Most assuredly, I say to you, before Abraham was, I AM.'"

The Old Testament says that Jehovah God is the creator (Isa. 40:28); the New Testament says of Jesus, "All things were made through Him, and without Him nothing was made that was made" (John 1:3). The Old Testament records Jehovah God saying, "'I, the LORD [Jehovah], am the first; and with the last I am He'" (Isa. 41:4); the New Testament records Jesus saying, "I am the First and the Last" (Rev. 1:17). The Old Testament says Jehovah is the One who forgives sins (Jer. 31:34); the New Testament records Jesus saying, "'But that you may know that the Son of Man has power on earth to forgive sins'—He said to the man who was paralyzed, 'I say to you, arise, take up your bed, and go to your house'" (Luke 5:24). These references show that Jesus of the New Testament is the Jehovah God of the Old Testament.

His Deity. Islam denies the deity of Christ. Muslims teach that Jesus Christ never claimed to be God or referred to Himself as the Son of God. They are especially repelled by the thought of Jesus Christ being referred to as the "Son of God." To them, this implies that God has a wife in order for a child to be born. This is understandably a blasphemous thought to them.

Biblical Christianity teaches that Jesus Christ is God, that He is the second Person of the Trinity. John 1:1 states, "In the beginning was the Word, and the Word was with God, and the Word was God." Verse 14 makes clear to whom this refers: "The Word became flesh and dwelt among us." Only Jesus Christ fits these qualifications.

Although He has existed from eternity past, the Lord Jesus Christ took upon Himself human form so that He could give His life on the cross for the sin of the world. When He came into the world, the Heavenly Father declared, "Let all the angels of God worship Him" (Heb. 1:6). The fact that worship is ascribed to Jesus Christ is an indication that He is God, for Jesus Himself told Satan, "'You shall worship the LORD your God, and Him only you shall serve'" (Matt. 4:10).

Biblical Christianity makes no claim that God "begot" Jesus in the physical sense of the word. That would be considered blasphemous

to Christians as well. As God, the Lord Jesus Christ has always existed. But in the miracle of the Incarnation, He took on Himself human form as He was born to Mary, who conceived by means of the Holy Spirit (Luke 1:26–35).

The angel Gabriel told Mary, "The Holy Spirit will come upon you, and the power of the Highest will overshadow you; therefore, also, that Holy One who is to be born will be called the Son of God" (v. 35).

AS GOD, THE LORD JESUS CHRIST HAS ALWAYS EXISTED.

Although the word *son* in Scripture is often used to mean "descendant," it does not always mean that. According to the flesh, Jesus was a descendant of David because He was born in the line of Judah.

As indicated in John 5:18, however, there is another sense in which the Father-Son relationship applied to Jesus. The Jews wanted to kill Jesus because He not only was healing on the Sabbath, but He also was calling God "His Father." How did the Jews understand Jesus' statement? (Calling God His Father was the same as saying He was the Son of God.) The Jews clearly understood that such a claim had nothing to do with being a descendant of God. They understood that He was "making Himself equal with God." This is why they wanted to kill Him. Had He not claimed to be equal with God, they would not have been so incensed. They highly revered Abraham, Moses and the prophets. Had Jesus claimed to be a prophet or someone highly regarded but less than God, it is unlikely the Jewish leaders would have sought to kill Him.

If Jesus Christ were only God, He could not have died on the cross for the sin of the world. If He were only man, His death could not have paid the penalty for the sins of others. It was necessary for Him to be the God-Man.

Throughout the centuries of church history, not all have agreed that Jesus Christ is the God-Man. Nestorius, patriarch of Constantinople for three years (A.D. 428–431), was such a person. He became the founder of the Nestorian Church, which had many followers in Persia (present-day Iran). Nestorius denied the biblical teaching that Jesus Christ was the God-Man come to earth to redeem fallen mankind. Church historian Earle E. Cairns points out that to Nestorius, "Christ was in effect only a perfect man who was morally linked to deity."[32]

The views of Nestorius were condemned in 431 at the Council of Nicea at Ephesus, 139 years before Muhammad was born. It was believed then—and should be remembered now—that if Jesus Christ were less than God, He would not have been able to save mankind. The views of Nestorius were not considered an orthodox view of Christianity from that time onward.

Muhammad's early contact with Christianity likely came from those who held the views of Nestorius about Jesus Christ: He was only a man and not God. This would have significantly influenced Muhammad regarding what he thought biblical Christianity taught.

His Atonement. Islam denies the death of Jesus Christ on the cross to pay for the penalty of sin. Muslims believe that God took Him to heaven before He had to go to the cross. They believe that whoever died on the cross was only someone who appeared to be like Jesus, but that it was not Him.

Hammudah Abdalati, a Muslim, says, "Islam rejects the doctrine of the Crucifixion of Jesus by the enemies of God and also the foundations of the doctrine. This rejection is based on the authority of God Himself as revealed in the Qur'an, and on a deeper rejection of blood sacrifice and vicarious atonement for sins."[33]

Because the blood of bulls and goats could not take away sin, the Lord Jesus Christ took upon Himself a human body so that He could shed His blood for the sins of the world (Heb. 10:4–5).

The Bible says, "And according to the law almost all things are purged with blood, and without shedding of blood there is no remission [forgiveness]" (Heb. 9:22). The Scriptures also reveal that "the blood of Jesus Christ . . . cleanses us from all sin" (1 John 1:7).

The Caner brothers say, "The greatest difference between Jesus Christ as God and Savior and Muhammad as prophet of Allah, comes at this point. Jesus Christ shed His own blood on the cross so that people could come to God. Muhammad shed other people's blood so that his constituents could have political power throughout the Arabian Peninsula.[34]

His Prophethood. Muslims see no difference between Jesus Christ and Muhammad, other than saying that Muhammad is the last (and the seal) of all the prophets. The Quran states:

> Say (O Muslims): We believe in Allah and that which is revealed unto us and that which was revealed unto Abraham, and Ishmael, and Isaac, and Jacob, and the tribes, and that which Moses and Jesus received, and that which the Prophets received from their Lord. We make no distinctions between any of them, and unto Him we have surrendered (2:136).[35]

How can the Muslims make no distinctions between Jesus Christ and Muhammad? The only way they can put Muhammad on the same level with Jesus Christ is to discredit the eyewitness reports of the New Testament concerning Christ.

No one can legitimately accuse Jesus Christ of any weakness, let alone any sin. The disciples, who were with Him constantly, never accused Him of a single fault. Jesus once asked an audience, "Which of you convicts Me of sin? And if I tell the truth, why do you not believe Me?" (John 8:46). The apostle Peter, who said that Jesus never committed a sin nor was He ever deceitful, emphatically expressed the testimony of the apostles (1 Pet. 2:22).

The reason such a testimony could be given concerning Jesus was that there was no sin in Him (Heb. 4:15; 1 Pet. 1:19; 1 John 3:5). The close companions of Muhammad made no such claims for their leader as the apostles made for the Lord Jesus Christ in their eyewitness reports. In fact, even the Quran tells Muhammad to ask forgiveness for his faults (40:55; 47:19).

Admittedly, it is one thing to claim to be sinless and to be God; it is quite another to prove those claims. The resurrection of Jesus Christ from the dead proved that His claims were true. In Paul's great sermon on Mars Hill, he proclaimed that God will someday judge the world through Jesus Christ. To confirm his statement, Paul added, "He has given assurance of this to all by raising Him from the dead" (Acts 17:31).

First Corinthians 15 is commonly called "The Resurrection Chapter" of the Bible. The apostle Paul recorded that after the resurrection of Jesus, He "was seen by Cephas [Peter], then by the twelve. After that He was seen by over five hundred brethren at once, of whom the greater part remain to the present, but some have fallen asleep" (vv. 5–6).

In effect, Paul was saying, "Even though some of this group have died, most are still living. If you don't believe what I'm saying about Christ's resurrection, go ask them."

Of all the founders of world religions, only the grave of the Lord Jesus Christ is empty. Although Jesus' tomb is empty—as verified by believers and unbelievers—Muhammad's remains are in the Prophet's Mosque in Medina. There is no valid comparison between Jesus Christ and Muhammad.

Holy Spirit

The Quran makes few references to the Holy Spirit. "Muslim theologians are at a loss to explain what is meant by the Holy Spirit," says Shorrosh.[36] In spite of what Muslims believe, Shorrosh accurately emphasizes, "Never once does the Holy Spirit in any text of the Bible refer to Muhammad, the Quran, or Islam."[37] The Scriptures reveal that the Holy Spirit is a person because He does things only a person can do. He convicts, guides, discloses things to come and glorifies Christ (John 16:7–15). He searches the depths of God and knows the thoughts of God (1 Cor. 2:10–11). It is also possible for the Holy Spirit to be grieved (Eph. 4:30).

The Bible also teaches that the Holy Spirit is God. In Acts 5:3–4 He is called God. The Holy Spirit does what only God can do—He regenerates by giving new birth to those who trust in Jesus Christ for salvation (John 3:3–8).

Man/Woman

Of all the contrasts between Islam and Christianity, one of the most apparent is the different attitude of men toward women. The Quran says:

> Men are in charge of women, because Allah hath made the one of them to excel the other, and because they spend of their property (for the support of women). So good women are the obedient, guarding in secret that which Allah hath guarded. As for those from whom ye fear rebellion, admonish them and banish them to beds apart, and scourge them (4:34).

Muslim writers make it seem that Islam has only positive benefits to womanhood, but those who are close observers do not share that opinion. Having seen the practical outworking of Islam, Shorrosh says, "A Muslim husband may cast his wife adrift without giving a single reason or even notice. The husband possesses absolute, immediate, and unquestioned power of divorce. No privilege of a corresponding nature is reserved for the wife."[38] Although some people debate how easy it is for a Muslim husband to divorce his wife, all agree that a Muslim wife does not have equal rights.

The Bible sets forth the equality of woman and man. They are considered "one in Christ" (Gal. 3:28), which gives equal standing before Him. Christian husbands are commanded to "love [their] wives, just as Christ also loved the church and gave Himself for it" (Eph. 5:25). The word translated "love" refers to an act of the will whereby the husband is to seek the highest good of his wife.

Muslims may claim that their men are seeking the highest good of the four wives and unlimited number of concubines (sexual partners) the Quran allows them, but others would seriously question this. The Bible nowhere indicates God's approval of sexual relationships between unmarried persons; instead, it commands believers to flee adultery and fornication (1 Cor. 6:18).

Sin

Islam believes that man is born into the world in a pure state and that what he becomes depends on external circumstances, according to Muslim Abdalati.[39]

In a debate about the distinctives of Islam vs. Christianity, Muslim Badru Kateregga says concerning the concept of sin and evil, "Muslims believe that man is fundamentally a good and dignified creature. He is not a fallen being. Muslims certainly would not agree that even prophets have participated in sinfulness!"[40]

Such views caused S. M. Zwemer, missionary to the Muslims in a past century, to say, "Islam denies the doctrine of the atonement and minimizes the heinousness of sin."[41] Except for the Lord Jesus Christ, all have sinned and come short of the glory of God (Rom. 3:23).

Biblical Christianity and Islam differ significantly on the concept of sin. The Bible teaches that when Adam and Eve faced a choice in the Garden of Eden, they chose to go their own way instead of God's way (Gen. 3). Because of this sin by the head of the human race (Adam), a sinful nature has been passed down to all descendants.

David acknowledged that he was brought forth in iniquity and that his mother had conceived him in sin (Ps. 51:5). He was not referring to any immoral act of his mother but to the sinful condition of mankind as they enter the world.

Romans 5:12 reveals that sin came into the world through one man (Adam) and that as a result, death passed to all men. Proof of this is that all eventually die. Romans 6:23 emphasizes that death is the result of sin. Muhammad's tomb in the Prophet's Mosque in Medina proves he is no exception.

SALVATION

Salvation in Islam is based on a works-righteousness. Each Muslim is viewed as having his deeds weighed on a giant scale. If the good deeds outweigh the bad, he is allowed to enter paradise.

"In Islam, it is believed that God judges people by their deeds or works, not by rites or ceremonies such as baptism. Islam further denies that a human can attain religious felicity on the basis of faith alone," says Isma'il R. Al Faruqi.[42]

Because salvation in Islam is always a goal in this life, not an attainment, Faruqi observes, "Religious justification is . . . the Muslim's eternal hope, never their complacent certainty, not for even a fleeting moment."[43]

Gene Edward Veith, cultural editor for *WORLD Magazine*, mentions that Mohammed Atta, the leader of the 9/11 terrorists, reportedly became addicted to pornography in Germany. Veith writes:

> His terrorist colleagues, in the days before 9/11, frequented strip clubs, buying lap dances and drinking alcohol, any one of which would earn them eternal damnation. But according to writings found after their attacks, they were confident in their salvation. By crashing the airplanes and murdering thousands, they were offering up human sacrifices and atoning for their own sins.[44]

The Bible reveals that because mankind is sinful, the only hope is to trust in the redemptive work of the Lord Jesus Christ. Any good works done by an individual are to no avail if the purpose is to obtain salvation on the basis of merit. The Old Testament Law system was based on works, but it was never intended to save anyone. The Book of Romans indicates that the works of the Law will save no one. Salvation is possible only through the righteousness that comes by faith in Jesus Christ (3:19–23).

Before trusting in Jesus Christ for salvation, mankind is viewed as dead in trespasses and sins (Eph. 2:1). To those hoping to be saved by good works, Ephesians 2:8–9 says, "For by grace you have been saved through faith, and that not of yourselves; it is the gift of God, not of works, lest anyone should boast."

Good works are important—not as a means of salvation but as an evidence of it. Ephesians 2:10 states, "For we are His workmanship, created in Christ Jesus for good works, which God prepared beforehand that we should walk in them." Good works are meaningless to God until a person acknowledges his sinful condition and trusts Christ as Savior.

Islam rejects what the Bible says about sin and salvation. Kateregga says, "Islam does not identify with the Christian conviction that man needs to be redeemed. The Christian belief in the redemptive sacrificial death of Christ does not fit the Islamic view that man has always been fundamentally good, and that God loves and forgives those who obey His will."[45]

In spite of such statements about man being fundamentally good, the Muslims see a need for special consideration by Allah. This is evident from their teaching concerning *Jihad*, or holy war. The Quran says, "And what though ye be slain in Allah's way or die therein? Surely pardon from Allah and mercy are better than all that they amass. What though ye be slain or die, when unto Allah ye are gathered?" (3:157–158).

Moderate Muslims emphasize that *Jihad* is only a personal inner struggle, but orthodox Islam teaches something else. Zacharias points out:

> However one might wish to interpret it, the sword and warfare are an intrinsic part of the Islamic faith. Even the best of apologists for Islam acknowledge the use of the sword in
> Islam but will mitigate it by saying that in each instance it was for defensive purposes. I suggest that the reader read the Koran and the history of Islam for himself to determine whether this was so.[46]

Concerning Islam and violence, Christian apologist Norman L. Geisler and former Muslim Abdul Saleeb say, "Christians who have engaged in violence are betraying the explicit teachings and examples of Jesus

HIS OWN FAMILY TRIED TO KILL HIM SEVERAL TIMES AFTER HE TURNED TO CHRIST.

Christ. On the other hand, Muslims who take upon themselves to destroy their alleged enemies in the name of God can rightly claim to be following the commands of God in the Qur'an and imitating their prophet as their role model."[47]

Mark A. Gabriel, a former Muslim, has written an excellent book to help one understand the true nature of Islam. *Islam and Terrorism: What the Quran Really Teaches about Christianity, Violence and the Goals of the Islamic Jihad* tells a heart-wrenching story about the author. Gabriel had memorized the Quran by the time he was 12 and went on to teach Islamic History at Al-Azhar University in Egypt—the "Harvard" of Islamic Universities. On his own he came up with contradictions in the Quran. When he made this known he was fired from the university and persecuted by the Egyptian Secret Police. Later someone gave him a New Testament, which started him on the path to trust Jesus Christ as his Savior. His own family tried to kill him several times after he turned to Christ. He came to the United States, was granted political asylum and changed his name for security reasons.

It is common for Muslims to point out that the verses for peace in the Quran far outnumber the ones for violence. However, Gabriel says that the verses for peace in the Quran refer to earlier revelations given to Muhammad and that those were all set aside by a later revelation that told him to destroy infidels. Gabriel writes:

> There are at least 114 verses in the Quran that speak of love, peace and forgiveness, especially in the surah entitled "The Heifer" (Surah 2:62, 109). But when Surah 9:5 was revealed later, it canceled out those previous verses. This verse states:
>
>> Fight and slay the Pagans wherever you find them, and seize them, beleaguer them, and lie in wait for them in every strategem (of war); but if they repent, and establish regular prayers and practise regular charity, then open the way for them: for Allah is Oft-forgiving, Most Merciful [Ali Translation].
>
> This is known as the verse of the sword, and it explains that Muslims must fight anyone who chooses not to convert to Islam, whether they are inside or outside of Arabia. It is considered to represent the final development of jihad in Islam.[48]

Gabriel maintains that our enemy is not Muslims but the Quran. Those who take this book seriously seek to do what the terrorists are doing today. Those in the U.S. who talk about Islam being a religion of peace are either deceived themselves or are purposely seeking to deceive Americans, Gabriel says. The terrorists are also opposed to Islamic governments who don't take the Quran seriously; that's why Muslim kills Muslim in this warfare.

In a book published by the Islamic Circle of North America, author Abul A'la Mawdudi (1903–1979) is described as a key person in the resurgence of contemporary Islam. Mawdudi says *Jihad* is used specifically in the language of Divine Law for the war that is waged against those who oppress Islam. If an Islamic country is attacked, the surrounding Islamic nations have the duty of offering help. And if they don't, then Muslims from the whole world must help.[49] On the same subject, Mawdudi adds, "What comparison would the loss of some lives—even if it were in the thousands or more—be to the calamity that would befall mankind as the result of the victory of evil over good."[50]

Jihad, with its concept of immediate entrance into paradise because of being a martyr in a holy war, reveals a religious system based on human merit. In fact, the only way salvation is guaranteed to a Muslim is if one dies as a martyr in *Jihad*.

But all systems of human merit fail. Some people may merit more than others, but none can merit right standing before a holy God. This is why Titus 3:5 says, "Not by works of righteousness which we have done, but according to His mercy He saved us."

FUTURE LIFE

Concerning the route to one's eternal destiny, one Muslim writer, Caesar E. Farah, says, "When the trial is over those destined to Hell or Paradise will be made to pass over a narrow bridge to their respective destinations. The bridge is so fashioned that the favored will cross with ease and facility while the condemned will tumble off into Hell."[51]

Norman Anderson, editor of *The World's Religions* and author of the section on Islam, describes the Muslim concept of paradise. After the judging of their deeds, Anderson says, "Some will be admitted to paradise, where they will recline on soft couches quaffing cups of wine handed to them by the Huris, or maidens of paradise, of whom each man may marry as many as he pleases. Others will be consigned to the torments of hell. Almost all, it would seem, will have to enter the fire temporarily, but no true Muslim will remain there for ever."[52] As mentioned previously, martyrs in a holy war are guaranteed immediate access into paradise.

Curiously, even as Muslim fanatics more and more are recruiting girls and young women to be martyrs, nothing is said about what is promised them after their death.

What They Believe

Biblical Christianity teaches "it is appointed for men to die once, but after this the judgment" (Heb. 9:27). Those who have trusted in Jesus Christ for salvation will be rewarded for their good deeds at the Judgment Seat of Christ (1 Cor. 3:11–15; 2 Cor. 5:10). This judgment, or evaluation, is not to determine salvation but rewards. Those who have rejected Christ as Savior will be given the sentence of judgment at the Great White Throne Judgment (Rev. 20:11–25).

Biblical Christianity offers the good news that those who trust Christ as Savior in this life can be assured of their salvation and future destiny. The apostle John wrote his first epistle so believers could know for certain that they had eternal life. Writing by inspiration, John penned, "These things I have written to you who believe in the name of the Son of God, that you may know that you have eternal life, and that you may continue to believe in the name of the Son of God" (1 John 5:13). You do not need to wait until some final judgment to be sure of your salvation.

CONCLUSION

Islam is more than a religion—it is a monotheistic philosophy of religion, politics and daily life. Many thinkers would question that Islam is a religion of peace after seeing the terrorizing and brutalizing of Kuwait by their Muslim brothers in Iraq. And that followed on the heels of the Iran-Iraq, eight-year war that pitted Muslim against Muslim and cost more than a million lives. And this does not even consider what has recently occurred in Afghanistan and Iraq. Sometimes little peace is found in Islam, even though its followers emphasize that the name means "peace."

Christians are concerned, however, about more than acquiring peace in this life; it is also needed for eternity. So the question that needs to be answered is, How does a person gain peace with God?

This kind of peace comes through a right standing with God by trusting Jesus Christ as Savior. Through this decision a person is delivered from condemnation, and he acquires peace with God. The Bible tells us, "Having been justified by faith, we have peace with God through our Lord Jesus Christ" (Rom. 5:1).

Any religion that makes the atoning work of Christ unnecessary and places emphasis on human merit cannot provide eternal salvation or peace with God.

But here is the crux of the matter: Does a person believe the Word of God is the Bible or the Quran? If the Bible is accepted as the source of authority, no choice is left but to reject all systems that deny the deity of Jesus Christ and His atoning work on the cross.

How, then, are we to reach Muslims with the Gospel of the death, burial and resurrection of the Lord Jesus Christ? Those who have worked in Muslim ministries for years affirm that it is not an easy task. They do give us some guidelines, however.

One person actively involved in a ministry to Muslims says, "Urge the Muslim friend to take the Gospel and compare the teachings of the Gospel to that of their Koran. Tell them to compare the Christ of the Gospel to the Christ of the Koran. Never be afraid that the Christ of the Gospel will come up second best—He never will. There have been many conversions to Christ by using this very method."

Francis R. Steele, retired associate director of Arab World Ministries, suggests, "If we do not believe that God is able to save Muslims, of course there is no sense in our trying to win them. But if we believe that He intended that they should be included in the outreach of the church, we must certainly believe that He is able to effect their salvation. This is the absolutely essential foundation to any effective witness to Muslims."[53]

Those who work with Muslims also emphasize that, above all else, love for the people must be genuine. Even though Muslims disagree with our message, we must not be unkind. As Christians, we should evidence the fruit of the Spirit, as mentioned in Galatians 5:22–23. We Christians must practice what we preach if we expect to receive a hearing from those who are seeking a relationship with God. Our lives must not make a lie out of what we believe.

Also, we must never depart from emphasizing the truth of the Scriptures. Although Muslims may reject that message, we are neither helpful to them nor faithful to ourselves or to the Lord if we stop proclaiming the truth of the Scriptures.

Only the Scriptures are able to make a person wise unto salvation. And that salvation is available only through faith in the Lord Jesus Christ (2 Tim. 3:15). There is no hope in any other plan of salvation. The Bible says, "Nor is there salvation in any other, for there is no other name under heaven given among men by which we must be saved" (Acts 4:12).

The key to our message must be the death, burial and resurrection of the Lord Jesus Christ, which were confirmed by eyewitnesses (1 Cor. 15:1–8). This is the Gospel, or good news, that we must proclaim to lost mankind, regardless of their religious affiliation. Regrettably, this is the very message that Muslims and the Quran deny.

But let us take hope. Many also doubted the resurrection of Christ in Paul's day, and the philosophers of Paul's time thought he was a babbler or proclaimed foreign gods "because he preached to them Jesus and the resurrection" (Acts 17:18). We must do the same. It is the resurrection of Christ that makes Christianity distinctly different from—and far superior to—other world religions.

David Wells, the Andrew Mutch Distinguished Professor of Historical and Systematic Theology at Gordon-Conwell Theological Seminary, was interviewed by *WORLD Magazine* in 2002. He was asked what was wrong with the ecumenism between Christians and Muslims since 9/11, about which he had expressed concern. His answer reveals the heart of the problem between Christians and Muslims:

> Islam denies that Christ was crucified and that He rose from the dead. It claims to esteem Christ as a prophet more highly than Christians because they don't believe God would give Him up to a criminal's death.
>
> There is no more serious attack on the essence and heart of the Christian faith than this. If Christ has not died for our sins and risen again, there is no forgiveness, no justification, no reconciliation, no salvation, no gospel, and no hope. Therefore to stand with a Muslim as if Christians and Muslims are both savingly related to the same God is to undermine the gospel and to deny Christ.[54]

Information and logic alone will not open closed hearts—only prayer is able to do that. It is significant that when Paul was preaching in Philippi, Luke recorded this concerning Lydia, "The Lord opened her heart to heed the things spoken by Paul" (Acts 16:14). Let us keep lovingly proclaiming the Gospel of Christ, while at the same time praying and depending on the Lord to open hearts.

Summary

Name of Religion: Islam
Name of Followers: Muslims
Founder: Muhammad (570–632)
Most Holy City: Mecca
Adherents: U.S.: 4–5 million
Worldwide: About 1 billion

What They Believe

Muslims: **Biblical Christians:**

Source of Authority

The Quran is their final authority. Also hold to other sources about Muhammad and Islam.

The Bible alone is their final authority.

Trinity

Consider belief in the Trinity to be polytheism.

The three Persons of the Godhead are one, though distinct.

God

The God of Quran loves only those who love him.

The God of the Bible loves everyone, even if they reject Him.

Jesus Christ

Deny the deity of Christ, His death on the cross for sin and His resurrection.

Jesus Christ is God and took on flesh to die for mankind's sin. He rose from the dead on the third day.

Holy Spirit

Quran makes few references to the Holy Spirit, and Muslim theologians seem at a loss to explain Him.

The Holy Spirit is a divine person of the Godhead who convicts, regenerates and teaches.

Man/Woman

Quran says that men are in charge of women.

Believe men and women are equal because they are "one in Christ."

Sin

Man is born into the world in a pure state, so he is fundamentally good and not a fallen being.

All mankind is born with a fallen nature and in need of salvation.

What They Believe

Salvation

A person cannot attain acceptance with Allah on the basis of faith alone. Male martyrs who die during a holy war gain immediate acceptance into heaven.

Salvation is possible only by believing in the finished work of Christ on the cross.

Future Life

Some believe eternal destiny is determined after a trial. Almost all will have to enter hell fire temporarily but no true Muslim will remain there.

Those who trust in Christ in this life for salvation have eternal life; those who reject Him will experience eternal death.

Recommended Reading

Anderson, Norman, ed. *The World's Religions*, 4th ed. Grand Rapids, Mich.: Eerdmans Publishing Company, 1975.

Answering Islam Web site, www.answering-islam.org.

Bickel, Bruce, and Jantz, Stan. *World Religions & Cults 101: A Guide to Spiritual Beliefs.* Eugene, Ore.: Harvest House Publishers, 2002.

Caner, Ergun Mehmet, and Caner, Emir Fethi. *Unveiling Islam: An Insider's Look at Muslim Life and Beliefs.* Grand Rapids, Mich.: Kregel Publications, 2002.

Carlson, Ron, and Decker, Ed. *Fast Facts on False Teachings.* Eugene, Ore.: Harvest House Publishers, 1994.

Eerdmans' Handbook to the World's Religions. Grand Rapids, Mich.: Wm. B. Eerdmans Publishing Company, 1982.

Enroth, Ronald, ed. *A Guide to New Religious Movements.* Downers Grove, Ill.: InterVarsity Press, 2005.

FaithFacts Web site, http://faithfacts.gospelcom.net.

Gabriel, Mark A. *Islam and Terrorism: What the Quran Really Teaches about Christianity, Violence and the Goals of the Islamic Jihad.* Lake Mary, Fla.: Charisma House, 2002.

Geisler, Norman L., and Saleeb, Abdul. *Answering Islam: The Crescent in Light of the Cross.* Grand Rapids, Mich.: Baker Books, 2002.

Gospelcom.net Web site, www.gospelcom.net (search for organizations and subject).

Katerrega, Badru D. *Islam and Christianity: A Muslim and a Christian in Dialogue.* Grand Rapids, Mich.: Eerdmans, 1981.

Martin, Walter. *The Kingdom of the Cults*. Ravi Zacharias, gen. ed. Minneapolis: Bethany House Publishers, 2003.

McDowell, Josh, and Stewart, Don. *Handbook of Today's Religions*. San Bernardino, Calif.: Here's Life Publishers, Inc., 1983.

Morey, Robert. *The Islamic Invasion: Confronting the World's Fastest Growing Religion*. Las Vegas: Christian Scholars Press, 1992.

Pipes, Daniel. *Militant Islam Reaches America*. New York: W. W. Norton and Company, 2002.

Saal, William J. *Reaching Muslims for Christ*. Chicago: Moody Press, 1991.

Shorrosh, Anis A. *Islam Revealed: A Christian Arab's View of Islam*. Nashville: Thomas Nelson Publishers, 1988.

Zacharias, Ravi. *Light in the Shadow of Jihad*. Nashville: Word Publishing, 2000.

_____. *Jesus Among Other Gods: The Absolute Claims of the Christian Message*. Nashville: Word Publishing, 2000.

ENDNOTES

[1] *Omaha World-Herald*, Nov. 15, 2003.

[2] Author's e-mail sent to the *Omaha World-Herald* Public Pulse, Nov. 17, 2003.

[3] Editor Jim Anderson's e-mail to the author, Nov. 28, 2003.

[4] Author's e-mail, Nov. 30, 2003.

[5] Bernard Lewis, *The Crisis of Islam: Holy War and Unholy Terror* (New York: The Modern Library, 2003), 24.

[6] *Omaha World-Herald*, Nov. 10, 2003, 1A.

[7] Seyyed Hossein Nasr, *Islam: Religion, History, and Civilization* (San Francisco: HarperSanFrancisco, 2003), 3.

[8] Ergun Mehmet Caner and Emir Fethi Caner, *Unveiling Islam: An Insider's Look at Muslim Life and Beliefs* (Grand Rapids, Mich.: Kregel Publications, 2002), 122.

[9] www.convertstoislam.org/introduction/howtobecomeaMuslim.htm, Aug. 20, 2003.

[10] Ibid.

[11] Caner and Caner, *Unveiling Islam*, 109–110.

[12] *WORLD Magazine*, Nov.–Dec. 2001, 12.

[13] *WORLD Magazine*, May 18, 2002, 44.

[14] *The World Almanac and Book of Facts 2005* (New York, N.Y.: World Almanac Education Group, Inc., 2005), 731.

[15] www.isna.net, "America Gets Another Muslim Friendly Campus," Sept. 24, 2003.

[16] www.isna.net, "Seeking Their Due," Sept. 24, 2003.

[17] Hammudah Abdalati, *Islam in Focus* (Indianapolis: American Trust Publications, 1975), 8.

What They Believe

[18] Anis A. Shorrosh says she was ten, *Islam Revealed: A Christian Arab's View of Islam* (Nashville: Thomas Nelson Publishers, 1988), 58; The Caners say she was nine, *Unveiling Islam*, 56.

[19] Nasr, *Islam*, 8.

[20] Ravi Zacharias, *Jesus among Other Gods* (Nashville: Word Publishing, 2000), 160.

[21] James R. White, "Examining Muslim Apologetics" in *Christian Research Journal*, Vol. 25, No. 3, 36.

[22] Ibid., 41.

[23] Patrick Johnstone and Jason Mandryk, *Operation World: 21ˢᵗ Century Edition* (United States: WEC International, 2001), 501.

[24] Shorrosh, *Islam Revealed,* 21.

[25] Ibid., 271.

[26] Comments about the five sources concerning what the Muslims draw on and teach were received by the author in an e-mail of September 17, 2001, just six days after the historic 9/11 event. I have especially drawn on what the sender wrote about the last four sources of authority in Islam. The name of the individual must remain confidential because of serving in Afghanistan at the time of this writing. This Christian leader, who holds an M.A. in World Christianity, has studied Islam for several years and has taught courses related to this religion. After citing the five sources, this person wrote, "All these sources for deciding what consists of a proper understanding of Islam agree that violence was a part of the expansion of Islam and is justifiable."

[27] G. W. Bromiley, "Trinity," in *Evangelical Dictionary of Theology*, Walter A. Elwell, ed. (Grand Rapids, Mich.: Baker Book House, 1984), 1,112.

[28] Fulton J. Sheen and Mervin Monroe Deems, "Apostles' Creed," in *The World Book Encyclopedia*, Vol. 1 (Chicago: World Book, Inc., 1986), 530.

[29] Robert Morey, *The Islamic Invasion: Confronting the World's Fastest Growing Religion* (Las Vegas: Christian Scholars Press, 1992), 64–65.

[30] *Fundamentalism: Contrasting Christianity and Islam* (Austin, Tex.: Christian Information Foundation, n.d.), 5.

[31] Caner and Caner, *Unveiling Islam*, 118.

[32] Earle E. Cairns, *Christianity through the Centuries: A History of the Christian Church* (Grand Rapids, Mich.: Zondervan Publishing House, 1954, 1981), 136.

[33] Abdalati, *Islam in Focus*, 159.

[34] Caner and Caner, *Unveiling Islam*, 49.

[35] All quotations from the Quran are taken from *The Meaning of the Glorious Koran: An Explanatory Translation by Mohammed Marmaduke Pickthall* (New York: New American Library, n.d.).

[36] Shorrosh, *Islam Revealed*, 219.

[37] Ibid., 221.

[38] Ibid., 167.

[39] Abdalati, *Islam in Focus*, 32.

[40] Badru D. Kateregga and David W. Shenk, *Islam and Christianity* (Ibadan, Nigeria: Daystar Press, 1980), 108.

[41] S. M. Zwemer, *The Moslem Doctrine of God* (New York: American Tract Society, 1905), 112.

[42] Isma'il R. Al Faruqi, *Islam* (Niles, Ill.: Argus Communications, 1979), 5.

[43] Ibid.

[44] *WORLD Magazine*, Feb. 22, 2003, 13.

[45] Kateregga and Shenk, *Islam and Christianity*, 141.

[46] Zacharias, *Jesus among Other Gods*, 159.

[47] Norman L. Geisler and Abdul Saleeb, *Answering Islam: The Crescent in Light of the Cross* (Grand Rapids, Mich.: Baker Books, 2002), 319. See also endnote 26 about violence in Islamic sources.

[48] Mark A. Gabriel. *Islam and Terrorism: What the Quran Really Teaches about Christianity, Violence and the Goals of the Islamic Jihad* (Lake Mary, Fla.: Charisma House, 2002), 30.

[49] Abul A'la Mawdudi, *Towards Understanding Islam: Islamic Circle of North America*, n.p., 1986), 125.

[50] Ibid., 139.

[51] Caesar E. Farah, *Islam: Beliefs and Observances*, 4th ed. (Woodbury, N.Y.: Barron's Educational Series, Inc., 1968), 116.

[52] Norman Anderson, ed., *The World's Religions*, 4th ed. (Grand Rapids, Mich.: Eerdmans Publishing Company, 1975), 117.

[53] Francis R. Steele, *Islam: An Analysis* (Upper Darby, Pa.: Arab World Ministries, n.d.), 5.

[54] *WORLD Magazine*, July–Aug. 2002, 53.

CHAPTER SEVEN

New Age Movement

The New Age Movement is eating away at the spiritual heart of America. Although not much is new about the New Age belief system, one needs to be aware that the terms associated with it have been twisted to mean something different than just a few decades ago.

How dangerous is the New Age Movement? Twenty years ago it was being called "more dangerous than secular humanism" by foremost Christian apologist Norman Geisler.[1] And the situation hasn't improved. In 1994 Ron Rhodes, president of Reasoning from the Scriptures Ministries, called the New Age Movement a "fast-growing spiritual cancer."[2]

The spiritual worldview of the New Age Movement has been around for a long time, but more and more influential individuals are aligning with it. Famous names such as Alice Bailey, Benjamin Creme, David Spangler, Levi Dowling, George Trevelyan, Fritjof Capra, Abraham Maslow, Marilyn Ferguson, Shirley MacLaine, George Lucas, Jessica Lipnack and Jeffrey Stamps have been associated with New Age beliefs. In addition, the mind-set of the New Age Movement has touched almost every area of life: education, culture, history, religion, politics, psychology, science and health.

The New Age Movement has no central headquarters; therefore, no leadership or membership lists are available. So we have no clear statistics that tell us how many people are followers of the New Age Movement. Some researchers have sought to determine the number of adherents by other means, such as by finding out how many people hold to one or more of the major beliefs of the New Age.

As to the number of people involved in the New Age, Ron Rhodes cites Marilyn Ferguson, author of *The Aquarian Conspiracy*, who was quoted in a 1993 article in the *Los Angeles Times*. Ferguson said that

What They Believe

"sociologists at UC Santa Barbara . . . estimate that as many as 12 million Americans could be considered active participants, and another 30 million are avidly interested. If all these people were brought together in a church-like organization, it would be the third-largest religious denomination in America."[3] Another source extrapolates from a 1990 CNN poll that "roughly 35–40 million people in the U.S. believe in one of the central tenets of New Age."[4]

In January 1987, the ABC-TV network aired a miniseries based on Shirley MacLaine's book *Out on a Limb*, which greatly popularized the beliefs of the New Age.

The New Age Movement emphasizes the mental and spiritual dimensions of mankind, and its beliefs are contrary to biblical Christianity. What has laid the groundwork for the New Age Movement?

BACKGROUND

Although the words *new age* would cause you to assume that the beliefs of this movement are modern, little, in fact, is new in the New Age Movement. The name is derived from the idea that the world is about to enter a utopian "Age of Aquarius." New Agers devote much attention to astrology, the belief that the heavenly bodies affect the mundane matters of humanity. It is from astrology that the Age of Aquarius is derived.

In their *Dictionary of Cults, Sects, Religions and the Occult*, Mather and Nichols say, "The age of Aquarius was to have begun in the nineteenth century. Some new agers see the twentieth century as 'the dawning of the age of Aquarius,' heralding the start of a new and cosmic worldview."[5] Regarding the spirituality of the New Age they add, "Such spirituality leaves behind the conceptual schema of the Judeo-Christian heritage characteristic of the last two thousand years of history. In its place comes the Aquarian age."[6]

The name *Aquarius* has become closely associated with the New Age Movement. In *The Aquarian Conspiracy,* Ferguson tells the story of the New Age Movement. She explains her choice of words in the title. At first she thought *conspiracy* was too strong a word. But then she said she realized that "conspire, in its literal sense, means 'to breathe together.' It is an intimate joining. To make clear the benevolent nature of this joining, I chose the word *Aquarian*. Although I am unacquainted with astrological lore, I was drawn to the symbolic power of the pervasive dream in our popular culture: that after a dark, violent age, the Piscean, we are entering a millennium of love and light—in the words of the popular song, 'The Age of Aquarius,' the time of 'mind's true liberation.'"[7]

The New Age Movement seems to be a reaction to the scientific age. Following a time when everything was so objective and particularized, the shift now is to emphasize the subjective and the whole. This has focused attention on "inner" feelings and on wholistic (or holistic) health, as well as on global matters rather than nationalistic ones.

Traditionally, the public education system of the United States—

A COUNTRY CAN RULE GOD OUT OF THE CLASSROOM AND THE SCIENCE LAB, BUT IT CANNOT RULE HIM OUT OF THE HEARTS OF PEOPLE.

from kindergarten through graduate level—has been based on an atheistic presupposition. Everything must be explainable apart from a supernatural God. Even though some fine Christian teachers and administrators have counter-balanced this presupposition somewhat, the system itself has made no room for God.

This educational system has produced scientists who have taken the same worldview. Again, although some scientists are outstanding Christians, the norm has been to explain everything in the experimental lab totally apart from God.

A country can rule God out of the classroom and the science lab, but it cannot rule Him out of the hearts of people. "[God] has put eternity in their hearts," the Bible declares (Eccles. 3:11). There is a spiritual vacuum within the heart of man that only God can fill. When people reject the true God, they begin to worship other objects. Secular humanism rejected a concept of God and turned to man himself. It sees man as only a highly evolved animal with no spiritual capacity.

The New Age Movement is a reaction to this atheistic view, but it is no closer to the truth than secular humanism is. Anyone who exchanges Secular Humanism for New Age thinking has simply swapped one spiritually bankrupt system for another. The New Age Movement has put an emphasis on the mind (as seen in its mysticism) and on the spirit (as seen in its worldview of God, matter and mankind). Let's now consider some of the basic beliefs of the New Age Movement as they compare with biblical Christianity.

BELIEFS

Douglas R. Groothuis, an associate professor of philosophy of religion and ethics at Denver Seminary, identifies six distinctives of New Age thinking: All is One; All is God; Humanity is God; A change in consciousness; All religions are one; and Cosmic evolutionary optimism.[8]

Similarly, George Mather and Larry Nichols see seven common themes of New Age beliefs: Monism; Pantheism; Reincarnation and Karma; Universal religion; Personal transformation; Planetary vision; and New Age eschatology.[9]

Robert J. L. Burrows cautions, "Issues New Agers address do not necessarily come with New Age ideology attached. Nor does the terminology they use. Holistic, holographic, synergistic, unity, oneness, transformation, personal growth, human potential, awakening, networking, energy, consciousness—such words occur with predictable regularity in New Age writings. It would, however, be erroneous to conclude that these words always indicate New Age commitment."[10]

Although there are many ways to approach an evaluation of the New Age Movement, this analysis will pursue what the Movement believes concerning its source of authority, God, Jesus Christ, sin and salvation, good and evil, and future life.

SOURCE OF AUTHORITY

Generally, New Agers do not speak of a source of authority. If such is referred to, it is not an external authority but an internal one. In the New Age Movement, the individual is considered to be the standard of truth. New Agers reject absolute objective truth for absolute subjective truth.

Actress Shirley MacLaine, although not the popular proponent of New Age beliefs that she once was, helped the public understand what the intellectuals were saying about the New Age Movement. She revealed the supposed power of the individual when commenting, "It's all my dream. I'm making all of it happen—good and bad—and I have the choice of how I'll relate to it and what I'll do about it."[11]

MacLaine echoed the belief of every New Ager when she said, "Perhaps everyone has his own truth, and truth as an objective reality simply does not exist."[12]

To the contrary, the Scriptures present objective truths. They are inspired (literally, "God-breathed"); therefore, they can be fully relied on. The *fact* of the inspiration of the Scriptures is seen in 2 Timothy 3:16: "All Scripture is given by inspiration of God, and is profitable for doctrine, for reproof, for correction, for instruction in righteousness." The *method* of inspiration is seen in 2 Peter 1:21: "Prophecy never came by the will of man, but holy men of God spoke as they were moved by the Holy Spirit." The *extent* of inspiration is seen in Matthew 5:18: "For assuredly, I say to you," said the Lord Jesus Christ, "till heaven and earth pass away, one jot or one tittle will by no means pass from the law till all is fulfilled."

So no individual is left to himself and his inner feelings as final authority; the Bible serves as this objective standard.

GOD

New Age thinkers show their true colors in what they believe about God. To them, God is not a Supreme Being distinct from creation— He is creation.

In developing a worldview about the material and immaterial world, New Agers reach a faulty conclusion. To them, there is only one essence in the universe, and everything and everyone is part of that essence. This is known as "monism," which comes from the Greek word *monos*, meaning "one."

Monism is a common view of Eastern religions, especially Hinduism. All creatures, as well as inanimate objects, are viewed as part of this divine essence. Some of the more commonly known groups in the United States that share this Hindu view with the New Agers are Christian Science, Transcendental Meditation (also known as the Science of Creative Intelligence) and Unity School of Christianity. In fact, in *The Aquarian Conspiracy*, Ferguson lists Unity churches under "discussion groups" of "Aquarian Conspiracy Resources."[13]

What They Believe

The monism of the New Age Movement is really pantheism, which is a belief that all (*pan*) is God (*theos*). Following this line of reasoning, whatever exists—whether living or nonliving—is part of God. This leads some observers to say that the worldview in the United States has switched from the atheism of secular humanism (there is no God) to the pantheism of the New Age Movement (everything is God).

Regarding the need to prevent pantheism from becoming a dominant philosophy in our society, Gordon R. Lewis, professor of theology and philosophy at Denver Seminary, wrote: "I realized the great importance of prevention as a visiting professor in India, where the results of a monistic world view and way of life have been entrenched for centuries. In a rural area of that poverty-stricken culture human life was cheap. I could see how difficult it is to evangelize pantheists who believe that they are already divine, have endless potential for self-improvement, are not inherently sinful, and not in need of the gracious, once-for-all provision of Jesus Christ's atonement."[14]

The god of the New Age Movement is an impersonal presence, not a person with intellect, emotions and a will, as the Bible presents God. Writing about the nature of divinity, New Ager Geoffrey Hodson says, "He does not bestow favors on some and withhold them from others; all his children are regarded equally."[15] Notice that Hodson uses personal pronouns (He, his) in referring to divinity even though he does not believe God is a person. This is seen by his footnote to "He" as it was used previously in the same paragraph: "The masculine is used for convenience only, the divine Principle being regarded as equally masculine, feminine, and androgyne [having male and female characteristics in one]."[16] When talking with a New Ager, do not be misled by an individual's use of personal pronouns when what is meant is a "divine Principle." New Agers should use the impersonal pronoun "it," not "he," when referring to their god.

Biblical Christianity is the common enemy of both secular humanism and the New Age Movement. Concerning the belief in monism by the latter two groups, Groothuis comments, "Secular humanism has a monism of matter and energy, while cosmic humanism (the One) has a monism of spirit—all is god."[17]

This reveals why New Agers cannot accept the teaching of the Bible. They are not able to get beyond the first five words: "In the beginning

God created" (Gen. 1:1). Because they confuse God with creation, New Agers see God as part of creation, not separate from it. Biblical Christianity clearly distinguishes between God and creation.

While rejecting the Bible's distinction between God and creation, New Agers accept and believe the lie of Satan. Eve told the Tempter that God had said they would die if she and Adam ate from the tree in the middle of the garden. But the Seducer said, "You will not surely die. For God knows that in the day you eat of it your eyes will be opened, and you will be like God, knowing good and evil" (Gen. 3:4–5).

Notice that not even Satan indicated they would "be" God—only that they would be "like" God. And even this was in only one aspect: "knowing good and evil" (although New Agers do not accept an ultimate distinction between these moral values). After the fall of Adam and Eve, God acknowledged what had occurred: "The man has become like one of Us, to know good and evil" (v. 22).

"This knowledge, as absolute, is an attribute of God (3:5), who is omniscient," wrote Hebrew scholar Merrill F. Unger. "But man, created with only the knowledge of good, acquired the experiential knowledge of evil through pride and disobedience, and in this manner fell into a state of sin and misery."[18]

Satan's lie—as verified by history—was, "You will not surely die" (v. 4). Adam and Eve immediately died spiritually, for their act of disobedience separated them from God. They later died physically as a result of their sin (Rom. 5:12).

Because New Agers believe all is One, this leads them to think they—and everything and everyone else—are part of this divine essence. They believe each person is "intertwined" with God.[19] New Agers even use the Bible to support their erroneous beliefs. They are especially fond of Jesus' words, "The kingdom of God is within you" (Luke 17:21). New Agers use these words to claim that each one has a divine spark within because he or she is part of the divine essence.

As in other instances where they use the Bible, New Agers twist the context and words to mean what they wish. Jesus Christ had come to earth to present Himself as the Messiah of Israel. The Pharisees were opposed to Him because He was ruining their established man-made rules, which they had added to Old Testament revelation. They were always trying to pose some question to disprove the deity of the Lord Jesus Christ. When they demanded of Him an answer concerning

when the kingdom of God would come (v. 20), He answered, "The kingdom of God is within you" (v. 21).

Jesus did not mean that these Pharisees had the kingdom of God inside of them. To the contrary, they were the enemies of everything the kingdom stood for. The word translated "within" is *entos*. Although it can have the meaning of "inside," it can also mean "in your midst." This latter possibility fits the context, as well as the rest of the Bible's teaching. Jesus Christ Himself was the King—the ruler of the kingdom. When the Pharisees asked Him when the kingdom would arrive, Jesus told them that the kingdom was in their midst, because the King (whom they rejected) was standing right in their presence.

NEW AGER BARBARA MARX HUBBARD SAYS WE NEED TO RECOGNIZE THAT THE "MESSIAH IS WITHIN."

JESUS CHRIST

Many counterfeit religious groups use the same tactic when explaining who Jesus Christ is: they deny His deity by distinguishing between "Jesus" and "Christ." Those who believe that "all is One" cannot accept the teaching of the Bible concerning Christ. The Bible teaches that Jesus Christ is God. It teaches that He took upon Himself human form for the purpose of redeeming mankind from the penalty of sin.

Typically, those who believe all is of one essence make "Christ" the cosmic principle, or ideal. Jesus was simply an unusual man, they say, who had this ideal within Him as we all do. New Ager Barbara Marx Hubbard says we need to recognize that the "Messiah is within."[20]

The human potential movement among New Agers is based on this faulty premise—that each person is god and needs only to have his consciousness enlightened so he will realize it. And the means to this enlightenment is meditation.

But the forms of meditation are many. Daniel Coleman, writing in *Psychology Today,* described 13 different forms of meditation. "Each of these approaches," wrote Coleman, "seeks the same basic psychological change in the meditator's awareness. This single aim is aptly summed up in the words of the Taoist Chuang Tzu, as translated by the Trappist Thomas Merton: No drives, no compulsions, / No needs, no attractions: / Then your affairs are under control. / You are a free man."[21]

The New Age Movement does not have the distinction of being the only group that emphasizes human potential. Biblical Christianity releases individuals to achieve their true potential in Jesus Christ by freeing them from the burden of sin and condemnation and by giving them untold optimism for this life. But biblical Christianity is also concerned about preparing people for eternity, not just preparing them to reach their maximum potential on earth.

Although the emphasis on human potential is selling well in the business world, when a person truly looks inside of himself, he finds self-centeredness and ugliness—not God. "The heart is deceitful above all things, and desperately wicked," says Jeremiah 17:9. "Who can know it?"

David Seamands, author of *Healing of Memories*, says, "I was a missionary to India, and the massive umbrella of pantheistic and monistic Hinduism was a tremendous challenge. It made me an absolute fanatic on Jesus Christ. The one place that I'm not going to budge is on the Incarnation, because I see the tremendous importance of it. 'Whether the Krishna existed or not,' says my Hindu friend, 'that's not important. It's the Krishna ideal that matters, so therefore it's the Christ ideal that matters. Whether or not Christ existed is not important.'

"To that I would and did say, 'No, we're not talking about the same thing. Whether Christ exists or not is not just important. It's absolutely paramount.'"[22]

We cannot separate the human Jesus from the divine Christ, as the New Agers attempt to do. They believe that the same Christ ideal, or spirit, dwelt in "Hercules, Hermes, Rama, Mithra . . . Krishna, Buddha, and the Christ."[23]

Sound confusing? It is. The Bible, however, does not leave a person wondering about who Jesus Christ is. The name *Jesus* means "Savior." Referring to the child who would be born to the virgin Mary, the angel told Joseph, "You shall call His name Jesus, for He will save His people from their sins" (Matt. 1:21).

The name *Christ* means "anointed one" or "Messiah." In Bible times, saying "Jesus Christ" was the same as saying "Jesus, the Messiah." After Andrew first began to follow Jesus, he went looking for his brother, Simon Peter. When he found him, Andrew announced, "We have found the Messiah." By inspiration, the apostle John added in his record of this event, "which is translated, the Christ" (John 1:41).

Jesus Christ is like no other. He was unique in His birth, life, death and resurrection. He was virgin born (Isa. 7:14; Matt. 1:23); He lived a sinless life (1 John 3:5); He died in the place of others to pay the penalty for sin (2 Cor. 5:21); and He was raised from the dead on the third day and ascended to the Heavenly Father (1 Cor. 15:3–4; Acts 1:11). None of these acts can be done by a divine Principle; He had to be a divine Person.

SIN AND SALVATION

If you try to find references to sin in New Age writings, you'll search in vain. Because New Agers believe that each person is god, they don't believe in sin as the Bible defines it. Any lack a person has, they say, is a lack of enlightenment. Their solution is to alter that person's consciousness so he will think properly about his oneness with the Force, or the impersonal presence.

New Agers don't believe that Adam fell into sin, as recorded in Genesis 3. One writer claims such erroneous thinking comes from misunderstanding the parable of the Prodigal Son (Luke 15). "As suggested throughout this interpretation," says Hodson, "the parable describes the journey of spirit outwards from the Source on the path of forthgoing, and inwards to the Source on the path of return."[24] This is a good example of how a Scripture story, which Jesus told as a lesson to the Pharisees who were angry because God was receiving sinners, is twisted by New Agers to mean something allegorical, even metaphysical. If we interpreted the words in their books in the way they interpret words in the Bible, we could make their statements mean anything we wanted them to mean as well.

Because they explain away sin, New Agers have no need for salvation in the biblical sense. In their minds, any salvation would simply be a more complete union with the One. "The true salvation of man, following his 'Fall,'" says Hodson, "is an ascent into full experience of this fact of oneness with God, implying ascension into conscious union with the Deity."[25]

But this is not what the Bible teaches. Genesis 3 reveals that mankind was separated from God when he disobeyed Him in the Garden. Because of this sin, a curse was placed on both mankind and nature (vv. 14–19). The New Testament confirms that each individual is a sinful being. "Therefore, just as through one man sin entered the world, and death through sin, and thus death spread to all men, because all sinned" (Rom. 5:12). Note that the reason death passed to all of us is that we have all been affected by sin.

Contrary to what the New Agers tell us, each person is not god; each person is not even inherently good. Instead, each person is separated from God.

Mankind needed a way back to God. People needed truth they could believe—not more of Satan's lies—and they needed eternal life. This is what Christ provided. "I am the way, the truth, and the life. No one comes to the Father except through Me," He said (John 14:6).

GOOD AND EVIL

The New Age Movement mimics Eastern religions, which distort the distinction between good and evil. Because of the New Age's monistic view that "all is One," how can it account for both good and evil? Is the one "essence," or "force" (the Hindu equivalent of God), both good and evil?

The God of the Bible stands in sharp contrast to the god of Eastern religions. In the One-is-all and all-is-One view of divine essence, there ultimately is neither good nor evil. "In the philosophy of the One ethical distinctions evaporate," says Groothuis, "supposed opposites—light and dark, good and evil, humans and God—merge and fuse."[26] This would explain why people whose values were shaped during the 1960s are primarily relativistic in outlook: the situation determines the rightness or wrongness, not a set standard of beliefs. Historian James Hitchcock sees the late 1960s as a time of significant shifting of worldviews in the United States. "Common attitudes, and especially the kinds of attitudes which are regarded as respectable, underwent a swift change between 1965 and 1970. Although it was perhaps only a minority who were most affected, they were the trend-setters. They either had little interest in religion or were hostile to it. They either rejected traditional morality or were willing to compromise it endlessly."[27]

Such a worldview sees no sharp distinctions between right and wrong, good and evil. Yet this is really an academic idealism by New Agers; they do not practice it in everyday life. When, for example, they are shortchanged by a cashier or a family member is threatened, they suddenly have values of right and wrong and insist on such distinctions.

The Bible clearly distinguishes between good and evil. The two never merge. Nor does a person ever transcend in his consciousness so he goes beyond the bounds of moral distinctions.

FUTURE LIFE

Although ultimately denying any distinction between good and evil, New Age thinkers are concerned about a future life—but not the future life known in the Bible. New Agers say that the way a person lives in this life will determine the way he will be reincarnated in the next. This is not a new concept; it is as old as the Eastern religions the New Agers follow. It also shows the natural bent of man's mind. He may think he can go beyond any moral boundaries of accountability, but somehow he still realizes the need to account for wrongdoing in this life.

Caryl Matrisciana of Great Britain was raised in India. In her book *Gods of the New Age*, this former New Ager shows the miseries of those living under Hinduism. She admits that her vegetarian diet and her crusading for animal rights and ecology were motivated by her worldview when she was a New Ager. "'Purity in eating leads to a purity in being, in essence, in mind, and in emotions' became my motto. This holistic guideline convinced me that my spiritual and physical being were one."[28]

She continues, "The theory behind vegetarian eating as the highest form of purity led me to campaign tirelessly for animal rights. Many times I placed animals high above human priorities."[29] Matrisciana reveals the thinking of some New Agers when she says, "*After all*, I believed, *these poor little creatures are reincarnated*"[30] (italics hers).

"I didn't realize until years later," admits Matrisciana, "that I was developing an attitude toward animals that I had rejected while growing up in India. Some animals were becoming sacred in my eyes. And I was placing them well above human beings!"[31]

This raises an important question. If teachings of the New Age Movement are so helpful to mankind, why haven't these same teachings helped improve life in the countries where such ideas originated? Robert J. L. Burrows is on target when he writes, "The vision [Fritjof] Capra believes will deliver us seems to thrive in cultures where misery is perpetually rampant and corruption is rife. India is a case in point. Christians know that the problem is perversity, not human perception—holiness, not holism."[32]

In Hinduism, the teaching of reincarnation involves the doctrine of karma, the law of sowing and reaping. They believe that whatever a person sows in this life, he will reap in the next life in his reincarnated state. New Ager L. H. Leslie-Smith quotes what apparently is a common saying to New Age devotees and adds his comment: "'Karma is the force that impels to Reincarnation, and that Karma is the destiny man weaves for himself.' In any one life we sow the seeds of the personality of the next incarnation. That is the hypothesis. Reincarnation is the method by which human karma, at any rate, works. The two are inseparably interwoven."[33]

But New Agers are not consistent at this point in borrowing from Eastern religions. As Groothuis points out, "The doctrine [of reincarnation] as conceived in Hinduism and Buddhism involves all forms of life and is called 'transmigration.' Westerners ignore this fact and color the idea with hopes for self-development. But according to the Eastern doctrine, one may come back as a dog, cow or gnat—something decidedly less attractive than a more fully realized 'human potential.'"[34]

How interesting it is that Shirley MacLaine admits that in her late teens she decided "God and religion were definitely mythological. . . . I couldn't believe in anything that had no proof."[35] And yet she is a strong believer in reincarnation. She has rejected the eyewitness reports contained in the Bible for the mythological mysticism of Eastern religions.

It is no wonder that she looked at her newborn daughter, Sachi, with all kinds of questions: "When the doctor brought her to me in the hospital bed on that afternoon in 1956, had she already lived many many times before, with other mothers? Had she, in fact, been one herself? Had she, in fact, ever been my mother? Was her one-hour-old face housing a soul perhaps millions of years old?"[36]

New Age thinkers who have borrowed the idea of reincarnation from ancient Eastern religions also have delved into the channeling business. In the world of the occult, channeling is the process of a person's body being used as the means—or channel—of communication from the spirit world. J. Z. Knight popularized channeling. She was supposedly a channel for Ramtha, a 35,000-year-old male spirit who calls himself "The Enlightened One." In an exposé of the New Age in a *Family Circle* article, Nancy Clark and Nick Gallo point out that an evening with Ramtha in a hotel ballroom "might cost $1,000 per person."[37]

In his critique of the channeling fad, Brooks Alexander writes, "The entities endlessly repeat the primal lie, the three-fold creed of error: There is no death; man is God; knowledge of self is salvation and power."[38]

The answer to man's future life is not karma but Christ. The Lord Jesus Christ paid the full penalty for sin so that each person can be completely delivered from condemnation by trusting Him as personal Savior. "There is therefore now no condemnation," says Romans 8:1, "to those who are in Christ Jesus." But, regrettably, those who reject God's provision for sin remain under sin's condemnation. When they pass from this life, it will not be to reincarnation but to condemnation. This is not God's fault. He has done all that is necessary to make a way of escape for sinful mankind. He sent His Son, Jesus Christ, to be the "propitiation for our sins, and not for ours only but also for the whole world" (1 John 2:2).

Those who reject Christ as Savior will have no second chance after passing from this world through death. "It is appointed for men to die once," says Hebrews 9:27, "but after this the judgment."

CONCLUSION

The concepts of the New Age Movement are not new—they are based on ancient erroneous beliefs about God, man and the world.

The Movement is to be commended for its spiritual concern, but it has turned away from the true God to gods of the spirit world. As Paul said of the Jewish leaders of his day, "They have a zeal for God, but not according to knowledge" (Rom. 10:2).

While we do not wish to minimize spiritual experience, the New Age Movement overemphasizes it. Experience and truth always must be kept in balance. We should not move from experience to truth, but from truth to experience. Only when we know the truth and respond to it can we have valid experiences that honor God.

Any believer who is tempted to delve into the teachings of the New Age Movement needs to heed the warnings of the Bible. Through Moses, God warned the Old Testament Israelites: "If there arises among you a prophet or a dreamer of dreams, and he gives you a sign or a wonder, and the sign or the wonder comes to pass, of which he spoke to you, saying, 'Let us go after other gods which you have not known and let us serve them,' you shall not listen to the words of that prophet or that dreamer of dreams, for the LORD your God is testing you to know whether you love the LORD your God with all your heart and with all your soul" (Deut. 13:1–3).

Notice from this passage that everything that is supernatural is not necessarily of God. If the message does not agree with the Scriptures, do not follow the messenger. The teachings of the New Age Movement clearly disagree with the Bible.

Before the Old Testament Israelites entered Canaan, Moses warned them: "When you come into the land which the LORD your God is giving you, you shall not learn to follow the abominations of those nations. There shall not be found among you anyone who makes his son or his daughter pass through the fire, or one who practices witchcraft, or a soothsayer, or one who interprets omens, or a sorcerer, or one who conjures spells, or a medium, or a spiritist, or one who calls up the dead. For all who do these things are an abomination to the LORD, and because of these abominations the LORD your God drives them out from before you" (Deut. 18:9–12).

New Agers are guilty of many of the things mentioned in this passage. Bookstores promoting their material usually have books dealing with witchcraft and other occult practices. In their excellent analysis of the New Age Movement, Dean Halverson and William Honsberger say, "One of the rising trends in New Age spirituality is Wicca, the religion of witchcraft. It is closely related to goddess worship and neo-paganism. All of these different groups hold to the divinity of nature and to the idea that spiritual power can be attained through the manipulation of these 'natural forces.' While Wicca originally attracted older adherents, it is quickly becoming a major attraction for young people. It promises power, mystery, self-gratification, and rebellion against Christianity."[39]

The message of the Bible to witchcraft and other occult practices is this: "All who do these things are an abomination to the Lord." God has given us His completed revelation, so we have no need to seek further information through the spirit world. Our need is to know the clear teachings of the Bible better.

Believers should be concerned about world peace, the environment, humane treatment of animals and reaching our full potential in Christ. Our concern should not be based, however, on the spiritual worldviews of Eastern religions—believing that all these things are part of the One, or the impersonal Force.

And we should not be naive when we hear a New Ager mention "God" or "Christ." He or she is not talking about the God and the Christ of the Bible.

Let us love those who have gone after other gods. Let us live before them as dynamic, caring Christians so they will see that Christianity is more than a creed; it is a life—eternal life. And let us be faithful in gently, but firmly, persuading them to turn to the Christ of the Bible, who has paid the penalty for their sins. Let us pray that they will trust in Him as Savior and be delivered from the hopelessness of their man-centered, pantheistic religion.

Summary

Name: New Age Movement
Name of Followers: New Agers
Number of Followers: U.S.: Probably more than 40 million

What They Believe

New Agers:	Biblical Christians:

Source of Authority

Truth as an objective reality does not exist. Internal, subjective feelings are absolute truth.	The Bible is the objective standard of truth. External, objective statements in the Bible are absolute truth.

God

Confuse creator with creation, thinking that creation is god. God is a divine Principle. Believe in monism—all is of one essence. Believe in pantheism—all is god.	God is a divine Person who exists entirely from creation and matter. Believe in theism—God is a Person and the Creator of mankind and the world.

Jesus Christ

Deny the deity of Christ by claiming that "Christ" is the cosmic principle, or ideal. Attempt to separate the human Jesus from the divine Christ.	Jesus Christ is God. The name "Jesus Christ" is an expression equal to "Jesus the Messiah."

Sin and Salvation

Each person is inherently good; therefore, no one is sinful. Any salvation is only a more complete union with the One.	Each person has a sin nature and on his own cannot measure up to God's standards. Salvation is possible only through believing in the finished work of Christ.

Good and Evil

Because all is one, there is ultimately no distinction between good and evil. Because of their belief in monism, the divine Principle is a composite of both good and evil, blending into one.	Good and evil are entirely separate and never lose their distinction. God has absolutely no evil in Himself, nor can He approve of evil of any kind.

Future Life

Believe in reincarnation—that through a long process of rebirths, a person can eventually reach perfection. Embrace the Hindu principle of karma—that what a person sows in this life he will reap in the next.	Only in this life is one given opportunity to receive salvation through Christ and become right with God. Sin has consequences, and the only way to become right with God is through Jesus Christ, not by karma.

Recommended Reading

Ankerberg Theological Research Institute Web site, www.ankerberg.org.

Bickel, Bruce, and Jantz, Stan. *World Religions & Cults 101: A Guide to Spiritual Beliefs.* Eugene, Ore.: Harvest House Publishers, 2002.

Carlson, Ron, and Decker, Ed. *Fast Facts on False Teachings.* Eugene, Ore.: Harvest House Publishers, 1994.

Enroth, Ronald, ed. *A Guide to New Religious Movements.* Downers Grove, Ill.: InterVarsity Press, 2005.

Geisler, Norman L. "The New Age Movement," *Bibliotheca Sacra.* Dallas: Dallas Theological Seminary, Jan.–March 1987.

_____, and Amano, J. Yutaka. *The Reincarnation Sensation.* Wheaton, Ill.: Tyndale House Publishers, 1986.

Groothuis, Douglas R. *Unmasking the New Age.* Downers Grove, Ill.: InterVarsity Press, 1986.

Gruss, Edmond C. *Cults and the Occult.* Phillipsburg, N.J.; P&R Publishing, 1994.

Halverson, Dean C., gen. ed. *The Compact Guide to World Religions.* Minneapolis: Bethany House Publishers, 1996.

Martin, Walter. *The Kingdom of the Cults.* Ravi Zacharias, gen. ed. Minneapolis: Bethany House Publishers, 2003.

Miller, Elliot. *A Crash Course on the New Age Movement.* Grand Rapids, Mich.: Baker Book House, 1989.

Rhodes, Ron. *New Age Movement.* Grand Rapids, Mich.: Zondervan Publishing House, 1995.

_____. *The Challenge of the Cults and New Religions.* Grand Rapids, Mich.: Zondervan, 2001.

_____. *The Culting of America.* Eugene, Ore.: Harvest House Publishers, 1994.

ENDNOTES

[1] Norman L. Geisler, "Background of the New Age Movement," cassette 1 of 3, *The New Age Movement* (Dallas: Quest Tapes, 1984).

[2] Ron Rhodes, *The Culting of America* (Eugene, Ore.: Harvest House Publishers, 1994), 17.

[3] Ibid., 19.

[4] Dean Halverson and William Honsberger, "The New Age Movement," in *The Com-*

pact Guide to World Religions, Dean Halverson, gen. ed. (Minneapolis: Bethany House Publishers, 1996), 160.

[5] Mather, George A., and Nichols, Larry A. *Dictionary of Cults, Sects, Religions and the Occult* (Grand Rapids, Mich.: Zondervan Publishing House, 1993), 24.

[6] Ibid.

[7] Marilyn Ferguson, *The Aquarian Conspiracy* (Los Angeles: J. P. Tarcher, 1980), 19.

[8] Douglas R. Groothuis, *Unmasking the New Age* (Downers Grove, Ill.: InterVarsity Press, 1986), 18–31.

[9] Mather and Nichols, *Dictionary of Cults, Sects, Religions and the Occult,* 202–204.

[10] Robert J. L. Burrows, "Americans Get Religion in the New Age," *Christianity Today*, May 16, 1986, 23.

[11] Shirley MacLaine, *It's All in the Playing* (New York: Bantam Books, 1987), 6.

[12] Ibid.

[13] Ferguson, *The Aquarian Conspiracy*, 428.

[14] Gordon R. Lewis, foreword to *Unmasking the New Age*, 10.

[15] Geoffrey Hodson, *The Hidden Wisdom in the Holy Bible*, Vol. 1 (Wheaton, Ill.: The Theosophical Publishing House, 1967), 68.

[16] Ibid.

[17] Groothuis, *Unmasking the New Age*, 53.

[18] Merrill F. Unger, *Unger's Commentary on the Old Testament*, Vol. 1 (Chicago: Moody Press, 1981), 20.

[19] MacLaine, *It's All in the Playing*, 331.

[20] Barbara Marx Hubbard, *The Evolutionary Journey* (San Francisco: Evolutionary Press, 1982), 157, cited in Groothuis, *Unmasking the New Age*, 30.

[21] Daniel Coleman, "Meditation Without Mystery," in *Psychology Today*, March 1977, 88.

[22] "Under Fire: Two Christian Leaders Respond to Accusations of New Age Mysticism," *Christianity Today,* Sept. 18, 1987, 19.

[23] Geisler, "The New Age Movement," *Bibliotheca Sacra*, Jan.–March 1987, 91.

[24] Hodson, *The Hidden Wisdom in the Holy Bible*, Vol. 1, 68.

[25] Ibid., 65.

[26] Groothuis, *Unmasking the New Age*, 154.

[27] James Hitchcock, *What Is Secular Humanism? Why Humanism Became Secular and How It Is Changing Our World* (Ann Arbor, Mich.: Servant Books, 1982), 60.

[28] Caryl Matrisciana, *Gods of the New Age* (Eugene, Ore.: Harvest House Publishers, 1985), 79.

[29] Ibid.

[30] Ibid.

[31] Ibid., 80.

[32] Burrows, "Americans Get Religion in the New Age," 19.

[33] V. Hanson, R. Stewart, and S. Nicholson, *Karma: Rhythmic Return to Harmony* (Wheaton, Ill.: The Theosophical Publishing House, 1990), 41.

[34] Groothuis, *Unmasking the New Age*, 150–151.

[35] Shirley MacLaine, *Out on a Limb* (New York: Bantam Books, 1983), 50.

[36] Ibid., 102.

[37] Nancy Clark and Nick Gallo, "Do You Believe in Magic?" in *Family Circle*, Feb. 23, 1993, 99.

[38] Brooks Alexander, "Theology from the Twilight Zone," *Christianity Today*, Sept. 18, 1987, 25.

[39] Halverson and Honsberger, "The New Age Movement," in *The Compact Guide to World Religions*, 162.

CHAPTER EIGHT

Roman Catholics

"He so loved the world." No, this is not a quote from John 3:16 about how much God loved the world. It's the headline of the *Omaha World-Herald* at the time of the death of Pope John Paul II (1920–2005).[1] He was succeeded by Cardinal Joseph Ratzinger of Germany, who adopted the name Benedict XVI.

Gene Edward Veith, cultural editor for *World* magazine, describes Benedict XVI:

> The new pope is a man who rails against 'the dictatorship of relativism.' He dismays ecumenists by insisting that Christ is the only way to salvation. He is heckled by gays for teaching that homosexuality is sinful. He says that there can be no human rights without the right to life. He has said that pro-abortion politicians should not be given communion and that voting for candidates because they are pro-abortion is a sin.[2]

It is yet to be seen how the new pope will rule the more than 1 billion Roman Catholics worldwide, about 66 million of whom are in the United States.[3]

Many positive things can be said about the Catholic Church—such as its emphasis on family values, pro-life views, opposition to euthanasia and the welfare of people worldwide. This evaluation, however, will focus on one key issue: how a person gets right with God. This will include a consideration about the source of authority for beliefs and views about God, sin, salvation and the future life.

People of many faiths say to their critics, "You're not telling the truth about what we believe." That's especially from those who follow the Catholic faith. Some Catholics are knowledgeable about what the Roman Catholic Church believes; others are not. However, it's not necessary to take an individual's word for what the Catholic Church teaches. The sources for the church's doctrines and beliefs are available for anyone who wishes to search them. One key source that will be used to document the information that follows is the Roman Catholics' own 1994 edition of the *Catechism of the Catholic Church*.[4] The introductory matter in this volume gives the approval of Pope John Paul II for the contents. This *Catechism* leaves no doubt about what Roman Catholics believe.

Another authoritative source is the *New Catholic Encyclopedia*.[5] The Roman Catholic Church produced this work after the Second Vatican Council (1962–1965), commonly referred to as Vatican II.

Roman Catholicism is the largest group in the world under the designation of "Christian." Used in the broad sense, "Christian" includes not only Roman Catholics but also Orthodox and Protestant groups. This term also distinguishes this religious belief system from other world religions, such as Buddhism, Islam, Judaism and Shintoism.

Although there are more than 1 billion Catholics worldwide, it must be realized that for the most part members are counted as they become baptized as infants. This is in contrast to the many Protestant groups that count membership from the time a person decides to trust in Christ and joins a local assembly.

How did the Roman Catholic Church originate? How does a person obtain salvation and receive the forgiveness of sin, according to this church? What is the significance of the Mass? What is the basis for the Church's belief in purgatory? Does the Roman Catholic Church accept any other authority besides the Bible? Have the changes since Vatican II been significant doctrinally?

Before answering these and other questions, consider the background of the Roman Catholic Church.

BACKGROUND

The Roman Catholic Church traces itself back to Christ's statement to the apostle Peter: "And I also say to you that you are Peter, and on this rock I will build My church, and the gates of Hades shall not prevail against it" (Matt. 16:18).

After citing this verse, the *Catechism of the Catholic Church* says, "Christ, the 'living stone,' thus assures his Church, built on Peter, of victory over the powers of death. Because of the faith he confessed Peter will remain the unshakeable rock of the Church."[6]

The question is, does the New Testament support this teaching? Was Peter the "rock" to which Christ referred?

In Matthew 16:18, two different words are used for "Peter" and "rock" in the original language of the New Testament (Greek). "Peter" is *petros*; "rock" is *petra*. The gender of these words is different. *Petros* is masculine; *petra* is feminine. The difference in gender of these words reveals they are not meant to be equivalent.

There are various interpretations of Matthew 16:18, but it is not correct to think that the only choice is that Peter was the "rock." The foundation of the Church was Christ Himself, of whom Peter said, "You are the Christ, the Son of the living God" (v. 16). As a child of God, Peter was a small segment of the rock cliff on which the true Church was to be built, but he was not the cliff itself. In this regard, it was Peter's confession that indicated the foundation of the church.

The Roman Catholic Church maintains that Christ placed Peter first among all the apostles and, in effect, made him the first pope. But the Scriptures reveal that Christ Himself rebuked Peter. In the same chapter in which Christ supposedly made Peter the first pope, He said to Peter, "Get behind Me, Satan! You are an offense to Me, for you are not mindful of the things of God, but the things of men" (v. 23).

There is no indication in the Bible that the other apostles considered Peter to have any special position of authority, nor is there any evidence that Christ granted him that position. The apostle Paul recorded an encounter he had with Peter: "But when Peter had come to Antioch, I withstood him to his face, because he was to be blamed" (Gal. 2:11). The incident involved Peter's behavior that confused New Testament believers about the Old Testament Law. If Paul could assign "blame" to Peter over a theological issue, then clearly his fellow apostles did not view Peter as a special authority.

Over the years the Roman Catholic Church has developed a hierarchical system of pope, cardinals, bishops and priests over the people. During the early centuries after Jesus' death, five geographical centers provided Christian leadership: Jerusalem, Antioch, Alexandria, Constantinople and Rome. Each center was important during different times. The local assemblies established after the time of Christ had overseers, or bishops, who were on an equal basis. As in the 21ˢᵗ century, however, smaller churches respected the opinions of the larger, established local churches and came to depend more and more on their counsel.

Rome was the largest city in the West during the early centuries. Christians considered the church in Rome important because of the significant events that had taken place there. The apostle Paul had suffered martyrdom there, and one of his longest New Testament letters, Romans, was written to the believers in that city.

The Roman Catholic Church considers Peter the first bishop in Rome, but the evidence is weak that Peter was or had been in Rome when Paul wrote his epistle to the Romans about A.D. 58. If so, as one author suggests, Paul surely would have sent greetings to Peter or at least mentioned his ministry in Rome.[7] Apparently Peter, as well as Paul, was martyred in Rome, however.[8]

The importance of Rome permitted the claim for authority by the Christian leaders there. According to church historian Earle Cairns, "The Council of Constantinople in 381 recognized the primacy of the Roman see. The patriarch of Constantinople was given 'the primacy of honor next after the bishop of Rome,' according to the third canon of the Council of Constantinople."[9]

Although the Roman bishops of this time were highly regarded, they did not make much of their prestige. Not until Gregory I ascended to the throne in 590 did a bishop of Rome claim primacy over other bishops.

As to the origin of the word *pope*, Cairns says, "Leo I, who occupied the Episcopal throne in Rome between 440 and 461, was the ablest occupant of that chair until Gregory I took that position in 590. His abilities won for him the name 'great.' He made much use of the title *papas* from which our word 'pope' is derived."[10]

The word *catholic* means "universal." During the early centuries after Christ, there were Christians in almost every part of the then-known world, and in this sense only were they called "catholic." They were not part of the Roman Catholic Church as we know it today, with its pope, cardinals, bishops and priests. It is in the sense of "universal" that the word *catholic* appears in some of the ecumenical creeds of Christendom. Concerning the Trinity, the Athanasian Creed says,

"And the catholic faith is this, that we worship one God in three persons and three persons in one God, neither confusing the persons nor dividing the substance."

The word *church* (*ekklēsia*) in the New Testament refers to an "assembly" or "called out group." In particular, the word most often referred to those who had trusted Jesus Christ as Savior. This is seen in the apostle Paul's greetings to the church at Corinth: "To the church [*ekklēsia*] of God which is at Corinth, to those who are sanctified in Christ Jesus, called to be saints, with all who in every place call on the name of Jesus Christ our Lord, both theirs and ours" (1 Cor. 1:2).

From 1 Timothy 3 it is evident that local churches, or assemblies, had their leaders, but there is no biblical evidence those leaders had binding authority on other believers outside of their own local assembly.

Something else to consider in the history of the Roman Catholic Church is that apparently the faith has expanded not by asking people to give up non-Catholic beliefs, but to add Catholicism to whatever they believe. *Operation World* is a prayer guide for the countries of the world. Under the listing for Haiti it says, "An estimated 75% of Catholics are also actively involved in Voodoo, a development of West African spiritism and witchcraft."[11]

THE WORD *CATHOLIC* MEANS "UNIVERSAL."

Although the Catholic Church is usually seen as peaceful in its relationship with other religions, *Operation World* says that in Ecuador "there have been sporadic, local incidents of mob violence, burning of churches and intimidation against Evangelicals."[12] Although this seems to be an inflammatory statement, *Operation World* is accepted as a source of integrity and is certainly not characterized by statements that are anti-Catholic.

A former student of mine and his wife, who are now missionaries in Ecuador, recently e-mailed me and said, "Lately a group of believers [has] undergone severe slander from the priest. He spreads many rumors about them, encourages people not to associate with them or even allow the believers to purchase food. Lately he even started trying to get their children kicked out of schools and encouraged other kids to bully them. It's worse than ever."[13]

And not all "Catholic countries" are supportive of the Church. Concerning Italy, where the headquarters of the Catholic Church is located, *Operation World* says, "Most Italians are Catholic in culture, but deeply cynical about the Church."[14]

Catholicism in the U.S. also needs to be distinguished from other countries. Theologian Loraine Boettner says, "American Catholicism, so different on the surface from that found in Spain, Italy, and Latin America, is nevertheless all a part of the same church, all run from Rome and by the same man who is the absolute ruler over all of the branches as he deems it safe or expedient."[15]

Boettner adds, "Undoubtedly Romanism in the United States would be much the same as that found in other countries were it not for the influence of evangelical Christianity as set forth by the Protestant churches."[16]

BELIEFS

Having briefly examined the background of the Roman Catholic Church, we need to consider what the Church believes and teaches. A look at some key doctrines enables one to compare the beliefs of the Catholic Church with those of biblical Christianity.

SOURCE OF AUTHORITY

One of the most crucial beliefs that any group has is what it uses as its source of authority. Some groups say the Bible is their final source of authority, but further research reveals it is the Bible as interpreted by some key leader. This means, of course, that the final source of authority is not the Bible but that person's interpretation of the Bible. To what do Roman Catholics look as the source of authority for the Church?

The Bible

The Roman Catholic Church accepts the Bible as one of its sources of authority, but to the 39 books of the Old Testament, the Catholic Church also adds the Apocrypha. The word *Apocrypha* literally means "hidden." This is a group of books considered outside of the canon, or standard, of what is considered Scripture by the masses of believers.

Before the time of Christ, the Jewish people did not consider the apocryphal books to be of equal authority with the 39 books, so they did not include them in the Hebrew Old Testament. Jerome's Latin Vulgate, composed in the late 4th century, gave only a secondary status to the Apocrypha. Even Roman Catholics did not consider the apocryphal writings as on the same level as the 66 books of the Bible until the leaders of the Reformation challenged such doctrines as papal authority, purgatory and the selling of indulgences.

At the Council of Trent (1545–1563), however, the Roman Catholic Church "recognized the Apocrypha, excepting I and II Esdras and the Prayer of Manasses, as having unqualified canonical status. Moreover, anyone who disputed this ecclesiastical decision was anathematized."[17]

The Council of Trent ranks as one of the three major councils of the Roman Catholics, along with Vatican I (1869–1870) and Vatican II (1962–1965). Concerning the Council of Trent, evangelical apologists Adolfo Robleto and John Hepp Jr. state:

> The Council of Trent . . . approved many superstitious and unbiblical beliefs of the Middle Ages, including the equal value of tradition and Scripture, the seven sacraments, communion by eating the bread only (and not drinking the wine), purgatory, indulgences, and the Mass as a propitiatory offering. Many decrees made by that council, to be believed under threat of 'anathema' and confirmed by Pope Pius IV, have ever since been considered infallible throughout the Catholic Church.[18]

Papal Infallibility

In addition to its belief in the Scripture as a source of authority, the Roman Catholic Church also believes in papal infallibility and views it as an equal source of authority. In *The New International Dictionary of the Christian Church*, Peter Toon defines "infallibility" as the "Roman Catholic doctrine that ecumenical councils of bishops and the pope speaking *ex cathedra* are immune from error when teaching concerning faith and morals."[19]

Ex cathedra is a Latin expression meaning "from the chair" and refers to something a pope says because of his position.

"Infallibility," says F. X. Lawlor in the *New Catholic Encyclopedia*, "is more than a simple *de facto* absence of error. It is a positive perfection, ruling out the possibility of error and entailing necessarily a central fidelity to the Christian revelation in the doctrine taught and accepted by the Church."[20]

In essence, the doctrine of papal infallibility means that Roman Catholics must accept what is taught by their Church regarding faith and morals, because the pope is considered free from error when speaking *ex cathedra*. Such teaching is considered as authoritative, if not more authoritative, than Scripture. Lawlor acknowledges that Vatican I defined the infallibility of the pope and Vatican II reaffirmed it."[21]

In addition to believing that Peter was the first bishop, or pope, of

JESUS CHRIST IS THE *ONLY* MEDIATOR BETWEEN MAN AND GOD.

Rome, the Roman Catholic Church relies heavily on Matthew 16:19 in its claim that Peter's successors possess binding authority. This verse records Christ's statement to Peter, "And I will give you the keys of the kingdom of heaven, and whatever you bind on earth will be bound in heaven, and whatever you loose on earth will be loosed in heaven."

The original language of the New Testament, however, does not support the claim the Roman Catholic Church bases on this verse. Julius R. Mantey was a coauthor of a Greek grammar widely used in Bible colleges and seminaries (*A Manual Grammar of the Greek New Testament*, New York: The MacMillan Company, 1927, 1955). Mantey gives the literal translation of Matthew 16:19, "I will give you the keys of the kingdom of heaven, but whatever you may bind ... on earth shall have been bound ... in heaven, and whatever you may loose ... on earth shall have been loosed ... in heaven."[22]

Verses similar to Matthew 16:19 are Matthew 18:18 and John 20:23. Mantey says, "During the first three centuries of the Christian era, no one, according to extant writings of the period, ever quoted John 20:23, Matthew 16:19 or 18:18 in favor of sacerdotalism [belief in the power of priests as essential mediators between God and man]. A thorough study of the Ante-Nicean Fathers reveals that no Greek-writing Church Father ever cited these passages to support such a doctrine."[23]

John 20:23 deserves special attention because it refers to forgiving sins. This verse records Jesus' words to His disciples: "If you forgive the sins of any, they are forgiven them; if you retain the sins of any, they are retained." The Lord Jesus spoke these words soon after His resurrection, but do they give authority to men to decide whose sins to forgive?

The words *forgiven* and *retained* are in the perfect tense in the Greek language. This tense emphasizes a completed act in the past with a continuing effect. As such, these expressions mean "they have been forgiven them" and "they have been retained."

The words of John 20:23 parallel Matthew 16:19. The disciples were not to make the decisions about whose sins to forgive and retain. Instead, they were to assure people of what was already true in heaven.

In talking to a person who had trusted in Jesus Christ as Savior, a disciple could assure the person that his sins were forgiven because they had already been forgiven in heaven. If a person had not trusted in Christ as Savior, a disciple could assure the individual that his sins were retained because they had been retained in heaven. Any believer today could do the same thing.

According to the Bible, God has never given authority to another person to decide whether or not an individual's sins will be forgiven. Jesus Christ is the *only* Mediator between man and God. The apostle Paul made this clear when he wrote, "For there is one God and one Mediator between God and men, the Man Christ Jesus" (1 Tim. 2:5).

Its belief in the infallibility of the pope when speaking *ex cathedra* on faith and morals reveals that the Roman Catholic Church accepts an authority that is not only outside of but also supersedes the Bible. Thus, the Catholic Church considers the Bible necessary but insufficient as a final guide.

The Magisterium

In addition to the Bible and papal infallibility, another source of authority for the Roman Catholic Church is the Magisterium of the

Church. The *Catechism of the Catholic Church* says, "The task of giving an authentic interpretation of the Word of God, whether in its written form or in the form of Tradition, has been entrusted to the living, teaching office of the Church alone."[24]

This confirms that the Roman Catholic Church does not consider the Bible as final authority; rather, the final authority is the person or group who determines how the Bible must be interpreted. The *Catechism* says, "This means that the task of interpretation has been entrusted to the bishops in communion with the successor of Peter, the Bishop of Rome."[25]

Interestingly, the *Catechism* tries to modify these strong comments with the statement, "Yet this Magisterium is not superior to the Word of God, but is its servant. It teaches only what has been handed on to it."[26] But it doesn't take a trained scholar to see that claiming authority in determining what a book means is superior to what the book says. And when tradition is added to the Scriptures as authority, a group has much latitude in adding to the Bible whatever it chooses. The *Catechism of the Catholic Church* says, "Sacred Tradition and Sacred Scripture make up a single sacred deposit of the Word of God."[27]

Other religious groups use a similar approach. Christian Science says the Bible is the final authority, yet relies on the interpretations of Mary Baker Eddy, especially as found in *Science and Health with Key to the Scriptures.*

The Way International, founded by Victor Paul Wierwille, claims the Bible as the final source of authority. The real authority for the group, however, is the writings of Wierwille, such as *Jesus Christ Is Not God.*

So, too, the current Seventh-day Adventist Church says the Bible is final authority but focuses special attention on the visions and testimonies of Ellen G. White, who died in 1915.

JESUS CHRIST

The Roman Catholic Church is to be commended for its strong stand on the deity of Christ. It clearly teaches that Christ is God, as revealed in the Bible. Its other teachings, however—particularly about purgatory—show that the Catholic Church does not believe in the sufficiency of Christ's death to pay the full penalty for sin. The Catholic Church teaches that each person must spend time in purgatory to atone for his sins.

The Bible teaches that only Christ's death can pay the penalty for sin and that He has paid the *full penalty*. Jesus' last words on the cross were, "It is finished!" (John 19:30). These words indicate that nothing needs to be added to what He accomplished at Calvary. All that is left for mankind to do is believe in His finished work. Jesus Himself said, "Most assuredly, I say to you, he who believes in Me has everlasting life" (John 6:47).

From the Book of Hebrews it is evident that Christ's sacrifice was different from all other sacrifices that had been made. His sacrifice was complete and effectual for all. "Every priest stands ministering daily and offering repeatedly the same sacrifices, which can never take away sins. But this Man, after He had offered one sacrifice for sins forever, sat down at the right hand of God" (10:11–12).

The Lord Jesus Christ offered one sacrifice forever, and then He sat down in heaven, indicating His redemptive work was finished.

MARY

Another theological issue that relates to Jesus Christ is what the Roman Catholic Church teaches concerning His earthly mother, Mary. Because of their reverence for Christ—which is to be commended—the Catholic Church gives honor to His mother that the Scriptures do not give—which is not to be commended.

The Catholic Church has declared Mary to be sinless, even though the Bible does not. The Church believes she was conceived without sin (Immaculate Conception), even as Jesus was. The Bible teaches, "All have sinned and fall short of the glory of God" (Rom. 3:23). The only exception is the Lord Jesus Christ. He knew no sin (2 Cor. 5:21), did no sin (1 Pet. 2:22) and was without sin (Heb. 4:15). The Bible does not make these kinds of statements about Mary. This is another indication that the Scriptures are not the final authority for the Catholic Church.

But the Catholic Church is bold in its claims about Mary's sinlessness. Writing in the *New Catholic Encyclopedia*, J. F. Murphy says, "In the case of Our Lady, this perfect sinlessness implies more than merely the absence of sin; it implies also a complete indefectibility in the moral order, or the *actual inability to sin* [italics mine]."[28] And the

What They Believe

Catechism of the Catholic Church says, "By the grace of God Mary remained free of every personal sin her whole life long."[29]

If sinlessness is claimed for the mother of the Lord Jesus Christ so she could be pure enough to bear the Savior, should it also be claimed for Mary's mother so she could be pure enough to bear Mary? Where does the process stop? The Bible stops it by claiming sinlessness only for the Lord Jesus Christ.

The dogma of the Immaculate Conception of Mary was proclaimed in 1854 by Pope Pius IX. Then in 1950, Pope Pius XII declared that after Mary completed her earthly life, both her body and soul were "assumed" into heavenly glory. This was the logical step to follow the belief that Mary was sinless. A person without sin could not experience decay. So the Church declared that Mary's body was assumed into heaven along with her soul. The Bible does not support this dogma, known as the Assumption of Mary.

The Roman Catholic Church claims it does not worship Mary. Yet it appears that the Church believes the surest way one has of reaching the ear of Jesus is by appealing to Him through Mary. To the casual observer, it seems that even Pope John Paul II was as devoted to Mary as to Jesus, if not more so. In his book, *Big Russ and Me*, NBC's moderator and managing editor of *Meet the Press*, Tim Russert, displays a picture of his family receiving a papal blessing. Russert is holding his son Luke in his arms at that time and points out, "Luke's T-shirt says 'Totus Tuus,' the pope's personal motto of 'all yours,' affirming his devotion to the Blessed Virgin."[30] Russert gives the background of the pope's motto, "In 1981, when the Holy Father was shot and almost killed by a Turkish gunman, he had said, 'Blessed Mother, if I live, I will rededicate my life to you. *Totus Tuus*.'"[31] We are pleased that the Pope's life was spared, but his expression reveals Roman Catholicism's view that the Scriptures are not the final authority. There is no biblical evidence that such devotion should be given to Mary.

Inasmuch as Jesus Christ is God, the Roman Catholic Church refers to Mary as "The Mother of God." It is true that Jesus Christ is God, but the expression "Mother of God" could lead one to think that if it were not for Mary, God would not exist.

In the original language of the New Testament, the word for "God" is *Theos*. This is the word used for "God" in John 1:1: In the beginning was the Word, and the Word was with God [*Theos*], and the

Word was God [*Theos*]. "Word" refers to the Lord Jesus Christ, as is evident from verse 14, "The Word became flesh and dwelt among us." So there is no question about Jesus Christ being God.

The word for "Lord" is *Kurios*, and the word for "Jesus" is *Iēsous*. On only four occasions in the New Testament is Mary referred to as the "mother of" someone divine—and it is never the "Mother of God." When the expectant Mary went to visit her cousin, who was also pregnant, Elizabeth referred to Mary as the "mother of my Lord" (*Kurios*) (Luke 1:43). Twice the apostle John referred to Mary as the "mother of Jesus" (*Iēsous*) (John 2:1,3). And Luke, the missionary companion of the apostle Paul and author of Acts as well as the gospel by his name, once referred to Mary as the "mother of Jesus" (*Iēsous*) (Acts 1:14). The Bible never refers to Mary as the "Mother of God [*Theos*]."

SIN

Depending on its gravity, the Roman Catholic Church distinguishes between "mortal and "venial" sins. James R. White has thoroughly studied this issue in Roman Catholic writings and has debated popular Catholic apologists. He is the director of Alpha and Omega Ministries, a Christian apologetics organization based in Phoenix, Arizona. In his excellent book evaluating Roman Catholicism, White says, "There is no clear and infallible guide as to just what is and is not venial sin, and the line between venial and mortal sin is difficult to trace with absolute certainty from Roman writings. Mortal sins destroy sanctifying grace and, unless they are confessed, bar one from entering into heaven."[32]

Both venial and mortal sin relate to "sanctifying grace." Venial sins don't deprive one of it; mortal sins do. A mortal sin results in the death of the soul. And sanctifying grace is entered into by baptism, which will be discussed next. Suffice it here to say that the Roman Catholic Church considers baptism to be the means by which one enters into salvation.

SALVATION

The Roman Catholic Church rejects the biblical teaching that salvation can be obtained only by grace alone through faith alone in Christ alone. During the Reformation, this was the key issue because Martin

Luther, a Catholic priest, took the position that salvation was by faith alone, not through faith plus works, as taught in the Catholic Church.

"The Council of Trent," says a Catholic theologian, "did not condemn the concept of faith-confidence itself, but it did reject the Reformers' claim that it alone suffices for justification...."[33]

According to the Roman Catholic Church, a person receives salvation through the Church and its sacraments—especially baptism. In the *New Catholic Encyclopedia*, M. Eminyan states:

> God's call to the kingdom does not reach man through reason alone, but through definite manifestations of God in history, through a positive sociological system vested with divine authority. Man must come into contact with this divine authority in order to be saved. And this contact is established through supernatural faith, without which 'it is impossible to please God' (Heb. 11:6), and through the Catholic Church which is the Mystical body of Christ, *outside of which there is no salvation*" [italics mine].[34]

Such statements reveal that the Roman Catholic Church does not consider faith alone in Christ's finished work to be sufficient for salvation. One must come not only through "supernatural faith" but also "through the Catholic Church." It is also clear in indicating that the Roman Catholic Church does not consider salvation possible outside the Church. This is clearly adding works to faith, which is the same error that the apostle Paul wrote about in his letters to the Romans and Galatians. Righteousness cannot be obtained by keeping the Law or through good works. Paul wrote, "I do not set aside the grace of God; for if righteousness comes through the law, then Christ died in vain" (Gal. 2:21).

According to the Bible, a person's works are evidence that he is saved, but they in no way help him to obtain salvation. "For by grace you have been saved through faith," Paul wrote, "and that not of yourselves; it is the gift of God, not of works, lest anyone should boast" (Eph. 2:8–9).

The Bible says everyone has sinned and does not measure up to the glory of God. People can do many good works through a church—including the Roman Catholic Church—but no one can do enough good to merit position before a holy, just God. Therefore, salvation can be obtained only by faith, as mentioned in Romans 3:21–23: "The righteousness of God apart from the law is revealed, being witnessed by the Law and the Prophets, even the righteousness of God, through faith in Jesus Christ, to all and on all who believe. For there is no difference; for all have sinned and fall short of the glory of God."

SACRAMENTS

The Roman Catholic Church has seven sacraments—baptism, confirmation, penance, holy Eucharist (the Mass), holy orders, matrimony and anointing the sick. For this evaluation, we will focus on the sacrament of baptism in order to answer the question, How does a person become right with God?

THE BIBLE IS CLEAR ABOUT THE PROPER PLACE OF BAPTISM.

The Catholic Church follows the decree of the Council of Trent, which declared, "If anyone says that baptism is optional, that is, not necessary for salvation, let him be anathema [accursed]."[35]

From its early history, the Roman Catholic Church has administered the sacrament of baptism to infants. The *Catechism of the Catholic Church* boldly quotes a statement "often repeated by the Church Fathers," which is, "Outside the Church there is no salvation."[36] And that salvation, according to the Catholic Church, comes through baptism. This is the means of justification for the Church, for their *Catechism* says, "All who have been justified by faith in Baptism are incorporated into Christ; they therefore have a right to be called Christians. . . ."[37]

The quotation above lacks clarity. Is it saying that one is "justified by faith in Baptism" or that once justified by faith, one is "in Baptism ... incorporated into Christ"? On the basis of the statement in the Council of Trent, previously quoted, it seems clear that baptism is the means of salvation for the Roman Catholic Church. Whichever way the *Catechism* intends the statement to be understood, the Bible is clear about the proper place of baptism. Romans 3:24 says we are "justified freely by His grace through the redemption that is in Christ Jesus." Romans 5:1 says, "Therefore, having been justified by faith, we have peace with God through our Lord Jesus Christ." And Galatians 2:16 says, "Knowing that a man is not justified by the works of the law but by faith in Jesus Christ, even we have believed in Christ Jesus, that we might be justified by faith in Christ and not by the works of the law; for by the works of the law no flesh shall be justified." Doing good deeds does not justify anyone; only belief in God does.

Even before the Mosaic Law, good works did not justify a person. Abraham lived before the time of the Law and of him it is said, "If Abraham was justified by works, he has something to boast about, but not before God. For what does the Scripture say? 'Abraham believed God, and it was accounted to him for righteousness'" (Rom. 4:2–3).

This demonstrates that the Roman Catholic Church goes outside of the Bible to establish its doctrine of salvation. The Bible teaches the need for baptism, but only for those who have already trusted in Christ as Savior. It is an evidence of salvation, not a means of it. Condemnation is based on the refusal to believe in Jesus Christ for salvation, not for refusal to be baptized.

Mark 16:15 records Jesus' words about believing and baptism in the first part of the verse: "He who believes and is baptized will be saved." The second part shows the basis of condemnation, "But he who does not believe will be condemned." And Jesus told Nicodemus, "He who believes in Him [Jesus Christ] is not condemned; but he who does not believe is condemned already, because he has not believed in the name of the only begotten Son of God" (John 3:18).

THE MASS

A *Catechism for Inquirers* states, "The mass is the sacrifice in which Jesus Christ, through the ministry of priests, perpetuates the sacrifice of the cross by his real presence under the appearances of bread and wine."[38]

In the Mass, the Roman Catholic Church believes that the elements—bread and wine—actually become the body and blood of the Lord Jesus Christ. This change, called "transubstantiation," allows Christ to offer Himself again as a sacrifice for sin. According to the Council of Trent, "In this divine Sacrifice which is performed in the Mass . . . Christ is contained in a bloodless sacrifice who on the altar of the cross once offered himself with the shedding of his blood: the holy Synod teaches that this sacrifice is truly propitiatory."[39]

Even though the Catholic Church believes Christ's sacrifice on Calvary and the Mass is the same sacrifice, White points out, "According to their doctrine, it is quite possible for a person to attend Mass every day of his life, commit a mortal sin the hour before his death, and be lost for eternity."[40] White states:

> The repetitive nature of the Mass stands in stark contrast to the completedness of the Cross. As the writer to the Hebrews said, if such a sacrifice as what is presented in the Mass were sufficient, wouldn't the persons drawing near be cleansed and have no more need of the offering? But the fact that they must come back over and over again shows that this sacrifice of the Mass has more in common with the old sacrifices of the Old Covenant than it does with the sacrifice of Jesus Christ on Calvary.[41]

The Book of Hebrews expressly states that the offering of Christ is not to be repeated. "Not that He should offer Himself often, as the high priest enters the Most Holy Place every year with blood of another—He then would have had to suffer often since the foundation of the world; but now, once at the end of the ages, He has appeared to put away sin by the sacrifice of Himself" (9:25–26).

Hebrews 10:10 says, "By that will we have been sanctified through the offering of the body of Jesus Christ once for all." Verse 12 says Jesus "offered one sacrifice for sins forever." And verse 14 adds that by this one sacrifice, Jesus Christ has "perfected forever those who are being sanctified."

Clearly, the Scriptures do not support the Roman Catholic teaching about the reoffering of Christ in the Mass. His offering was once-for-all, never to be repeated.

At the time of Vatican II, Stuart P. Garver was the editor of *Christian Heritage*, a magazine of Protestant-Catholic affairs, and was an accredited journalist at Vatican II. Concerning the sacraments of the Roman Catholic Church, Garver writes:

> By insisting the sacraments are essential to salvation . . . the Roman Catholic theologian perverts the pure Gospel of Christ. Faith in Christ, of course, is said to be essential; but

such faith, to have any saving value, must be complemented by the meritorious performance of the sacraments. To faith is added the merits of one's good works; this is work righteousness. It is a perversion of the gospel of grace.[42]

FUTURE LIFE (PURGATORY)

Perhaps no other teaching of the Roman Catholic Church so clearly shows that it does not rely on the authority of the Bible alone as does its teaching about purgatory. Few other dogmas make it so apparent that the Catholic Church does not believe that faith in the finished work of Christ on the cross is sufficient to completely deliver from condemnation.

In the *New Catholic Encyclopedia,* J.F.X. Cevetello describes purgatory as:

The state, place, or condition in the next world, which will continue until the last judgment, where the souls of those who die in the state of grace, but not yet free from all imperfection, make expiation for unforgiven venial sins or for the temporal punishment due to venial and mortal sins that have already been forgiven and, by so doing, are purified before they enter heaven.[43]

Notice especially in the preceding statements that "those who die in a state of grace" still suffer consequences for sins that have "already been forgiven." It is necessary for these believers to spend time in purgatory for further purging, or purification, "before they enter heaven."

The Reformers challenged this teaching of the Roman Catholic Church. Writing in the *New Catholic Encyclopedia,* R.J. Bastian reminds readers, however, that the Council of Trent "reiterated the revealed character of the existence of purgatory against the reformers, who had denied that there was any basis for it in Sacred Scripture."[44]

In spite of this decree by the Council of Trent, Cevetello admits now, even after Vatican II, "The doctrine of purgatory is not explicitly stated in the Bible" and, "In the final analysis, the Catholic doctrine on purgatory is based on tradition, not Sacred Scripture."[45] This is precisely what the Reformers claimed and what the Roman Catholic Church denied at the time.

To this weak view of grace and of the finished work of Christ is added agony for anyone who thinks about loved ones who have been "forgiven" but who must yet spend time in purgatory being purified for heaven. And how can the loved ones help these in purgatory? Bastian says, "The Church has also authoritatively defined that the souls detained there can be helped by the prayers and other good works of the faithful on earth."[46] But how many prayers does it take? How many good works?

The agony of those left on earth is not lessened when the same author admits, "The manner in which these prayers and good works of the faithful are applied to the souls in purgatory has not been authentically determined by the Church."[47]

As Catholics admit, their doctrine of purgatory is not found in the Bible. Instead, the Bible teaches, "He who believes in Him [Jesus Christ] is not condemned" (John 3:18). No one will be condemned who trusts Christ alone for salvation. The Bible teaches that when a believer is absent from the body, he is present with the Lord (2 Cor. 5:6–8). The believer does not need to spend any time in purgatory after death because Jesus Christ has fully paid the penalty for sin.

VATICAN II AND AFTER

To understand the significance of the Second Vatican Council (1962–1965), we must understand a basic distinction in beliefs that the Roman Catholic Church holds.

Garver, as noted, was the editor of *Christian Heritage* and an accredited journalist at Vatican II. Writing in 1973, he explained some basic beliefs of the Catholic Church:

> In the Roman Catholic Church there is an essential core of theology by which it is not only identified but fully certified as authentic Catholicism. That essential core of theology is preserved in the *de-fide* doctrines of the Church of Rome. These *de-fide* doctrines must be received on faith; failure to believe any one of these is to commit a mortal sin and dying therein one will suffer the pains of eternal punishment.
>
> There is, however, a vast body of Roman Catholic theology that does not fall into this de-fide definition, doctrines which have not been fully defined by the Church and may, therefore, be debated as opinions, theologically certain conclusions, or *proxima fidi*, that is, close to being defined as official *de-fide*

teaching of the Church. Hence there is an *official* Catholic theology to which all its teachers must give full consent and a
still undefined body of theology which Catholic theologians
may question and debate without anywise repudiating their
essential Catholicism.[48]

Having made these distinctions, Garver concludes: "Vatican Council
II offered no new doctrines, neither did it repudiate or change any of
the essential teaching of the Church. Only pastoral disciplinary and
liturgical patterns of its ministry were dealt with in order to up-date
its service to the People of God and all the world."[49]

A significant development since Vatican II has been the formation of
ECT (Evangelicals and Catholics Together). Both evangelical and
Roman Catholic leaders participated in and endorsed the controversial
ECT statement released March 29, 1994.

Soon after the publication of the statement, more controversy ensued. In 1995, Protestant evangelical Charles Colson of Prison
Fellowship and Roman Catholic Richard John Neuhaus of Institute on
Religion and Public Life served as editors for a book to handle some
of the varying opinions. Entitled *Evangelicals and Catholics Together: Toward a Common Mission*, this book includes the ECT statement. Some
comments in the statement are especially significant, such as, "We reject any appearance of harmony that is purchased at the price of
truth."[50] The ECT statement also declares, "We affirm together that we
are justified by grace through faith because of Christ."[51] This comment
especially drew fire from some evangelicals who stress that the word
"alone" is significantly missing because the Roman Catholic Church
adds works to belief in salvation by grace through faith.

And in what seems a proclamation that Protestants should not try to
convert Catholics nor Catholics convert Protestants, the ECT statement declared, "In view of the large number of non-Christians in the
world and the enormous challenge of our common evangelistic task,
it is neither theologically legitimate nor a prudent use of resources for
one Christian community to proselytize among active adherents of another Christian community."[52]

Evangelical J. I. Packer of Regent College (British Columbia) writes
in Colson and Neuhaus's book and seems surprised that some of his
fellow evangelicals challenged him for endorsing the ECT statement.
Packer reports that after the original ECT statement came out in

March 1994, a group met to come up with "Resolutions for Roman Catholic and Evangelical Dialogue," also known as "The CURE Statement of August 1994." CURE is an acronym meaning Christians United for Reformation. Reading the seven statements of CURE makes one wonder if the original ECT would have been agreed to had these statements been on the table then. For instance, point 2 of the CURE statement says, "The doctrine of justification by grace alone through faith alone because of Christ alone has since the Reformation been acknowledged by mainstream Protestants as 'the article by which the Church stands or falls.'"[53]

On January 19, 1995, evangelicals released another declaration, called "Statement by Protestant Signers to ECT." This seems to be another attempt for evangelicals to sharpen the distinctions that were confused in the original ECT. In this new statement, evangelicals clarified their meaning of justification through faith in Christ by emphasizing it had to do with "the substitutionary atonement and imputed righteousness of Christ, leading to full assurance of eternal salvation."[54] While rejecting proselytizing as mentioned in the original ECT, the evangelicals specified, "Evangelism and church planting are always legitimate."[55]

To those who thought he had gone too far in endorsing the ECT statement, Packer says, "At this point I must state explicitly that I am not and could not become a Roman Catholic because of certain basic tenets to which the Roman system, as such, is committed."[56]

In 1995, the same year Colson and Neuhaus's book was released, a book by Norman L. Geisler and Ralph E. MacKenzie was published entitled *Roman Catholics and Evangelicals: Agreements and Differences.*[57] Geisler is one of the foremost Christian apologists and current president of Southern Evangelical Seminary. MacKenzie is a graduate of Bethel Theological Seminary West. They divided their book in three parts: areas of doctrinal agreement, areas of doctrinal differences and areas of practical cooperation. Roman Catholic James Akin says that this book "offers a comprehensive and balanced discussion and should retire older, sensationalistic works."[58]

In the last appendix of their work, Geisler and MacKenzie evaluate what they call the "Colson-Neuhaus Declaration." Geisler and MacKenzie write, "In the final analysis, then, the question is this: is Roman Catholicism (since Trent) a false church with significant truth in it, as the Reformers believed, or is it a true church with significant

error in it? Since 'a true church' must proclaim the 'true gospel' (Gal.
1:8; 2:4), the answer will depend on what is essential to the true gospel."[59]

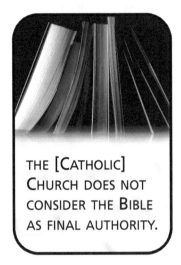

**THE [CATHOLIC]
CHURCH DOES NOT
CONSIDER THE BIBLE
AS FINAL AUTHORITY.**

After offering some distinctions, Geisler and MacKenzie conclude:

The bottom line, then, is whether there is anything in what Roman Catholicism has infallibly proclaimed that denies an essential element of the true gospel. According to the Reformers, the answer was affirmative, since Catholicism denies salvation is 'by grace alone through faith alone, based on Christ alone.' For Trent demanded that meritorious works are a necessary condition for receiving the gift of eternal life (= entering heaven). Thus, while affirming the necessity of grace, Catholicism denies the exclusivity of grace as a condition for receiving the gift of eternal life. . . . This, in the eyes of historic Protestantism, is a false gospel.[60]

CONCLUSION

Regardless of the surface changes of the Roman Catholic Church, its basic theological position remains the same. Even if the Catholic Church encourages the reading of it, the Church does not consider the Bible as final authority. This Roman system considers many teachings binding on Catholics that are not taught in the Bible, such as papal infallibility, Mary's Immaculate Conception and her assumption into heaven, Christ's sacrifice in the Mass and purgatory.

Particularly, the Roman Catholic Church rejects the teaching of the Bible concerning salvation by grace through faith in Christ alone. This is seen throughout the Catholic system of sacraments and its requirements of certain acts to obtain merit. It is especially seen in the Church's teaching concerning purgatory.

The message here is not that every Roman Catholic is unsaved. Any person who trusts Christ *alone* for salvation receives complete forgiveness of sin and has eternal life—regardless of his or her earthly religious affiliation. In fact, there seem to be many within the Catholic Church who would be considered "evangelical" rather than "Catholic." Under the entry of "Holy See: Vatican City State" in *Operation World* it says, "A large proportion of the Catholic missionary force is charismatic. The Evangelical Catholic movement has been gaining in influence and number with its more biblical interpretation of faith."[61]

It is gratifying to know there are those in the Catholic Church who believe salvation is by grace alone through faith alone in Christ alone. It is regrettable, however, that so many of these seem blind to the official teachings of the counterfeit religious system they serve.

The most important question anyone must answer is, How can I come into a right relationship with God? The Bible says, "Christ died for our sins" (1 Cor. 15:3). Jesus Himself said, "He who hears My word and believes in Him who sent Me has everlasting life, and shall not come into judgment, but has passed from death into life" (John 5:24).

Some of the nicest people you would ever want to meet are Roman Catholics. But just being nice does not qualify one to enter the presence of a holy God. The word of the Roman Catholic Church says good works need to be added to faith in Christ. The Word of God says, "Now to him who works, the wages are not counted as grace but as debt. But to him who does not work but believes on Him who justifies the ungodly, his faith is accounted for righteousness" (Rom. 4:4–5).

Summary

Name:	Roman Catholic Church
Head of the Church:	The Pope (Benedict XVI)
Worldwide Headquarters:	The Holy See, Vatican City State, Rome, Italy
Membership (2005):	U.S.: 66 million; Worldwide: 1 billion

What They Believe

Roman Catholics:	Biblical Christians:

Source of Authority

The Bible is an authority, along with the Pope, speaking *ex cathedra*, the Magisterium and sacred tradition.

The Bible alone is the source of authority.

Jesus Christ

Christ is God. Do not believe in the sufficiency of Christ's death to pay the full penalty for sin, as indicated by belief in purgatory.

Christ is God. His sacrifice was complete and effectual for all (Heb. 10:11–12).

Mary

Mary was sinless when conceived and never sinned her entire life. She has been bodily assumed into heaven and is the "Mother of God."

Only Jesus is sinless. There is no biblical reference to Mary's bodily assumption or for her being the "Mother of God."

Sin

Distinguish between "mortal" and "venial" sins, but the difference is difficult to trace.

Believe that "all have sinned and fall short of the glory of God" (Rom. 3:23), and "the blood of Jesus Christ His Son cleanses us from all sin" (1 John 1:7).

Salvation

Reject biblical teaching that salvation can be obtained only by grace alone through faith alone in Christ alone. A person receives salvation through the Church and its sacraments, especially baptism.

Believe that "by grace you have been saved through faith, and that not of yourselves; it is the gift of God, not of works, lest anyone should boast" (Eph. 2:8–9). Also believe that "to him who does not work but believes on Him who justifies the ungodly, his faith is accounted for righteousness" (Rom. 4:5).

Sacraments

The Church has seven sacraments—baptism, confirmation, penance, holy Eucharist (the Mass), holy orders, matrimony and anointing the sick. There is no salvation apart from baptism in the Church, based on the Council of Trent. "The mass is the sacrifice in which Jesus Christ, through the ministry of priests, perpetuates the sacrifice of the cross by his real presence under the appearances of bread and wine."

Baptism is an evidence of salvation, not a means of it. Claim that the offering of Christ is not to be repeated (Heb. 9:25–26).

Future Life/Purgatory

Purgatory is for "those who die in a state of grace" where they suffer consequences for sins that have "already been forgiven." Admit the Church doctrine on purgatory is based on tradition, not Scripture.

A believer does not need to spend any time in purgatory after death because Jesus Christ has fully paid the penalty for sin. The "purging" all believers receive is when Jesus "purged our sins, sat down at the right hand of the Majesty on high" (Heb. 1:3).

Recommended Reading

Boettner, Loraine. *Roman Catholicism*. Philadelphia: P&R Publishing, 2000.

Colson, Charles and Neuhaus, Richard John, eds. *Evangelicals and Catholics Together: Toward a Common Mission*. Dallas: Word Publishing, 1995.

Geisler, Norman L., and MacKenzie, Ralph E. *Roman Catholics and Evangelicals: Agreements and Differences*. Grand Rapids, Mich.: Baker Academic, 1995.

Millheim, John E. *Let Rome Speak for Herself*. Schaumburg, Ill.: Regular Baptist Press, 1982.

Ridenour, Fritz. *So What's the Difference?* Ventura, Calif.: Gospel Light Publications, 2001.

White, James R. *The Roman Catholic Controversy: Catholics and Protestants—Do the Differences Still Matter?* Minneapolis: Bethany House Publishers, 1996.

Zacchello, Joseph. *Secrets of Romanism*. Neptune, N.J.: Loizeaux Brothers, Inc., 1989.

ENDNOTES

[1] *Omaha World-Herald*, April 3, 2005, 1K.

[2] *WORLD Magazine*, April 30, 2005, 22.

[3] *World Almanac and Book of Facts 2005* (New York: World Almanac Education Group, Inc., 2005), 732, 734

[4] *Catechism of the Catholic Church* (New Hope, Ky.: Urbi et Orbi Communications, 1994).

[5] *New Catholic Encyclopedia* (Washington, D.C.: The Catholic University of America, 1967).

[6] *Catechism of the Catholic Church*, section 552.

[7] H. A. Whaley, "Rome, Church At," *The Zondervan Pictorial Encyclopedia,* Merrill C. Tenney, ed. (Grand Rapids, Mich.: Zondervan Publishing House, 1976), V:169.

[8] Ibid.

[9] Earle Cairns, *Christianity through the Centuries* (Grand Rapids, Mich.: Zondervan Publishing House, 1981), 158.

[10] Ibid., 159.

[11] Patrick Johnstone and Jason Mandryk with Robyn Johnstone, *Operation World: 21ˢᵗ Century Edition* (Cumbria, United Kingdom: Paternoster Lifestyle, 2001), 298.

[12] Ibid., 231.

[13] E-mail to the author, June 10, 2004.

[14] Johnstone, Mandryk, Johnstone, *Operation World: 21ˢᵗ Century Edition*, 365.

[15] Loraine Boettner, *Roman Catholicism* (Philadelphia: P&R Publishing, 2000), 4.

[16] Ibid.

[17] D. H. Wallace, "Apocrypha," in *Evangelical Dictionary of Theology*, Walter A. Elwell, ed. (Grand Rapids, Mich.: Baker Book House, 1984), 66.

[18] Adolfo Robleto and John Hepp Jr., *Roman Catholic Doctrine in the Light of Vatican II* (Houston: Lit-International, 1977), 190–191.

[19] Peter Toon, "Infallibility," *The New International Dictionary of the Christian Church* (Grand Rapids, Mich.: Zondervan Publishing House, 1974), 508.

[20] F. X. Lawlor, "Infallibility," *New Catholic Encyclopedia* (Washington, D.C.: The Catholic University of America, 1967), 7:496.

[21] Ibid.

[22] Julius R. Mantey, *Was Peter a Pope?* (Chicago: Moody Press, 1949), 70.

[23] Ibid., 56.

[24] *Catechism of the Catholic Church*, section 85.

[25] Ibid.

[26] Ibid., section 86.

[27] Ibid., section 97.

[28] J. F. Murphy, *New Catholic Encyclopedia*, 9:347.

[29] *Catechism of the Catholic Church*, section 493.

[30] Tim Russert, *Big Russ & Me: Father and Son Lessons of Life* (New York: Miramax, 2004), picture section.

[31] Ibid., 298.

[32] James R. White, *The Roman Catholic Controversy: Catholics and Protestants—Do the Differences Still Matter?* (Minneapolis: Bethany House Publishers, 1996), 126.

[33] L. Villette, "Sacraments as Signs of Faith," *New Catholic Encyclopedia*, 12:815.

[34] M. Eminyan, "Salvation, Necessity of the Church for," *New Catholic Encyclopedia*, 12:995, 996.

[35] T.M. De Ferrari, "Baptism (Theology of)," *New Catholic Encyclopedia*, 2:63.

[36] *Catechism of the Catholic Church*, section 846.

[37] Ibid., section 818.

[38] Joseph I. Mallory, *A Catechism for Inquirers*, revised by Edward H. Peters (New York: Paulist Press, 1977), 50.

[39] J.G.G. Norman, "Mass, the," *The New International Dictionary of the Christian Church*, 641.

[40] White, *The Roman Catholic Controversy*, 179.

[41] Ibid., 179–180.

[42] Stuart P. Garver, *Watch Your Teaching!* (Hackensack, N.J.: Christ's Mission, Inc., 1973), 58.

[43] J.F.X. Cevetello, "Purgatory," in *New Catholic Encyclopedia*, 11:1034.

[44] R.J. Bastian, "Purgatory," in *New Catholic Encyclopedia*, 11:1035.

[45] Cevetello, "Purgatory," 11:1034.

[46] Bastian, "Purgatory," 11:1035.

[47] Ibid.

[48] Garver, *Watch Your Teaching!*, ix.

[49] Ibid., ix, x.

[50] Charles Colson and Richard John Neuhaus, eds. *Evangelicals and Catholics Together: Toward a Common Mission* (Dallas: Word Publishing, 1995), xvii.

[51] Ibid., xviii.

[52] Ibid., xxx.

[53] Ibid., 158.

[54] Ibid., 161.

[55] Ibid.

[56] Ibid.

[57] Norman L. Geisler and Ralph E. MacKenzie, *Roman Catholics and Evangelicals: Agreements and Differences* (Grand Rapids, Mich.: Baker Books, 1995).

[58] Ibid., back cover.

[59] Ibid., 502.

[60] Ibid.

[61] Johnstone, Mandryk, Johnstone, *Operation World: 21ˢᵗ Century Edition*, 301.

CHAPTER NINE

Rosicrucians

Of all the counterfeit religious groups in existence today, probably none is more complex or confusing than Rosicrucianism. Even researchers who have spent many years studying various religious groups find the doctrines of Rosicrucianism complicated and foreign.

In his excellent book *The Kingdom of the Cults*, Walter Martin stated, "Of all the cult systems under discussion in this book, the Rosicrucians most certainly qualify, along with the spiritists, Theosophists and Swedenborgians, as the most mystically minded. More than any of the others, they are also devoted to a detailed system of doctrine composed of so many strains of other cult viruses, as to be almost beyond the point of comprehension, much less analysis."[1]

A study of the doctrines of the Rosicrucians soon reveals how much they have borrowed from a wide variety of other religions and philosophies. Because the Rosicrucians teach and practice everything from spiritism to astrology to reincarnation to the doctrine of the Trinity, researchers are often uncertain as to how to classify them. While Martin included the group in his book on the cults, he placed them in a special appendix.[2] In their book on religions, Josh McDowell and Don Stewart listed the Rosicrucians as an occult group.[3] Irvine Robertson considered them to be a movement that was an outgrowth of old religions, especially Hinduism and Buddhism.[4] In his book *The Encyclopedia of American Religions*, J. Gordon Melton discussed the Rosicrucians under the heading "The Psychic and New Age Family."[5]

You will understand the confusion about Rosicrucianism if you have read the previous chapters in this book about Christian Scientists, Masons and the New Age Movement, and when you read the succeeding chapters about Transcendental Meditation and Unity School of Christianity. By comparing these groups, you'll find an amazing similarity of the belief systems—and one similarity is their claim that they do not have a belief system!

What They Believe

Within the larger group known as Rosicrucians exist several branches, each having its own unique doctrines and interpretations. Some of the best-known branches include the Ancient and Mystical Order of the Rosae Crucis (AMORC), Societas Rosicruciana in America, Rosicrucian Fellowship and Lectorium Rosicrucianum. Each group follows different leaders and has its own headquarters and publishing house in various cities in the United States and throughout the world.

Despite this diversity in people, places and philosophies, Rosicrucianism contains some elements that are common to all. Exactly who are the Rosicrucians, and what do they believe?

BACKGROUND

The Rosicrucians are a secret order of men and women who claim to possess wisdom that has been handed down from ancient times. It is difficult to determine how many adherents there are. The official Rosicrucian Web site claims that "hundreds of thousands of Rosicrucian students" have taken a home study since 1915.[6] In 1985 Martin indicated there were probably about 60,000 worldwide. In 1990, however, the *Los Angeles Times* reported that there were about 250,000 AMORC members worldwide, a number that the revised Martin book, published in 2003, cites as well.[7] Perhaps this is because, like the New Age Movement, some of their major beliefs are held by many people who do not consider themselves Rosicrucians. The Rosicrucians claim many well-known people of the past as their followers, including such men as Isaac Newton, Benjamin Franklin and Francis Bacon.

The term *Rosicrucian* means "rosy cross." One of the symbols of the Rosicrucians is a cross on which a rose is superimposed. But do not be misled by the beauty of the rose nor in thinking the cross has anything to do with the cross of Christ. In their excellent work *Dictionary of Cults, Sects, Religions and the Occult*, Mather and Nichol suggest, "The rose cross most likely derived its symbolic significance from alchemy."[8] Alchemy is referred to often in the Rosicrucian writings. In *The Encyclopedia of Secret Knowledge*, Charles Walker defines the term this way: "Alchemy is the art of transformation, and may be described as a method of investigating nature in a spiritually creative way. Just as an artist takes colour pigments and oil from the earth and combines these so as to incorporate on canvas his own inner vision (thus transforming nature into mental images), so the alchemist seeks to work with the material of nature, and impress upon it something of the power of the invisible spirit."[9]

One of the Rosicrucian leaders says of the rosy cross, "Esoterically, the Rose represents Secrecy and Evolution, while the Cross represents the Labor and Burdens of Life and the karma which we must endure in our earthly existence."[10] So the cross of the Rosicrucians is not to be confused with the cross of Christianity.

The name *Rosicrucian* is derived from a legendary character of the Middle Ages by the name of Christian Rosenkreuz (also spelled Rosenkreutz or Rosencreutz). The earliest known document that mentions the Rosicrucians is a booklet entitled *Fama Fraternitatis* ("Account of the Brotherhood"). This booklet is usually referred to as *Fama*. Published in Germany in 1614, it "purports to recount the life of a medieval knight, Christian Rosenkreuz, who traveled to Morocco and the Near East to acquire secret wisdom and an elixir of life."[11]

According to *Fama*, on his trips to the Mediterranean basin "Rosenkreuz acquired secret wisdom . . . which he subsequently imparted to three others after his return to Germany. The number of his disciples was later increased to eight, who went to different countries."[12]

Although he was supposedly born in 1378 and was said to have lived for 106 years, Rosenkreuz "is now generally regarded to have been a symbolic rather than a real character, whose story provided a legendary explanation of the order's origin."[13] Some believe the character Christian Rosenkreuz was based on the life of Swiss alchemist and physician Paracelsus (1493?–1541).[14]

According to J. Gordon Melton, "Many commentators have suggested that a Lutheran pastor, Valentin Andreae (1586–1654), was the author of the pamphlet, since he was [the] admitted author of the 1616 novel *The Hermetic Romance or the Chemical Wedding; written in High Dutch by Christian Rosencreutz*."[15] *The New Encyclopaedia Britannica* says, "There is, however, no reliable evidence to date the order's history earlier than the 17th century."[16]

An examination of early Rosicrucian documents reveals that several other groups prevalent in England and other parts of Europe in the

1700s greatly affected Rosicrucian doctrines and practices. Foremost among these were the Freemasons, a guild of bricklayers and stone artisans originally formed in the Middle Ages who gradually became an occult order. According to Melton, "The Freemasons added a Rosicrucian degree to their initiations, and the Rosicrucians were greatly influenced by the Freemasons."[17] He added that "modern Rosicrucian teachings are like those of Theosophy and Freemasonry, and can be seen as a form of Christian gnosticism and mysticism. Transmutation, psychic development and meditative/yogic disciplines are stressed."[18]

The oldest group of Rosicrucians in the United States was founded by Paschal Beverly Randolph in 1868. Known as the Fraternitas Rosae Crucis, it also operates under the names "Aeth Priesthood" and the "Church of Illumination." Of this order, Melton wrote: "The inner circle of the Fraternity is the Aeth Priesthood, in which is taught 'the highest occultism known to man.' The Church of Illumination is an Outer Court group, which means it interacts with the public and from its members a select few are chosen to join the inner group."[19] Their teachings include reincarnation, karma and the belief that health can be maintained by removing all thoughts of weakness and age. Following his death, Randolph was succeeded by R. Swinburne Clymer, whose extensive writings have attracted many to the group. The headquarters for this order were in Quakertown, Pennsylvania, although it is not listed among current Rosicrucian groups.[20]

MUCH OF THIS PHILOSOPHY CENTERS ON ASTROLOGY.

The Rosicrucian Fellowship was founded in 1907 by Carl Louis Van Grasshof, better known as Max Heindel. He was an active Theosophist (Theosophy is a religious movement that is an outgrowth of the Eastern religions, particularly Hinduism and Buddhism). During Heindel's trip to Germany in 1907, a celestial being supposedly appeared to him and led him to the Temple of the Rosy Cross, where he was given the material for his book *The Rosicrucian Cosmo-Conception*, the primary text of the group. Heindel later wrote *The Rosicrucian Philosophy* as well. Much of this philosophy centers on astrology. The headquarters for the Rosicrucian Fellowship is located near Oceanside, California.

The most widely publicized of the Rosicrucian groups is the Ancient and Mystical Order of the Rosae Crucis (AMORC), founded by H. Spencer Lewis in 1915. AMORC seems to be the least secretive of the Rosicrucian orders. The group launched a public relations campaign shortly after its formation and has actively continued to seek new members. Its official Web site said, "We are a nonsectarian body of men and women devoted to the investigation, study and practical application of natural and spiritual laws. Our purpose is to further the evolution of humanity through the development of the full potential of each individual. Our goal is to enable everyone to live in harmony with creative, cosmic forces for the attainment of health, happiness, and peace."[21]

Lewis was a prolific writer, and many people may have been attracted by his books. He wrote such works as *Mansions of the Soul: A Cosmic Conception, Rosicrucian Questions and Answers With Complete History of the Rosicrucian Order* and *The Secret Doctrines of Jesus*. The main office of AMORC is located at Rosicrucian Park in San Jose, California.

The core beliefs of the various groups of Rosicrucians are similar. Do not be misled by their statements that they do not have a belief system. The AMORC home page says, "We do not propose a belief system, nor a dogmatic decree, but a personal, practical approach to living that each student must learn and master through their own experiences. Our teachings do not attempt to dictate what you should think—we want you to think for yourself. What we provide are simply the tools to enable you to accomplish this."[22]

Even though Rosicrucians claim otherwise, they do have a belief system. Any group that has definite views about God and mankind has a belief system even though it may be difficult to determine what it is. For instance, if you would ask, "Do you believe that Jesus Christ is the only way of salvation?" and the group answers no, it shows the group has a belief system.

BELIEFS

The mysterious and unusual practices of the various Rosicrucian groups seem similar to the Masons. In determining whether or not they are biblically based, what matters most are their views about their source of authority, the Trinity, Jesus Christ, the Holy Spirit, man, sin and salvation, and the future life.

SOURCE OF AUTHORITY

Biblical Christianity accepts the Bible as the final source of authority. "All Scripture is given by inspiration of God" (2 Tim. 3:16). Jesus Christ told us, "Do not think that I came to destroy the Law or the Prophets. I did not come to destroy but to fulfill. For assuredly, I say to you, till heaven and earth pass away, one jot or one tittle will by no means pass from the law till all is fulfilled" (Matt. 5:17–18).

But what do the Rosicrucians say about their standard of truth? "To get at the true explanation concerning pain and sorrow," Max Heindel explained, "we will first take the purely occult information, and then see what light the Bible gives."[23] From this statement we see that the mysteries and teachings of Rosicrucianism are considered superior to the wisdom of the Bible.

In Rosicrucian literature, you frequently encounter the word *occult*. By this Heindel was referring to hidden, or secret, wisdom that only those in that system of thought supposedly possess. "As there is an outer, *orthodox*, or every-day Bible interpretation and application with which most of us are familiar," R. Swinburne Clymer wrote, "so is there an inner, *esoteric* or *Spiritual* interpretation"[24] (emphasis his). Varying degrees of knowledge are contained within this esoteric wisdom. This "spiritual" insight is available only to those in the inner circle of Rosicrucians—the initiates.

Thus, whenever a statement in the Bible contradicts their theology, Rosicrucians give it a mystical, esoteric interpretation in order to explain away the normal meanings of the words. The language of the Bible is used, but the meaning is twisted into something entirely different from what the Bible intended. If we were to interpret the words in their writings the way the Rosicrucians interpret words in the Bible, we could make their words mean anything we want them to mean— as they have done with the Scriptures. The philosophies and special wisdom of the inner circle of Rosicrucians always take precedence over the Scriptures.

THE TRINITY

Biblical Christianity holds that there is one God existing in three Persons—Father, Son and Holy Spirit. The term *Trinity* signifies "that within the one essence of the Godhead we have to distinguish three 'persons' who are neither three gods on the one side, nor three parts or modes of God on the other, but coequally and coeternally God."[25] Each Person of the Godhead has intellect, emotions and will. Each possesses the attributes of God—such as omnipotence, omnipresence and omniscience—and each receives worship.

While the Rosicrucians teach the doctrine of the Trinity, their interpretations of it are far different from what the Bible teaches. As Clymer wrote, "God is the Father; The Holy Ghost is the Mother, Feminine side; the Son is the *Christos*, or Christic principle; the outer manifestation is Man"[26] (emphasis his).

Like so many other false religions, including Christian Science, the New Age Movement and Unity School of Christianity, Rosicrucianism believes that God is a principle—not a person. Rosicrucians teach a form of pantheism in which "God" is merely a collection of spirits and ideas. In describing their interpretation of the Trinity, Walter Martin wrote: "It is a historic affirmation of Rosicrucianism, that God is an impersonal being, composed of seven spirits, which manifest themselves as a 'triune godhead,' or, Father, Son and Holy Spirit. . . . In such a semantic jungle, the nature of God, the holy Trinity, or Triune Deity of Biblical revelation undergoes total, if not complete, mutilation. It becomes a type of occult pantheism, culminating in an impersonal spirit-being, who is 'collectively' God."[27]

JESUS CHRIST

Again, like many other false religions, Rosicrucians make a distinction between the names *Jesus* and *Christ*. They say that Jesus was an ordinary man and that Christ was merely a divine principle. Thus, they deny His deity.

The Rosicrucians have twisted and reinterpreted almost every aspect of Christ's life in order to make Him fit their philosophies. They claim that He belonged to the Essenes, a secret order of men who lived together in settlements and devoted their lives to study. They teach that Mary and Joseph were Gentiles, not Jews, and that Joseph was a widower with two sons before he agreed to take Mary. While they do not deny the virgin birth of Christ, they say that Buddha, Krishna and other Eastern leaders were also born in this manner. Likewise, they teach that Jesus spent His early years studying under the Essenes and preparing for His ministry as a mystic. Rosicrucians deny that Christ's miracles were supernatural, believing that anyone who had received training in mysticism would be able to do them.

Rosicrucians also deny the death and resurrection of Jesus, thus eliminating His atonement for our sins. They are supporters of the "swoon" theory, which teaches that Christ did not die on the cross but merely fainted and was later revived. According to H. Spencer Lewis,

> The storm soon broke and delayed the removal of the body of Jesus for a few hours, but in that time food and drink were given Him, and support was placed under His body to prevent it from pulling too greatly upon the nails which tortured His flesh. The few faithful ones noted with great anxiety that a somber stillness and a numbness was passing over the body, and that gradually Jesus lost consciousness. At the earliest possible moment, when the storm quieted, torches were brought and an examination of the body revealed that Jesus was not dead. The blood flowing from the wounds proved that the body was not lifeless, and so the cross was immediately taken down and the body removed from it. . . . The body was placed in a special part of the tomb which had been prearranged for its reception, and physicians connected with the Essene Brotherhood were at hand to render every possible assistance in caring for the wounds.[28]

Thus, in Rosicrucian theology, Jesus was merely a man—God's messenger and mystic who taught the divine Christ principle. The doctrines of Rosicrucianism are very similar to Gnosticism, which was a combination of Greek philosophy and Eastern religious thought.[29] In fact, Clymer associated their doctrines of Christ with those of the Gnostics: "Is this Christ not the *Christos* of the Gnostics and of the present new Church of the Illuminated?"[30] (emphasis his). The answer is yes, of course, but if the question is, Is this the Christ of the Bible? the answer is an emphatic no.

The Greek word *Christos* means "anointed one," and it was used to refer to Jesus as the Messiah. The apostle John recorded that when

Andrew found his brother, Peter, he told him, "We have found the Messiah" (which is translated, the Christ)" (John 1:41).

The Bible teaches that Jesus Christ is God and that God is a divine Person, not an impersonal principle. A principle cannot die for someone's sins. If Jesus were only a man—even with a *Christos* principle in Him—His death would not have paid the penalty for sin, nor would He have risen from the dead. However, the Bible clearly states that His death propitiated, or satisfied, the Heavenly Father for "our sins, and not for ours only but also for the whole world" (1 John 2:2). The Christ of the Church of the Illuminated bears little, if any, resemblance to the Christ of the Bible.

THE HOLY SPIRIT

The Bible teaches us that the Holy Spirit is the third Person of the Trinity—not merely an impersonal force, as so many groups claim. The Holy Spirit has all the attributes of a person and of God. He does things only a person can do and some only God can do. The Holy Spirit regenerates (John 3:6), teaches about God (14:26), convicts us concerning sin, righteousness and judgment (16:8), and baptizes into the body of Christ (1 Cor. 12:13). The Bible also refers to the Holy Spirit as God. When Ananias lied about giving all the price he had received for a piece of property, Peter asked him, "Why has Satan filled your heart to lie to the Holy Spirit?" (Acts 5:3). And then the apostle added, "You have not lied to men but to God" (v. 4).

The Rosicrucians, on the other hand, teach that the Holy Spirit is merely a principle, or essence, of life. Clymer wrote: "In God, or as part of God, is the Holy Ghost, or the *Light* which is the *life* of the Soul. It is also the mother side of the Trinity; it is the fire or light of the universe; the floor of the world, the Sustainer, for without this *Light*, this fire, i.e., heat or warmth of the fire, there could be no life either in man, animals, or vegetables."[31] He later added, "God is the Spirit in the sense that He is the *principle* of Life"[32] (emphasis his). The Rosicrucians have taken words that Christ used to describe the Holy Spirit's work and have made these the Holy Spirit Himself. Thus, instead of being a person, He becomes an "it"—light, fire—an impersonal force in the universe.

MAN

Understanding what the Rosicrucians believe about the nature of man reveals much about their entire system of thought. Their concept of man is woven into their understanding of the soul. "To man," Clymer wrote, "God gave a part of Himself with an intent of what should be done with that part. Man was also given carefully planned Laws to be followed that this Spark from God might attain its highest degree of perfection.

"If man obeys, if he follows the dictates of the Law, then this *Divine Spark*, which is universally and erroneously called the 'Soul,' may be developed and awakened into Consciousness"[33] (emphasis his).

Like the followers of Christian Science, Hinduism, Theosophy, Unity and the New Age Movement, the Rosicrucians teach the concept of monism—that the universe is made up of only one impersonal element that constitutes ultimate reality. Each person is simply a part of the impersonal divine principle. In writing about this concept, H. Spencer Lewis stated, "The Rosicrucians have always believed that there is but one soul in the universe, and that is the universal soul or the universal consciousness of God."[34]

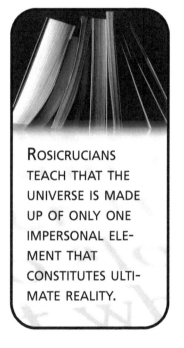

ROSICRUCIANS TEACH THAT THE UNIVERSE IS MADE UP OF ONLY ONE IMPERSONAL ELEMENT THAT CONSTITUTES ULTIMATE REALITY.

Thus, man is part of this "universal consciousness." In other words, man can achieve godhood. However, man has not yet become perfect. This perfection is obtained through evolution, reincarnation and obedience to God's laws, say the Rosicrucians. Gradually, man works his way to this consciousness. Note how the Rosicrucians have reinterpreted the Bible's teachings about the new birth: "To BE RE-BORN of the Spirit is to have *become* Spiritually Awakened or Soul Conscious. The prime requisite is the *awakening*, bringing into Consciousness that part of God—*Flame* of God—which was given, or drawn into the body at the moment of birth and is known as the *Divine Spark*, or the *Christos*. This *Christos*, awakened and brought into Consciousness, is the Christ; the Immortal part of man"[35] (emphasis theirs).

H. Spencer Lewis added, "Our Cosmic conception shows us that the Soul of man and all conscious creatures is a form of Divine Consciousness, which has certain attributes or functions. It may, therefore, be called *Infinite Mind*."[36] These uncertain reasonings are far from the clear revelation of Jesus' words recorded in John 14:6: "I am the way, the truth, and the life. No one comes to the Father except through Me."

SIN AND SALVATION

The Scriptures make it clear that sin separates from God and excludes us from His kingdom. The Bible emphatically states, "All have sinned and fall short of the glory of God" (Rom. 3:23). Therefore, man can never earn his salvation, for "the wages of sin is death." However, we still have hope because "the gift of God is eternal life in Christ Jesus our Lord" (6:23). But only those who believe in the finished work of Christ on the cross will receive this gift. John 1:12 states, "As many as received Him, to them He gave the right to become children of God, to those who believe in His name."

The Rosicrucians have twisted the Bible's clear teachings about sin and salvation to fit their mystical and secret beliefs. They deny the existence of sin and, hence, the need for salvation. While the Scriptures teach that every person is born as a sinful descendant of Adam, the Rosicrucians teach that each person is born with the "divine spark." All that remains is for him to fan the flame—to have his soul awakened to the divine nature within him.

Rosicrucianism is a system of self-salvation through self-reformation. "Before the Neophyte is prepared to walk in the path of the Occult Initiate," Clymer stated, "it is necessary for him to thoroughly purge himself of pride, of purely selfish ambitions and of avarice, which most frequently manifests itself in jealousies."[37]

Max Heindel left no mystery as to what he believed constitutes sin and salvation: "There is but one sin—Ignorance," he wrote, "and but one salvation—Applied Knowledge."[38] "All sorrow, suffering and pain," he continued, "are traceable to ignorance of how to act, and the school of life is as necessary to bring out our latent capabilities as is the daily school which evokes those of the child."[39]

What They Believe

Rosicrucians teach that, because each person is a part of the divine, no one will be lost. According to Heindel, "A 'lost soul' is an impossible conception when we consider that we are all a part of God."[40] He went on to explain, "We could not exist outside God, in a Hell, and if a single soul were lost, that would mean that a part of God would be lost."[41]

By teaching that every person is part of the universal consciousness known as "God," Rosicrucians rid themselves of the problems of sin and hell. However, this only poses a greater problem for them—what to do with the Bible's many teachings about hell. Heindel recognized this discrepancy in their teachings and confronted the issue in his usual evasive manner: "But then, it may be asked, what may be the meaning of the number of passages which in the New Testament speak of 'everlasting' salvation and condemnation? The passages are easily understood when properly illuminated by a dictionary and a knowledge of the occult teaching."[42]

Like so many followers of false religions, the Rosicrucians have twisted many key doctrines of the Scriptures to fit their "mysteries." However, their "mysteries" are not new. Their belief in an impersonal God, a deified humanity and a self-salvation is merely the age-old teachings of the Eastern religions wrapped in a different package.

Future Life

Closely linked with the Rosicrucians' teachings concerning salvation is their belief in reincarnation, a doctrine common to many Eastern religions.

Heindel defined reincarnation as "a slow process of development carried on with *unwavering persistence* through repeated embodiment in human forms of increasing efficiency, whereby all beings are in time brought to a height of spirituality inconceivable to our present limited understanding"[43] (emphasis his). But one only has to read the daily newspaper or to watch the evening news to realize mankind is not on its way to a "height of spirituality" but to depths of sin that is "inconceivable to our present limited understanding."

In Rosicrucianism, salvation through Jesus Christ is replaced with the Hindu belief in karma—the law of sowing and reaping. They teach that what is sown in this life is reaped in the next. Therefore, the goal of life is to be as good as possible so that, after death, you can be reborn in a higher state. Through this continuous cycle of rebirths, a person eventually reaches ultimate reality—total consciousness of the impersonal divine principle, or Brahman, within him.

Thus, according to the Rosicrucians, Christ's death was not needed to atone for our sins, since we can each free ourselves from our past sins through reincarnation. In their book *The Living Christ*, the Rosicrucians leave little doubt about their view of the purpose of reincarnation: "The *Church of the Illumination* maintains that this is the LAW OF JUSTICE. It offers every Soul the opportunity, time and again, to free itself of its accumulated evils"[44] (emphasis theirs). To the Rosicrucians, the cross is not a symbol of Christ's death and the freedom that it brings. Rather, it is a mystical symbol of man's own death to his past and his evolution—past, present and future—toward his final state of total consciousness.

Considering the fact that sin and hell are nonexistent according to the Rosicrucians, it seems strange that they would teach that atonement for our past is necessary. Yet this is exactly what they teach. In referring to their "Law of Exact Justice," they state, "This is the demand upon man that he MUST pay to 'the uttermost farthing' all that he is indebted for and cannot be free, economically, morally or Spiritually, until he has so paid. Both the Law of Karma and Reincarnation are involved, otherwise there would be no future opportunity for man to retrieve his past"[45] (emphasis theirs). Why would people who are born with the divine nature of God need to pay for their past? This is just one example of the many contradictions that exist in Rosicrucianism.

Reincarnation is contrary to the teachings of God's Word. Only one death and resurrection could ever fully pay the penalty of sin—that of the God-Man, Jesus Christ. The only way to be freed from our sin is through belief in Him. "He who believes in Him is not judged; he who does not believe has been judged already, because he has not believed in the name of the only begotten Son of God" (John 3:18). And we have only one life in which to make this all-important decision: "It is appointed for men to die once and after this comes judgment" (Heb. 9:27).

CONCLUSION

While the Rosicrucians claim to be a nonreligious order, their philosophies and views present a specific religious belief system. If you would strip Rosicrucianism of its concepts of the divine principle and the deity of man, little would be left. In reality, Rosicrucianism has borrowed teachings from almost every religion. As mentioned previously, this system of belief has been especially influenced by Theosophy, a religious movement founded in India by Madame Helena Petrovna Blavatsky (1831–1891) and Henry Steel Olcott (1832–1907) that is an outgrowth of Eastern religions, particularly Hinduism and Buddhism.

Rosicrucians also claim that many renowned people have been followers of their teachings. They will cite statements from these famous people as supposed proof of their belief in Rosicrucian principles. However, considering how the Rosicrucians have made the Bible fit their interpretations, it is possible that they have merely forced the statements of these famous people into their system as well.

Likewise, the Rosicrucians seek to justify their mysteries and secret knowledge by claiming that Jesus had secret teachings. While on occasion Jesus did use parables to conceal His teachings from the masses, He did not do this to preserve secrets for His initiates. He did so because these people had rejected Him as the promised Messiah of Israel. In their hardened condition, it was useless to attempt to communicate with them further (Matt. 13:10–15). But to those who were open to the truth, Jesus had no secret doctrines. He told His disciples on another occasion, "Whatever I tell you in the dark, speak in the light; and what you hear in the ear, preach on the housetops" (10:27).

Nor does the Bible use the term *mystery* as the Rosicrucians do. In the original language of the New Testament, the word *musterion* occurs 27 times—five in the plural (mysteries) and 22 in the singular (mystery). In each case the word always refers to some truth that was previously unrevealed but has since been made known to all. It is never used to describe some secret knowledge that is given only to a few privileged people.

For example, the apostle Paul said, "By revelation He made known to me the mystery (as I wrote before in a few words, by which, when you read, you may understand my knowledge in the mystery of Christ), which in other ages was not made known to the sons of men, as it has now been revealed by the Spirit to His holy apostles and prophets" (Eph. 3:3–5). Did Paul and the other apostles keep this mystery for an inner circle of people? No. In the following verse, Paul stated what the mystery was so that all could read it: "That the Gentiles should be fellow heirs, of the same body, and partakers of His promise in Christ through the gospel" (v. 6). No mention was made in the Old Testament of the fact that God desired Gentile believers in Christ to be fellow-heirs with Jewish believers. This truth was not revealed until the New Testament.

Likewise, Colossians 1:26 refers to another "mystery which has been hidden from ages and from generations, but now has been revealed to His saints." What was this mystery? Paul did not keep it a secret but explained, "which is Christ in you, the hope of glory" (v. 27). While God did not reveal all information to the Jews in the Old Testament, the truths were in no way "secret." The Lord was simply waiting for their fulfillment in Christ. Once the prophecies were fulfilled, these truths were given to all without reservation.

The Rosicrucians claim to have the key to the "mysteries" of the Bible, but that's impossible: as we have seen, God has already revealed His truths in the Scriptures. The Bible contains no secrets. The Lord has made His will plain to all. The "secrets" that the Rosicrucians supposedly possess are not biblical truths but myths. Any "revelation" that contradicts the Scriptures cannot be from God. Paul warned that the time would come when people would "turn their ears away from the truth, and be turned aside to fables" (2 Tim. 4:4). Groups like the Rosicrucians are a fulfillment of this prophecy.

The apostle Paul also described false teachers of the last days as "having a form of godliness but denying its power" (2 Tim. 3:5). And what should be the Christian's response toward such teachers? Paul said, "From such people turn away!" (v. 5).

The strange and erroneous teachings of the Rosicrucians definitely qualify as myths, and Christians should avoid such false doctrines.

Summary

Name:	Rosicrucians
Main Organizations:	Ancient and Mystical Order of the Rosae Crucis (AMORC) San Jose, California
	Lectorium Rosicrucianism Bakersfield, California

Rosicrucian Fellowship
Oceanside, California

Membership (2003): About 250,000 worldwide
Web Site: www.amorc.org

What They Believe

Rosicrucians: **Biblical Christians:**

Source of Authority

The "mysteries" and teachings are superior to the wisdom of the Bible. The Bible has an outer, orthodox interpretation but also an inner, esoteric or spiritual interpretation.

The Bible alone is final authority. Its words are to be interpreted in the way they were used normally when written.

The Trinity

God is not a person but a principle. "Trinity" refers to many impersonal spirit beings who are collectively God and it represents the idea of father, mother (Holy Spirit) and Christic principle (Christ).

God is a divine Person. Accept the trinitarian view of Godhead expressed in the Apostles' Creed, used as early as A.D. 150. The three Persons of the Godhead are one, yet distinct—with each being coequally and coeternally God.

Jesus Christ

Jesus was a man and Christ was merely a principle, not God. Deny the death and resurrection of Christ, saying that He only fainted and was later revived.

Jesus Christ is a divine Person. He died on the cross, was buried and rose again after three days.

The Holy Spirit

The Holy Spirit is not a person but a principle of life. He is an impersonal force, the fire and light of the universe.

The Holy Spirit is a divine Person, the third Person of the Trinity who does such works as regenerates, convicts of sin and baptizes believers into the Body of Christ.

Man

Believe in the deity of man—that every person is part of the universal divine consciousness known as "God." Each person has a divine spark within him or her.

Man is not now and never becomes God. Believe in the sinful nature of mankind that results in death for all.

Sin and Salvation

Deny the existence of sin; therefore, no salvation is needed. Any lack can be overcome by self-reformation and applied knowledge. No one can be lost because this would mean a part of God is lost, since every person is part of God.

All have sinned so every person needs salvation. Only faith in Christ can deliver from sin's condemnation. All will be eternally lost who do not trust in Christ for salvation.

Future Life

Believe in the Eastern concept of reincarnation—that through a slow process of death and rebirth in new forms of life, man can gradually reach spiritual perfection. Embrace the Hindu law of karma—that what we sow in this life is reaped in the next.

Reject any idea of reincarnation or second chance for salvation after this life. There are consequences to sin but all who believe in Christ are delivered from condemnation.

Recommended Reading

Ankerberg, John, and Weldon, John. *Encyclopedia of Cults and New Religions.* Eugene, Ore.: Harvest House Publishers, 1999.

Gruss, Edmond C. *Cults and the Occult.* Grand Rapids, Mich.: P&R Publishing, 1994.

Martin, Walter. *The Kingdom of the Cults.* Ravi Zacharias, gen. ed. Minneapolis: Bethany House Publishers, 2003.

Mather, George A., and Nichols, Larry A. *Dictionary of Cults, Sects, Religions and the Occult.* Grand Rapids, Mich.: Zondervan Publishing House, 1993.

McDowell, Josh, and Stewart, Don. *Handbook of Today's Religions.* San Bernardino, Calif.: Here's Life Publishers, Inc., 1983.

Robertson, Irvine. *What the Cults Believe.* Chicago: Moody Press, 1991.

ENDNOTES

[1] Walter R. Martin, *The Kingdom of the Cults* (Minneapolis: Bethany House Publishers, 1985), 507.

[2] Ibid., 507–512.

[3] Josh McDowell and Don Stewart, *Handbook of Today's Religions* (San Bernardino, Calif.: Here's Life Publishers, Inc., 1983), 221–224.

[4] Irvine Robertson, *What the Cults Believe*, 4th ed.; (Chicago: Moody Press, 1983), 167–168.

[5] J. Gordon Melton, *The Encyclopedia of American Religions*, Vol. 2 (Wilmington, N.C.: McGrath Publishing Company, 1978), 177–183.

[6] AMORC—The Worldwide Rosicrucian Order, www.amorc.org, Oct. 25, 2005.

[7] Edmond C. Gruss, *Cults and the Occult* (P&R Publishing, 1994), 159, and Walter R. Martin, *The Kingdom of the Cults*. Ravi Zacharias, gen. ed. (Minneapolis: Bethany House Publishers, 2003), 645.

[8] George A. Mather and Larry A. Nichols, *Dictionary of Cults, Sects, Religions and the Occult* (Grand Rapids, Mich.: Zondervan Publishing House, 1993), 234.

[9] Charles Walker, *The Encyclopedia of Secret Knowledge* (London: Random House, 1995), 32.

[10] H. Spencer Lewis, *Rosicrucian Manual* (San Jose, Calif.: Rosicrucian Press, 1947), 42, cited in Edmond C. Gruss, *Cults and the Occult*, 161.

[11] Robert S. Ellwood Jr., "Rosicrucians," in *Abingdon Dictionary of Living Religions*, Keith Crim, ed. (Nashville: Abingdon, 1981), 631.

[12] "Rosicrucian," in *The New Encyclopaedia Britannica, Micropaedia*, Vol. 10 (Chicago: Encyclopaedia Britannica, Inc., 1993), 188.

[13] Ibid.

[14] Ellwood, 631.

[15] Melton, 178.

[16] *The New Encyclopaedia Britannica, Micropaedia*, Vol. 10, 188.

[17] Melton, 178.

[18] Ibid., 179.

[19] Ibid., 180.

[20] see listing of major Rosicrucian Orders under "Rosicrucians," Mather and Nichols, 235.

[21] www.amorc.org, July 5, 1997.

[22] Ibid.

[23] Max Heindel, *The Rosicrucian Christianity Lectures* (Oceanside, Calif.: The Rosicrucian Fellowship, 1939), 227.

[24] R. Swinburne Clymer, *The Teachings of the Masters: The Wisdom of the Ages* (Quakertown, Pa.: The Philosophical Publishing Company, 1952), 11.

[25] G. W. Bromiley, "Trinity," in *Evangelical Dictionary of Theology*, Walter A. Elwell, ed. (Grand Rapids, Mich.: Baker Book House, 1984), 1,112.

[26] Clymer, 11.

[27] Martin (1985), 509–510.

[28] Ibid., 265–266.

[29] For discussion of this subject see G. L. Borchert, "Gnosticism," in *Evangelical Dictionary of Theology*, 444–447.

[30] Clymer, 11.

[31] Ibid., 26.

[32] Ibid., 27.

[33] Ibid., 18.

[34] H. Spencer Lewis, *Rosicrucian Questions and Answers with Complete History of the Rosicrucian Order* (San Jose, Calif.: Supreme Grand Lodge of AMORC, Inc., 1929, 1941, 1965, 1971, 1977), 258.

[35] *The Living Christ; His People . . . His Church* (Quakertown, Pa.: The Church of the Illumination, 1955), 40.

[36] H. Spencer Lewis, *Mansions of the Soul: A Cosmic Conception* (San Jose, Calif.: Rosicrucian Press, 1930), 58.

[37] R. Swinburne Clymer, *A Compendium of Occult Laws* (Quakertown, Pa.: The Philosophical Publishing Company, 1938), 267.

[38] Heindel, 20.

[39] Ibid.

[40] Ibid., 326.

[41] Ibid.

[42] Ibid., 326–327.

[43] Ibid., 14.

[44] *The Living Christ,* 51.

[45] Ibid., 53.

CHAPTER TEN

Secular Humanism

"Sixty years ago could we have imagined that unborn children would be killed by the millions here in our own country? Or that we would have *no freedom of speech* when it comes to speaking of God and biblical truth in our public schools? Or that every form of sexual perversion would be promoted by the entertainment media? Or that marriage, raising children, and family life would be objects of attack?"[1] These words, written by the late Francis Schaeffer in 1984, seem even more applicable today than when he wrote them.

After raising these questions, Schaeffer concluded, "Sadly we must say that very few Christians have understood the battle that we are in."[2]

The stakes are high. There is reason for alarm because the battle is being waged on the front lines of spiritual warfare, and the enemies of biblical Christianity rejoice over any ground they gain as the atheistic viewpoint of secular humanism continues to spread. "One of the most significant historical dilemmas of the twentieth century has been the collapse of Western Christianity, especially in the United States," says John Whitehead, a leading constitutional attorney in America.[3]

But what can possibly be wrong with humanism, you ask. Generally, humanism is associated with being humane, about caring for others. But that is where the difficulty first arises—understanding what the terminology means as well as understanding the background and beliefs that have brought us to this present stage of spiritual warfare.

BACKGROUND

As Delos McKown points out in *The Humanist*, the chief periodical promoting contemporary secular humanism, the word *human* was originally spelled "humane."[4] McKown goes on to say that what is believed—or not believed—by secular humanists today is far more specific than just being humane to other human beings.

What They Believe

Encyclopaedia Britannica explains: "In recent years the term *humanism* has often been used to refer to value systems that emphasize the personal worth of each individual but that do not include a belief in God. There is a certain segment of the Unitarian Universalist Association that is nontheistic and yet uses religious forms to promote distinctive human values."[5]

What makes things even more confusing is that there are several kinds of humanism. Christian apologist Norman Geisler refers to nine varieties of humanism: evolutionary, behavioral, existential, pragmatic, Marxist, egocentric, cultural, Christian and secular.[6] By examining the common views of the different kinds of humanism, Geisler shows where humanism conflicts with biblical Christianity.

Important terms that need to be understood in the debate include not only *humanism* but also *theistic, atheistic* (or *nontheistic*) and *secular.*

The Greek word for "God" is *theos*, from which is derived the word *theist*—that is, one who believes in God. The Greek language negates a word by placing an "a" before it, such as in the term *asocial* to refer to someone who is not social. Thus, an atheist is one who does not believe in God. Literature of contemporary secular humanists also frequently uses the term *nontheist*—a neutral-sounding term that tends to moderate the fact that they are actually anti-theists. A true nontheist would simply ignore God, but the literature of secular humanists reveals their preoccupation with attacking God and every concept related to Him.

A vast difference exists between humanism that is theistic and secular humanism that is nontheistic or atheistic. Humanist McKown states, "Secular humanists, in short, are agnostic or atheistic."[7]

How did we get to a situation in North America where atheism is replacing theism as the dominant belief? An astute observer of the beliefs and history of American religious groups, J. Gordon Melton observes, "In the early twentieth century an aggressive humanist orientation developed among supporters of the American Unitarian Association, the Free Religious Association, and the American Ethical Union. At the time, members of these groups were still theistic. By the 1920s, however, some Unitarians had become anti-theists."[8]

The Unitarians (now Unitarian Universalists) have figured prominently in the promotion of secular humanism in North America. Edd

Doerr, in reviewing books in *The Humanist*, stated, "Half of the signers of the 1933 *Humanist Manifesto I* were Unitarian Universalist ministers, as were the first four presidents of the American Humanist Association, the AHA's first executive director, and this journal's first editor."[9] Doerr further commented, "There has been a long overlapping then, between organized humanism and the Unitarian Universalist movement."[10] After referring to various surveys, Doerr noted "that at least three-fourths of all Unitarian Universalists are humanists, making the UUA the largest organization of humanists in the United States."[11]

The Unitarian Universalist Association (UUA) is not a large group, relatively speaking. Its 214,738 members are found in 1,010 congregations.[12] But numbers are not as important as the strategic and influential places of leadership that humanists hold.

In his book *What Is Secular Humanism?*, historian James Hitchcock addresses the shift in worldviews held by Americans. The period from just before the Civil War until World War II was a time of theism. "Even most non-church members believed in God and were respectful of the Bible and other kinds of religious authority," writes Hitchcock.[13] This is not to say that everyone was a Christian in the biblical sense, but the country was theistic in its worldview.

THE PERIOD FROM JUST BEFORE THE CIVIL WAR UNTIL WORLD WAR II WAS A TIME OF THEISM.

"The period 1945–1965," Hitchcock continues, "was a morally conservative time in American life. Traditional values were publicly honored and to a considerable extent lived by."[14] Still mainly theistic in worldview, the country emphasized high family values during these two decades.

Hitchcock sees 1965–1970 as a significant time of shifting worldviews in the United States. "Common attitudes, and especially the kinds of attitudes which are regarded as respectable, underwent a swift change between 1965 and 1970. Although it was perhaps only a minority who were most affected, they were the trendsetters. They either had little interest in religion or were hostile to it. They either rejected traditional morality or were willing to compromise it endlessly."[15] Perhaps the "me generation" was a logical consequence for a Western culture that embraced evolution, which made man the highest creature totally apart from a supernatural God.

These attitudes provided fertile soil for the atheistic views of secular humanism to grow. The "me generation" meshed perfectly with what humanists believe: "As secular humanists we believe in the central importance of the value of human happiness here and now."[16]

But organized humanism was far from new. In 1933 a group of 34 American humanists set forth their philosophy and beliefs in 15 affirmations called the *Humanist Manifesto I*. Melton summarizes this document: "The statement called for a radical change in religious perspectives. Religion was seen as a tool for realizing the highest values in life. A religion adequate to the twentieth century regards the universe as self-existing, not created, and regards man as part of nature evolved in its processes. Mind-body dualism, supernaturalism, theism, and even deism are rejected."[17]

The American Humanist Association was formed in 1941 "to bring some coordination and fellowship nationally to the various independent humanist efforts."[18]

Forty years after the signing of *Humanist Manifesto I*, humanists from many countries signed *Humanist Manifesto II*, which had 17 affirmations. Geisler comments on *Humanist Manifesto II*: "Like its predecessor, the second manifesto is atheistic, naturalistic, evolutionistic, socialistic, relativistic, and still optimistic that man can save himself. There is, however, a much stronger international emphasis in the second statement."[19]

This should not surprise anyone who realizes the Western world has long taught the evolutionary theory of origins. Anyone who believes that by chance and long ages, totally apart from a miracle-working God, mankind came on the scene is humanistic to the core. And to believe in such an evolutionary theory is to make a blind leap of faith. But how did such humanistic views originate? "Humanism traces its roots from ancient China, classical Greece and Rome, through the Renaissance and the Enlightenment, to the scientific revolution of the modern world," says *Humanist Manifestos I and II*.[20] In fact, secular humanism is also called "scientific humanism or naturalistic human-ism," acknowledges McKown.[21]

Whereas the term *humanism* makes man the measure of all things, Whitehead explains that "the word 'secular' comes from the Latin *saecularis*, meaning 'a race, generation, age, the times of the world.' Its basic meaning is this: The secular is the worldly or temporal as against the spiritual or eternal."[22]

For those who think that secular humanism is not to be taken seri-ously, Whitehead warns, "Secularism is a closed system. As such, it will eventually seek to eliminate alternative viewpoints. The secular state wants no competition in the arena of ideas."[23] This is common among groups that claim to be broadminded and progressive: they cannot permit the freedom of a more narrow view, only of a broader view. So believers in Christ and the Bible can expect opposition to their views even by those who supposedly welcome all views.

The roots of secular humanism show the shift in worldviews that has brought us to this time of spiritual warfare. It is the beliefs of sec-ular humanism, however, that reveal how antagonistic it is to biblical Christianity and how intense the spiritual struggle really is.

BELIEFS

In comparing the beliefs of secular humanism with biblical Christianity, we must evaluate what each says concerning source of authority, religion, God, Jesus Christ, man, sin, salvation and the future life.

SOURCE OF AUTHORITY

Biblical Christianity accepts the Bible—and the Bible alone—as its final authority. It is the standard by which all doctrines and practices are judged. The 39 books of the Old Testament and the 27 books of the New Testament are held to be inspired by God in the original manuscripts (Matt. 5:18; 2 Tim. 3:16; 2 Pet. 1:21).

Secular humanists strongly oppose any special consideration of the Bible as the Word of God. Those who hold a high position of the Bible are called "bibliolaters" by the secular humanists.[24] "To accept the Bible as inerrant," they say, "is to be committed to a belief in false-hoods and contradictions."[25] Furthermore, let there be no misunderstanding: Secular humanists in key positions of leadership in government, media and the public education system will do all they can to stamp out biblical Christianity.

Even though the Bible has given timeless truths, which are as relevant

in the 21st century as they were in the first, the humanists ridicule the Bible as being hopelessly out-of-date. They seem to forget that their own *Humanist Manifesto I* had to be revised in a short 40 years because it was considered out-of-date by the humanists themselves. They were forced to admit that "it did not go far enough. It did not and could not address itself to future problems and needs."[26]

TO THE SECULAR MIND-SET, THERE IS NO SUCH THING AS ABSOLUTE TRUTH.

The preface of *Humanist Manifesto II* states: "It is forty years since *Humanist Manifesto I* (1933) appeared. Events since then make that earlier statement seem far too optimistic. Nazism has shown the depth of brutality of which humanity is capable."[27]

And the ink on the 1973 *Humanist Manifesto II* was hardly dry when they decided another declaration was needed, so *A Secular Humanist Declaration* was drafted by Paul Kurtz, endorsed by 58 humanists and published in 1980.

Not only do the humanists fail to acknowledge the weak authority and short span of their own finite views, but they also fail to realize that Nazism under Adolf Hitler, to which they refer, was influenced by humanism, not religion. Hitler was thoroughly an evolutionist, and social Darwinism took its awful toll under his regime.[28]

Not only is the Bible rejected as the final authority, but neither can truth serve as the humanists' source of authority. To the secular mind-set, there is no such thing as absolute truth—although humanists make absolute statements about everything being relative. *Humanist Manifesto I* says: "Humanism . . . does insist that the way to determine the existence and value of any and all realities is by means of intelligent inquiry and by the assessment of their relation to human needs."[29] This is situation ethics—that right and wrong depend on the situation. There are no moral absolutes; everything is relative.

"Under relativism," says John Whitehead, "the concepts of truth and nontruth become blurred. As a consequence, people, once they accept relativism, by definition cannot know what the truth is. Instead, they can only guess as to the best course to follow. Thus, it becomes easier to sell nontruth to such a society."[30] With the shift in worldviews in the United States, perhaps we should not be surprised by politicians and others who claim to have done no wrong. Having been educated in the religious views of secular humanism, most of them probably do not believe there is a standard for right and wrong.

In emphasizing the importance of free inquiry, the humanists say, "The guiding premise of those who believe in free inquiry is that truth is more likely to be discovered if the opportunity exists for the free exchange of opposing opinions."[31] Yet humanists strongly oppose the "free exchange of opposing opinions" of those who believe in God and consider Him to be the Creator of humanity and the universe. Like Pilate of old, they ask, "What is truth?" (John 18:38). And also like Pilate, they reject the One who said, "I am the way, the truth, and the life. No one comes to the Father except through Me" (John 14:6).

The Bible also declares, "The heart is deceitful above all things, and desperately wicked; who can know it?" (Jer. 17:9). Thinking individuals know by experience and observation that this statement is true. Yet humanists say, "Secular humanism places trust in human intelligence rather than in divine guidance."[32]

Secular humanists deify man by placing his needs and experiences above the authority of God's Word. They boldly declare, "We believe … that traditional dogmatic or authoritarian religions that place revelation, God, ritual, or creed above human needs and experience do a disservice to the human species."[33]

RELIGION

Most secular humanists disdain religion in general and God in particular. McKown, writing in *The Humanist*, says, "Informed people of good will must recognize that secular humanism is not a religion but a system of disbelief in all religions."[34]

McKown seems not to remember that the United States Supreme Court has decreed that secular humanism is a religion.[35] Specifically, in the case of *Torcaso v. Watkins* (1961), the Supreme Court justices identified secular humanism as a religion: "Among religions in this country which do not teach what would generally be considered a belief in the existence of God are Buddhism, Taoism, Ethical Culture, Secular Humanism and others."[36]

In 1987 U.S. District Court Judge W. Brevard Hand banned more than 40 textbooks from the Alabama school system because they taught the religion of Secular Humanism. *Christianity Today* reported that the judge had issued the ruling in the "class-action suit brought by 624 Christian parents and teachers in Mobile County. They charged that the state had illegally established secular humanism as a religion by using texts that minimize or ignore the role of religion in American history and contemporary culture."[37]

Concerning separation of church and state, *The Secular Humanist Declaration* says, "The lessons of history are clear: wherever one religion or ideology is established and given a dominant position in the state, minority opinions are in jeopardy. A pluralistic, open, and democratic society allows all points of view to be heard."[38] But the humanists disregard their own statement when Christians speak up about the teaching of values, origins and sex education. The theistic view of Christians is quickly becoming the minority opinion in jeopardy.

Secular humanists believe that the state "should not favor any particular religious bodies through the use of public monies, nor espouse a single ideology and function thereby as an instrument of propaganda or oppression, particularly against dissenters."[39] But they do not believe the state should discriminate against their views. The atheistic view of the secular humanists is fast becoming—if it has not already become—the unofficial state religion of the United States, for it is taught in the public schools from kindergarten through the graduate level. Although many Christian teachers and administrators contribute positively to students in the system, the underlying beliefs of the public school system serve as enemies of the gospel of Christ. Furthermore, that which is now most successfully competing with atheistic views for dominance in the public school classroom is not the theistic views of Christians but the pantheistic views of the New Age Movement. There is a continuing shift from believing in no god to believing everything is god.

Secular humanists somehow feel compelled to commend various religions, yet they have the underlying suspicion that religion is responsible for many, if not most, of the evils in the world. "Although [religions] have helped to build hospitals and schools and, at their best, have encouraged the spirit of love and charity," they say, "many have also caused human suffering by being intolerant of those who did not accept their dogmas or creeds."[40]

Historian James Hitchcock reminds us, "Secular Humanists have often manipulated public opinion in their favor by charging that religion has a history of bloody persecution, while Humanism has always been tolerant."[41] But he continues, "Modern Secular Humanism has been stained with blood from its very birth."[42] Referring to the so-called Reign of Terror in the mid-1790s after the French Revolution, for example, during which thousands of Frenchmen were guillotined, Hitchcock writes: "At first the Revolution seemed willing to tolerate the church if the clergy would promise to be loyal to the regime. Soon the government embarked on a systematic 'de-Christianizing' campaign. Churches were closed and converted to profane uses, like stables for horses. Religious symbols were destroyed. The religious press was outlawed. All religious services were forbidden. Priests and nuns were rounded up in large numbers and sent into exile, imprisoned, or executed. The aim of the government was to wipe out every remaining vestige of Christianity."[43]

Let us not be so naive as to think that secular humanists have always been tolerant or that they are now tolerant of those who embrace biblical Christianity.

Humanists also think that religion should bow to the authority of science. Part of the fifth affirmation of *Humanist Manifesto I* says: "Religion must formulate its hopes and plans in the light of the scientific spirit and method."[44] In their zeal to dethrone religion with its supernatural God, the secular humanists have made science their god.

GOD

By their own admission, "secular humanists may be agnostics, atheists, rationalists, or skeptics, but they find insufficient evidence for the claim that some divine purpose exists for the universe. They reject the idea that God has intervened miraculously in history or revealed himself to a chosen few, or that he can save or redeem sinners."[45]

The anti-God stand of the humanists is underscored by their statement that "secular humanists have no dealings with the sacred and do not believe in either the divine or the demonic."[46]

What They Believe

Furthermore, the preface to *Humanist Manifesto II* says, "As in 1933, humanists still believe that traditional theism, especially faith in the prayer-hearing God, assumed to love and care for persons, to hear and understand their prayers, and to be able to do something about them, is an unproved and outmoded faith."[47]

From this statement, one would assume that the humanists believe only what is provable. They are intellectually dishonest, however, because they believe in evolution, which is unprovable by the scientific method that they hold as their authority. For instance, in order for evolution to have occurred, nonliving matter had to produce living matter. Since the days of Louis Pasteur (1822–1895), science has taught that such spontaneous generation is impossible. To believe in evolution in spite of this scientific knowledge is to take a blind leap of faith, unsupported by any evidence. But secular humanists, with their atheistic presuppositions, cannot explain origins in any other way.

While secular humanists say that they "recognize the importance of religious experience,"[48] they also say, "We deny, however, that such experiences have anything to do with the supernatural."[49] Because humanists do not recognize the supernatural—either divine or demonic—they must give everything a naturalistic explanation. This eliminates God from the classrooms and negates any moral accountability to a supreme being.

JESUS CHRIST

Biblical Christianity accepts that Jesus Christ is God. The Council of Nicea in A.D. 325 condemned as heresy the views of Arius, who taught that Jesus Christ is not God. Although his views continued to flourish for a while, by A.D. 381 "the question was officially settled by the church."[50]

Secular humanists, on the other hand, declare, "We reject the divinity of Jesus, the divine mission of Moses, Mohammed, and other latter-day prophets and saints of the various sects and denominations."[51]

Because the humanists do not believe in the supernatural, they do not believe that Jesus Christ is God and that the Bible, which tells about Him, is reliable. As the apostle John wrote about Jesus, "He came to His own, and His own did not receive Him" (John 1:11). Fortunately for us John added, "But as many as received Him, to them

He gave the right to become children of God, to those who believe in His name" (v. 12).

MAN

The second affirmation of *Humanist Manifesto I* states, "Humanism believes that man is a part of nature and that he has emerged as the result of a continuous process."[52]

A Secular Humanist Declaration states, "Although the theory of evolution cannot be said to have reached its final formulation, or to be an infallible principle of science, it is nonetheless supported impressively by the findings of many sciences."[53]

Bowing at the throne of science and technology, secular humanists "believe the scientific method, though imperfect, is still the most reliable way of understanding the world."[54] Christians should not be so quick to think that something is true just because some "scientist" has declared it so. Many scientists are creationists, but the impression of the man on the street is that only the evolutionary theory is scientific.

HUMANISTS DECEIVE THEMSELVES IF THEY THINK THE THEORY OF EVOLUTION IS ESTABLISHED BY THE "SCIENTIFIC METHOD."

Yet humanists deceive themselves if they think the theory of evolution is established by the "scientific method." Henry Morris, a trained scientist (Ph.D., University of Minnesota) and founder of the Institute for Creation Research, explains: "True science is supposed to be observable, measurable, and repeatable. Evolution, however, even if it were true, is too slow to observe or measure and has consisted of unique, non-repeatable events of the past. It is therefore outside the scope of genuine science and has certainly not been *proven* by science"[55] (emphasis his).

Humanists claim to be advocates of the freedom of speech and academic freedom, but they want to restrict the rights of others to express views that represent a theistic point of view concerning origins.

Some humanists are so insecure about their beliefs and threatened by a free exchange of ideas about origins that they say, "If successful, creationists may seriously undermine the credibility of science itself."[56]

Humanists confuse the facts of science with the interpretation of scientific data. Scientists must deal with the available data. Theories about how the data originated are not part of the pure discipline of science. If they were, all scientists would have to be either creationists or evolutionists to be competent. But the university system of the United States has both creationists and evolutionists who are competent scientists. This is because serious scientists are not dealing with theories of origins but with what is "observable, measurable, and repeatable."[57] If secular humanists were intellectually honest, they would tell you that the theory of origins is beyond the scientific process; that evolution is based on faith just as creationism is; and that when a scientist talks about origins he is in the field of philosophy and religion, not science.

A good example of a non-scientific statement by scientists is what was said about photos from the Pathfinder spacecraft, which landed on Mars on July 4, 1997. Reported by the *Orlando Sentinel*, the statement reads: "A flood of biblical proportions—enough to fill the Mediterranean Sea—gushed down from the highlands of Mars a billion or so years ago, the latest pictures from the Pathfinder spacecraft confirmed Monday."[58] That is quite a statement for those who don't even believe in a biblical flood! And no scientist working with what is observable, measurable and repeatable could ever agree to such a statement about a flood on Mars "a billion or so" years ago. Do not be mistaken. The conflict in views is not between science and religion; it is a conflict between two religious views—atheism and theism.

Morris wrote in 1989, "That humanism is merely a more genteel term for atheism is confirmed by the current president of the American Humanist Association, Dr. Isaac Asimov, who is also probably the most prolific writer in the whole world of science, having authored approximately three hundred books, covering every scientific field." Morris cited a 1982 interview in which Asimov said, "I am an atheist, out and out. It took me a long time to say it. I've been an atheist for years and years."[59]

Although secular humanists claim to believe in academic freedom, their practice betrays their true feelings. They believe that only the various views about the origins of life that are based on the theory of evolution should be taught in the classroom. (The views are various because evolutionists do not agree among themselves.)

Strangely, humanists think that allowing theists to speak on these issues would endanger academic freedom. When a group is afraid to let others address an issue, it indicates the adherents are unsure of the validity of their position. Those who believe in a standard for truth don't believe truth will be hurt by letting others express their views, no matter how erroneous those views are. But notice how insecure the humanists are: "We deplore the efforts by fundamentalists . . . to invade the science classrooms, requiring that creationist theory be taught to students and requiring that it be included in biology textbooks. This is a serious threat both to academic freedom and to the integrity of the educational process."[60]

How strange that the expression of different views is a "threat . . . to academic freedom." Unless differing views are allowed to be expressed, there is no such thing as academic freedom. This clearly reveals that the humanists are for freedom of speech and academic freedom for atheistic views of secular humanism, but not for the theistic views of others.

Free-speech attorney Whitehead, of the Rutherford Institute, says, "If religious people do not regain their right to free speech in the public schools and other public places, then religion will be totally *privatized*, much as it is in countries like the Soviet Union. There 'freedom' of religion is allowed only in a controlled church"[61] (emphasis his).

The evolutionary view is an endeavor to explain what exists completely apart from a miracle-working God. The public schools, under the domination of secular humanists, shelter their students by presenting only one main view of origins. In this regard private Christian schools actually present a broader education because most of them explain not only what creationists say about origins but also what evolutionists say.

Humanists also contradict themselves about human life. On the one hand they say, "The preciousness and dignity of the individual person is a central humanist value."[62] Yet on the other hand they say that the "right to . . . abortion . . . should be recognized."[63] How does killing an unborn child maintain "the preciousness and dignity of the individual person"?

What They Believe

This is how secular humanists justify abortion: "We have found no convincing evidence that there is a separable 'soul' or that it exists before birth or survives death."[64]

Concerning sexual behavior, secular humanists say, "Without countenancing mindless permissiveness or unbridled promiscuity, a civilized society should be a *tolerant* one"[65] (emphasis theirs). What is actually practiced, however, is that sexual behavior that deviates from the biblical norm is tolerated, but attitudes about sexual behavior based on the Bible are not tolerated. Movies and television programs that present aberrant sexual behavior are justified in this pluralistic society by those who claim various views must be presented and that attempts to restrict are "censorship."

SIN

Biblical Christianity believes that "all have sinned and fall short of the glory of God" (Rom. 3:23). This is because sin has been passed down to us from Adam: "Just as through one man sin entered the world, and death through sin, and thus death spread to all men, because all sinned" (Rom. 5:12). We are not only sinners by nature, but we are also sinners by action. All of us need forgiveness of sin and eternal life.

Secular humanism believes none of this. When man is deified on the one hand, or only considered a high-level animal on the other hand, there is no such thing as sin. The view that man is only a high-level animal is seen frequently in explaining why man behaves like he does. It is seen in the explanation of the 29 marriages of Glynn Wolfe, who made it into the *Guinness Book of World Records* as the world's most married man. As one anthropologist said of Wolfe, "This behavior was an evolutionary throwback unable to quell his primitive craving for endless variety in partners."[66]

Instead of recognizing any corruptness of the human heart, humanists boast, "We are responsible for what we are or will be."[67] Whatever one thinks about sin influences what he believes about salvation.

SALVATION

If there is no such thing as sin, there is nothing from which to be saved. Humanists think they need no salvation apart from themselves because whatever needs they have can be met by their own efforts.

In his preface about *Humanist Manifesto II*, Paul Kurtz wrote, "What more pressing need than to recognize in this critical age of modern science and technology that, if no deity will save us, we must save ourselves?"[68]

No one will ever become right with God by self-works. The apostle Paul reminded believers, "By grace you have been saved through faith, and that not of yourselves; it is the gift of God, not of works, lest anyone should boast" (Eph. 2:8–9).

In the first century there were those who thought they could become right with God through the works of the Law. But Paul reminded them that "by the deeds of the law no flesh will be justified in His sight, for by the law is the knowledge of sin" (Rom. 3:20).

To the anti-theist positions of *Humanist Manifestos I and II, A Secular Humanist Declaration* added its voice by affirming that secular humanists "reject the idea that God . . . can save or redeem sinners."[69]

Furthermore, evangelicals need to realize that humanists do not believe their biblical views make a positive contribution to themselves or to society. On the contrary, humanists believe, "Salvationism, based on mere affirmation, still appears as harmful, diverting people with false hopes of heaven hereafter."[70] Secular educators and psychologists view evangelicals as those who have been harmed, not helped, by their faith in a God who provides salvation. "Promises of immortal salvation or fear of eternal damnation are both illusory and harmful," say the secularists.[71] This is hardly encouraging news for evangelicals getting ready to attend their next PTA meeting.

FUTURE LIFE

Biblical Christianity teaches that everyone will be resurrected after death. It believes that all who accept God's offer of salvation through Christ will enjoy eternal bliss, but all who reject the salvation He offers will suffer eternal judgment. All who believe in Jesus Christ for salvation have forgiveness of sins and eternal life. "He who believes in Him [God's Son] is not condemned; but he who does not believe is condemned already, because he has not believed in the name of the only begotten Son of God" (John 3:18).

But, as mentioned before, secular humanists boldly say, "We have found no convincing evidence that there is a separable 'soul' or that it

. . . survives death."[72] In this view, man is no more than an animal. But the Bible reveals that every person has an eternal destiny—either in heaven or hell (Matt. 25:46; John 5:29).

CONCLUSION

What must Christians do if Christianity is to survive with vitality? John Whitehead says, "Christians have been drawn off into many minor battles because they lack priorities. If we are to survive the coming years, it will be because Christians and others have focused on the key issues."[73]

Whitehead says the key issues in the order of their importance are "the sanctity of human life; the protection of the traditional family, the church and the private school; the freedom of the public arena (including public schools); and the need to assist those who are oppressed for their faith in totalitarian states."[74]

As Francis Schaeffer so aptly put it, "If the truth of the Christian faith is in fact *truth*, then it stands in antithesis to the ideas and the immorality of our age, and it must be *practiced* both in teaching and practical action"[75] (emphasis his).

Concerning the matter of truth, Schaeffer wrote so eloquently: "Here is the great evangelical disaster—the failure of the evangelical world to stand for truth as truth. There is only one word for this—namely *accommodation*: the evangelical church has accommodated to the world spirit of the age"[76] (emphasis his).

Schaeffer especially lamented that many who call themselves evangelicals no longer take a strong stand for all that the Bible teaches nor on matters of life and death.[77]

As Geisler summarizes concerning the secular humanists, "Although they claim to be humane, they promote the killing of innocent life (abortion, euthanasia). Although they claim to be scientific, they violate basic laws of science. Although they claim to be rational, they violate fundamental principles of reason. Although they claim that all ethics is relative, they do so with an absolute statement. In the final analysis, then, secular humanism is not a consistent position."[78]

The basic problem of the secular humanists is that they have "exchanged the truth of God for the lie, and worshiped and served the creature rather than the Creator" (Rom. 1:25).

Christians are engaged in a spiritual warfare. Worldviews in North America have shifted from theism to atheism—and even to pantheism of the New Age Movement. Freedom of speech for the believers of biblical Christianity is being lost. More than ever we need to heed the apostle Paul's injunctions concerning spiritual warfare:

> Be strong in the Lord and in the power of His might. Put on the whole armor of God, that you may be able to stand against the wiles of the devil. For we do not wrestle against flesh and blood, but against principalities, against powers, against the rulers of the darkness of this age, against spiritual hosts of wickedness in the heavenly places. Therefore take up the whole armor of God, that you may be able to withstand in the evil day, and having done all, to stand (Eph. 6:10–13).

Summary

Name: Secular Humanists
Also Known As: Humanists
Headquarters: American Humanist Association
                     Washington, D.C.
Web sites: www.americanhumanist.org
Publication: *The Humanist Magazine*
                     www.thehumanist.org

What They Believe

Secular Humanists: **Biblical Christians:**

Source of Authority

Make absolute statements about all truth being relative. Human needs, experience and science are above revelation, God, ritual or creed.

The Bible alone is final authority. It is the standard by which everything else is judged.

What They Believe

Religion

Claim not to be a religion, even though the U.S. Supreme Court has declared Secular Humanism is a religion. Foundation of beliefs is atheism—that there is no God.

Admit being a religion based on the teachings and works of the Lord Jesus Christ. Foundation of beliefs is theism—that God exists and created the universe.

God

Do not believe in either the divine or the demonic.

Believe in the almighty, sovereign God as revealed in the Bible.

Jesus Christ

Jesus Christ is not a supernatural Person.

Jesus Christ is a divine Person, the second member of the Trinity and the Messiah of Israel.

Man

Man is a product of biological evolution. Claim to be advocates of free speech but are not open to those who present theistic view of man's origin.

God created man in His own image. Believe that for the sake of intellectual fairness creationism should get an equal opportunity to be expressed along with evolutionary theory.

Sin

Sin does not exist.

All people are sinners by nature and actions and have fallen short of God's standards.

Salvation

No deity will save humans; people must save themselves, even though they don't think there is anything to be saved from. Believe that teaching about salvation is harmful.

Salvation from eternal condemnation is possible only through believing in Jesus Christ. Only when one is right with God is he prepared to fully live for time and eternity.

Future Life

There is no future life and no convincing evidence a separable soul survives death.

A person is a spiritual being as well as a material being, and each person will live either in heaven or hell for eternity.

Recommended Reading

Bickel, Bruce, and Jantz, Stan. *World Religions & Cults 101: A Guide to Spiritual Beliefs.* Eugene, Ore.: Harvest House Publishers, 2002.

Geisler, Norman L., and Brooks, Ron. *When Skeptics Ask.* Wheaton, Ill.: Victor Books, 1990.

Halverson, Dean C., gen. ed. *The Compact Guide to World Religions.* Minneapolis: Bethany House Publishers, 1996.

Johnson, Phillip E. *Reason in the Balance: The Case against Naturalism in Science, Law & Education.* Downers Grove, Ill.: InterVarsity Press, 1995.

McDowell, Josh, and Stewart, Don. *Handbook of Today's Religions.* San Bernardino, Calif.: Here's Life Publishers, Inc., 1983.

Morris, Henry M. *The Long War against God: The History and Impact of the Creation/Evolution Conflict.* Grand Rapids, Mich.: Baker Book House, 1989.

Schaeffer, Francis A. *A Christian Manifesto.* Westchester, Ill.: Crossway Books, 1981.

_____. *The Great Evangelical Disaster.* Westchester, Ill.: Crossway Books, 1984.

ENDNOTES

[1] Francis A. Schaeffer, *The Great Evangelical Disaster* (Westchester, Ill.: Crossway Books, 1984), 23.

[2] Ibid.

[3] John W. Whitehead, *The End of Man* (Westchester, Ill.: Crossway Books, 1986), 16.

[4] Delos B. McKown, "Humanism, Disbelief, and Bibliolatry," in *The Humanist,* May/June 1990, 7.

[5] *Encyclopaedia Britannica, Micropaedia*, Vol. 6 (Chicago: Encyclopaedia Britannica, Inc., 1993), 137.

[6] Norman L. Geisler, *Is Man the Measure? An Evaluation of Contemporary Humanism* (Grand Rapids, Mich.: Baker Book House, 1983), 7.

[7] McKown, "Humanism, Disbelief, and Bibliolatry," in *The Humanist*, May/June 1990, 7.

[8] J. Gordon Melton, *The Encyclopedia of American Religions*, 2nd ed. (Detroit: Gale Research Company, 1987), 469.

[9] Edd Doerr, "Book Reviews," in *The Humanist*, May/June 1990, 45.

[10] Ibid.

[11] Ibid.

[12] *The World Almanac and Book of Facts 2005* (New York: World Almanac Education Group, Inc., 2005), 732.

[13] James Hitchcock, *What Is Secular Humanism? Why Humanism Became Secular and How It Is Changing Our World* (Ann Arbor, Mich.: Servant Books, 1982), 55.

[14] Ibid.

[15] Ibid., 60.

[16] *A Secular Humanist Declaration*, reprint from *Free Inquiry* magazine, Vol. 1 No. 1, Winter, 1980, 15.

[17] Melton, *The Encyclopedia of American Religions*, 469.

[18] Ibid.

[19] Geisler, *Is Man the Measure?*, 118.

[20] *Humanist Manifestos I and II*, Paul Kurtz, ed. (Buffalo, N.Y.: Prometheus Books, 1973), 15.

[21] McKown, "Humanism, Disbelief, and Bibliolatry," in *The Humanist*, May/June 1990, 7.

[22] John W. Whitehead, *The Stealing of America* (Westchester, Ill.: Crossway Books, 1983), 97.

[23] Ibid., 99.

[24] McKown, "Humanism, Disbelief, and Bibliolatry," in *The Humanist*, May/June 1990, 8.

[25] Ibid., 9.

[26] *Humanist Manifestos I and II*, 3.

[27] Ibid., 13.

[28] see Henry M. Morris, *The Long War against God: The History and Impact of the Creation/Evolution Conflict* (Grand Rapids, Mich.: Baker Book House, 1989), 75–80.

[29] *Humanist Manifestos I and II*, 8.

[30] Whitehead, *The Stealing of America*, 33.

[31] *A Secular Humanist Declaration*, 11.

[32] Ibid., 24.

[33] *Humanist Manifestos I and II*, 15–16.

[34] McKown, "Humanism, Disbelief, and Bibliolatry," in *The Humanist*, May/June 1990, p. 7.

[35] see Geisler, *Is Man the Measure?*, 162–165.

[36] Whitehead, cited in Geisler, *Is Man the Measure?*, 164.

[37] *Christianity Today*, April 3, 1987, 42.

[38] *A Secular Humanist Declaration*, 12.

[39] *Humanist Manifestos I and II*, 19–20.

[40] *A Secular Humanist Declaration*, 19

[41] Hitchcock, *What Is Secular Humanism?*, 41.

[42] Ibid., 41.

[43] Ibid.

[44] *Humanist Manifestos I and II*, 8.

[45] *A Secular Humanist Declaration*, 18.

[46] McKown, "Humanism, Disbelief, and Bibliolatry," in *The Humanist*, May/June 1990, p. 7.

[47] *Humanist Manifestos I and II*, 13.

[48] A *Secular Humanist Declaration*, 17.

[49] Ibid.

[50] "Arius," in *The Wycliffe Biographical Dictionary of the Church*, by Elgin Moyer, rev. by Earle E. Cairns (Chicago: Moody Press, 1982), 17.

[51] *A Secular Humanist Declaration*, 18.

[52] *Humanist Manifestos I and II*, 8.

[53] *A Secular Humanist Declaration*, 21.

[54] Ibid., 20.

[55] Morris, *The Long War against God*, 23.

[56] *A Secular Humanist Declaration*, 22.

[57] Morris, *The Long War against God*, 23.

[58] cited by the *Omaha World-Herald*, July 8, 1997, 6-A.

[59] Morris, *The Long War against God*, 114.

[60] *A Secular Humanist Declaration*, 21.

[61] Whitehead, *The Stealing of America*, 122.

[62] *Humanist Manifestos I and II*, 18.

[63] Ibid.

[64] *A Secular Humanist Declaration*, 19.

[65] *Humanist Manifestos I and II*, 18.

[66] *Los Angeles Times,* cited in the *Omaha World-Herald*, July 13, 1997, 5-A.

[67] *Humanist Manifestos I and II*, 23.

[68] Ibid., 3–4.

[69] *A Secular Humanist Declaration*, 18.

[70] *Humanist Manifestos I and II*, 13.

[71] Ibid., 16.

[72] *A Secular Humanist Declaration*, 19.

[73] Whitehead, *The Stealing of America*, 112.

[74] Ibid.

[75] Schaeffer, *The Great Evangelical Disaster*, 37.

[76] Ibid.

[77] Ibid.

[78] Geisler, *Is Man the Measure?*, 161.

CHAPTER ELEVEN

Seventh-day Adventists

If you're looking for a good neighbor, you would be pleased to live next to a Seventh-day Adventist. Members of this wholesome group are known for their emphasis on health, families, elementary and secondary schools, colleges and fine hospitals.

The teachings of the Seventh-day Adventists are not on the same level as the erroneous beliefs of other groups evaluated in this book, such as the Jehovah's Witnesses and the Latter Day Saints (Mormons). But there are enough concerns about the beliefs of Seventh-day Adventists that a chapter about them is necessary. On the one hand they seem to say what orthodox Christians believe; on the other hand they say things that make one wonder.

Ruth A. Tucker, associate professor of Missiology at Calvin Theological Seminary, says, "No reputable scholar would claim that the Seventh-day Adventists are 'cultic' to the same degree as the Mormons, for example. Yet the history, and even present-day doctrine, of this group could be said to have cultic characteristics."[1]

According to the Seventh-day Adventist Web site, in 2003 the church group had 53,502 churches in the world with a membership of baptized adults numbering nearly 13 million.[2] The *World Almanac and Book of Facts 2005* gives a U.S. membership for the Seventh-day Adventists of nearly 919,000.[3] As pointed out on the Adventist Web site, "Less than 10 percent of Seventh-day Adventists live in the United States."[4] The Adventists are a prominent part of the religious population in the Caribbean islands. For instance, those affiliated with the SDA Church rank in the top five denominations in the Bahamas, Barbados, British Virgin Islands, Cayman Islands, Jamaica, Puerto Rico, St. Lucia and the U.S. Virgin Islands. The only groups outranking the Adventists in four of these countries are Anglican (Barbados), United (Cayman Islands) and Roman Catholics (Jamaica and St. Lucia).[5]

What They Believe

The key primary sources that will be used for this evaluation of the Seventh-day Adventists are *Seventh-day Adventists Answer Questions on Doctrine, Annotated Edition: Notes with Historical and Theological Introduction by George R. Knight*[6]; *Handbook of Seventh-day Adventist Theology: Commentary Reference Series, Vol. 12*[7]; and *Seventh-day Adventists Believe . . . : A Biblical Exposition of 27 Fundamental Doctrines.*[8]

The term "Adventists" refers to those who especially emphasize the Second Advent of Christ. Not all Adventists are Seventh-day Adventists. According to the *Handbook of Denominations in the United States*, there are five Adventist groups: Advent Christian Church, Branch Davidians, Church of God General Conference, Church of God (Seventh Day), and the largest group, the Seventh-day Adventists.[9] In this chapter, a reference to "Adventists" means the Seventh-day Adventists.

In the church name, "Seventh-day" refers to the day on which they think all believers should worship. Rather than worshiping on the first day of the week (Sunday), on which the Lord Jesus Christ rose from the dead, they believe we should worship on the seventh-day (Saturday), as instructed in the Old Testament Mosaic Law. This idea is not original with James and Ellen White; Adventists were sold on the idea by another early SDA leader, Joseph Bates (1792–1872). This belief will be discussed later under "Sabbath-Keeping."

BACKGROUND

Although many people were involved in the early days of what became the Seventh-day Adventist Church, we will consider three specific individuals.

William Miller (1782–1849). A Baptist minister, William Miller was the leader of a group referred to as the "Millerites." This movement was the forerunner of modern Seventh-day Adventists. Miller was a zealous Bible student who yearned for the return of the Lord. As he studied the Scriptures, Miller interpreted the 2,300 days referred to in Daniel 8:14 to be literally 2,300 years. This verse says, "For two thousand three hundred days [lit., evenings and mornings]; then the sanctuary shall be cleansed."

But why did Miller interpret 2,300 days as being 2,300 years? There is no basis for interpreting "days" as "years" in Daniel 8:14. David R. Reagan was a professor of international law and politics before leaving that profession to preach the soon return of Christ, first on radio and now on his TV program, *Christ in Prophecy*. Regarding Miller's interpretation of Daniel 8:14, Reagan says:

> This is a prophecy about a prophetic type of the Antichrist, a Greek tyrant by the name of Antiochus Epiphanes, who stopped the sacrifices in the Jewish Temple in 168 BC. Many scholars believe the reference to 2,300 evenings and mornings refers to 1,150 days (composed of 1,150 mornings and evenings). If so, then the time period would constitute the three years and 55 days from Tishri 168 BC, when the sacrifices ceased, to Chislev 165 BC (December 25th), when the Temple was cleansed and the sacrifices resumed.
>
> But Miller ignored the context of the passage and jumped to the conclusion that the '2,300 evenings and mornings' stood for 2,300 days, which, in turn, were symbolic of 2,300 years. Then, assuming the date of the prophecy was 457 BC, Miller added 2,300 years and concluded that the Lord would return in 1843.[10]

MANY OF THE BE-LIEFS OF SEVENTH-DAY ADVENTISTS ARE BASED ON THEIR INTERPRETATION OF PROPHECY.

Miller estimated that Christ would return between March 21, 1843, and March 21, 1844. But why did he begin with a starting date of 457 B.C.? The Adventists agree that a key to the beginning date of the prophecy is the prophecy of the 70 Weeks of Daniel (9:24–27). The decree of Artaxerxes is commonly considered to have begun these 70 weeks. But the date others use for this decree is around 445, not 457 B.C.[11] Thus, the beginning date is crucial to Miller's reckoning.

This indicates that many of the beliefs of Seventh-day Adventists are based on their interpretation of prophecy. Commonly used terms in their writings are such words as *types, symbols* and *prefigures*. In fact, Tucker's chapter title for her evaluation of the beliefs of this group is, "Seventh-day Adventism: Eschatological Confusion."[12] There are legitimate types and symbols in the Bible, but they have to be based on the clear teaching of Scripture about those matters before one can properly interpret what the types and symbols mean. Without a plain passage on which to base one's teachings, types and symbols can be made to refer to about anything the interpreter wishes. In this regard, the true source of authority is not the Scriptures but the interpreter.

When Miller's date of Christ return passed, some of his followers attributed it to a miscalculation. They set another date: October 22, 1844. The appearance of the Savior still did not occur, however. This incident became known as the "Great Disappointment."

Miller became disillusioned, according to some, after the failure of his prediction. The Millerites disbanded and several smaller groups formed. The group that eventually developed into present-day Seventh-day Adventists took Miller's teachings and reinterpreted them. They said Miller was right about the time of the fulfillment of the prophecy, but that he was wrong about the event of Christ's visible return. Instead of Christ returning to the earth, they said, He changed His position in heaven from the Holy Place to the Holy of Holies to begin an investigative judgment. There is little evidence that Miller agreed with the theories and movements that developed from his teaching.

James S. White (1821–1881). Not as well known as his famous wife, James White had met Ellen Gould Harmon by the time of the Great Disappointment but their relationship developed later. They were married by a Justice of the Peace on August 30, 1846. James began to publish *Present Truth* in 1849 and took part in selecting the Seventh-day Adventist name in 1860.

Ellen G. White (1827–1915). Widely recognized as the prophetess of modern Seventh-day Adventists, Ellen G. White far outstripped her husband in importance to the movement.

Sadly, young Ellen was hit in the head with a stone thrown by a school mate. At first it was feared this might end her life. It did not, but it did end her formal schooling when she was only nine years old.

When she was 17, Ellen had the first of about 2,000 visions over her lifetime. More will be said about these visions under "Source of Authority." At 18, she married James White, and both were founders and leaders in what was to be the Seventh-day Adventist Church.

BELIEFS

Evangelicals have long been divided regarding the beliefs of the Seventh-day Adventists. The debate is about whether the Adventists should be considered as evangelicals or as a counterfeit religious group.

In 1957, in order to respond to questions posed by evangelicals, the SDA published *Seventh-day Adventists Answer Questions on Doctrine*, commonly referred to as *Questions on Doctrine*, or QOD. Some evangelical leaders, such as Walter Martin and Donald Barnhouse, accepted the explanations and welcomed the Seventh-day Adventists as fellow evangelicals. Others, such as M. R. De Haan, founder of Radio Bible Class (now RBC), remained unconvinced.

After analyzing *Questions on Doctrine*, theologian John Gerstner concluded, "We are sorry that after reading this volume we are still unconvinced of Seventh-day Adventists' adequate creedal orthodoxy."[13]

In 2003 Andrews University Press published an annotated edition of *Questions on Doctrine*. This volume, part of the Adventist Classic Library, reproduces the full text of the 1957 edition and has "Notes with Historical and Theological Introduction by George R. Knight." References to *Questions on Doctrine* in this presentation will be cited according to the page number(s) found in the annotated edition.

The Seventh-day Adventists agree with orthodox Christianity on many doctrines, but on others they differ. The special topics under consideration in this evaluation of their beliefs are source of authority, investigative judgment, Satan—the sin-bearer, annihilation of the wicked, soul sleep and Sabbath-keeping.

SOURCE OF AUTHORITY

Seventh-day Adventists claim to accept the Bible as final authority. In the introduction to their Fundamental Beliefs on their Web site, they say, "Seventh-day Adventists accept the Bible as their only creed."[14] This is also the belief of orthodox Christianity.

One cannot fully understand Seventh-day Adventists, however, without grasping how they view the many visions of Ellen G. White. Many of her teachings were based on these visions.

Under the heading of "The Gift of Prophecy" in the Fundamental Beliefs of SDA, it is emphasized that her writings "make clear that the Bible is the standard by which all teaching and experience must be tested."[15] On the surface, this statement agrees with orthodox Christianity, but the attitude of the Adventist Church toward her many visions seems to indicate something else. Even if one does not consider Seventh-day Adventists a counterfeit religious group, the strong emphasis on one woman's writings and visions is a cultic characteristic comparable with the Christian Scientists (Mary Baker Eddy), Jehovah's Witnesses (Charles Taze Russell) and the Mormons (Joseph Smith).

It is not unusual for Christian groups who believe in the gift of prophecy today to have many in their fellowship who exercise this gift. Strangely, however, SDA focuses the most attention—indeed, almost all the attention—on Ellen G. White, who passed away 90 years ago. There are many well-trained pastors and theologians in the SDA movement. Reading their works reveals their knowledge of the original languages of the Bible. Why are not some of them singled out as having the gift of prophecy?

We must evaluate to what extent White's visions are considered authoritative by the SDA church. For instance, a key reason that the Sabbath is strongly emphasized as the day of worship by the Adventists is because of one of her visions. When she was 19, she saw "the law of God in the ark of the heavenly sanctuary with a halo of light encircling the fourth commandment."[16] By this we see that the Adventists' belief in worshiping on the Sabbath is not just that it is mentioned in Exodus 20:8, but that White had a vision concerning it. This is an instance of looking beyond the Scripture for a source of authority. This goes beyond what biblical Christianity teaches.

The Seventh-day Adventists would have us believe that White's visions only corroborated what they already believed the Bible taught. But some of her visions had nothing to do with what is in the Scriptures. Nancy J. Vyhmeister serves on the SDA Biblical Research Institute Committee and is professor of missions at Andrews University. She wrote the first chapter in *Handbook of Seventh-day Adventist Theology* and refers to White's first vision when she was only 17. In this vision, Vyhmeister acknowledges that White saw "a representation of the journey of the Adventist people to heaven."[17] This is not in the Bible.

In another vision, White saw "the Second Advent and the glories of the New Jerusalem."[18] These topics are in the Bible, but what she saw in her vision may not be.

In her early 20s, she also had a vision that she and her husband, James, should begin to print what later became *Present Truth*.[19] This is not in the Bible.

Time magazine tells of dress rules resulting from visions that White had. "For ten years she struggled to get her Adventist sisters to wear their skirts nine inches above the floor, over long trousers. But her 'dress reform' caused complaints and embarrassment till a new vision told her to become silent on the subject. She gratefully complied."[20] These visions were not based on the Bible.

Yet it is stated that during the late 1840s the Whites attended Bible conferences and that at these meetings her visions corroborated the conclusions reached by studying the Bible, "leading to confidence in the positions taken."[21] If it is agreed by mature, knowledgeable Bible students that a position taken is based on the Scripture, why is it necessary to have it corroborated by a vision of one who had no formal education after age nine and had been having visions since she was 17? Can you imagine how quickly the leaders of SDA would discount my evaluation of their beliefs if they learned I had no formal education after age nine? And would it help if I had visions to support my views? I don't think so. Why, then, do they make such an exception for her?

The distinctive beliefs of orthodox Christianity were developed over the early centuries and have been expressed in The Apostles' Creed, The Nicene Creed, The Athanasian Creed and the Chalcedonian Definition. Some of these creeds resulted from "ecumenical councils"; that is, representatives of Christianity in the then-known world. These councils did not decide what was to be believed; they expressed what was commonly held by those who accept the Bible as the Word of God.

None of these creeds needed to be "corroborated" by visions. In this regard, the Seventh-day Adventists are outside of orthodox Christianity when they look especially to the visions of one woman to confirm their beliefs.

Seventh-day Adventists also have an unusual view of the inspiration of the Scriptures. Believers in Christ commonly use the word *inspira-*

tion in a non-theological sense as well as a theological sense. In a non-theological sense, some might say, "The composer of that music was inspired." In a theological sense, some would say, "The writers of

Scripture were inspired of God," and cite 2 Timothy 3:16 as a basis for their comments. This verse says, "All Scripture is given by inspiration of God, and is profitable for doctrine, for reproof, for correction, for instruction in righteousness."

When Seventh-day Adventists refer to Ellen G. White as "inspired," one must determine the sense in which they use the term. They make an attempt to distinguish her inspiration from that of the Scriptures, but they draw a very fine line—and sometimes an indistinguishable line—in making this distinction.

WHITE DID NOT BE-LIEVE THE WORDS OF THE BIBLE WERE INSPIRED, ONLY THE WRITERS.

White did not believe the words of the Bible were inspired, only the writers. She wrote, "It is not the words of the Bible that are inspired, but the men that were inspired. Inspiration acts not on the man's words or his expressions but on the man himself, who, under the influence of the Holy Ghost, is imbued with thoughts."[22]

Notice that her emphasis was on "thoughts," not "words." But a thought cannot be expressed apart from words, and to change the words is to change the thought. Evangelical Christianity believes in "verbal, plenary inspiration"—that the words of the entire Bible were God-breathed. It holds that God superintended in such a way that He produced an infallible record through fallible men, not that the men themselves were inspired.

Of her own writings, White said, "Although I am as dependent upon the Spirit of the Lord in writing my views as I am in receiving them, yet the words I employ in describing what I have seen are my own."[23]

When Adventists refer to the Scripture writers as being inspired, that makes what they believe about White similar to what she believed about the human authors of the Bible. It is common for the Adventists to refer to her as "inspired."

For instance, in 1971 her book *The Great Controversy* was distributed to Tennessee residents under the title *The Triumph of God's Love* (which is an example of the way the Adventists promote old material as if it is new). In a descriptive blurb on the back cover, the publishers told of her fame as an author and said, "She is considered to have been inspired of God."[24] The publishers referred to her in the same way she referred to the writers of Scripture.

And on their Web site, the Seventh-day Adventists say of White, "Her writings are a continuing and authoritative source of truth which provide for the church comfort, guidance, instruction, and correction.[25]

Notice their words about her writings being "a continuing . . . source of truth," as well as an "authoritative source of truth." This is an unusual claim. The evangelical world is thankful for the writings of past "giants" of the faith, but no one claims that their writings are a "continuing and authoritative source of truth." Only the Bible holds that high position in the minds of evangelicals.

Yet the SDA in the same paragraph say that her writings "also make clear that the Bible is the standard by which all teaching and experience must be tested." This seems like doublespeak and must be confusing to the followers of SDA. Are her writings a "continuing and authoritative source of truth," or is the Bible the "continuing and authoritative source of truth"?

And although White wrote the *Great Controversy* in 1888, Adventists still refer to it as "one of our standard works."[26]

The Seventh-day Adventists seek to distinguish between White's writings and those of biblical prophets, yet they see her "gift of prophecy" on a level with such people as John the Baptist.

Acknowledging that White is not on the same level as the writers of canonical Scripture (those accepted as inspired books of the Bible), Seventh-day Adventists indicate there were many other prophets in the Old Testament and "Simeon, John the Baptist, Agabus, and Silas in the New." And of this list of New Testament prophets, the church says, "It is in this latter category of messengers that we consider Ellen G. White to be."[27]

But again we must ask, why are the Seventh-day Adventists still focusing on the visions and testimonies of one who died 90 years ago?

Two books were published in 1976 and 1982 that hit the Seventh-day Adventists like bombshells. These books were written by men who had been sympathetic to the teachings of White, but they sought to know the truth about her revelations and why her writings were so similar to other authors who wrote before her visions were published.

In 1976 Ronald L. Numbers, whose late father was an SDA minister, published *Prophetess of Health: A Study of Ellen G. White*. Numbers had a complete Adventist parochial education and taught in two Adventist universities (Andrews and Loma Linda), and he holds a Ph.D. in the history of science from the University of California at Berkeley. This volume was revised and enlarged in 1992 under the title, *Prophetess of Health: Ellen G. White and the Origins of Seventh-day Adventist Reform*.[28] The revision has an introduction by Jonathan M. Butler telling of what happened when Numbers was writing the first volume. This introduction reads like a mystery novel as it documents how SDA leaders sought to squelch any suggestion that White was not who the Adventists traditionally present her as. Why? Because Numbers reveals how many of White's supposed divine revelations were similar to what others had written. His book is extensively researched and thoroughly documented.

In 1982 a book by Walter T. Rea, *The White Lie*, was published.[29] Rea was a devoted follower of White and had written commentaries on Daniel and Revelation that were based on her writings. Later, however, he was shocked when he came across the writings of others that were similar—sometimes identical—to her writings. Just as Numbers did, Rea thoroughly documents how SDA leadership sometimes acknowledged the problems with White's writing but would not officially admit such and continued to push the concept of her inspiration from God. In fact, the leadership even disciplined and defrocked some of those bringing these documented charges of plagiarism or "borrowing" to light. The dedication of Rea's book is "to all those who would rather believe a bitter truth than a sweet lie." The extensive appendices in Rea's book reveal how close many of White's writings about her supposed visions are to others who wrote before her.

These books by Numbers and Rea are so well documented that it seems impossible for any educated person to read them and assume that SDA leaders are telling the truth about White. As mentioned, only a small percent of SDA followers live in the United States. Rea says that most Adventists outside of the United States "have not had her writings in total or do not care to use them, or at least interpret them somewhat different from the way the American adherent does."[30]

Given what Numbers and Rea have presented, it would seem logical for SDA leaders to at least back off a little from its unreserved support of Ellen G. White. But this is not the case.

Her prominence is seen in the recently published *Handbook of Seventh-day Adventist Theology*. The front matter of this book explains that each author writing on a topic was to give biblical data, then a historical overview of the doctrine, and then end his or her presentation with "a compilation of representative statements from Ellen G. White."[31]

In teaching a men's Bible study, I sought to emphasize positive characteristics of the current Adventist scholars, although they seem to explain away some of the clear problems associated with the statements of White. One of the men in the Bible study asked, "Why don't they get rid of her writings and just go by the Bible?" Good question.

Anthony Hoekema carefully considered what the Adventists said in the 1957 edition of *Questions on Doctrine*, especially concerning the authority of the Bible and their views about the visions of White. After giving various reasons for his conclusion, he wrote, "On the question of their source of authority, therefore, we must reluctantly insist that the Seventh-day Adventists do not bow before the Scriptures as their ultimate authority in matters of faith and life."[32]

INVESTIGATIVE JUDGMENT

A basic doctrine of the Seventh-day Adventists is the teaching that Christ, as part of His atoning work, has been conducting an "investigative judgment" in the heavenly sanctuary since 1844. This teaching is even more doctrinally significant than their teaching about the Sabbath. Tucker says the investigative judgment "distinctively gives the movement cultic characteristics."[33]

The doctrine of the investigative judgment was formulated after Christ failed to return on October 22, 1844, as had been predicted. The next day, it occurred to Hiram Edson, a member of the date-setting movement, "That instead of our High Priest *coming out* of the Most Holy of the heavenly sanctuary to come to this earth on the tenth day of the seventh month, at the end of 2300 days, he for the first time *entered* on that day the second apartment of that sanctuary and that he had a work to perform in the Most Holy before coming to earth" [emphasis his].[34]

Adventists seem to have missed the biblical point that Christ has been in the Holy of Holies since He ascended to the Father. Reagan, referred to earlier, sums it up succinctly when he says, "The whole concept of 'the investigative judgment' is foreign to the Bible. Jesus entered the Holy of Holies in Heaven immediately after His ascension (Hebrews 1:3; 6:19–20; 8:1; 9:6–12, 24; and 12:2), and not in 1844."[35]

Ellen G. White described the investigative judgment that Christ is supposedly conducting at this time:

> As the books of record are opened in the judgment, the lives of all who have believed on Jesus come in review before God. . . . When any have sins remaining upon the books of record, unrepented of and unforgiven, their names will be blotted out of the book of life, and the record of their good deeds will be erased from the book of God's remembrance. . . .

> All who have truly repented of sin, and by faith claimed the blood of Christ as their atoning sacrifice, have had pardon entered against their names in the books of heaven; as they have become partakers of the righteousness of Christ, and their characters are found to be in harmony with the law of God, their sins will be blotted out, and they themselves will be accounted worthy of eternal life."[36]

Seventh-day Adventists believe that although a person's past sins are forgiven when he accepts Christ, his sin is not blotted out until the process of the investigative judgment. Thus, a believer's salvation is never certain. They say, "It seems to us abundantly clear that the acceptance of Christ at conversion does not seal a person's destiny. His life record after conversion is also important."[37] But since no one is perfect, what is needed to "seal a person's destiny"? How can anyone be sure of forgiveness of sins and eternal life?

The Bible teaches that Jesus Christ completely paid the penalty for sin—past, present and future. Jesus "offered one sacrifice for sins forever" (Heb. 10:12). He said that anyone who believes in Him "shall not come into judgment, but has passed from death into life" (John 5:24).

If, after receiving Christ as Savior, a believer commits a sin, he is not in danger of having his name blotted out of the Book of Life if he does not repent of it. Confession of sin after salvation is necessary to *maintain* fellowship with the Father but not to *retain* salvation. If confession of each sin were required for salvation, no one would be saved because no one is capable of remembering and confessing every sin.

On the one hand, the SDA Fundamental Beliefs state, "Abiding in Him [Christ] we become partakers of the divine nature and have the assurance of salvation now and in the judgment."[38] On the other hand, a faith-plus-works type of salvation is revealed in Ellen G. White's words quoted earlier, "As they have become partakers of the righteousness of Christ, and their characters are found to be in harmony with the law of God, their sins will be blotted out, and they themselves will be accounted worthy of eternal life."[39]

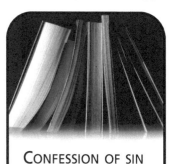

CONFESSION OF SIN AFTER SALVATION IS NECESSARY TO *MAINTAIN* FELLOWSHIP WITH THE FATHER BUT NOT TO *RETAIN* SALVATION.

According to the Scriptures, character does not determine one's salvation; rather, one's salvation determines character. It is not until a person receives Jesus Christ as Savior and becomes a "new creature" (2 Cor. 5:17) that he can have a character that pleases God. Such a person is Christ's "workmanship, created in Christ Jesus for good works" (Eph. 2:10). But no amount of good works will please God until a person has received salvation by trusting Christ as Savior.

The Scriptures speak of individuals being judged, but the time of these judgments is in the future, not the present. Those who know Jesus Christ as Savior will someday "appear before the judgment seat of Christ, that each one may receive the things done in the body, according to what he has done, whether good or bad" (2 Cor. 5:10). This is a judgment to determine rewards, however, not salvation. Of this same judgment, Paul wrote, "If anyone's work is burned, he will suffer loss; but he himself will be saved, yet so as through fire" (1 Cor.

3:15). Only those who have been saved will appear before the Judgment Seat of Christ. Those who have not accepted Christ will appear before the Great White Throne to have their works evaluated and then will be cast into the lake of fire (Rev. 20:11–15).

The Bible contains no basis for the doctrine of investigative judgment taught by the Seventh-day Adventists. This teaching reveals they do not accept the Bible as final authority and that they are not in agreement with orthodox Christianity on this doctrine.

Sharp differences of opinion exist within Adventism regarding the investigative judgment. Adventists who have opposed the doctrine of investigative judgment, or the other teachings of White, experience the disapproval of fellow members. Among others, Australian theologian Desmond Ford and American theologian Smuts van Rooyen have been censured and have had their ordinations annulled for claiming the investigative judgment is not taught in the Bible.[40] Any such men who have remained in the Adventist camp are certainly in the evangelical wing instead of the traditional one.[41] The disciplinary action taken against their own members shows the extent to which traditional Adventists hold to the teachings of White, regardless of their lack of biblical basis.

Satan—The Sin-Bearer

The Adventists make comments about sins being laid on Satan that cause non-Adventists to question if they believe he's part of atoning for sin. On the one hand, Adventists say, "Satan makes no atonement for our sins"; on the other hand, they say, "But Satan will ultimately have to bear the retributive punishment for his responsibility in the sins of all men, both righteous and wicked."[42]

It is one thing if Satan must bear responsibility for what he has done; it is quite another if he must bear the responsibility of sins that others have committed. But what does the SDA's main prophetess say?

In writing about the sin offering and the sacrifice of the scapegoat in Leviticus 16, White wrote:

> When the investigative judgment closes, Christ will come, and His reward will be with Him to give to every man as his work shall be. . . . As the priest, in removing the sins from the sanctuary, confessed them upon the head of the scapegoat, so

Christ will place all these sins upon Satan, the originator and instigator of sin. The scapegoat, bearing the sins of Israel, was sent away 'unto a land not inhabited' (Leviticus 16:22); so Satan, bearing the guilt of all the sins which he has caused God's people to commit, will be for a thousand years confined to the earth, which will then be desolate, without inhabitant, and he will at last suffer the full penalty of sin in the fires that shall destroy all the wicked.[43]

SDA leaders say Satan doesn't bear mankind's sins, but White refers to him as "bearing the guilt of all the sins which he has caused God's people to commit." Whom do we believe? Do we believe the current leaders or their key prophetess? Her words are so clear these leaders cannot successfully explain them away.

Commenting on White's teaching, Hoekema says, "These statements leave us with no choice but that of concluding that, according to the prophetess of Seventh-day Adventism, sin is not really eradicated from this earth until it has been laid on Satan."[44]

Although other Bible scholars have disagreed with Hoekema's conclusion, many are still uncertain about the Adventists' teaching in this area. Part of this confusion is the result of ambiguity and disagreements within the writings of Adventists themselves.

The Scriptures teach that Christ bore the full penalty of our sins because he became the propitiation (satisfaction) for them and also for the sins of the whole world (1 John 2:2). Those who refuse to receive Christ as their sin-bearer will suffer everlasting punishment (Luke 13:5; John 3:18–19). In speaking of Christ, the prophet Isaiah stated, "The LORD has laid on Him the iniquity of us all. . . . He bore the sin of many, and made intercession for the transgressors" (Isa. 53:6,12).

In His agonizing hours on the cross, Christ was actually "made . . . to be sin for us" (2 Cor. 5:21). Inasmuch as all our sins were placed on Him, we can be delivered from all condemnation by receiving Him as our Savior. Jesus did not die to take these sins from us in order to place them—or the guilt of them—on another; He died to suffer the full condemnation for our sins. Satan will be judged for his own sin, but Christ "bore our sins in His own body on the tree" (1 Pet. 2:24).

ANNIHILATION OF THE WICKED

Another false doctrine held by the Seventh-day Adventists is the belief that the wicked will cease to exist at death. Adventists teach that only the believer is promised eternal existence; therefore, the wicked will not be raised from the dead to suffer everlasting punishment. The Adventists reason that a loving God would not permit anyone to suffer for eternity. Their number one reason for rejecting eternal punishment is: "Because everlasting life is a gift of God (Rom. 6:23). The wicked do not possess this . . . no murderer hath eternal life abiding in him (1 John 3:15)."[45] No one says the wicked possess eternal life; the question is whether they will be eternally punished.

True, God is described as a God of love in the Scriptures (John 3:16; 1 John 4:7–10). Because of His love, God gave His Son to bear the penalty for our sin so we would not need to suffer condemnation. All who trust in Him receive forgiveness of sins and eternal life. Those who reject what Christ has accomplished in their behalf will be punished for their sin because "the wages of sin is death, but the gift of God is eternal life in Christ Jesus our Lord" (Rom. 6:23).

God's Word says the punishment experienced by unbelievers will be eternal. In describing events at the end of the Tribulation, Jesus said, "And these will go away into everlasting punishment, but the righteous into eternal life" (Matt. 25:46). No distinction can be made in this verse between the words everlasting and eternal—as the Adventists have sought to do—for they are only different translations of the same Greek word. If the "everlasting punishment" described in this passage is to be denied, then logically one must also deny the "eternal life" that it proclaims.

For those who accept the Bible as final authority, a comparison of Revelation 19:20 and 20:10 proves that the wicked do not cease to exist. The beast and the false prophet, who will deceive many during the Great Tribulation, will be cast into the lake of fire before Christ begins his 1,000-year rule on earth. At the end of the 1,000 years, Satan will also be cast into the lake of fire to join the beast and false prophet, who are still there. They will not cease to exist but will remain there for eternity.

Soul Sleep

Similar to the Jehovah's Witnesses, the Seventh-day Adventists deny the immortality of the soul. The Adventists believe a person *is* a soul but that he does not *have* a soul. A SDA encyclopedia says, "Man is a soul, as for example, in Num. 19:18, where the plural of *nephesh* is translated 'persons.'"[46] Thus, Adventist doctrine teaches that the soul does not exist apart from the body.

It is true that the Hebrew word for "soul" (*nephesh*) can sometimes be translated "person" or "persons," as it is in Numbers 19:18. This is similar to the expression, "There were 200 souls at the service." But this concept cannot be used to support an entire doctrine as the Adventists have done. The Scriptures reveal in other places that the soul *can* exist apart from the body and spirit. Matthew 10:28 records the words of Jesus: "And do not fear those who kill the body but cannot kill the soul. But rather fear Him who is able to destroy both soul and body in hell." If there is no soul when there is no life in the body, then Jesus' words are not correct. But according to His words, the soul exists even after the body dies.

The Seventh-day Adventists teach the doctrine commonly known as "soul sleep," or what some of them refer to as "death sleep." This is the belief that a person has no conscious existence from the time of death until the resurrection from the dead. Although they talk of "assurance," their theology does not allow the followers to know for sure they are secure for eternity. Such a belief does not agree with the inspired words of the apostle John, who wrote that it is possible to "know" one has eternal life. John wrote:

> This is the testimony: that God has given us eternal life, and this life is in His Son. He who has the Son has life; he who does not have the Son of God does not have life. These things I have written to you who believe in the name of the Son of God, that you may know that you have eternal life, and that you may continue to believe in the name of the Son of God (1 John 5:11–13).

And in John 5:24, the same apostle records the words of Jesus that also show one can be assured during this life of having eternal life. Jesus said, "Most assuredly, I say to you, he who hears My word and believes in Him who sent Me has everlasting life, and shall not come into judgment, but has passed from death into life."

What They Believe

The Adventists base their teaching of the unconsciousness of the dead on such verses as Ecclesiastes 9:5: "For the living know that they will die; but the dead know nothing, And they have no more reward, for the memory of them is forgotten." However, we must remember that although the Book of Ecclesiastes is inspired by God and accurately records what He desired, it was written to express that everything under the sun is vanity apart from God. From the perspective of an unbeliever, life is a useless cycle that ends in death where the dead know nothing.

In *Correcting the Cults*, Norman L. Geisler and Ron Rhodes say about such verses as Ecclesiastes 9:5: "The passages that say there is no knowledge or remembrance after death are speaking of memory *in this world*, not of no memory *of this world*. Solomon clearly qualified his comment by saying it was 'in the grave' (Eccles. 9:10) that there was 'no remembrance'"[47] (emphasis theirs).

Those who know God realize there is life after death because when the believer is absent from the body he is present with God (2 Cor. 5:1–8; Phil. 1:23–24).

First Thessalonians 4:14–16 also reveals that those "in Jesus" or "in Christ" go to be with Him at death. No believer in the Old Testament is referred to as being "in Jesus" or "in Christ," nor is any believer in Revelation 4–22. This is terminology for the present age, when God is working with the Gentiles and calling out a people for His name (Acts 15:14).

Of course, this is one of the problems with Seventh-day Adventists. They do not believe in a distinct Church age in contrast to Old Testament Israel. In fact, as Hans K. LaRondelle, Professor Emeritus at Andrews University, points out, the Adventists really see themselves as a "faithful remnant of Israel that inherits the covenant promises and responsibilities."[48] The covenant promises are seen in Genesis 12:1–3, which involves land, physical descendants and blessings. Do the Adventists really believe they will someday inherit the land promised to Abraham and his descendants?

The apostle Paul understood the Church and Israel to be distinctly different when he wrote, "Give no offense, either to the Jews or to the Greeks or to the church of God" (1 Cor. 10:32).

When Christ comes to rapture the church from the earth, He will bring *with Him* the believers who have died (1 Thess. 4:14). This proves they are not in an unconscious state in the grave; they are in the presence of the Lord Jesus Christ. When they return with Christ they will receive their bodies from the grave. Those caught up at this time are only those "in Christ" (v. 16). When the physical body dies, the believer's soul and spirit are immediately in the presence of Christ. The true essence of the person does not sleep in an unconscious state in the grave.

Sabbath-Keeping

When most people are asked to describe the beliefs of the Seventh-day Adventists, they usually think first of the Adventists' practice of worshiping on the seventh day of the week (from which the group derives part of its name). As mentioned, the earliest leaders did not observe Sabbath-keeping at first. By the Adventists' own testimony, "In 1846 Joseph Bates convinced James and Ellen White that the fourth commandment should be restored in the true worship of God."[49]

Their observance of the fourth commandment is just one example of how the Seventh-day Adventists so highly regard the authority of White. Their special focus on this commandment did not come from studying the Bible's teachings on the subject but instead was the result of one of White's visions. As pointed out earlier, on April 3, 1847, when she was 19 years old, White had a vision in which she saw "the law of God in the ark of the heavenly sanctuary with a halo of light encircling the fourth commandment."[50]

Commenting on the significance of this vision, Adventist writers say, "This view confirmed the confidence of the Sabbathkeeping Adventists in their position and brought a clearer understanding of the Sabbath's significance."[51] Such comments reveal the Adventists' belief that White's visions shed light on the Scriptures, although they prefer to describe her visions as "corroborating" the Scriptures. Instead of examining her visions and testimonies in the light of the Scriptures and allowing God's Word to be the judge, they accept these visions as from one considered inspired to speak for God.

Adventists usually stress the Sabbath doctrine more than any other teaching. It is probably safe to assume that those in the pew of Adventist churches know far more about the importance of keeping the Sabbath than they do about the investigative judgment, for instance.

The greatest concern for evangelicals is not that this group desires to worship on a different day but that they make the keeping of this day, as well as the keeping of other laws, a criterion for a person's relationship with the Lord—even to the extent of evidence of his salvation.

The Adventists say that salvation is by faith in Christ. But to faith in Christ, they add the works of the Law. This is the same error for

THE SEVENTH-DAY ADVENTISTS ERR IN FOCUSING PRIMARILY ON THE TEN COMMANDMENTS.

which Paul condemned the Galatians. Seventh-day Adventism is 21st century Galatianism, and the Book of Galatians needs to be studied carefully to see the proper relationship of the Law to salvation. Paul denounced those who were teaching a gospel of faith plus works (Gal. 1:8; 3:1–11).

The Adventists add works to faith when they say, "We regard the observance of the Sabbath as a test of our loyalty to Christ."[52] Salvation cannot be obtained by both faith and works. The Bible says, "For by grace you have been saved through faith, and that not of yourselves; it is the gift of God, not of works, lest anyone should boast" (Eph. 2:8–9). Romans 11:6 indicates that it is impossible for anything to be obtained by both faith and works because one excludes the other. The Word of God teaches that salvation can be received only through faith in Christ apart from the works of the Law (Rom. 3:21–24). A person produces good works because he *has* everlasting life, not in order to obtain it or retain it.

Because they believe so strongly in Sabbath-keeping, the Adventists have gone so far as to say that "Sunday-keeping" will be the mark of the beast in the future. In their *Handbook of Seventh-day Adventist Theology*, LaRondelle quotes J. N. Andrews, who said, "Sundaykeeping is not yet the mark of the beast, and will not be until the decree goes forth causing men to worship this idol Sabbath. The time will come when this day will be the test, but that time has not come yet."[53]

The Adventists have failed to see how the New Testament teaching affects the Old Testament practice concerning the day of worship.

During Old Testament times, God did not command the patriarchs in pre-Mosaic times to keep the Sabbath. This command was not given until the Law was given through Moses, as recorded in Exodus 20:8–11. Even then, the Gentiles were under no obligation to observe this day. God specifically gave the Sabbath as a token of His covenant with Israel. The same book that records the fourth commandment also records God's statement, "Therefore the children of Israel shall keep the Sabbath, to observe the Sabbath throughout their generations as a perpetual covenant. It is a sign between Me and the children of Israel forever" (Ex. 31:16–17). When Christ came as the Messiah of Israel and was rejected by the nation, God temporarily set aside the nation from His active program (Rom. 10–11). Thus, the token of God's covenant with Israel—the Sabbath—was also set aside. That is why there is no specific reference to the keeping of the Sabbath in the epistles written to the Body of Christ, the Church.

The New Testament teaches, "Therefore let no one judge you in food or in drink, or regarding a festival or a new moon or sabbaths, which are a shadow of things to come, but the substance is of Christ" (Col. 2:16–17). The Old Testament Sabbath Day was only a picture of the rest that a person enters when he places his faith in Christ and ceases from his own works (Heb. 4:9–11).

In commemoration of the day on which Christ rose from the grave, the New Testament Christians met for worship on the first day of the week (Acts 20:7). Paul also instructed the Corinthian Christians to set aside their offerings on the first day of the week for the work of the Lord (1 Cor. 16:2). These practices were not performed in order to merit salvation but because these individuals already knew Christ as their Savior and wanted to fellowship together in the Lord on the day He had risen from the dead.

The Seventh-day Adventists err in focusing primarily on the Ten Commandments. No Jew in the Old Testament would think of selecting the Ten and neglecting the others. And by common Jewish count, there were 613 commandments in the Law. This is the argument of James when he writes, "For whoever shall keep the whole law, and yet stumble in one point, he is guilty of all" (2:10). That is also Paul's argument when he tells the Galatians, "I testify again to every man who becomes circumcised that he is a debtor to keep the whole law" (Gal. 5:3).

Seventh-day Adventists are confused about the purpose of the Law. According to the New Testament, the Old Testament Law is made for the lawless. The apostle Paul wrote, "Knowing this: that the law is not made for a righteous person, but for the lawless and insubordinate, for the ungodly and for sinners, for the unholy and profane, for murderers of fathers and murderers of mothers, for manslayers" (1 Tim. 1:9). For those who have trusted Christ as Savior, Paul said, "For sin shall not have dominion over you, for you are not under law but under grace. What then? Shall we sin because we are not under law but under grace? Certainly not!" (Rom. 6:14–15). The evidence of a changed life is not that a person observes a particular day, but that he shows the fruit of the Spirit—"love, joy, peace, longsuffering, kindness, goodness, faithfulness, gentleness, self-control. Against such there is no law" (Gal. 5:22–23).

Adventists equate "commandments" only with the Ten Commandments of the Old Testament Law. But what about the commands that Jesus gives us in the New Testament? First John uses the word *commandments* seven times in six verses (2:3–4; 3:22, 24; 5:2–3), and these references clearly have more in mind than the Ten Commandments. Paul told the Thessalonians, "For you know what commandments we gave you through the Lord Jesus" (1 Thess. 4:2). A reading of 1 Thessalonians 5 reveals many commands that God did not give to Moses with the Ten Commandments.

Seventh-day Adventists are outside of orthodox Christianity when they put such an emphasis on Old Testament Law, and they fail to be consistent when they emphasize only the Ten Commandments.

CONCLUSION

The distinctive doctrines of the Seventh-day Adventists are not normally presented in their media ministries. It is not until one begins receiving their literature or picks up a copy of *Signs of the Times* that he sees how their teaching differs from orthodox Christianity. Their doctrinal distinctives are not evident to the average viewer in their television programs, *Faith for Today* and *It Is Written*.

For this reason, Christians should know what literature is published by the Seventh-day Adventists. When in doubt, check the publisher. Some of the major publishing houses for the Seventh-day Adventists are listed in the summary at the end of this chapter.

The Seventh-day Adventist teachings concerning the investigative judgment, the visions of Ellen G. White, Satan's part in bearing the final guilt for sin, and obedience to Old Testament Laws as an evidence of salvation, reveal their gospel is not the same as revealed in the Word of God. Because of these deviations it is not recommended that one become a part of this church group.

This does not mean that every person in the Seventh-day Adventist movement is unsaved. One who trusts Christ *alone* for salvation has forgiveness of sins and eternal life no matter with what earthly group he is affiliated. It is regrettable, however, that so many in this movement are blind to mixed messages that the Seventh-day Adventists leaders present to their followers, especially regarding their prophetess.

As Rea has written, "One can hope that the administrators and supersalesmen of the Seventh-day Adventist system will yet learn a lesson from the past—that they will be willing to join the people in going beyond their veil of Ellen G. White. If they have the courage to do this, they may yet find that Christ who eluded the Millerites and whose delay so tantalized the early advent believers."[54]

Summary

Name:	Seventh-day Adventists
Also Known As:	SDA, Adventists
Founder:	Ellen G. White (1827–1915)
Cofounder:	James S. White (1821–1881)
Headquarters:	Seventh-day Adventist Church Silver Spring, Maryland
Current World President:	Jan Paulsen
Membership (2003):	U.S.: About 919,000; Worldwide: About 13 million
Major Publishing Houses:	Pacific Press Publishing Association Nampa, Idaho
	Review and Herald Publishing Association Hagerstown, Maryland
	Andrews University Press Berrien Springs, Michigan
Web Site:	www.adventist.org

What They Believe

Seventh-day Adventists:	Biblical Christians:
Source of Authority	
Visions of Ellen G. White "corroborate" the Bible.	The Bible alone is the source of authority and needs no corroboration.
Salvation	
Christ is carrying out an investigative judgment to see who is "worthy of salvation."	All who trust Christ alone have salvation at that moment.
Sin	
Sin must finally be cast upon Satan to cause him to bear the guilt of all sins which he has caused God's people to commit.	All sin was laid on Christ when He died on the cross for mankind's sin; Christ alone has borne the penalty for all sin.
Punishment of the Wicked	
The wicked will be annihilated (cease to exist).	All who reject salvation in Christ will suffer eternally.
Soul Sleep	
The believer is thought to be in a "death sleep" from death to the resurrection.	Those who "sleep in Jesus" are with Him and will return for their bodies at the Rapture.
Sabbath-Keeping	
Sabbath-keeping is an evidence of salvation; in the future Sunday-keeping will be the "mark of the beast."	Old Testament laws and holy days were a shadow of things to come; the reality is Jesus Christ. Now we are not to judge others based on special days or ceremonies.

Recommended Reading

Geisler, Norman L, and Rhodes, Ron. *Correcting the Cults.* Grand Rapids, Mich.: Baker Books, 1997.

Gerstner, John H. *The Theology of the Major Sects.* Grand Rapids, Mich.: Baker Book House, 1979.

Hoekema, Anthony A. *Four Major Cults.* Grand Rapids, Mich.: Wm. B. Eerdmans Publishing Company, 1963.

Lamb & Lion Ministries Web site, www.lamblion.com/articles/doctrinal/ Cults/Cults-11.php.

Numbers, Ronald L. *Prophetess of Health: Ellen G. White and the Origins of Seventh-day Adventist Health Reform*. Knoxville, Tenn.: University of Tennessee Press, 1992.

Rea, Walter T. *The White Lie*. Turlock, Calif.: M & R Publications, 1982.

Tucker, Ruth A. *Another Gospel: Alternative Religions and the New Age Movement*. Grand Rapids, Mich.: Zondervan Publishing House, 1989.

ENDNOTES

[1] Ruth A. Tucker, *Another Gospel: Alternative Religions and the New Age Movement* (Grand Rapids, Mich.: Zondervan Publishing House, 1989), 93.

[2] www.adventist.org/world_church/facts_and_figures/index.html.en, Oct. 15, 2005.

[3] *World Almanac and Book of Facts 2005* (New York: World Almanac Education Group, Inc., 2005), 731.

[4] www.adventist.org/world_church/facts_and_figures/history/index.html.en, July 27, 2005.

[5] Figures are from Patrick Johnstone and Jason Mandryk, *Operation World*: 21st Century Edition (United States: WEC International, 2001).

[6] George R. Knight, ed. *Seventh-day Adventists Answer Questions on Doctrine, Annotated Edition* (Berrien Springs, Mich.: Andrews University Press, 2003).

[7] Raoul Dederen, ed. *Handbook of Seventh-day Adventist Theology: Commentary Reference Series*, Vol. 12 (Hagerstown, Md.: Review and Herald Publishing Association, 2000).

[8] *Seventh-day Adventists Believe . . . . : A Biblical Exposition of 27 Fundamental Doctrines* (Washington, D.C.: Ministerial Association General Conference of Seventh-day Adventists, 1988).

[9] Frank S. Mead and Samuel S. Hill, rev. by Craig D. Atwood. *Handbook of Denominations in the United States*, 11th ed. (Nashville: Abingdon Press, 2001).

[10] David A. Reagan, www.lamblion.com/articles/doctrinal/Cults/Cults-11.php, July 20, 2005.

[11] See J. Dwight Pentecost, *Things to Come* (Grand Rapids, Mich.: Zondervan Publishing House, 1958), 244–246, and John F. Walvoord, *Endtimes* (Nashville: Word Publishing, 1998), 115–116.

[12] Tucker, *Another Gospel*, 93.

[13] John H. Gerstner, *Theology of the Major Sects* (Grand Rapids, Mich.: Baker Book House, 1977), 10.

[14] www.adventist.org/beliefs/fundamental/index.html, July 22, 2005.

[15] Ibid.

[16] Don F. Neufeld, ed., "White, Ellen Gould (Harmon)," *Seventh-day Adventist Encyclopedia: Commentary Reference Series*, 2nd rev. ed., Vol. 11 (Hagerstown, Md.: Review and

What They Believe

Herald Publishing Association, 1996), 874.

[17] Nancy J. Vyhmeister, "Who Are Seventh-day Adventists?" *Handbook of Seventh-day Adventist Theology*, 7.

[18] Ibid.

[19] Ibid.

[20] "Prophet or Plagiarist?" *Time*, Aug. 2, 1976, 43.

[21] Vyhmeister, "Who Are Seventh-day Adventists?" *Handbook of Seventh-day Adventist Theology*, 7.

[22] Neufeld, "Inspiration of Scripture," *Seventh-day Adventist Encyclopedia*, Vol. 10, 770.

[23] *Review and Harold*, Oct. 8, 1867, as quoted on www.ellenwhite.org/egw4.htm, Oct. 18, 2005.

[24] Ellen G. White, *The Triumph of God's Love* (Mountain View, Calif.: Pacific Press Publishing Association, 1971), back cover.

[25] www.adventist.org

[26] Knight, ed. *Seventh-day Adventists Answer Questions on Doctrine Annotated Edition*, p. 335.

[27] Ibid., 80.

[28] Ronald L. Numbers, *Prophetess of Health: Ellen G. White and the Origins of Seventh-day Adventist Reform* (Knoxville, Tenn.: The University of Tennessee Press, 1992).

[29] Walter T. Rea, *The White Lie* (Turlock, Calif.: M & R Publications, 1982).

[30] Rea, *The White Lie*, 124.

[31] "Preface" *Handbook of Seventh-day Adventist Theology*, x.

[32] Anthony A. Hoekema, *Four Major Cults* (Grand Rapids, Mich.: Wm. B. Eerdmans Publishing Company, 1963), 108.

[33] Tucker, *Another Gospel*, 98.

[34] LeRoy E. Froom, *The Prophetic Faith of Our Fathers* (Washington, D.C.: Review and Herald Publishing Association, 1954), 4:881.

[35] Reagan, www.lamblion.com/articles/doctrinal/Cults/Cults-11.php, July 20, 2005.

[36] Ellen G. White, *The Great Controversy* (Mountain View, Calif.: Pacific Press Publishing Company, 1911), 483.

[37] Knight, ed. *Seventh-day Adventists Answer Questions on Doctrine Annotated Edition*, 334.

[38] www.adventist.org/beliefs/fundamental/index.html, July 22, 2005.

[39] White, *The Great Controversy*, 483.

[40] James C. Hefley, "Adventist Teachers Are Forced Out in a Doctrinal Dispute," *Christianity Today*, March 18, 1983, 3–25. "Another Adventist Professor Is Ejected for His Views," *Christianity Today*, June 12, 1981, 35.

[41] see the Internet Christian Library, www.iclnet.org/pub/resources/text/cri/cri-jrnl/web/crj0005b.html.

[42] Knight, ed. *Seventh-day Adventists Answer Questions on Doctrine Annotated Edition*, 319.

43 White, *The Great Controversy*, 485–486.

44 Hoekema, *Four Major Cults*, 120–121.

45 Knight, ed. *Seventh-day Adventists Answer Questions on Doctrine Annotated Edition*, 419.

46 Neufeld, "Soul," in *Seventh-day Adventist Encyclopedia*, Vol. 11, 629.

47 Norman L. Geisler and Ron Rhodes, *Correcting the Cults* (Grand Rapids, Mich., Baker Books, 1997), 75.

48 Hans K. LaRondelle, "The Remnant and the Three Angels' Messages," *Handbook of Seventh-day Adventist Theology*, 864.

49 Ibid., 886.

50 Neufeld, "White, Ellen Gould (Harmon)," *Seventh-day Adventist Encyclopedia*, Vol. 11, 874.

51 Ibid.

52 Knight, ed. *Seventh-day Adventists Answer Questions on Doctrine Annotated Edition*, 132.

53 LaRondelle, "The Remnant and the Three Angels' Messages," *Handbook of Seventh-day Adventist Theology*, 886.

54 Rea, *The White Lie*, 278.

CHAPTER TWELVE

Transcendental Meditation

TM, SCI, MIU, MUM—it's hard to understand the organization without a glossary. TM, or Transcendental Meditation, is the most commonly known among these initials. What is not so commonly known, however, is the origin of the teachings of TM.

Maharishi Mahesh Yogi preached TM in the United States in the late 1950s and early '60s. But the value changes of the '60s—when the emphasis was on self instead of spiritual values—were not helpful to Maharishi's views any more than they were to traditional values. He was more shrewd, however, than most others in recovering. After returning to his native India for a time, he came back to the United States with an emphasis on science that greatly aided his organization. America was shifting its values away from religion to science, so that anything that was said to be scientific was thought to be true. A naive public did not realize that much of what was being said in the name of science was in fact philosophy and religion, not science.

Whether intentionally or unintentionally, the Maharishi capitalized on this interest in science when he called his views "Science of Creative Intelligence"—or SCI for short. Concerning this stage in Maharishi's life, George Mather and Larry Nichols say in their *Dictionary of Cults, Sects, Religions and the Occult*: "He changed his strategy completely, omitting from the movement's vocabulary all religious terminology and replacing it with the language of psychology."[1]

Although Maharishi founded the Maharishi International University (MIU) in California, in 1974 it moved to Fairfield, Iowa, a town of nearly 10,000 people in the southeastern part of the state. Now known as the Maharishi University of Management (MUM), the university will celebrate its 35th anniversary in 2006. Its Web site details the beliefs and writings of the Maharishi and the offerings of the university, which is an accredited institution of higher learning.

What They Believe

On its 25th anniversary in 1996, Maharishi University published a *Silver Jubilee Commemorative Volume* that included tributes from local, state and international personalities. And what a commemorative volume it is—an 8.5 x 11-inch book with a coated four-color cover. The theme of the book is "Celebrating Twenty-Five Years of Maharishi's Consciousness-Based Approach to Education." Key words in the book are "Natural Law" and "Unified Field of Natural Law." The university's Web site refers to the "unified field of natural law" as something the students experience as the "deepest level of their own intelligence" while practicing the Maharishi's TM.[2]

In highlights of a recent message given by Maharishi (most often referred to as "His Holiness Maharishi Mahesh Yogi") to the MUM community, he says, "We are very proud of our knowledge that Guru Dev gave us, and we think that we used the knowledge very well, and the world will never be the same—we will soon have a world free from problems, in full enlightenment and bliss."[3]

The president of Maharishi University, Dr. Bevan Morris, describes what students can expect at MUM: "Through practicing the Maharishi Transcendental Meditation and TM-Sidhi programs, including Yogic Flying, students experience the Self—pure consciousness, Transcendental Consciousness, self-referral consciousness—the basis of all education, and engage the managing intelligence of the universe for increasing effectiveness, good fortune and success in all aspects of their personal and professional lives."[4]

The reference to "Yogic Flying" is somewhat misleading. Three people in the *Commemorative Volume* are shown enjoying what is called "bubbling bliss" during twice-daily TM sessions.[5] The camera caught them suspended in mid-air. Is this yogic flying?

The first public demonstration of yogic flying took place in Washington in what was called the "First Olympics of the Age of Enlightenment." Reporting for the *Omaha World-Herald*, Cate Peterson described the scene before the "race" began. "The competitors sat cross-legged on 6-inch foam rubber pads that covered the large auditorium floor."[6] Peterson reported that some seemed to warm up by swaying; others by half-bounces, but once the bell tones sounded, "the practitioners had 'transcended' into the first stage of yogic flying: hopping." An organizer admitted to Peterson that no one had gone on to the second stage of hovering or to the third stage, which is actual

276

flying. Regarding hovering and flying, Peterson reported, "They know it can be done, organizers said, because it has been described in ancient Indian writings."[7]

Twenty-two young men took part in the "games" that day, while 2,800 attended the 10-day TM conference. Watching the event caused Peterson to write, "What was billed as the first-ever public demonstration of 'yogic flying' looked more like a scene from 'The Human Frogs.'"[8]

The last three pages of the *Silver Jubilee Commemorative Volume* have pictures of selected facilities in North America and around the world. Twenty facilities are pictured from North America, and six are pictured from the Netherlands, England, Switzerland, Australia, India and Thailand.

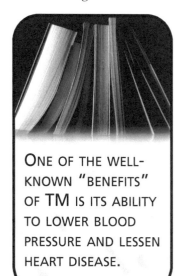

ONE OF THE WELL-KNOWN "BENEFITS" OF TM IS ITS ABILITY TO LOWER BLOOD PRESSURE AND LESSEN HEART DISEASE.

One of the well-known "benefits" of TM is its ability to lower blood pressure and lessen heart disease. The fact that scientists have verified the connection between TM and better health has made a desperate public susceptible to a meditation that is more than meditation.

The Maharishi also has received attention in the press from his statements about lowering, if not eliminating, crime in America's cities. Remember, he has said, "The world will never be the same—we will soon have a world free from problems, in full enlightenment and bliss."[9]

It is one thing for Hindu-based philosophies like the New Age Movement and Transcendental Meditation to gain a following in areas where they are not well known, but how effective are they where they are best known? How effective are they with the enormous population of India and the small town of Fairfield, Iowa?

Of the Hindu-based New Age Movement, Robert J. L. Burrows writes about one of its proponents: "The vision [Fritjof] Capra believes will deliver us seems to thrive in cultures where misery is perpetually rampant and corruption is rife. India is a case in point. Christians know that the problem is perversity, not human perception—holiness, not holism."[10]

In the fall of 1992 Maharishi was offering, for a price, professional meditators for hire who could create harmony and eliminate crime. Des Moines city manager Cy Carney learned the charge would be "10 cents per person per day, or $7 million for a year."[11] Omaha's cost would be $22.7 million a year.[12]

But how has the crime rate changed in Fairfield, with a population of only about 10,000? Surely the hometown of Maharishi University since 1974 would notice a sharp decline, if not the total elimination, of crime. In 1993 *Omaha World-Herald* reporter Jeff Gauger wrote a story on Fairfield. Concerning crime, he cited Fairfield's Police Chief Randy Cooksey, who said, "I personally don't see any difference in what it was like prior to MIU coming."[13]

If TM is not effective in reducing crime, then one wonders about its supposed health benefits. The emphasis on the need to calm one's emotions to lower blood pressure, prevent heart disease and cope with life provided the hotbed in which Transcendental Meditation could grow. Even Christian doctors who do not recommend TM have long been urging Christians to do those things that stimulate sound mental health and reduce anxiety. "Set aside time for personal mental health," say Drs. Frank B. Minirth and Paul D. Meier, "because you won't be of much use to God, family, or others if you don't have good mental health yourself. This includes time to unwind and relax."[14]

Meditation is not a new subject to biblical Christians. God told Joshua, "This Book of the Law shall not depart from your mouth, but you shall *meditate* in it day and night, that you may observe to do according to all that is written in it. For then you will make your way prosperous, and then you will have good success" (Josh. 1:8, emphasis mine).

The psalmist often used the word *meditate*. Referring to the man who is blessed, he wrote, "His delight is in the law of the Lord, and in His law he meditates day and night" (Ps. 1:2). The psalmist told God, "I will meditate on Your precepts, and contemplate Your ways" (119:15). He also said, "I remember the days of old; I meditate on all Your works" (143:5). Notice in these verses that the psalmist was focusing on who God is and what He has done. He was not emptying his mind but filling it by thinking on God and His mighty acts.

In accordance with the Bible's emphasis on meditation, Bible teachers and preachers throughout church history have urged believers to meditate on God and on the Scriptures. Many have encouraged a daily time of meditation, frequently referred to as "daily devotions" or "quiet time." What is normally meant by these expressions is that the believer should seek a quiet place where he can be alone to read the Bible, meditate on—or think about—its truths and talk to God in prayer.

But another kind of meditation—TM—has been brought from the Eastern world and has become popular in the West. It is "transcendental" because the person transcends, or goes beyond, specific thoughts and arrives at what TM's founder calls the "source of thought." It is "meditation" because the person withdraws from the busy world for 20 minutes twice a day to take part in a procedure designed to release stress and unfold his full potential.

The meditation encouraged by Christianity and the meditation practiced in TM are not the same. In TM, meditation is a passive opening of the mind. The mind is to be at complete rest as the person attempts to gain union with pure awareness, or the source of thought. In contrast to this, Christianity teaches that a person is *not* to open his mind to anything and everything. The Bible says believers are to bring "every thought into captivity to the obedience of Christ" (2 Cor. 10:5). The Scriptures specifically instruct believers in what type of thoughts to allow: "Finally, brethren, whatever things are true, whatever things are noble, whatever things are just, whatever things are pure, whatever things are lovely, whatever things are of good report, if there is any virtue and if there is anything praiseworthy—meditate on these things" (Phil. 4:8).

BACKGROUND

Transcendental Meditation owes its popularity to Maharishi Mahesh Yogi. Born in India in the early 1900s (possible birth dates range from 1910 to 1918) as Mahesh Brasad Warma, he graduated from Allahabad University in India in the early 1940s with a degree in physics. He then became the favorite disciple of Guru Dev. (*Guru* means "leader" and *Dev* means "divine.") Guru Dev was associated with a

Hindu monastery. Under his tutelage, Maharishi mastered yoga (the process by which one comes into union with Brahman—the Hindu concept of God). That is why he added the name "Yogi," meaning "one who is devoted to yoga."

At the feet of Guru Dev, Maharishi was taught the Hindu monistic worldview—the absolute unity of all being. This view is reflected in such statements as "all is One." Monism is a common view of Eastern religions, especially Hinduism. All creatures, as well as all inanimate objects, are viewed as a part of the "divine essence." Ultimately, those who believe in monism would say there is no difference between God and a person because they are part of the same divine essence. Some commonly known groups in the United States that share this Hinduistic view with TM are Christian Science, Unity School of

ALL CREATURES, AS WELL AS ALL INANIMATE OBJECTS, ARE VIEWED AS A PART OF THE "DIVINE ESSENCE."

Christianity and the New Age Movement. As to the effect of Hinduism on modern America, John Ankerberg and John Weldon say, "By itself Maharishi Mahesh Yogi's Transcendental Meditation, a form of advaita Vedanta Hinduism, has over three million graduates."[15] Since founding TM in 1957, Maharishi has trained 40,000 teachers in the Science of Creative Intelligence (SCI).[16]

Transcendental Meditation's view of life is pantheistic, because adherents believe that God is all and all is God. Or put another way, they believe that God is in everything and that everything is God. It's easy to see that the god of Hinduism is not the personal God of the Bible; it is an impersonal "Being" or "essence" of the universe.

Concerning the practical results of pantheism and the need to prevent it from infiltrating our homes, schools, businesses and churches, Gordon R. Lewis, professor of theology and philosophy at Denver Seminary (Colorado), has written: "I realized the great importance of prevention as a visiting professor in India where the results of a monistic world view and way of life have been entrenched for centuries. In a rural area of that poverty-stricken culture human life was cheap. I could see how difficult it is to evangelize pantheists who believe that they are already divine, have endless potential for self-improvement, and are not inherently sinful, and not in need of the gracious, once-for-all provision of Jesus Christ's atonement."[17]

Maharishi Mahesh Yogi came to the United States in 1958 and has been utilizing mass media to sell TM as a scientific and secular discipline rather than a religion. TM has been promoted as a harmless discipline that will improve health, increase productivity and creativity, and reduce stress and tension. But Transcendental Meditation is not a neutral discipline; it is religious worship.

Transcendental Meditation is a technique of meditating in which the subject chants silently a teacher-assigned "mantra" (a secret word from Sanskrit, the classical language of India) until an altered state of awareness called "cosmic (or bliss) consciousness" is realized. Maharishi believes "the perfect orderliness of the Sanskrit language creates orderliness and balance in the brain physiology, expands the memory, and purifies the physiology."[18] Thus, numerous books are for sale, and even online dictionaries are available, to help devotees learn about Sanskrit, with an emphasis on its alphabet.

The mantra in Sanskrit is enough to reveal that TM is religious, for the personal mantra is actually the name of a Hindu deity. This is why Walter Martin concluded, "The repeating of the mantra results in worshiping the Hindu deity."[19] The participants might plead ignorance to this, but "Maharishi himself admits that the use of the mantra invokes gods and spirits from the spirit world."[20]

Allegedly, each person is assigned his or her own mantra. Theoretically, however, several people could have the same one and not know it, because no one is to tell what his mantra is. Calvin Miller, author of *Transcendental Hesitation*, was able to successfully guess the mantra of an individual because he had learned that mantras are sometimes assigned on the basis of age—not on the supposed "vibes" of the participant.[21]

One former teacher of TM says that instructors were told to lie to the unknowing public concerning TM, especially about the significance of the mantra.[22] This agrees with what Irvine Robertson, a former faculty member at Moody Bible Institute and a critic of TM, maintains: "[Maharishi] capitalized on a statement from the popular Hindu scripture called the Bhagavad Gita. There the Lord Krishna [the eighth or ninth incarnation of a Hindu deity] says, 'Let not him who knows the whole disturb the ignorant who knows only a part.'"[23] Any person who operates by such a philosophy cannot be counted on to tell the truth. He could reason, "What you don't know won't hurt you." But, as we have all learned from experience, what we don't know can hurt us.

Besides the mantra, the Puja ceremony also reveals that TM is religious. After receiving personal instruction, an individual must attend the Puja ceremony in order to receive his personal mantra. "*Puja* is the Hindi word commonly used in north India to indicate Hindu idol worship. (It is not used by Christians living in India)," says Irvine Robertson.[24]

The Puja ceremony is recited in Sanskrit, so most people do not know what is actually being said. An *English Translation of Transcendental Meditation's Initiatory Puja* (Berkeley, Calif.: Spiritual Counterfeits Project, n.d.) reveals the religious nature of this ceremony. Irvine Robertson summarizes the ceremony: "The first of the three stages of the ritual begins with the invocation 'To Lord Narayana' and progresses through a sequence of references to historical and legendary personages until it reaches Shri Guru Dev. He, of course, is the immediate teacher of Maharishi, the founder of TM.

"During the second stage, some seventeen items [such as flowers, fruit and a white handkerchief] are offered before the image of Guru Dev, the Divine Master. Each offering is accompanied by the words 'I bow down.'"[25] What a participant says in the Puja ceremony clearly shows that he is bowing down to, and worshiping, a Hindu deity.

TM has been promoted as a science, without any religious connotations, and it has thus made inroads into the public school system, the government and the military. Even some religious leaders have been misled into thinking TM is only a neutral discipline rather than a religion in disguise.

In 1977, however, a New Jersey federal court decision barred the teaching of Transcendental Meditation in that state's schools. It ruled that "the teaching of SCI/TM and the Puja are religious in nature; no other inference is permissible or reasonable."[26]

David Haddon, who has studied counterfeit religious groups, says, "Maharishi's Science of Creative Intelligence (SCI), the theoretical aspect of TM, is a restatement in semiscientific language of the principles of Shankara's monism. Thus, Hindu monism or pantheism is the underlying philosophy of the entire movement."[27] Shankara was a ninth century Hindu reformer who believed and taught the philosophy of monism.

Most people would undoubtedly be better off physically, mentally and emotionally if they took some time out of each day's hectic pace to withdraw to a quiet place and relax. Most would probably discover new energy and enthusiasm for living, even if they had never heard of Transcendental Meditation. The Christian especially would be helped if he consistently spent 20 minutes twice a day—or even once a day—thinking about the truths of Scripture and about the character and wonderful works of God. During these minutes one could read from the Scriptures, use a daily devotional guide and follow a list to pray for family, friends, missionaries and government leaders. Some people follow the acronym ACTS as a pattern in praying—**A**doration, **C**onfession, **T**hanksgiving, **S**upplication. Others recommend reading a great hymn of the faith. Still others recommend recording in a journal your thoughts about God and His Word and what He's doing—or needs to do—in your life. Having a set place and set time where this is done adds consistency to the schedule, but all of this is vastly different from what is suggested by TM.

BELIEFS

Is Christianity reconcilable with Transcendental Meditation? This is the crucial question anyone who accepts historic biblical Christianity needs to ask. The answer is found by examining the beliefs of TM and its founder, Maharishi Mahesh Yogi.

GOD

Christianity believes that God is a divine Person because it can be easily demonstrated from the Bible that He has intellect, emotions and a will. He knows, feels and makes decisions on His own. He is almighty and sovereign. He exists apart from creation because "in the beginning God created the heavens and the earth" (Gen. 1:1).

As mentioned, TM is based on Hinduism, which is pantheistic in its view about God. Maharishi speaks of a personal as well as an impersonal God, but it is clear from his statements that only the impersonal

God is really God. He speaks of the impersonal God as "the supreme Being of absolute eternal nature."[28] The personal God eventually "merges into the impersonal absolute state of the Supreme."[29] TM's pantheistic view that "all is God and God is all" cannot be reconciled with the Bible. The Bible makes a clear distinction between God, the Creator, and all that He has created.

Because TM is pantheistic, man is considered part of God. Maharishi believes the life in everyone is the absolute Being, but this is not a personal God. Therefore, his idea should not be confused with the Bible's teaching that the Holy Spirit indwells those who trust Christ as Savior. "The impersonal God is that Being which dwells in the heart of everyone," Maharishi says. "Every individual in his true nature is the Impersonal God."[30] Maharishi teaches that through TM it is possible for a person to gain total, complete unity with the impersonal God or Being of the universe. In essence, through TM man becomes one with God. This is Hinduism, not Christianity.

MAN

TM maintains that man is inherently good, so the process of meditation is intended to bring to the surface the good in each person. Promoters of TM sometimes tell others, "The kingdom of God is within you." This reflects the view of Maharishi that the true nature of each person is "the impersonal God."

The phrase "the kingdom of God is within you" refers to Jesus' statement recorded in Luke 17:21. When the Lord Jesus Christ made this remark, He was addressing the Pharisees, who had adamantly opposed His claims that He was the Son of God and the Messiah of Israel. When Jesus said that the kingdom of God was within them, He did not mean that each of the unbelieving Pharisees was individually God. Nor did He mean that God was indwelling them. They were rejecting what God wanted to do for them. Jesus Christ Himself had come to be the Messiah of Israel. He was simply telling them, since they were concerned about the kingdom, that the kingdom was in their midst because He, the King, stood in their midst. The Greek words translated "within you" can justifiably be rendered "among you" or "in your midst," which would better reflect the meaning in its context.

Instead of man being inherently good, the Bible reveals that he is inherently evil. "All have sinned," says Romans 3:23, "and fall short of the glory of God." And Romans 5:12 says, "Through one man sin en-tered the world, and death through sin, and thus death spread to all men, because all sinned."

Good and Evil

With its roots in Eastern religions, TM also distorts the distinction between good and evil. Because of its monistic view that "all is One," how can it account for both good and evil? Is the one "essence," or "force" (the Hindu equivalent of God), both good and evil?

The God of the Bible stands in stark contrast to the god of Eastern religions. In the One-is-all and all-is-One view of divine essence, there ultimately is neither good nor evil because both merge into one. "In the philosophy of the One ethical distinctions evaporate; supposed opposites—light and dark, good and evil, humans and God—merge and fuse."[31]

The Bible clearly distinguishes between good and evil. The two never merge. Nor does a person ever transcend in his consciousness so that he goes beyond the bounds of moral distinctions.

Sin and Accountability

TM holds out the promise of happiness without facing the sin issue. The Bible reveals that man will never be happy or possess joy unless he faces his sin problem and comes into a right relationship with Jesus Christ. Imagine the happiness and joy of the person who real-izes that "there is therefore now no condemnation to those who are in Christ Jesus, who do not walk according to the flesh, but according to the Spirit" (Rom. 8:1). The believer has happiness and joy in his fel-lowship with God: "For the kingdom of God is not food and drink, but righteousness and peace and joy in the Holy Spirit" (Rom. 14:17). Any theory for happiness that does not take into consideration man's separation from God because of sin is programmed for failure—with eternal consequences.

Christianity and TM are also far apart concerning accountability. Be-cause TM reflects the Hindu philosophy of Maharishi that the supreme God is not a personal God, adherents understandably sense no responsibility to give account to anyone other than themselves. This is in line with the Vedas, a large collection of Hindu scriptures that tend to deify man and minimize sin. Because followers of TM are taught the all-is-One view where good and evil merge and where adherents can become one with God, they believe that they will eventually be beyond sin. Such a belief is worshiping their own divinity. No wonder TM does not emphasize the individual's responsibility or accountability to a personal God.

In contrast to this, the Bible reveals that each individual will give an account to God. Those who believe in Jesus Christ as their Savior will some day give account, not to be judged for their sin but to be rewarded for living in such a way as to please Jesus Christ (Rom. 14:12; 1 Cor. 3:10–15; 2 Cor. 5:10). Those who reject Jesus Christ as personal Savior will stand before the Great White Throne to give account and then will be thrown into the lake of fire (Rev. 20:11–15).

This is not an act of cruelty on God's part; rather, it is the result of a person rejecting what a loving God has provided for him in the Person of Jesus Christ. The Lord Jesus Christ has already paid the penalty for the sin of the world, but it is applied to a person's account only when he recognizes his sinful condition and believes in Jesus Christ as his Savior (John 1:12; 3:36; 5:24).

SALVATION

The Bible reveals that the way of salvation is by believing in Jesus Christ, who is "the propitiation [satisfaction] for our sins, and not for ours only but also for the whole world" (1 John 2:2). Because Jesus Christ paid the full penalty for sin, anyone who trusts Him as Savior receives forgiveness of sin and inherits eternal life. "He who hears My word," said Jesus, "and believes in Him who sent Me has everlasting life, and shall not come into judgment, but has passed from death into life" (John 5:24).

In TM, we find no salvation as the Bible speaks of it. Because each individual has the impersonal divine Being within him, he is not considered in need of salvation. As we have already seen, those who practice TM feel they are beyond sin; therefore, they have no need of salvation or a Savior. According to Maharishi, "Fulfillment of Life lies in gaining the status of divine life and living the life of eternal freedom in fulness of all values of human existence."[32] Fulfillment supposedly comes when man—by "transcendental deep meditation"—attains the state of pure consciousness, or the state of absolute pure Being, and is able to maintain himself in that state.[33] Such a view is not biblical nor in any way a view of historic biblical Christianity.

FUTURE LIFE

As would be expected from his background in Hinduism, Maharishi Mahesh Yogi believes in reincarnation—that through a slow process of death and rebirth in new forms of life, man can gradually reach spiritual perfection.

This also shows the natural bent of man's mind. On the one hand, he denies the distinction between good and evil; on the other hand, he somehow realizes the need to account for wrongdoing in this life. But salvation through Jesus Christ is replaced with the Hindu belief in karma—the law of sowing and reaping. If a person experiences adverse circumstances in this life, it is said to be because of his past in another life.

Biblical Christians also believe that people reap what they sow (Gal. 6:7), but this is far different from reincarnation. Biblical Christianity realizes the truth of Scripture that we have all sinned and come short of God's glory (Rom. 3:23). However, those who trust in Jesus Christ as their Savior are forgiven of their sins and given eternal life, and are not doomed to the fatalistic karma of Hinduism. Thus, Galatians 6:8 says, "He who sows to the Spirit will of the Spirit reap everlasting life."

Karma is cyclical, because one reincarnation occurs after another. Man's goal is to break out of this cycle by becoming one with the universal Being. "The force of karma," says the Maharishi, "keeps maintaining the life in the relative field, and the individual is constantly kept out of the realm of pure Being."[34] Those who reach full union with the "pure Being" are no longer reincarnated.

Reincarnation and karma are Hindu in origin, not Christian. According to the Bible, this one life on earth is all anyone has to prepare for eternity. If a person does not believe in Christ as Savior during this life, he has no hope for the future. "It is appointed for men to die once," says Hebrews 9:27, "but after this the judgment."

RELIGION

The view of Hinduism is that all religions are of equal value. This concept is also promoted by TM. Students are told, for instance, to remain in whatever religion they are in and just add on the techniques of TM. Certainly, many people see no distinction between different religions, but the significance of this point in TM is that it reflects the Hindu concept of religion held by Maharishi Mahesh Yogi. "Transcendental deep meditation," says the Maharishi, "is the practice to live all that the religions have been teaching through the ages; it is through this that man readily rises to the level of divine Being, and it is this that brings fulfillment to all religions."[35]

The Bible nowhere teaches that all religions are the same. It says, "There is one God and one Mediator between God and men, the Man Christ Jesus" (1 Tim. 2:5). Jesus said of Himself, "I am the way, the truth, and the life. No one comes to the Father except through Me" (John 14:6). And the apostle Peter said of Jesus Christ, "Nor is there salvation in any other, for there is no other name under heaven given among men by which we must be saved" (Acts 4:12). The Bible makes it clear that man cannot become a god. He can, however, reestablish the relationship with God that was lost through sin. But that is by one means only—faith in the Lord Jesus Christ. Any other religious belief will end in disappointment and will have eternal consequences.

CONCLUSION

Those who have carefully studied counterfeit religious groups leave no doubt about their view of Transcendental Meditation. David Haddon says that the Maharishi has "persistently concealed from the public both the religious basis and the ultimate spiritual goal of TM—the annihilation of personal existence in the impersonal Absolute."[36]

"TM is only a beginning," says Irvine Robertson, "a gradual movement from matter to mind, and then to supermind. This final attainment is explained as being 'union with the Divine,' the 'glorious Cosmic Consciousness,' the realization of the self, which is the impersonal god who is in every man, being, and object. *This* is the purpose of TM"[37] (emphasis his).

And for those who think that TM is only an innocent form of meditation, note what those who have studied it warn: "TM . . . is not a neutral discipline that can be practiced without harm to the individual," say Josh McDowell and Don Stewart. "In actuality, TM is a

Hindu meditation technique that attempts to unite the meditator with Brahman, the Hindu concept of God."[38]

In this day of philosophical and theological confusion, the Christian needs to be guided by the objective statements of the Scriptures rather than by the subjective feelings of an antibiblical system, even though those feelings may seem good at the moment. Any believer who is tempted to delve into the teachings of TM needs to heed the warnings of the Bible.

Through Moses, God warned the Old Testament Israelites: "If there arises among you a prophet or a dreamer of dreams, and he gives you a sign or a wonder, and the sign or the wonder comes to pass, of which he spoke to you, saying, 'Let us go after other gods which you have not known and let us serve them,' you shall not listen to the words of that prophet or that dreamer of dreams, for the LORD your God is testing you to know whether you love the LORD your God with all your heart and with all your soul" (Deut. 13:1–3).

This passage clearly teaches that everything that is supernatural is not necessarily from God. If the message does not agree with the Scriptures, avoid the message and the messenger. How does Deuteronomy 13:1–3 relate to TM? Even if an army of followers of TM actually could do yogic flying, or even if crime could be eliminated from a major city, TM should not be followed because its message does not agree with God's Word. Helping people for time is admirable, but offering no hope for eternity is horrible.

Also, God's warnings in the Book of Exodus apply to TM because of its use of a mantra and the Puja ceremony—both linked to Hindu deities. God commanded, "You shall have no other gods before Me" (20:3). And He later added, "Make no mention of the name of other gods, nor let it be heard from your mouth" (23:13). The person who believes in the God of the Bible for salvation—and apart from Him there is no salvation—should have absolutely nothing to do with TM.

Regardless of the contrary claims of the proponents of Transcendental Meditation, it clearly has a religious basis. And that religious basis is not historical Christianity, but Hinduism. Those who follow TM in ignorance are seeking to solve this world's problems, but it's at the expense of spiritual truths that could give them true rest and relaxation —not only for time but also for eternity.

Summary

Name:	Transcendental Meditation (TM)
Also Known As:	Science of Creative Intelligence (SCI)
	Maharishi University of Management (MUM)
Founder:	Maharishi Mahesh Yogi (c. 1910?–)
U.S. Headquarters:	Asbury Park, New Jersey
Membership:	U.S.: About 1 million; Worldwide: 6 million
Web Sites:	www.maharishi.org
	www.mum.edu

What They Believe

TM Practitioners:	Biblical Christians:
Source of Authority	
Follow the teachings of Maharishi Mahesh Yogi and Hindu Vedic scriptures.	The Bible alone is the final authority of faith and practice of all else.
God	
Believe in Brahman, the Hindu concept of God, and pantheism, that God is everything and everything is God. Believe in an impersonal God that is the essence or Being of the universe.	God is a Trinity—the three Persons of the Godhead are coequally and co-eternally God. God is also a divine Person, not a force, who exists apart from creation.
Man	
Man is inherently good and TM brings that goodness to the surface. The kingdom of God is within each person.	Man is inherently sinful; even though he does many good things, on his own he can never do enough to be accepted by God. God indwells only those who trust in Christ as their Savior.
Good and Evil	
Belief in monism (all is one) causes TM followers to conclude that ultimately good and evil blur together without distinction.	Good and evil are entirely separate and never lose their distinction, and God has absolutely no evil in Himself nor can He approve of evil of any kind.

Sin and Accountability

Mankind is inherently good and has no sin as described in the Bible. Because God is only an essence or Being there is no personal accountability.

All are inherently sinful, which results in sinful acts, even though good is also done. Everyone must some day give account to a personal, holy God.

Salvation

There is no need for salvation because every person has the divine essence within him. Fulfillment comes by attaining and maintaining oneself in the state of the absolute pure Being.

All must trust in Jesus Christ for salvation in order to have forgiveness of sins and eternal life. One becomes right with God through salvation provided in Jesus Christ, and man never becomes God.

Future Life

Believe in reincarnation, that man can eventually reach perfection through a long process of rebirths. Embrace the Hindu law of karma, that what we sow in this life we reap in the next.

Believe in resurrection—to eternal blessing for those who have trusted in Christ; to eternal condemnation for those who have rejected Him. Sin has consequences, but only in this life does one have opportunity to become right with God; after this life is the judgment.

Recommended Reading

Ankerberg, John, and Weldon, John. *Encyclopedia of Cults and New Religions.* Eugene, Ore.: Harvest House Publishers, 1999.

_____. *The Facts on Hinduism.* Eugene, Ore.: Harvest House Publishers, 1991.

Boa, Kenneth. *Cults, World Religions & the Occult.* Wheaton, Ill.: Victor Books, 1990.

Carlson, Ron & Decker, Ed. *Fast Facts on False Teachings.* Eugene, Ore.: Harvest House Publishers, 1994.

Enroth, Ronald, and others. *A Guide to Cults and New Religions.* Downers Grove, Ill.: InterVarsity Press, 1983.

Martin, Walter. *The Kingdom of the Cults.* Ravi Zacharias, gen. ed. Minneapolis: Bethany House Publishers, 2003.

Mather, George A., and Nichols, Larry A. *Dictionary of Cults, Sects, Religions and the Occult.* Grand Rapids, Mich.: Zondervan Publishing House, 1993.

What They Believe

McDowell, Josh, and Stewart, Don. *Handbook of Today's Religions.* San Bernardino, Calif.: Here's Life Publishers, Inc., 1983.

Rhodes, Ron. *The Challenge of the Cults and New Religions.* Grand Rapids, Mich.: Zondervan, 2001.

Robertson, Irvine. *What the Cults Believe.* Chicago: Moody Press, 1991.

ENDNOTES

[1] George A. Mather, and Larry A. Nichols, *Dictionary of Cults, Sects, Religions and the Occult* (Grand Rapids, Mich.: Zondervan Publishing House, 1993), 277.

[2] www.mum.edu/Maharishi.html, July 17, 1997.

[3] *Maharishi University of Management Silver Jubilee Commemorative Volume* (Fairfield, Iowa: Maharishi University of Management Press, 1996), n.p.

[4] Ibid.

[5] Ibid.

[6] Cate Peterson, *Omaha World-Herald*, July 10, 1986.

[7] Ibid.

[8] Ibid.

[9] *Maharishi University of Management Silver Jubilee Commemorative Volume*, n.p.

[10] Robert J. L. Burrows, "Americans Get Religion in the New Age," *Christianity Today*, May 16, 1986, 19.

[11] *Omaha World-Herald*, Jan. 16, 1993.

[12] Jeff Gauger, *Omaha World-Herald*, Feb. 7, 1993, 10.

[13] Ibid.

[14] Frank B. Minirth, M.D., and Paul D. Meier, M.D., *Happiness Is a Choice* (Grand Rapids, Mich.: Baker Book House, 1978), 145.

[15] John Ankerberg and John Weldon, *The Facts on Hinduism* (Eugene, Ore.: Harvest House Publishers, 1991), 8.

[16] *Maharishi University of Management Silver Jubilee Commemorative Volume*, 5.

[17] Gordon R. Lewis, foreword to *Unmasking the New Age*, by Douglas R. Groothuis (Downers Grove, Ill.: InterVarsity Press, 1986), 10.

[18] www.mum.edu/PRESS/Sanskrit/sanskrit.html, July 1997.

[19] Walter Martin, *The New Cults* (Ventura, Calif.: Regal Books, 1980), 92.

[20] Mahesh Yogi, *Meditations of Maharishi Mahesh Yogi*, 17–18, cited by Walter Martin, *The New Cults*, 96.

[21] Calvin Miller, *Transcendental Hesitation* (Grand Rapids, Mich.: Zondervan Publishing Company, 1977), 57–58.

[22] Joan Harrison, cited by Dave Hunt, *The Cult Explosion* (Eugene, Ore.: Harvest House Publishers, 1980), 11.

[23] Irvine Robertson, *What the Cults Believe* (Chicago: Moody Press, 1991), 122.

[24] Ibid., 124.

[25] Ibid.

[26] United States District Court, District of New Jersey, Civil Action No. 76–341.

[27] David Haddon, "Transcendental Meditation" in *A Guide to Cults and New Religions*, by Ronald Enroth and others (Downers Grove, Ill.: InterVarsity Press, 1983), 136.

[28] Maharishi Mahesh Yogi, *Transcendental Meditation*, formerly titled *The Science of Being and the Art of Living* (Bergenfield, N.J.: New American Library, 1963), 265.

[29] Ibid., 271.

[30] Ibid., 269.

[31] Douglas R. Groothuis, *Unmasking the New Age* (Downers Grove, Ill.: InterVarsity Press, 1986), 154.

[32] Yogi, *Transcendental Meditation*, 245.

[33] Ibid.

[34] Ibid., 41.

[35] Ibid., 255.

[36] Haddon, *A Guide to Cults and New Religions*, 148.

[37] Robertson, *What the Cults Believe*, 126.

[38] Josh McDowell and Don Stewart, *Handbook of Today's Religions* (San Bernardino, Calif.: Here's Life Publishers, Inc., 1983), 81.

CHAPTER THIRTEEN

Unification Church

Though many people in the United States have heard of the Reverend Sun Myung Moon, the outspoken and powerful leader of the Unification Church, today he seems to enjoy more popularity outside of the United States.

But the group still has significant influence inside the U.S. Officially known as The Holy Spirit Association for the Unification of World Christianity (HSA-UWC), this group owns the *Washington Times* newspaper in the nation's capital, and Moon seems to have access to some top U.S. leaders. *The Handbook of Denominations* reports, "In a speech at a U.S. Congressional reception in 2004, Rev. Moon was officially crowned, and he then declared that he 'is none other than humanity's Savior, Messiah, Returning Lord, and True Parent.'"[1]

Moon's unorthodox teachings and questionable recruiting practices have made this church a source of controversy for many years. Likewise, the Unification Church has been the subject of much national publicity in recent years as a result of Moon's conviction in 1982 (and subsequent imprisonment) on charges of conspiracy to defraud the federal government and of filing false income tax returns. After his release from prison, Moon was even bolder in claiming to be the Lord of the Second Advent to the world.[2]

The Unification Church is a relatively new movement as far as world religions go, having been founded in 1954. Since then, however, the group has made substantial inroads in many countries, including America, although Moon did not come to the United States until the mid-1960s.

BACKGROUND

A study of the Unification Church must naturally begin with Sun Myung Moon, the founder of the group and its spiritual leader. His influence is so strong, in fact, that his followers are commonly referred to as "Moonies."

Moon was born on January 6, 1920, in what is now North Korea. When he was 10 years old, his family converted to Presbyterianism. Then on Easter morning in 1936, at the age of 16, Moon claims to have received a vision while praying on a mountainside. In it Jesus Christ supposedly appeared to him and told Moon that he "had an important mission to accomplish in the fulfillment of God's providence."[3] Just as Mormonism got its start when 14-year-old Joseph Smith received a vision, this world religion also began in the mind of a teenager.

Mose Durst, the president of the Unification Church of America, relates what followed that Easter morning encounter: "Rev. Moon spent the next nine years praying and desperately studying the Bible. Through this search, he received the revelation that is now recorded in the Divine Principle."[4]

Moon began to preach his new "revelations" shortly after the end of World War II. Then came the partitioning of Korea and the Communist takeover of the north. Moon was arrested in 1948 and spent the next two years in a Communist labor camp. When he and the other prisoners were freed by a United Nations landing party on October 14, 1950, Moon supposedly carried one of his fellow prisoners "on his back on a bicycle the six hundred miles to Pusan."[5]

In 1954, following several years of preaching in Pusan and the surrounding region, Sun Myung Moon formally organized the Unification Church under the official name of The Holy Spirit Association for the Unification of World Christianity. As of 1984—its 30th anniversary—the Unification Church claimed to have "three million members in more than 120 countries."[6] Membership in the United States was reported about that time to be between 40,000 and 45,000. Some researchers, however, believe these U.S. figures were grossly exaggerated.[7] It is estimated that there are only about 10,000 followers in the U.S.[8]

After several difficult years in Korea, the Unification Church began to experience growth and prosperity. The church sent missionaries to Japan and several European countries. In 1959 Moon's first missionary, a woman by the name of Dr. Young Oon Kim, came to the United States. She located first in Oregon and then in California around the

San Francisco Bay area, where the first Unification church in America had its birth.[9]

Moon came to the United States in 1965 and gave impetus to what later became a worldwide movement by visiting every state in the union.[10] Taking advantage of the social unrest of the time, the movement soon gained many adherents among the country's youth. The group established headquarters in New York and began an all-out publicity campaign. Moon held huge meetings in major cities across the country.

To train those who were interested in joining the movement, the church established the Unification Theological Seminary on a 250-acre campus in Barrytown, New York. The group claims that this training center provides its students with "a unique experience in ecumenical Christian education."[11] The goal of the movement is to unify all theological beliefs; thus, the reason for calling it the "Unification" church. The education that students receive at their seminary is no doubt ecumenical, as well as unique. It is highly questionable, however, whether the education received could be considered Christian.

Moon has launched a number of business, political, educational and cultural—as well as religious—ventures to help promote the goals of the Unification Church. Some of these investments, and the group's fund-raising techniques, eventually caused the United States government to question Moon's tax-exempt status and business practices. In 1982 Moon was convicted of conspiracy to defraud the federal government and of filing false income tax returns. He was sentenced to 18 months in prison and fined $25,000. He did not begin serving his term, however, until the summer of 1984.

Before being imprisoned in Danbury, Connecticut, Moon told his followers, "I am going the road of confinement for the purpose of unity. Inside the prison I will work even harder to bring about greater unity with the Unification movement and the Christian community. Also I am working to bring unity between the Unification movement, the Christian community, and other religions. That is the purpose of my going to prison today."[12]

While Moon was in prison, the Unification Church made a major move to sell religious leaders on its views. It mailed packages of public relations materials to 300,000 pastors and Christian leaders. The packets contained three videotapes and a guide entitled "The Unification Principle," copies of *Divine Principle* and *God's Warning to the World: Reverend Moon's Message From Prison,* and a pamphlet entitled *Word and Deed*, which was written to commemorate the organization's 30th anniversary. (In some packages, *Divine Principle* was replaced with *Outline of the Principle Level 4*.) The cost of this public relations effort was estimated to be from $4.5 million to $10 million.[13]

Moon is especially concerned about disseminating his message in the United States because he believes America will be the future base of operations for the Lord of the Second Advent. "The end of the world signifies that the time of the arrival of the Lord of the Second Advent is near," he said. "He must have a base somewhere, some foundation prepared upon which he can begin to fulfill his mission. America is meant to be that base."[14] Speaking in Washington, D.C.,

Moon said, "The movement for world salvation must begin in this country. America is the base and when America fulfills her mission you will be eternally blessed."[15] To that end, Moon has been a permanent resident of the United States since 1973.

MOON'S TEACHINGS REVEAL THAT HE DOES NOT CONSIDER THE BIBLE TO BE THE INSPIRED WORD OF GOD.

BELIEFS

Much of the controversy surrounding the Unification Church has involved its doctrines and practices. In writing about this group and its strange beliefs, *The New York Times Magazine* stated, "While church members accept Moon's theology as revealed truth, nonmembers generally find it a mind-boggling mixture of Pentecostal Christianity, Eastern mysticism, anti-Communism, pop psychology and metaphysics."[16] What does Sun Myung Moon and the Unification Church believe about the basic doctrines of historical Christianity?

SOURCE OF AUTHORITY

Moon speaks with self-confidence about his authority: "You may again want to ask me, 'With what authority do you say these things?' I spoke with Jesus Christ in the spirit world. And I spoke also with John the Baptist. This is my authority."[17]

Moon also claims to have had "visionary chats with Moses, Buddha and assorted Biblical luminaries."[18]

Moon's teachings reveal that he does not consider the Bible to be the inspired Word of God or the final source of authority. "The Bible . . . is not the truth itself," Moon stated, "but a textbook teaching the truth. Naturally, the quality of teaching and the method and extent of giving the truth must vary according to each age. . . . Therefore, we must not regard the textbook as absolute in every detail."[19]

While the Unification Church uses the Bible, it is not its only source of authority. According to Durst, its president, "*The Divine Principle*, along with the Old and New Testaments serve as the scriptures of the Unification faith."[20] *Divine Principle* is the book that supposedly contains the new truths Moon received through special revelation to him alone.[21]

Like many counterfeit religious groups, the Unification Church emphasizes continuing revelation. The followers believe that Moon has received truths that have been hidden from others. Thus, the writings and teachings of Moon take precedence over the Bible. In writing about his belief that John the Baptist was responsible for Christ's death, Moon emphatically stated, "These are hidden truths presented to you as new revelations. You have heard me speak from the Bible. If you believe the Bible you must believe what I am saying."[22] In placing his personal "revelations" and interpretations above the authority of the Bible, Moon has left his followers with no choice but to consider him to be the absolute and infallible source of authority.

No one needs be confused about what the Unification Church considers to be the absolute source of authority. A two-page advertisement in the *Omaha World-Herald* on January 7, 1997, printed the text of Moon's speech that he presented on November 23, 1996, at the Buenos Aires Sheraton Hotel. The introduction to this expensive advertisement stated: "The words that follow are not concepts of one man's thinking. Rather, they are a direct revelation from God especially for this age."[23] The claim of "direct revelation" shows that the words of Moon are to be held on a level equal to, if not higher, than the Bible. And when Moon interprets the Bible, his method of interpretation allows him to come up with meanings that are unique to him.

METHOD OF INTERPRETATION

For words to have understandable meaning they must be interpreted in their usual, customary sense at the time they are written or spoken. Even figures of speech must be interpreted in this way if they are to convey the intended meaning. Rather than interpreting the language of the Scriptures according to its normal historical and cultural setting, Moon often allegorizes statements to make them fit his unusual teachings.

For instance, note Moon's interpretation of Christ's crucifixion: "The thief crucified on Jesus' right side foreshadowed the democratic world, and the thief crucified on Jesus' left side represented the Communist world."[24] Thus, according to Moon, the practice of referring to democracy as being on the "right" and Communism as being on the "left" is derived from Scripture.

Further, Moon claims that the word *resurrection* does not refer to raising someone from the dead. Instead, he teaches, "Resurrection means accepting the word of God to become the possessor of God's love."[25] This is term-twisting. There is no basis in historical Christianity (the only religion whose founder has been resurrected) for using the term in this manner.

In addition, Moon teaches that the expression "end of the world" is not referring to the actual destruction of the earth. Rather it only means that "evil is going to end."[26]

We find no biblical support for Moon's interpretations of these and many other teachings of Scripture. His interpretations are not based on the normal use of language in Bible times. The fact that Moon's followers wholeheartedly accept the validity of these strange teachings shows that they consider Moon's interpretations to be the final source of authority, not the Bible.

The Unification Church is based on the philosophies and concepts of a man rather than on the Scriptures. Because God possesses absolute power and knowledge, He has the ability and wisdom necessary to communicate His revelation to man as He wanted it to be understood.

The Bible is God's final and complete revelation. Jude referred to the faith as "once for all delivered to the saints" (1:3). The apostle John warns those who would add to or take away from the Book of Revelation (22:18–19). Because Revelation has more Old Testament quotations than any other New Testament book, one could not change Revelation without affecting the entire Bible.

Dualism

One cannot understand Moon's underlying views without understanding dualism. Josh McDowell and Don Stewart, in their *Handbook of Today's Religions,* wrote of Moon's views, "All of existence is dual: Father God and Mother God; Male and Female; Light and Dark; Yin and Yang; Spirit and Flesh. Each part of existence has its dual aspect. Moon's God (with dual male/female aspects) always acts in a dual manner with his dual creation."[27]

Moon's dualism is expressly seen in his view of the Fall. J. Isamu Yamamoto, a specialist in evaluating counterfeit religious groups, summarizes Moon's interpretation: "God's highest expression of this duality within creation itself was to be the relationship between man and woman. The first man was Adam; the first woman was Eve. God created them spiritually immature as brother and sister. He intended for them to assume a subject/object relationship with himself in their growth to spiritual perfection. Thereafter, as husband and wife, Adam and Eve were supposed to establish the Kingdom of Heaven on earth through their offspring."[28]

According to Moon, there were two falls of man—one physical and one spiritual. Both involved sexual sins. Moon teaches that Eve was the first victim of Satan. He tempted Eve to have an illicit sexual relationship with him. This caused her to fall spiritually because she was given spiritual insight into her failure. To cover her sin, she tempted Adam and committed the same sin with him. This caused them both to fall physically.

Because Moon believes in a dual fall of man, he teaches that God's redemption is also dual in nature—that both physical and spiritual salvation are necessary. He reasons that since the first Adam failed in his relationship with God, and thus could not raise perfect spiritual children, a second Adam was needed to marry and bear children to produce the perfect, sinless race. This is where Jesus Christ becomes the key figure.

JESUS CHRIST

In determining whether a group can be considered distinctively Christian or not, it is essential to examine its teachings concerning Jesus Christ. Do the leaders claim that He is God? Do they teach that He completely paid the penalty for sin at His first coming with His death and resurrection? Do they believe He will come again?

You do not have to look long at the teachings of the Unification Church before you discover that they are vastly different from what the Bible teaches. Moon does not believe that Jesus Christ is God. "Jesus was a man, one with God, but he was not God the Father. When he returns to earth he will come as a man in the position of the third Adam."[29]

The question is not, "Was Jesus the Father?" but, "Was Jesus God?" And Moon clearly denies the deity of Jesus. In *Divine Principle*, Moon emphatically stated, "Jesus is the man of this value. However great his value may be, he cannot assume any value greater than that of a man. . . . It is plain that Jesus is not God Himself."[30]

This directly contradicts the Bible's many teachings about Christ. For example, when Jesus told the people that He was the Son of God, the Jewish leaders clearly understood the meaning—He was claiming to be equal with God (John 5:18). This is why they wanted to have Him crucified. The Scriptures indicate that although there is only one God, He exists as three Persons—Father, Son and Holy Spirit. In John 1:1–14, Jesus is referred to as the "Word": "In the beginning was the Word, and the Word was with God, and the Word was God" (v. 1).

Likewise, Moon has denied Christ's purpose for coming to earth, saying that He failed to fulfill God's plan: "Jesus failed in His Christly mission. His death on the cross was not an essential part of God's plan for redeeming sinful man."[31] Moon claims that Satan entered Christ's body on the cross and that His death was Satan's greatest victory.

In addition, Moon teaches that John the Baptist was actually responsible for Christ's death. According to Moon, the people were looking for Elijah to return to earth before the coming of the Messiah. When the people asked Jesus about Elijah, He indicated that John the Baptist was Elijah. However, when they questioned John about it, he denied everything. Moon further claims that John's testimony was more readily accepted than Christ's words. Therefore, according to Moon's logic,

John's lack of faith led directly to the crucifixion of Jesus.

Throughout the Scriptures, God's plan of salvation is clearly laid out. From the beginning, Christ knew that He would die for the sins of mankind. He was in total control and gave His life willingly. Jesus stated, "I lay down My life that I may take it again. No one takes it from Me, but I lay it down of Myself. I have power to lay it down, and I have power to take it again. This command I have received from My Father" (John 10:17–18). Therefore, John the Baptist was in no way directly responsible for Christ's death.

IN UNIFICATION THEOLOGY, GOD'S PLAN OF SALVATION IS NOT YET COMPLETE.

Likewise, Moon does not believe that Jesus was physically resurrected after His crucifixion. He teaches that Christ's postresurrection appearances were those of a spirit.[32] The Bible, however, reveals that Jesus had a body. This was evidenced by His invitation to Thomas to touch His wounds, thus verifying that He was the crucified Christ (John 20:24–29).

So what, then, was the Lord's reason for coming to earth? According to Moon, "Jesus was the second Adam. It was God's will for him to be blessed in heavenly matrimony with the second Eve, his restored bride. God intended him to bring forth upon this earth his own sinless children. Then Jesus and his bride would have become the True Parents for humankind, and all humankind would have found life by grafting onto them."[33] But Moon thinks John the Baptist thwarted God's plan, and Jesus was crucified before He was able to marry and bear sinless children. So in Unification theology, God's plan of salvation is not yet complete.

Because God's will supposedly was thwarted at the coming of the second Adam (Jesus Christ), Moon claims we are to look for a "third Adam" (the Lord of the Second Advent), who will marry and produce the sinless race.[34] Moon stated, "The Messiah is destined to come to earth as the Son of Man in the flesh. He comes as the third Adam. He will take a bride and thereby bring about the most joyful day of heavenly matrimony, referred to as 'the marriage supper of the Lamb' in the book of Revelation. They will fulfill the role of the True Parents."[35]

At the Second Coming, Moon does not expect the Messiah to appear from heaven but to be born into this world as Jesus was at His first coming. This "third Adam" will then grow to adulthood and marry to produce the sinless race.

Thus, according to Moon, we are still waiting for God's salvation to be revealed. Jesus Christ's death did not pay the penalty for sin or save us. A "third Adam" must still come and marry his bride.

Who is the "third Adam"? At first, Moon did not expressly lay claim to the title, although he strongly hinted at it. For instance, he has long taught that the Messiah will be born in Korea—which just happens to be the place of his birth. Likewise, in the Unification Church, Moon has been given the title "The Lord of the Second Advent." Moon's marriage in 1960 to Hak Ja Han is considered to be "the marriage of the Lamb" mentioned in Revelation 19. He and his wife are also called the "True Parents" by his followers. All these examples point to the fact that the Unification Church—and Moon himself—consider him to be God's new savior.

In 1990 Moon admitted his claim to be "The Lord of the Second Advent." In a San Francisco speech he referred to himself as the Messiah. In addition, he said, "I have been called upon by God . . . I have suffered persecution and confronted death with only one purpose in mind, so that I can live with the heart of true parents to love races of all colors in the world."[36]

The marriage of the "True Parents" is seen in a different light, however, if one realizes that Moon had divorced his first three wives and that he was 40 years old when he married 17-year-old Hak Ja Han. As Mather and Nichols so aptly point out, "Moon's fourth wife . . . was declared to be the 'perfect mother' after the first three Eves proved to be failures."[37]

Regarding a third Adam, the Bible teaches us that Jesus Christ is the "last Adam." "So it is written," says 1 Corinthians 15:45, "'The first man Adam became a living being.' The last Adam became a life-giving spirit." Jesus Christ is the first, last and only Savior. He has paid the price completely. We need only to believe in Him to be saved.

THE HOLY SPIRIT

Because Moon's views concerning Jesus Christ are not in harmony with the Bible, it raises the question of what he teaches about the third Person of the Trinity.

Moon believes that Jesus came as the "True Father." To this he added, "However, a father alone cannot give birth to children. There must be a True Mother with a True Father, in order to give rebirth to fallen children as children of goodness. She is the Holy Spirit."[38] Moon further stated, "Thus, the Holy Spirit is a female Spirit, consoling and moving the hearts of the people."[39]

Although the Greek word for "spirit" (*pneuma*) is neuter, masculine pronouns are used in referring to the Holy Spirit in such passages as John 15:26 and John 16:13–14. Nowhere does the Bible state that the Holy Spirit is the "True Mother" or "female Spirit." Likewise, the Scriptures never refer to a union of Jesus Christ and the Holy Spirit in the way that Moon describes. There is no biblical basis for Moon's assertions.

THE TRINITY

Because the followers of Unification teach that Jesus was simply a man and that the Holy Spirit is His spiritual wife, they likewise have reinterpreted the biblical doctrine of the Trinity.

In the 1968 edition of *Divine Principle*, we find the following explanation of the Trinity:

> Through divine marriage in Perfection, Adam and Eve would have formed a trinity with God. This trinity was to be the pattern for all future marriages. . . . Having united with Satan, Adam and Eve failed to establish the trinity with God. By uniting with the Holy Spirit, Jesus established the trinity for the first time—but only in spirit. The divine ideal of trinity will be completely realized when the Lord comes in the glory of his Father. . . . Then he will be with his Bride, inviting all people to the marriage supper of the Lamb (Rev. 19:7–9). He and his Bride will be the true Parents. All mankind will be restored to God by forming trinities with Him.[40]

Thus, in Unification theology, Jesus Christ and the Holy Spirit are not God. In fact, the Son and the Holy Spirit supposedly did not even fulfill the true purpose of the Trinity. While not specifically stated, it is apparent from their use of terms that the followers of Moon believe that the first true trinity has been formed between Moon, his wife and God. They also teach that, through marriage, men and women can form a trinity with God.

SALVATION

One of the principal doctrines of the Unification Church is the "Law of Indemnity"—that God's children must pay the debt for their sins. Moon teaches that we must pay all we can before God will step in and forgive the rest of our debt.

In *Divine Principle*, we find the following explanation of indemnity:

> God does not and cannot forgive man unconditionally because it is contrary to the Divine Principle. It is not enough simply to desire to return to Him from Satan's domain. Like the prodigal son, we must make our way painfully and step by step from the far country to our Father's house. Only when we get within sight of that house will our Father run to meet us. . . . However, He does make concessions which result in man's compensating for only a fraction of his total debt. When man fulfills this condition, his whole debt is discharged and he is acknowledged by God as though he had not sinned at all.[41]

The Unification Church teaches a salvation based on works. A variety of methods for "restitution" are stressed, including fasting, fund-raising and recruiting new members. This is why the followers of Moon are willing to spend many long days and years selling items for the church. They believe that the more they sell, the faster they will pay their sin debt and reach perfection.

In Unification theology, indemnity is only the first stage of the salvation process. As stated earlier, Moon teaches that both a spiritual and a physical salvation are needed. According to Moon, Christ originally came to provide a physical salvation for mankind by marrying and fathering sinless children. When He failed in His mission, God used His death to provide a spiritual salvation for mankind.

However, this spiritual redemption was not adequate. Physical salvation is still needed. Thus, when mankind has paid its share of the debt, God will then send the "third Adam" to establish the kingdom of heaven on earth. He will marry, and he and his wife will become the True Parents. Those who have prepared themselves through indemnity and are ready for marriage will then be reborn and will be able to have sinless children. Moon stated, "By the restoration of True Parents we will be reborn as children of our heavenly Father, God, with full salvation into His sonship. . . . All men will be made new through their True Parents. All will be made capable of bringing sinless children into the world."[42]

Because of his comments, one might wonder if Moon offers a salvation based on sex. In his November 1996 speech in Buenos Aires, he told world leaders: "If you start a campaign to secure absolute sex [in contrast to free sex] in your country, your families and your nation will go straight to Heaven."[43]

The Unification Church has replaced salvation through faith in Jesus Christ and His finished work on the cross with a salvation based on good works, including marriage and raising children—not just children but sinless children. Clearly this is not what the Bible teaches.

MARRIAGE

Throughout Moon's teachings, we find an emphasis on the dualism of male/female and on marriage. "Marriage is the most important means of establishing God's kingdom on earth," he wrote.[44]

In fact, Moon doesn't think that Jesus has entered the Kingdom of Heaven because He wasn't married. He says, "Jesus came as Savior of humankind but could not enter the Kingdom of Heaven. He instead went to Paradise. In order to enter the Kingdom of Heaven, Jesus would have had to form a family. That is why Jesus wants to come again. Jesus was to marry, form a family, serve and live with God in that family, and then enter the Kingdom of Heaven with that family. He could not enter the Kingdom of Heaven by himself alone."[45]

Much attention has been focused on Moon's own marriage to his fourth wife in 1960 and on the mass marriages he has performed since that time. Mose Durst wrote, "The first wedding in Unification Church history was that of Rev. and Mrs. Sun Myung Moon in 1960. This marriage is considered the cornerstone for all later church weddings. Since 1961, there have been successively larger weddings of Unification Church members."[46]

What They Believe

Little was known about the Unification Church's marriage practices and teachings until 1982, when two marriage ceremonies attracted the attention of many in the United States. On July 1, 1982, Moon conducted a mass ceremony, or "blessing," for 2,075 couples in Madison Square Garden. According to Durst, it "was the first large wedding to take place outside Korea. On October 16, 1982, Rev. and Mrs. Moon officiated at the marriage of 5,800 couples in Seoul, Korea."[47] In August 1992 Moon united 30,000 couples—20,000 in Seoul, Korea, and about 10,000 of them outside of Korea via simultaneous satellite hookups.[48]

MARRIAGE IS AN INTEGRAL PART OF UNIFICATION'S SYSTEM OF SALVATION.

Marriage is an integral part of Unification's system of salvation. J. Gordon Melton stated, "The Unification Church impresses on the new member from the day he joins the importance of the marriage process, or blessing. Without the blessing no one is saved or qualified for the kingdom of heaven. Everything prior is mere preparation."[49] Melton has provided the following details about their marriage practices and teachings.

Many of those who join the Unification Church are single. These members spend their first few years in the group preparing for the "blessed life." They work on overcoming racial prejudices and on building interpersonal relationships. They seek to bring spiritual children (new recruits) into the church as preparation for becoming physical parents. Members also must pay indemnity by working for the church. In return, the church gives them just enough to live on.

Finally, after two to seven years of preparation, the member may apply for a "matching." The application goes to the blessing committee. If the candidate meets the requirements and is accepted, he is then enrolled in the next matching session. While candidates may request a certain person or racial preference, most leave the decision up to Moon, who pairs the couples in a matching ceremony. Most of these pairings are interracial or intercultural, since Moon believes this is the way to achieve the unity that is the goal of the Unification Church.

Following the matching, the couple participates in three ceremonies to complete the marriage process. The first is the wine ceremony, the closest parallel in the Unification Church to the Lord's Supper. The couple drinks a wine mixture containing more than 20 ingredients, supposedly including a small amount of blood from Moon and his wife. According to Melton, the wine ceremony "begins the reversal of the Eden events. It changes the satanic blood lineage of the couple and restores them to the heavenly lineage Adam and Eve had before the Fall. . . . Also, after this ceremony until the marriage is consummated, the men view their future spouses as 'mother' figures who lead them to their full status in the kingdom. The wine ceremony binds the couple as surely as marriage. The bond can only be broken by one partner's leaving the church or committing adultery."[50]

The wine ceremony begins an engagement period that can last anywhere from a few days to a few years. During this time, the couple separates and becomes acquainted with each other through phone calls, letters and occasional visits. The second step in the marriage process is the blessing ceremony itself, in which all the matched couples make their vows public and receive the blessing of Moon. This is immediately followed by a 40-day separation period, where each partner meditates on the seriousness of his or her calling. Then they are allowed to consummate the marriage in a private three-day ceremony. Following the marriage, the couple embarks on the "blessed life," in which the restoration process is completed by parenting "perfect" children to achieve the physical salvation left undone by Jesus. Braswell, in his *Understanding Sectarian Groups in America,* points out that over the years Moon has changed the delay of time in consummating the marriage. There was a 40-day waiting period in 1970 and then a three-year waiting period in 1975.[51]

One wonders how these children of the "Moonie" marriages turned out. Some born of the couples for whom Moon performed the ceremony in 1982 would be in their 20s now. Were these offspring perfect spiritual children, or did they act like typical kids and teenagers? And once they get ready to marry, will they have to have their marriages purified by Moon and his wife? What if these "Parents" are no longer living by then?

The marriages and the many children Moon encourages his couples to bear are outgrowths of his interpretation of the Second Coming.

SECOND COMING

While the Unification Church speaks a great deal about the Second Coming, its concept of Christ's return is far different from God's revelation in His Word.

In a statement of faith released by the Unification Theological Seminary in Barrytown, New York, we discover the Unification Church's views on eschatology:

> The Second Coming of Christ will occur in our age, an age much like that of the First Advent. Christ will come as before, as a man in the flesh, and he will establish a family through marriage to his Bride, a woman in the flesh, and they will become the True Parents of all mankind.
>
> Through our accepting the True Parents (the Second Coming of Christ), obeying them and following them, our original sin will be eliminated and we will eventually become perfect. True families fulfilling God's ideal will be begun, and the Kingdom of God will be established both on earth and in heaven. That day is now at hand.[52]

To comprehend the full impact of this statement, we must first understand the meaning behind the terms used by the Unification Church. First, even though they speak of the "Second Coming of Christ," they are not referring to Jesus Christ, the Son of God. The word *Christ* means "Messiah," and Moon's followers are using the word in its literal sense but not to refer to the Jesus Christ of the Bible.

Thus, the Unification Church claims that God will send a new messiah, the third Adam, to achieve what Jesus Christ failed to do in the First Advent. Unification writers make it abundantly clear that the third Adam is not Jesus: "Jesus said in reference to the Second Advent that 'the Son of man' would come. In Revelation it is said that he will bear a new name. . . . If Jesus is to come, why should he have a different name which no one knows but himself? Jesus' name is known to the world. It is thus clear that not Jesus but someone else will come, bearing a new name."[53]

Likewise, Unificationists teach that the third Adam will not come in the clouds, as the Bible states in 1 Thessalonians 4:16–17, but that he will be born another time in the flesh. Rather than taking the believers to heaven, say the Unificationists, he will establish the Kingdom of

God on earth through marriage. The followers of Moon also believe that the Second Advent already has occurred.

All of this adds up to an unspoken—but very real—view among Unification members that Rev. Sun Myung Moon is the "Lord of the Second Advent" and that he is in the process of establishing God's eternal kingdom on earth.

CONCLUSION

God has not told us all that we wish to know about many things. When He has remained silent, however, it is best that we be content with whatever information He has revealed in His infallible, inerrant Word. When we claim "special revelations" and use these to interpret the Scriptures, our interpretations will almost always be erroneous. Also, the revelations usurp the Bible as the final source of authority.

According to the Bible, Adam and Eve's fall was not the result of some sexual sin. It occurred because they disobeyed God's command and ate the fruit of the forbidden tree (Gen. 2:16–17; 3:1–13). They chose to go their own way instead of God's way, and this spirit of in-dependence is the essence of sin. Having become sinners, Adam and Eve passed on a sinful nature to all of their descendants, including the result of sin—death (Rom. 5:12).

The sacrifices of the Old Testament pointed forward to a time when God would send the perfect Sacrifice to take away sin. Before the eter-nal Son of God was born in human flesh, an angel told Joseph, "She [Mary] will bring forth a Son, and you shall call His name Jesus, for He will save His people from their sins" (Matt. 1:21). Throughout the Bible, the purpose of Christ's mission is evident—He came to die for the sins of the world. Rather than denying who Jesus was, as Moon claims he did, John the Baptist affirmed the Lord's ministry. When he saw Jesus approaching, John told the crowd, "Behold! The Lamb of God who takes away the sin of the world!" (John 1:29).

Jesus Christ willingly laid down His life as a substitute for all peo-ple. In so doing, He propitiated (satisfied) the Heavenly Father concerning sin (John 10:17–18; 1 John 2:2). Any person who realizes he is a sinner and trusts in the finished work of Christ receives for-giveness of sin and inherits eternal life (John 5:24).

Those who accept Jesus Christ as their personal Savior during this age become part of His Body, the Church (Eph. 1:22–23). At a future time, the Lord Jesus Christ will return, and all believers will rise to meet Him in the air (1 Thess. 4:16–17). Later He will come triumphantly to the earth and stand on the Mount of Olives, from which He ascended to the Father after His resurrection (compare Acts 1:11–12 with the prophecy of Zechariah 14:3–4).

Regardless of how a person might classify the teachings of Sun Myung Moon, they are not biblical Christianity. Although he refers to the Scriptures and weaves his interpretations of them into his own system, Moon does not believe that Christianity is the answer to the world's problems.

Moon's opinion of Christianity is revealed in a statement he made in 1974—and there is no indication that he has changed his mind: "God is now throwing Christianity away and is now establishing a new religion, and this new religion is Unification Church. . . . We have only one way."[54]

Summary

Name of Organization: The Holy Spirit Association for the Unification of World Christianity (HSA-UWC)
Also Known As: Unification Church, "Moonies"
Founder: Sun Myung Moon (1920–)
Membership (2003): U.S.: About 10,000; Worldwide: About 3 million
Web Site: www.unification.org

What They Believe

Moonies: **Biblical Christians:**

Source of Authority

Consider *Divine Principle*, along with the Bible, as their scriptures. Believe in continuing revelation. Sun Myung Moon's interpretations and teachings are the final and absolute source of authority.

The Bible alone is their final authority. The 66 books of the Bible complete God's revelation to mankind. No one person or church is the "official" interpreter of the Bible.

God/The Trinity

Everything in existence has a dual aspect, even the supreme being, who is Father God and Mother God. The "third Adam," his bride and God formed the first trinity, and mankind will be restored by forming trinities with God through marriage.

Dualism arises out of man-made world religions, not biblical Christianity. The Father, Son and Holy Spirit form the Trinity and each is co-equally and coeternally God.

Jesus Christ

Jesus was only a man, not God. Christ's purpose in coming was to marry and produce perfect children; however, He was killed before He could accomplish His mission. Do not believe in the physical resurrection of Jesus; claim He returned as a spirit. Christ was the second Adam but a "third Adam" must yet appear to fulfill God's program by marrying and producing a sinless race.

Jesus is God and is the first, last and only Savior. Christ became a man to live a perfect life and die on the cross to pay for the sin of mankind, and His mission was accomplished. Believe in the physical resurrection of Jesus, which was verified by eyewitnesses.

The Holy Spirit

The Holy Spirit is a female Spirit— the "True Mother" and spiritual wife of Jesus.

The Greek word for "spirit" (*pneuma*) is neuter, but masculine pronouns are used in referring to the Holy Spirit.

Salvation

A person can earn his salvation through fasting, fund-raising, recruiting and other works. The "third Adam" will provide physical salvation by marrying and producing sinless children. Only those who receive the marriage blessing will be saved, or qualified, for the kingdom.

Salvation can be attained only by grace alone through faith in Christ alone. Salvation is from sin's condemnation, and any physical salvation is obtained when believers are delivered from the presence of sin at death. Anyone can have salvation by believing in Jesus Christ.

Second Coming

Jesus Christ will not return. Instead, God will send another man as the "third Adam." Moon is the "third Adam" and he has begun to establish God's kingdom.

Believe in the physical, visible return of Christ. He will return as the King of kings and Lord of lords.

Recommended Reading

Ankerberg, John, and Weldon, John. *Encyclopedia of Cults and New Religions.* Eugene, Ore.: Harvest House Publishers, 1999.

What They Believe

Boa, Kenneth. Cults, *World Religions & the Occult*. Wheaton, Ill.: Victor Books, 1990.

Bjornstad, James. *Sun Myung Moon and the Unification Church*. Minneapolis: Bethany House Publishers, 1984.

Braswell, George W., Jr. *Understanding Sectarian Groups in America*. Nashville: Broadman & Holman Publishers, 1994.

Enroth, Ronald, and others. *A Guide to Cults and New Religions*. Downers Grove, Ill.: InterVarsity Press, 1983.

_____, ed. *A Guide to New Religious Movements*. Downers Grove, Ill.: InterVarsity Press, 2005.

Gruss, Edmond C. *Cults and the Occult*. Phillipsburg, N.J.: P&R Publishing, 1994.

Martin, Walter. *The Kingdom of the Cults*. Ravi Zacharias, gen. ed. Minneapolis: Bethany House Publishers, 2003.

Mather, George A., and Nichols, Larry A. *Dictionary of Cults, Sects, Religions and the Occult*. Grand Rapids, Mich.: Zondervan Publishing House, 1993.

McDowell, Josh, and Stewart, Don. *Handbook of Today's Religions*. San Bernardino, Calif.: Here's Life Publishers, Inc., 1983.

Rhodes, Ron. *The Challenge of the Cults and New Religions*. Grand Rapids, Mich.: Zondervan, 2001.

Robertson, Irvine. *What the Cults Believe*. Chicago: Moody Press, 1991.

Yamamoto, J. Isamu. *Unification Church*. Grand Rapids, Mich.: Zondervan Publishing House, 1995.

ENDNOTES

[1] Frank S. Mead, Samuel S. Hill and Craig D. Atwood, *Handbook of Denominations in the United States*, 12th edition (Nashville: Abingdon Press, 2005), 383.

[2] "Causa Seminar Speech," Aug. 29, 1985, 7–8, cited by James A. Beverley, *Evangelizing the Cults*, Ronald Enroth, ed. (Ann Arbor, Mich.: Servant Publications, n.d.), 73.

[3] Sun Myung Moon, *Christianity in Crisis: New Hope* (Washington, D.C.: The Holy Spirit Association for the Unification of World Christianity, 1974), 117.

[4] Mose Durst, *Word and Deed—The Unification Movement: Toward an Ideal World* (New York: HSA Publications, n.d.), 10.

[5] Moon, *Christianity in Crisis*, 120.

[6] Durst, *Word and Deed*, 16.

[7] Art Toalston, "The Unification Church Aims a Major Public Relations Effort at Christian Leaders," *Christianity Today*, April 19, 1985, 51.

[8] *Christian Century*, Sept. 11–18, 1996, 845, and www.adherents.com, Oct. 28, 2005.

[9] George W. Braswell Jr., *Understanding Sectarian Groups in America* (Nashville: Broadman & Holman Publishers, 1994), 100.

[10] Ibid., 101.

[11] Durst, *Word and Deed*, 16.

[12] Sun Myung Moon, *God's Warning to the World: Reverend Moon's Message from Prison* (New York: Rose of Sharon Press, 1985), 159.

[13] Toalston, *Christianity Today*, April 19, 1985, 50.

[14] Moon, *Christianity in Crisis*, 62.

[15] Ibid., 67.

[16] Berkeley Rice, *The New York Times Magazine*, May 30, 1976, 18–19.

[17] Moon, *God's Warning to the World*, 128.

[18] Berkeley Rice, "The pull of Sun Moon," *The New York Times Magazine*, May 30, 1976, 145.

[19] *Divine Principle* (Washington, D.C.: The Holy Spirit Association for the Unification of World Christianity, 1973), 9.

[20] Durst, *Word and Deed*, 7.

[21] Ibid., 10.

[22] Moon, *God's Warning to the World*, 129.

[23] *Omaha World-Herald*, Jan. 7, 1997, 6.

[24] Moon, *God's Warning to the World*, 89.

[25] Ibid., 137.

[26] Ibid., 109.

[27] Josh McDowell and Don Stewart, *Handbook of Today's Religions* (San Bernardino, Calif.: Here's Life Publishers, Inc., 1983), 101.

[28] J. Isamu Yamamoto, "'Unification Church' (Moonies)," *A Guide to Cults and New Religions* (Downers Grove, Ill.: InterVarsity Press, 1983), 157.

[29] Moon, *God's Warning to the World*, 42.

[30] *Divine Principle*, 255, 258, cited by Josh McDowell and Don Stewart, *Understanding the Cults* (San Bernardino, Calif.: Here's Life Publishers, Inc., 1982), 137.

[31] Ibid., 142–143, cited by McDowell and Stewart, *Understanding the Cults*, 136.

[32] *Divine Principle*, 360.

[33] Moon, *God's Warning to the World*, 42.

[34] Ibid., 43.

[35] Ibid., 148.

[36] *The San Francisco Chronicle*, cited in the *Omaha World-Herald*, Aug. 17, 1990, 3.

[37] Mather and Nichols, *Dictionary of Cults, Sects, Religions and the Occult*, 283.

[38] *Divine Principle*, 215.

[39] Ibid.

[40] *Divine Principle* (1968), 77–78.

[41] Ibid., 48.

What They Believe

[42] Moon, *Christianity in Crisis*, 28.

[43] *Omaha World-Herald*, Jan. 7, 1997, 7.

[44] Moon, *God's Warning to the World*, 37.

[45] *Omaha World-Herald*, Jan. 7, 1997, 7.

[46] Durst, *Word and Deed*, 14.

[47] Ibid.

[48] *Omaha World-Herald*, Aug. 25, 1992.

[49] J. Gordon Melton, "What's Behind the Moonie Mass Marriages," *Christianity Today*, Dec. 16, 1983, 28.

[50] Ibid., 30.

[51] Braswell, *Understanding Sectarian Groups in America*, 124.

[52] Frederick Sontag, *Sun Myung Moon and the Unification Church* (Nashville: Abingdon, 1977), 105.

[53] *Divine Principle* (1968), 183.

[54] "Moon Landing in Manhattan," *Time*, Sept. 30, 1974, 68.

CHAPTER FOURTEEN

Unitarian Universalists

Imagine belonging to a denomination that does not care what you believe. For instance, you can choose your sexual preference because homosexuals and lesbians are welcomed and same-sex marriages are endorsed by some churches in the denomination, or association, as the followers prefer to call it. Better yet, you don't have to worry about any judgment in the future because the church teaches that no one will suffer eternal condemnation no matter how he lives or what he believes. Of course, if you believe in biblical Christianity you won't find the church so friendly toward you—which means that in this church you can believe about anything you want except the truth of historic biblical Christianity.

Such a denomination is not a figment of your imagination. It's the Unitarian Universalist Association (UUA).

This church sees nothing worthy of salvaging from biblical Christianity. In 1964 Jack Mendelsohn, a highly respected minister in the Unitarian Universalist movement, wrote in *Why I Am a Unitarian Universalist*, "I am willing to call myself a Christian only if in the next breath I am permitted to say that in varying degrees I am also a Jew, a Hindu, a Moslem, a Buddhist, a Stoic, and an admirer of Akhenaten, Zoroaster, Confucius, Lao-Tse and Socrates."[1] Mendelsohn's statement also points to the extreme theological liberalism of Unitarian Universalists. They consider themselves to be the "bridge" for the world's religions.

In his book Mendelsohn added, "We are open to all that is ethically best in the world's religions, and through freedom, reason, and tolerance we feel prepared to touch each of the great faiths and draw together their moral fervor."[2] The Unitarian Universalist Church claims to have no creeds. Anyone can be a member of the church, regardless of his beliefs. As a result, many who belong to this group do not want to be known as "Christians." Others may accept the title, but they do not believe in biblical Christianity.

BACKGROUND

The history of the Unitarian Universalist Association is the story of two separate religious groups—the American Unitarian Association and The Universalist Church of America. These groups merged in 1961 to form the UUA.

Both groups trace their roots back to the early years of Christianity,

THE BOOK CREATED SUCH A STIR THAT HE SPENT THE NEXT 20 YEARS IN HIDING.

but a standard work on denominations in the United States says, "Unitarianism, as we know it today … began with the Protestant Reformation, among Anti-Trinitarians and Socinians [followers of Faustus Socinus]."[3]

In 1531 Michael Servetus published a book entitled *On the Errors of the Trinity*. The book created such a stir that he spent the next 20 years in hiding. He was finally imprisoned and burned at the stake on October 27, 1553. Following his death, anti-Trinitarian churches began to spring up in Poland and Transylvania (now part of Romania) under the leadership of Faustus Socinus and Francis David.

The doctrines of Unitarianism and Universalism soon spread to England, where the movements gained momentum and became more organized. A number of leaders arose in the 17th and 18th centuries, including Unitarians John Biddle, Theophilus Lindsey and Joseph Priestly and Universalists James Relly and John Murray. Around the middle of the 18th century, Relly founded a Universalist center in London. In 1759 he published a book entitled *Union*, which outlined the teachings of Universalism and became one of the movement's key works. In 1774 Lindsey, a former Church of England clergyman, established the first Unitarian society in Great Britain.

One of the first members of Lindsey's church was scientist Joseph Priestly. When Priestly's house and laboratory were burned by a mob, he immigrated to America and became a key figure in the American Unitarian movement. Under his leadership, the first permanent Unitarian church in America was founded in Philadelphia in 1796.

During the 19th century, the Unitarian church experienced some of its greatest growth and influence. In 1802 the oldest Pilgrim church in America—founded at Plymouth in 1620—became a Unitarian church. The American Unitarian Association was organized in 1825.[4]

Much of this early growth can be attributed to the leadership of three men: William Ellery Channing (1780–1842), Ralph Waldo Emerson (1803–1882) and Theodore Parker (1810–1860). In their speeches and writings these men spoke out against many of the basic doctrines of Christianity. As a result of their influence, Unitarianism in America "reacted against Calvinistic doctrines that emphasized human sinfulness, as well as the Trinity. Unitarians argued that such doctrines were inconsistent with the Bible and contrary to reason."[5] Notice from this statement that the early Unitarians argued using the Bible as their basis, even though biblical Christians believe their arguments were flawed. Present-day Unitarians would be embarrassed by the appeal of early Unitarians to the Bible, for they have now completely rejected the Bible as an authoritative document. Alan Gomes, associate professor of historical theology at Talbot School of Theology, points out that Unitarian Universalism had Christian roots. Key people he cites in the development of Unitarianism from the Continent, England and America are Faustus Socinus (1539–1604), who was from the Minor Reformed Church, John Biddle (1615–1662) and William Ellery Channing (1780–1842), a New England Congregationlist.[6]

According to David Robinson, a professor of English and director of American Studies at Oregon State University, "William Ellery Channing is the single most important figure in the history of American Unitarianism."[7] Channing's boyhood gave him ample reasons to champion the cause of social reform—a distinctive of Unitarianism. Mendelsohn says of Channing: "As a youngster he watched his mother struggle in genteel but real poverty to feed and clothe a large family. Though wiry and muscular enough as a boy to defend himself, he was shaken to the roots of his young being by the brutality of teachers to pupils, larger student to smaller student. Occupying British troops had left much of his home town of Newport a sorry, stripped-down shambles."[8]

What They Believe

In 1819 Channing preached a message entitled "Unitarian Christianity." Robinson acknowledges the significance of this message by saying it "stands as the defining statement of the movement, and in its wake the American Unitarian Association was formed in 1825."[9]

American essayist and poet Ralph Waldo Emerson was also a significant leader in the Unitarian movement. The son of a Unitarian minister, Emerson's early life was marked by sickness and poverty. His father died when he was young, leaving his mother to raise their five sons. In 1829 he was ordained as Unitarian pastor of the Second Church of Boston.

Emerson's views, such as his unwillingness to administer the Lord's Supper, were too radical even for the Unitarians of his day, so he resigned the pastorate in 1832 to pursue a career as a writer and lecturer. In 1838 he delivered his famous Divinity School Address at Harvard. In this address Emerson "criticized the historical Christianity of Andrews Norton and other Unitarians and caused a storm of controversy."[10] Prior to this event, many followers of the Unitarian movement were still in sympathy with biblical Christianity. Emerson's address served to liberalize Unitarian doctrines even further and is considered by Unitarians to be "a major event in the history of religious liberalism."[11]

Joining Emerson in his efforts to liberalize Christianity was Unitarian pastor Theodore Parker. He is best known for his 1841 address entitled "A Discourse on the Transient and Permanent in Christianity." In this address he argued "that most of the traditional supports of Christian belief such as the biblical miracles, the inspiration of the scriptures, and the divinity of Jesus were transient rather than permanent and necessary parts of religion."[12]

Like Emerson, Parker's views were too strong for the Unitarians of his time, and he was rejected. His radical views, however, became a rallying point for advancing liberalism within the Unitarian movement.

During this period, the Universalist movement also was gaining influence in America under the leadership of John Murray (1741–1815), Hosea Ballou (1771–1852) and others.

Like many of the leaders of the Unitarian and Universalist movements, Murray was born and raised in England. He came from a family of strict Calvinists. As a young man, Murray reacted against the teachings of Calvinism regarding predestination and eternal damnation. He became an avid follower of James Relly. According to Robinson, "The key to Murray's development was his reading of James Relly's *Union* (1759) and his subsequent listening to his preaching. Relly argued that all humanity actually achieved union with Christ in his death and therefore had already paid the price for sin."[13]

Believing that "all humanity actually achieved union with Christ in his death" means that the world needs no evangelistic message because it is not lost. The messenger need only tell people they are already right with God. In effect, Unitarian Universalism says to sinful humanity, "Be happy; you have all the relationship with God that you'll ever get." Of course, for the most part, contemporary Unitarianism rejects the concept of God altogether.

Murray's beliefs caused many of his friends in England to ostracize him. A number of personal tragedies, among them the death of his wife and child, led him to come to America in 1770. Murray began to preach extensively and found many supporters. In 1779 he helped organize the first Universalist church in Gloucester, Massachusetts.

While John Murray is considered the founder of American Universalism, Robinson considers Hosea Ballou to be "the single most important leader in the denomination's history."[14] Ballou's book, *A Treatise on Atonement* (1805), was a watershed theological work for the denomination. The Unitarian Universalist Association describes it as "the first book published in America openly rejecting the doctrine of the Trinity."[15] In addition, Ballou attempted "to undermine what he believed was the basis of the entire Calvinist system, the notion of the vicarious [substitutionary] atonement of Christ for the sins of humankind."[16]

Although the American Unitarians and Universalists were at odds with each other throughout much of their history, they eventually decided that their similarities outweighed their differences. This led to the merger of the two denominations in 1961, which resulted in the further liberalization of their views. According to a report in *Time* magazine, "A compromise hammered out during the merger eliminated the name of Jesus from the association's statement of principles, which were said to be 'immemorially summarized in the Judeo-Christian heritage as love to God and love to man.' In the 1970s, 'man' was changed to 'humankind.'"[17]

What They Believe

Before their merger, the Unitarians claimed a membership of 109,508, and the Universalist Church numbered 70,542. After joining forces in 1961, membership rose to 210,648 in 1975 and now stands at about 218,000.[18]

Furthermore, the Baby Boomer generation has been drawn to the church—initially, because of the church's anti-authority attitude, but now because this generation is searching for spiritual meaning. In 1991 *Newsweek* magazine quoted UUA President William Schulz as saying, "The quintessential boomer church may well be the Unitarian Universalist Association, which emphasizes that each individual is the ultimate source of authority."[19] Anyone searching for meaning in the New Age Movement would also find a home in the UUA church, because Schulz's statement sounds like something a New Ager would say.

While the history of the Unitarian Universalists is interesting, the theology of the group is more important than its facts and figures.

BELIEFS

The word *beliefs* is perhaps too strong a word to use when describing the views of Unitarian Universalists since it is an unwritten creed that they do not believe in creeds. Despite the changes that have taken place in the movement, they still hold to the proclamation of the 1894 National Conference of Unitarians that "'nothing in this constitution is to be construed as an authoritative test,' thus declaring the denomination to be uncompromisingly noncreedal."[20]

That statement reveals the group's thinking that all truth is relative and that no belief should be binding on all. It is apparent when reading their books, however, that the Unitarian Universalists have some definite beliefs—even though most of them take the form of denials.

SOURCE OF AUTHORITY

Like many non-Christian groups, the Unitarian Universalists deny the divine inspiration and authority of the Bible, although early in their history they adhered to it. Mendelsohn expressed the views of the group when he wrote, "Churches, Bibles and creeds are the creations of men who once exercised their freedom to create."[21] He added, "The Bible is replete with inaccuracies, inconsistencies, and errors."[22]

In his book *Challenge of a Liberal Faith*, George Marshall echoed this view. In answering the question "What do Unitarians and Universalists think about the Bible?" he replied, "It is not necessary as a source of divine authority, nor is it regarded by us as a verbally inspired book. . . . Different parts of it are to be taken more seriously than others, and we should use our intellect in interpreting and judging its contents. While it is quoted by us and may be used in our services, it is often read in conjunction with other books, including those from other religious traditions and secular fields."[23]

Many people and movements have made similar accusations against the Word of God. But even after centuries of attack, the Bible still remains not only a valid historical document but also a revelation of God's way of salvation through Jesus Christ. Although some passages may appear to be contradictory at first glance, a careful study reveals that the Bible fits together as a unit without any inaccuracies. Events predicted many years in advance have been literally fulfilled. This would not have been the case if the Bible were only a work of man and not the Word of God.

The *fact* that the Bible is God's inspired Word is revealed in 2 Timothy 3:16: "All Scripture is given by inspiration of God, and is profitable for doctrine, for reproof, for correction, for instruction in righteousness." The *method* of inspiration is given in 2 Peter 1:21: "Prophecy never came by the will of man, but holy men of God spoke as they were moved by the Holy Spirit." The *extent* of inspiration is seen in Matthew 5:18: "For assuredly, I [Jesus] say to you, till heaven and earth pass away, one jot or one tittle will by no means pass from the law till all is fulfilled."

For the majority of Unitarian Universalists, human reason and experience have replaced the Bible. Mendelsohn wrote, "With us reason holds the place that is ordinarily accorded to revelation in orthodox religions!"[24] However, even reason is not considered to be final or authoritative. Mendelsohn added, "This does not mean that we are unmindful of the limitations of human reason, nor that we look upon it as an infallible guide. In our way of life there are *no* infallible guides" [25] (emphasis his). Notice this absolute statement that there are no absolutes! Everyone lives by someone's absolutes. Many groups, not just the Unitarians, want us to reject the absolutes of the Bible and live by their absolutes.

What They Believe

THE TRINITY

The name *Unitarian* indicates a belief that God exists in one person rather than three. Thus, one of the key doctrines of the Unitarian Universalists is a denial of the Trinity. They claim that the Trinitarian doctrine is not taught in the Bible but was later added by the Council of Nicea in A.D. 325. In William Ellery Channing's sermon entitled "Unitarian Christianity," delivered in Baltimore in 1819, he placed "Jesus well above humans but well below God, by holding, as he put it, 'the most exalted views of Jesus Christ, which are consistent with the supremacy of the Father.'"[26] The Unitarian Universalists consider Channing's sermon to be "a landmark statement of Unitarian principles."[27]

What the Unitarian Universalists have failed to realize, however, is that those who believe in the Trinity do not deny the unity of God. The word *trinity* means "three in one." As theologian G. W. Bromiley says, the word "signifies that within the one essence of the Godhead we have to distinguish three 'persons' who are neither three gods on the one side, nor three parts or modes of God on the other, but co-equally and coeternally God."[28]

Moses declared, "Hear, O Israel: The LORD our God, the LORD is one!" (Deut. 6:4). When the scribes asked Jesus what commandment was most important, He answered, "The first of all the commandments is: 'Hear, O Israel, the LORD our God, the LORD is one'" (Mark 12:29). While these statements by Moses and Jesus emphasize the unity of God, they are not denials of the Trinity.

Contrary to the Unitarians' claim that the Trinitarian doctrine was later added, we find a number of references to the Trinity in the Bible (although the word *trinity* is not used in the Bible, just as the word *Unitarian* is not used). God frequently uses plural pronouns—us, our—in referring to Himself (Gen. 1:26; 11:7). The New Testament

> THE UNITARIAN UNIVERSALIST CHURCH DOES NOT HAVE ONE SPECIFIC VIEW OF GOD.

more clearly reveals that God is a trinity (Matt. 28:19). Each member of the one Godhead—Father, Son and Holy Spirit—is a Person because each has intellect, emotions and will. Each Person has the attributes of God, for each has all power, all knowledge and is everywhere present.

Of course, the Bible's teachings concerning the Person of God and the Trinity are beyond our limited understanding and must be accepted by faith. The Unitarian Universalists' denial of the Trinity clearly reveals their elevation of human reason over God's revelation in His Word.[29]

GOD

In the past, Unitarian Universalists acknowledged the power, nature and personhood of God. In recent years, however, their liberalism has reached the point where some in the movement are not only denying the personality of God but are even questioning His existence.

Because of the "freedom" that exists in the Unitarian Universalist church, they do not have one specific view of God. In summarizing their various positions concerning God, George Marshall wrote:

> There are a multitude of beliefs held by us, because there is no set dogma or doctrine. It is probable there may be some Unitarian Universalists who believe in the type of jealous, nationalist God of Old Testament accounts, and some who believe in the loving father of Jesus' concept. Some would agree with Jesus, 'God is love.' Others would join with Gandhi in saying 'God is truth.' Others join with scientists in saying God is 'the first cause,' or with philosophers in calling God 'the center of focus in the universe.' Others define God as the integrating force, that which makes meaning in our experience, that which makes sense out of life, the power for good, etc. Generally speaking Unitarian Universalists find God within the natural order, not outside of it. God becomes a natural force rather than supernatural.

> All Unitarian Universalists do not agree in the necessity for belief in God. Some are humanists who feel it is more important to deal with human and social concerns and to apply their attention to the ethical issues of life, rather than draining

it off in theological and philosophical speculation. Many say it is not a matter of rejecting the idea of God, but that this idea means many different things to different people.[30]

Such views of God make the Unitarian Universalists wide open to the view of the New Age Movement, with its emphasis on God being only an impersonal force and that all things and people are of the one essence (monism). In fact, Gomes sees the UUAs as having swung from Christianity to humanism to now emphasizing a new spiritualism. Gomes says, "The UUA's seventh principle in its *Statement of Principles and Purposes* also embodies the New Age thrust when it speaks of the UUA's 'respect for the interdependent web of all existence.'"[31]

JESUS CHRIST

In light of their denial of the Trinity and their views concerning God, it is not surprising to discover that Unitarian Universalists also deny the deity of Christ. They teach that Jesus was merely a very good man and teacher. They do not believe that He is God or our Savior. They overlook that He claimed to be God—and the fact that if that claim was a lie, He couldn't have been a good man and teacher.

Unitarian Universalists teach that Christ's followers claimed more for Him than He did for Himself. Mendelsohn wrote, "Most of us believe that on the basis of the evidence available to us, Jesus, at most, thought of himself as the Jewish Messiah. It was later followers and interpreters, like the apostle Paul, who transformed Jesus into a Christian Saviour atoning to God for the sins of mankind."[32]

In order to explain away the Bible's clear teachings about Jesus Christ, the Unitarian Universalists claim that the passages concerning the deity of Christ and His atonement were added later by the apostles and other Christian writers. Such thinking reveals not only their rejection of the authority and inspiration of the Scriptures but also their lack of understanding of Christ's teachings about Himself. Not only did Jesus claim to be the Jewish Messiah, but He also made it clear that He and God are one (John 10:30; 17:21–22). The Jewish leaders understood Christ's claims of deity, which was why they wanted to crucify Him: "Therefore the Jews sought all the more to kill Him, because He not only broke the Sabbath, but also said that God was His Father, making Himself equal with God" (5:18).

Jesus also taught that His purpose for coming to earth was to provide salvation for mankind, or "humankind," if you prefer, "for the Son of Man has come to save that which was lost" (Matt. 18:11). In John 6:37 He added, "All that the Father gives Me will come to Me, and the one who comes to Me I will by no means cast out."

As the time of His death and resurrection approached, Christ plainly revealed God's plan of salvation to the people:

> I am the good shepherd; and I know My sheep, and am known by My own. As the Father knows Me, even so I know the Father; and I lay down My life for the sheep. And other sheep I have which are not of this fold; them also I must bring, and they will hear My voice; and there will be one flock and one shepherd. Therefore My Father loves Me, because I lay down My life that I may take it again. No one takes it from Me, but I lay it down of Myself. I have power to lay it down, and I have power to take it again. This command I have received from My Father (10:14–18).

Jesus also declared that this salvation is available only through Him: "I am the way, the truth, and the life. No one comes to the Father except through Me" (14:6).

SALVATION

Since the Unitarian Universalists deny both the deity of Christ and His role as Savior, it is to be expected that they would also reject the Bible's teachings regarding salvation through faith in Him. Acts 16 tells of the Philippian jailer who asked Paul and Silas, "Sirs, what must I do to be saved?" (v. 30). They answered, "Believe on the Lord Jesus Christ, and you will be saved, you and your household" (v. 31).

Mendelsohn's response to Paul's answer reveals the thinking of the Unitarian Universalists concerning salvation by faith in Christ alone:

> Here was the track of authoritarianism on which orthodox Christianity would run from Paul's day to our own. It did not occur to Paul that the jailer might have some thoughts and insights of his own worth probing and nurturing. Paul saw no reason whatever for encouraging the man to think, to use his own mind, to exercise his reason, to ponder the experiences of heart and conscience for satisfying religious answers. Paul

said none of the words that might have moved Christianity in the direction of freedom and personal responsibility. Instead, he uttered a dogma. He said, in effect, this is not something to discuss, to weigh, to test by experience. No, this is something you simply accept. Unitarian Universalists will have none of it.[33]

For Unitarian Universalists, salvation is not a matter of being delivered from the penalty of sin and eternal condemnation by trusting Christ as personal Savior. To them, salvation involves character development. "We believe," stated Mendelsohn, "that religion has no higher object than to teach us how to get from Sunday to Monday; how to take our Sunday professions into our Monday behavior, in short, when we talk of salvation, we talk of making religion a real force in our daily lives."[34] True Christianity also emphasizes making religion a force in one's daily life by applying the Word of God to life situations so that we live what we believe, but it moves from doctrine to experience and does not make experience equal to religion.

George Marshall added, "We are concerned with the ethical relations and understanding of life, not about the salvation of souls. For us, salvation is by character; religion is a matter of deeds, not creeds; and this natural world is the center of our lives."[35] One wonders what standards Marshall would use to decide if proper "ethical relations" have been attained. And notice the creedal statement by this non-creedalist about how salvation is obtained—"by character." This shows how the Unitarian Universalists view the nature of man: that it is possible for him, or her, to attain some standard by self-effort. But who knows what that standard is? The only thing we know is that it is not a biblical standard.

The ethical and moral viewpoints of the Unitarian Universalist Association became evident on June 25, 1996, when it became the first U.S. denomination to endorse the legalization of same-sex marriages. The UUA did allow, however, for each church in the association to decide if it would follow suit.

Those who believe in biblical Christianity should be concerned about integrity of character in all areas of life, but this is a result of salvation—not a means to it. Ephesians 2:8–9 emphasizes that salvation is by grace through faith, completely apart from good works. Verse 10 reveals what should characterize the believer's life after salvation: "For we are His workmanship, created in Christ Jesus for good works, which God prepared beforehand that we should walk in them."

HELL

The term *universalist* in the UUA indicates their belief in the universal salvation of mankind—that no one will face eternal condemnation. It seems now to have come to refer to a belief in universal religion. Because they accept reason as the highest authority and because it does not seem reasonable to them that a loving God would send anyone to a place of eternal torment, they reject the Bible's teachings about hell.

Hosea Ballou, a key leader in the history of the Universalist movement, rejected endless punishment in *A Treatise on Atonement* (1805). In fact, according to David Robinson, "Ballou's eventual position, which came to be known as 'ultra-Universalism,' was that the consequences of sin manifested themselves in this life only."[36]

> UNITARIAN UNIVERSALISTS REJECT THE BIBLE'S TEACHINGS ABOUT HELL.

For biblical Christianity, however, the authority is revelation—not reason. The fact that God would purposely send His Son to die for our sin defies human logic and reason; however, this is exactly what He did. Nor is it reasonable to some that we can be delivered from the condemnation of sin by believing in Jesus Christ, but John 3:16–18 reveals that we can. Jesus Christ is "Himself is the propitiation [satisfaction] for our sins, and not for ours only but also for the whole world" (1 John 2:2). Love, not logic, motivated the Lord to lay down His life to provide what we needed—God's free and unmerited offer of salvation.

Those who reject the Son of God, however, reject the offer of God's love. "Who is a liar but he who denies that Jesus is the Christ? He is antichrist who denies the Father and the Son. Whoever denies the Son does not have the Father either; he who acknowledges the Son has the Father also" (1 John 2:22–23).

What They Believe

The Bible tells us that those who do not trust in Jesus Christ for salvation will be condemned, while those who believe in Him will not be condemned (John 3:16–18). Jesus Himself will judge those who reject Him because the Father "has committed all judgment to the Son" (5:22).

All unbelievers will someday stand before the Great White Throne to be judged (Rev. 20:11–15). Because their names will not be written in the Book of Life, they will be thrown into the lake of fire. The Scriptures also make it clear that they will not be immediately annihilated but instead will suffer eternal torment. The Book of Revelation describes how two individuals (the beast and the false prophet) will be thrown into the lake of fire before the 1,000-year rule of Christ begins (19:20–21). At the end of this millennial period, Satan will also be cast into the lake of fire, where he will join the beast and false prophet. They will not have ceased to exist after 1,000 years (20:10).

As contrary to human reason as it might seem, the Bible reveals that those who have trusted in Jesus Christ alone for salvation will receive eternal life. Those who do not have a right relationship with God through Christ will receive punishment that lasts forever. Both of these truths are taught in the Scriptures. Matthew 25:46 states, "These [the condemned] will go away into everlasting punishment, but the righteous into eternal life." It is not reasonable to deny eternal punishment unless one also denies eternal life. As Christian theologian Leon Morris has aptly noted, "The punishment is just as eternal as the life. The one is no more limited than the other."[37]

Unitarian Universalists need to accept what the Bible teaches about hell. As Morris says, "If Jesus wished to teach something other than eternal retribution, it is curious that he has not left one saying which plainly says so. In the [New Testament] there is no indication that the punishment of sin ever ceases."[38]

CONCLUSION

The Unitarian Universalists have a commitment to and involvement in social concerns that many Christians could do well to emulate. They are to be commended for their willingness to speak out against social injustice (even if we can't agree with some of their positions on moral issues).

In their attempts to be freethinking and non-creedal, however, they have become so liberal that they deny almost every doctrine of the Christian faith. They have replaced the worship of God with a worship of self. They teach that human reason and experience take precedence over the Word of God. They have rejected God's offer of salvation through faith in Christ and have replaced it with a salvation of personal development and good works. Their beliefs allow every person to do whatever is right in his own eyes as long as he is sincere about it.

The fact that the Unitarian Universalist Association has become progressively more liberal through the years shows us what happens when we do not have an absolute standard of truth on which to base our lives. And for the Christian, the Bible must be that standard. Each person must carefully choose his standard, realizing that his choice will have eternal consequences.

Summary

Name of Organization: Unitarian Universalist Association (UUA)
Also Known As: Unitarians
U.S. Headquarters: Boston, Massachusetts
Membership (2005): U.S.: 217,970
Web Site: www.uua.org

What They Believe

Unitarians: **Biblical Christians:**

Source of Authority

The Bible contains many errors. Make absolute statements about there being no absolutes to follow. | The Bible is without error in the original manuscripts. It sets forth absolutes for faith and practice.

The Trinity

Deny the doctrine of the Trinity. | God exists in three Persons who are one yet distinct, with each being co-equally and coeternally God.

What They Believe

God

Hold a variety of liberal views about God: some believe that God is a not a person; others deny entirely that God exists.

God is a divine Person with intellect, emotions and will.

Christ

Jesus was only a man, not God. Apostles and other Christian writers added the teachings about Christ's atonement for sin.

Jesus Christ is God, the second Person of the Trinity, who became man to die for the sins of the world. Believe that early Christians who died for the faith rather than deny Christ would not have died for a lie.

Salvation

If any salvation is needed it is attained by character development, not faith in Jesus Christ.

Salvation is attained only by faith alone in Christ alone.

Hell

No one will be eternally condemned. People suffer the consequences of sin in this life only.

Hell is a real place and the destination of those who reject the salvation God has provided in Christ. Those who reject the saving work of Jesus Christ suffer eternal consequences.

Recommended Reading

Ankerberg, John, and Weldon, John. *Encyclopedia of Cults and New Religions.* Eugene, Ore.: Harvest House Publishers, 1999.

Bowman, Robert M., Jr. *Why You Should Believe in the Trinity. Grand* Rapids, Mich.: Baker Books, 1989.

Gomes, Alan. *Unitarian Universalism.* Grand Rapids, Mich.: Zondervan Publishing House, 1996.

Martin, Walter. *The Kingdom of the Cults.* Ravi Zacharias, gen. ed. Minneapolis: Bethany House Publishers, 2003.

Mather, George A., and Nichols, Larry A. *Dictionary of Cults, Sects, Religions and the Occult.* Grand Rapids, Mich.: Zondervan Publishing House, 1993.

Mead, Frank S., Hill, Samuel S., and Atwood, Craig D. *Handbook of Denominations in the United States*, 12th ed. Nashville: Abingdon Press, 2005.

Ridenour, Fritz. *So What's the Difference?* Ventura, Calif.: Regal Books, 1979.

Rhodes, Ron. *The Challenge of the Cults and New Religions.* Grand Rapids,

Mich.: Zondervan, 2001.

ENDNOTES

[1] Jack Mendelsohn, *Why I Am a Unitarian Universalist* (New York: Thomas Nelson & Sons, 1964), 75.

[2] Ibid., 76.

[3] Frank S. Mead, *Handbook of Denominations in the United States*, rev. by Samuel S. Hill (Nashville: Abingdon Press, 1995), 285.

[4] Harry Barron Scholefield, ed., *The Unitarian Universalist Pocket Guide* (Boston: Beacon Press, 1963), 59.

[5] "Unitarians," in *The World Book Encyclopedia*, Vol. 20 (Chicago: World Book, Inc., 1987), 19.

[6] Alan W. Gomes, "Unitarian Universalists and the Second Law of Theological Thermodynamics: The Rise of Militant Pluralism," *Trinity Journal*, Fall 1996, 151–154.

[7] David Robinson, *The Unitarians and the Universalists* (Westport, Conn.: Greenwood Press, 1985), 229.

[8] Jack Mendelsohn, *Channing: The Reluctant Radical* (Boston: Little, Brown and Company, 1971), 7.

[9] Robinson, *The Unitarians and the Universalists*, 229.

[10] Ibid., 253.

[11] *The Unitarian Universalist Pocket Guide*, 59.

[12] Robinson, *The Unitarians and the Universalists*, 302.

[13] Ibid., 297.

[14] Ibid., 215.

[15] *The Unitarian Universalist Pocket Guide*, 59.

[16] Robinson, *The Unitarians and the Universalists*, 61.

[17] "Deleted Deity," *Time*, June 27, 1983, 63.

[18] "Unitarian Universalist Association Statistical Summary," www.uua.org/aboutuua/statistics.html, Oct. 28, 2005.

[19] *Newsweek*, Dec. 17, 1991.

[20] Robinson, *The Unitarians and the Universalists*, 7.

[21] Mendelsohn, *Why I Am a Unitarian Universalist*, 34.

[22] Ibid., 132.

[23] George N. Marshall, *Challenge of a Liberal Faith* (New Canaan, Conn.: Keats Publishing, Inc., 1970, 1980), 230–231.

[24] Mendelsohn, *Why I Am a Unitarian Universalist*, 37.

[25] Ibid.

[26] Robinson, *The Unitarians and the Universalists*, 31.

[27] *The Unitarian Universalist Pocket Guide*, 59.

[28] G. W. Bromiley, "Trinity," in *Evangelical Dictionary of Theology*, ed. by Walter A. El-

well (Grand Rapids, Mich.: Baker Book House, 1984), 1,112.

[29] For more information concerning the Trinity, see Lewis Sperry Chafer, *Major Bible Themes*, rev. by John F. Walvoord (Grand Rapids, Mich.: Zondervan Publishing House, 1926, 1953, 1974).

[30] Marshall, *Challenge of a Liberal Faith*, 229–230.

[31] Gomes, "Unitarian Universalists and the Second Law of Theological Thermodynamics," *Trinity Journal*, Fall 1996, 160.

[32] Mendelsohn, *Why I Am a Unitarian Universalist*, 43.

[33] Ibid., 29–30.

[34] Ibid., 31.

[35] Marshall, *Challenge of a Liberal Faith*, 237.

[36] Robinson, *The Unitarians and the Universalists*, 215.

[37] Leon Morris, "Eternal Punishment," in *Evangelical Dictionary of Theology*, 369.

[38] Ibid., 370.

CHAPTER FIFTEEN

Unity School of Christianity

How would you like to have happiness, health, prosperity and peace of mind? It would be difficult to find anyone who wouldn't want all these things. And those things are precisely what the Unity School of Christianity claims to offer.

Known more simply as "Unity," this group was founded by Charles and Myrtle Fillmore. Charles believed that he could cure himself of physical ailments by using a process of mental healing that is the hallmark of this group and others like it. Supposedly he and his wife both healed themselves of debilitating injuries and diseases using this process.

But the Unity School of Christianity is much more than a health organization. It is a religion whose beliefs bear little resemblance to the name it wears—Christianity. This group has borrowed teachings from many different religions and philosophies: Hinduism, Spiritism, Theosophy, Christian Science and Christianity. At the heart of these teachings is a "health and wealth" philosophy that is attractive to many people. As a result, the Unity School of Christianity is one of the largest counterfeit religious groups today, with adherents worldwide numbering perhaps a million or more, even though only 31,000 are members of the denomination in the United States.[1]

BACKGROUND

Charles Fillmore was born on an Indian reservation near St. Cloud, Minnesota, on August 22, 1854. While still a young boy, he destroyed his hip socket in a skating accident. As a result, his leg stopped growing and the muscles withered. He was further crippled by a curvature of the spine.

In 1881 Fillmore married Mary Caroline (Myrtle) Page. The early years of their marriage were marked by financial troubles. In 1884 they lost their prosperous real estate business in Colorado and moved to Kansas City, Missouri, to start again. But their real estate business there soon failed as well, and they were left penniless.

The Fillmores were also plagued by physical problems. Charles continued to struggle with his injuries. Then Myrtle contracted tuberculosis and was given only a few months to live. However, in the spring of 1886, they attended a lecture that changed their lives. The speaker was E. B. Weeks, a representative of the Illinois Metaphysical College.[2] This college had been founded by Emma Curtis Hopkins, who was described by Unity writer James Freeman as "one of the most unusual figures that has appeared in the whole metaphysical movement," and who at one time had been associated with Mary Baker Eddy as an editor of the *Christian Science Journal*.[3]

The lecture left a profound impression on Mrs. Fillmore. As she left the hall, the speaker's words kept ringing in her ears and later became her prayer. In fact, Unity's Web site reported, "Myrtle discovered that by repeating the affirmative prayer, 'I am a child of God, therefore, I do not inherit sickness,' and praying for perfect health for two years, she was healed of terminal tuberculosis."[4]

Notice the words "repeating the affirmative prayer." This is similar to the technique of Transcendental Meditation whereby a word or phrase is repeated over and over to produce the desired state of mind in which a person can get in tune with the one essence of the universe (or "God," as some people refer to that one essence).

Charles Fillmore did not accept this healing process as readily as his wife did. He decided to investigate some other religions and practices first. He immersed himself in Hinduism, Buddhism and other Eastern religions. He also studied Rosicrucianism, Theosophy, New Thought, Christian Science and Christianity. Finally, he agreed to try his wife's meditation technique and claimed to receive healing from it as well. Excited by their "discovery," the Fillmores began to share their meditation techniques with others. Gradually they formed the doctrines that became the Unity School of Christianity, borrowing many of the teachings of the various groups they had studied.

In 1889 the Fillmores published a magazine called *Modern Thought*, which was the voice of their new movement. The name of the magazine—and group—was changed several times in the next few years.

Finally in 1891 they officially adopted the name "Unity." The group joined the International New Thought Alliance, along with Christian Science and New Thought, and was a member of this organization until 1922.

Shortly after his wife's death in 1931, Charles Fillmore married Cora Dedrick, his personal secretary. They continued to lead the group until Fillmore's death in 1948. Control of the organization was then assumed by Fillmore's two sons, Lowell and W. Rickert. Since then, Unity has experienced tremendous growth. Today the group conducts its worldwide work from a large complex known as Unity Village in Lees Summit, Missouri (a suburb of Kansas City). Unity Village has its own ZIP code, library, bookstore and chapel, and publishes more than 75 million copies of booklets, brochures and magazines each year.[5] Among their publications are *Unity Magazine* and *Daily Word*.

BELIEFS

When you study the beliefs of the Unity School of Christianity, you soon discover many similarities between their doctrines and the teachings of Christian Science and New Thought. The reason is that all three groups have a common source (although their followers wouldn't agree)—a mental healer named Phineas P. Quimby (1802–1866). *Encyclopaedia Britannica* says of Quimby, "[He] practiced mesmerism (hypnotism) and developed his concepts of mental and spiritual healing and health based on the view that illness is a matter of the mind."[6] Mary Baker Eddy, the founder of Christian Science, and Julius Dresser, the founder of New Thought, were both students of Quimby. Likewise, the Fillmores were greatly influenced by Quimby's writings, as well as by Emma Curtis Hopkins and her Illinois Metaphysical College.

Those who have carefully studied these different groups agree on their similarities. "They are as much alike as triplets," J. K. Van Baalen wrote.[7] "Borrowing heavily from Christian Science and New Thought," McDowell and Stewart assessed, "the Fillmores added their own interpretations, including the Eastern concept of reincarnation."[8] Walter Martin, a leading authority in counterfeit religious groups until his death in 1989, wrote, "A careful perusal of the *Metaphysical Bible Dictionary* published by the Unity School will quickly show that Christian Science, Unity and New Thought (which *does* recognize

Quimby) have an almost interchangeable vocabulary, a fact denied by only the uninformed and those who are unwilling to study the facts of history and semantics"[9] (emphasis his).

In order to better understand the teachings of the Unity School of Christianity and others like it, we need to examine the philosophy of New Thought, which is at the root of Unity beliefs. According to theologian John H. Gerstner, "New Thought is a modified pantheism. Eastern religions, Theosophy, and Christian Science identify or tend to identify, metaphysically, the individual with the whole."[10]

The term *pantheism* is derived from the Greek words *pan* (all) and *Theos* (God); hence, it is the belief that all is God. Pantheists cannot agree with the first verse of the Bible, which says, "In the beginning God created" (Gen. 1:1), because they believe God is the creation. Proponents of this philosophy teach that since God is in everything, then mankind and matter also must be part of the divine essence, or part of God. This concept is seen in one of Unity's goals of "becoming conscious of our oneness with God" and considering prayer and meditation as the primary means to that end.[11]

> UNITY ALSO HAS MANY BELIEFS IN COMMON WITH THE NEW AGE MOVEMENT.

In addition, Unity has adopted many other concepts and practices of Eastern religions. Followers believe in reincarnation and practice Hindu-type meditation and dietary habits, including vegetarianism. Unity also has many beliefs in common with the New Age Movement. In fact, in *The Aquarian Conspiracy*, Marilyn Ferguson lists Unity churches under "discussion groups" of "Aquarian Conspiracy Resources."[12] In seeking to combine Christianity with pantheism and Eastern religions, Unity School of Christianity has formed a theology that is not only confusing but also dangerous from the perspective of biblical Christianity. You don't have to look far to see that their beliefs bear little resemblance to the teachings of God's Word.

SOURCE OF AUTHORITY

The Unity School of Christianity does not believe in the inspiration or absolute authority of the Bible. Its *Statement of Faith* says, "We believe the Scriptures are the testimonials of men who have in a measure apprehended the divine Logos but that their writings should not be taken as final."[13]

True to their desire to unify all religions into one, Unity followers say, "We believe there is truth in all teachings. Unity leaves all people free to find the truth for themselves."[14] This reveals that Unity holds to no absolutes other than subjective feelings about what constitutes truth—yet they are not without specific beliefs themselves.

Because they believe in continuing revelation ("the continuing revelations of the Christ Presence"[15]), the followers of Unity do not even consider their own teachings to be permanently binding. Charles Fillmore waited almost 30 years before publishing a statement of faith. When the statement was finally adopted in 1921, the following disclaimer appeared with it: "We are hereby giving warning that we shall not be bound to this tentative statement of what Unity believes. We may change our mind tomorrow on some of the points, and if we do, we shall feel free to make a new statement."[16]

Even the parts of the Bible used by Unity followers in their teachings are not interpreted in their context based on normal rules of language. Fillmore taught that "beginning with the very first chapter of Genesis, the Bible is an allegory."[17] Because of its allegorical interpretation of the Bible, Unity has twisted obvious truths and teaches something entirely different than the normal use of language would convey. If words are not understood in their normal, customarily accepted meanings, they can be made to mean and represent anything.

Just as the Christian Scientists have done, the followers of Unity have given spiritual, metaphysical meanings to many people, places and events in the Bible. For instance, Fillmore wrote: "The 'upper room' is the very top of the head. Jesus was in this 'upper room' of his mind when Nicodemus came to see him 'by night'—meaning the ignorance of sense consciousness."[18] He also stated, "The breastplate (of the High Priest) had on it twelve precious stones, representing the twelve tribes of Israel. This clearly means that the twelve faculties of the mind must be massed at the great brain center called the solar plexus."[19] With such abstract interpretations of even the most obvious teachings of Scripture, the followers of Unity can make the Bible fit any doctrine they wish to believe.

These examples also show us the emphasis that Unity places on the mind. Like the Eastern religions and other groups based on them, the followers of Unity believe in the concept of a "universal consciousness." They teach that each person is part of this "infinite mind," which is virtually omnipotent. However, man's mind is not yet perfect, and he must work to reach this ultimate state of consciousness. Problems that arise, such as sickness or financial loss, are attributed to a lack of mind control. "What we need to realize above all else," wrote Fillmore, "is that God has provided for the most minute needs of our daily life and that if we lack anything it is because we have not used our mind in making the right contact with the supermind and the cosmic ray that automatically flows from it."[20]

Thus, Unity's final authority is not the Scriptures but reason or, more accurately, the imagination of the mind. Fillmore said, "The one important thing which the student of spiritual science must learn, is to trust the logic of the mind."[21]

THE TRINITY

Historical Christianity believes that God is a Trinity—one God, existing in three Persons: Father, Son and Holy Spirit. References to the Trinity were made as early as A.D. 150 in the Apostles' Creed. While the followers of Unity use this same terminology, their meaning of the Trinity is vastly different. "The Holy Trinity," Fillmore wrote, "is known as the Father, the Son, and the Holy Spirit. Metaphysically, we understand the Trinity to refer to mind, idea, and expression, or thinker, thought, and action."[22] This is similar to the view of Christian Science, which says the Trinity is "Life, Truth, and Love."[23]

True to its pantheistic background, Unity teaches a belief in an impersonal God. Unity members do not believe that God is a person who has intellect, emotions and will. Instead, He is merely a "principle."[24] In *Lessons in Truth*, one of Unity's primary books of doctrine, the group's beliefs concerning God are clear: "God is not a . . . person having life, intelligence, love, power. God is that invisible, intangible, but very real something we call life. God is perfect love and infinite power. God is the total of these, the total of all good, whether manifested or unexpressed."[25] Thus, in Unity theology, God is not a person who loves us but rather is love itself. It is true that the Bible says "God is love" (1 John 4:8), but it is not true that this can be reversed to mean "love is God," as is done by Unity and others who depersonalize God. They like to emphasize Jesus' words in John 13:34, "A new commandment I give to you, that you love one another; as I have loved you, that you also love one another." But this verse is not to assume that Jesus gave permission for people to believe heresy about Him and excused it because they loved each other.

JESUS CHRIST

Like many false religions, Unity separates Jesus from Christ. And, like other groups that are based on Eastern religions, Unity teaches that Christ is a principle—not a person. According to Unity, "Christ is the only begotten Son of God, the one complete idea of perfect man and divine Mind. This Christ or perfect-man idea existing eternally in divine Mind is the true, spiritual, higher-self of every individual."[26]

The difference between the Person of Christ and the Christ Presence is seen in the statement by the Association of Unity Churches: "We believe in universal principles and spiritual values as revealed and demonstrated by Jesus Christ and the continuing revelations of the Christ Presence."[27] What is "the Christ Presence"? It is common for groups like the New Age Movement and Christian Science to refer to the Christic Principle that is within each person. This is the theology of the divine spark being within each person, a view that Scriptures do not support.

Thus, the followers of Unity teach that Jesus of Nazareth was not God but a man who possessed the Christ principle—the highest state of consciousness. James Freeman stated, "Jesus was undoubtedly the greatest of all exponents of the impersonal I AM, which is revealed to man when he opens up the supermind within his own soul."[28] These statements show us not only how Unity has attempted to humanize God but also how it has deified man.

For example, notice Fillmore's explanation of miracles: "God never performs miracles, if by this is meant a departure from universal law. Whatever the prophets did, was done by the operation of laws inherent in Being, and open to the discovery of every man. Whatever Jesus of Nazareth did, it is likewise the privilege of every man to do."[29]

Such a statement reduces Jesus Christ to the level of sinful man. However, because Unity believes that every person is divine, its followers would say that this statement is lifting us all to the level of the divine principle.

In Unity theology, Jesus Christ was merely the perfect man—the example of what we can become. Unity writer Elizabeth Turner stated, "The difference between Jesus and us is not one of inherent spiritual capacity, but in difference of demonstration of it. Jesus was potentially perfect, and He expressed that perfection; we are potentially perfect, and we have not yet expressed it."[30] Clearly the Christ of Unity is not the Christ of the Bible.

SIN AND SALVATION

With its pantheistic view of God, it comes as no surprise that Unity denies the sinfulness of man and his need for salvation. According to the teachings of Unity, evil is not real; it is only a figment of man's imperfect mind. In his book *Christian Healing*, Charles Fillmore wrote: "1. I deny that I have inherited disease, sickness, ignorance or any mental limitation whatsoever. 2. I deny that I am a child of the flesh. I deny all belief in evil, for God made all that really is and pronounced it good. 3. Therefore no such deception as a belief in evil can darken my clear understanding of Truth."[31]

Thus, in Unity theology, "salvation" is a process in which we gradually unite our minds with the "divine Mind." As we gain control of our thoughts—pushing the belief in sin out of our minds—we eventually achieve perfection. In other words, we become equal with God. Fillmore emphatically stated, "In man a wonderful being is in process of creation. This being is spiritual man, who will be equal with God, when he overcomes or handles with wisdom and power, the faculties of the body."[32]

Unity teaches a salvation based on works and right thinking, not on a personal relationship with Christ. However, the Bible declares, "There is none righteous, no, not one. . . . For all have sinned and fall short of the glory of God" (Rom. 3:10,23). No one can ever achieve salvation through works, because our works are like filthy rags in God's eyes—they will never be good enough to merit His favor (Isa. 64:6). Only the sacrifice of God through His Son, Jesus Christ, could pay the full penalty for sin. Forgiveness of sin and eternal life come only by receiving Him as Savior (John 1:12; 5:24).

HELL

Since Unity does not believe that anyone is a sinner in the biblical sense of the word, it also denies the existence of hell as a place of punishment for sinners. In his book *The Unity Way of Life*, religion analyst Marcus Bach asked the followers of Unity what they found in the group. In addition to physical healing, prosperity and other benefits, the following response was frequently given: "No talk about sin or punishment."[33]

The biblical doctrine of sin and punishment is not popular today. People want to believe that sin doesn't exist and, therefore, that there will be no penalty for it. As a result, they are attracted to groups that teach such a philosophy. The apostle Paul warned that this would eventually happen: "The time will come when men will not put up with sound doctrine. Instead, to suit their own desires, they will gather around them a great number of teachers to say what their itching ears want to hear" (2 Tim. 4:3, NIV).

> TO SOME PEOPLE IT IS NOT REASONABLE THAT THERE WOULD BE A PLACE CALLED "HELL."

In speaking of heaven and hell, Unity's *Metaphysical Bible Dictionary* states, "Both are states of mind, and conditions, which people experience as a direct outworking of their thoughts, beliefs, words, and acts."[34] Once again, the followers of Unity have given the Bible's clear teachings a metaphysical interpretation. However, hell is more than a "state of mind." It is a real place of physical and spiritual torment. God's Word makes this plain (Matt. 10:28; Mark 9:43; Rev. 20:10–15).

To some people it is not reasonable that there would be a place called "hell." On the other hand, it is not reasonable that God would send His only, sinless Son to suffer and die on the cross to pay the penalty for the sin of mankind. If God did not allow His Son to bypass the cross in providing redemption, what makes us think He will not punish those who reject His enormously gracious offer of salvation?

SICKNESS

Many of the doctrines of Unity center around physical healing. Unity followers claim to be able to heal themselves through a process of denial. When sickness strikes, they deny the victory of the disease and death, saying, "Pain, sickness, poverty, old age, death cannot master me, for they are not real."[35]

In a recommended treatment for "cold, grippe, and influenzas," Fillmore instructed the afflicted person to affirm, "Spirit is not subject to heat nor cold. I am Spirit. I am the positive force of Being, and I put out of my consciousness all negative thoughts. I do not believe in that thing called 'a cold,' nor do I admit for a moment that it has any power over me. I am a Spirit, free-flowing life, and my circulation is equalized in God."[36] Just as the Christian Scientists do, Unity followers believe the means to overcome sickness is to keep repeating, as a mantra, an "affirming prayer," which is to remind the person that God is within and that the person can deny the disease. Christian Scientists believe disease is an illusion of the mind, whereas Unity adherents believe in the reality of disease but think it can be overcome by right thinking. On the other hand, Unity does not take an anti-medical position as does Christian Science.

REINCARNATION

In a clear rejection of the beliefs of biblical Christianity about sin, salvation and the future life, Unity follows Eastern religions in its belief of reincarnation. From his study of Eastern religions, Fillmore adopted this teaching into Unity theology. In Unity's Statement of Faith, this belief is clearly stated: "We believe that the dissolution of spirit, soul and body, caused by death, is annulled by rebirth of the same spirit and soul in another body here on earth. We believe the repeated incarnations of man to be a merciful provision of our loving Father to the end that all may have opportunity to attain immortality through regeneration, as did Jesus."[37]

The followers of Unity are, of course, free to believe whatever they choose. But the teaching about reincarnation and Jesus attaining immortality through regeneration did not originate from the Bible. Unity takes advantage of the biblically illiterate when it uses expressions from the Bible to support its views that have their origin in Eastern religions.

In the teachings of Unity, reincarnation takes the place of salvation in Christ and eternity in heaven for the redeemed. Unity emphasizes the idea that God never intended for mankind to die. Therefore, they say, when a person dies, he immediately comes back to earth in another form. He is given a chance to make up for the mistakes of his past life and to improve himself. Gradually, through a series of reincarnations, the person eventually becomes perfect. He reaches the highest level of consciousness and becomes one with the "divine Mind." He then becomes part of the "universal consciousness"—a state of peace and tranquillity that lasts forever.

Be sure to note that although Unity at times refers to God as if He is a person, the followers do not believe this. Instead, they believe in monism—that everything is ultimately of one essence. To them, God is only a principle, not a person. So any comment about what the God of Unity "intended" or "never intended" is misleading.

The Bible tells us, however, that while God did not wish for mankind to experience death, it entered the world as a result of the Fall. Romans 5:12 states, "Therefore, just as through one man sin entered the world, and death through sin, and thus death spread to all men, because all sinned." Unity leaders have attempted to explain away the real meaning of this verse with their metaphysical definitions.

Nowhere in the Bible do we find the doctrine of reincarnation. The Scriptures state emphatically that each person experiences physical death only once. And after we die, our chances for salvation are gone. "It is appointed for men to die once, but after this the judgment," says Hebrews 9:27. We seal our eternal future when we accept or reject Christ while on earth.

Instead of reincarnation, the Word of God teaches the resurrection of the body. When Christ returns, those who have accepted Him as Savior will receive their bodies back from the grave as incorruptible, glorified bodies. They will then spend eternity with the Lord (1 Cor. 15:35–58; 1 Thess. 4:13–18). Those who have rejected Jesus Christ as their Savior will receive their bodies back at a later resurrection to stand before the Great White Throne Judgment. They will then be cast into the lake of fire (Rev. 20:11–15).

CONCLUSION

The Unity School of Christianity is the result of positive thinking in its most dangerous extreme. It is an emphasis on the innate goodness of mankind with a divine twist that all and everything is of the same divine essence. The followers of this movement are so intent on looking for the good that they have become blind to the reality of sin and their need for a Savior. They have replaced God's plan of salvation through Christ with a system based on human merit and mental enlightenment. Unity's followers have no need for a personal God, since they believe that each person is God in miniature—that each one has the Christ Presence within.

While the followers of Unity call their group a "School of Christianity," they have rejected many major doctrines of the Bible. They have ignored or have reinterpreted God's clear revelation in His Word concerning the fall of man and His divine plan of redemption through the sacrifice of His only Son. They have replaced the Bible's message of a personal God with belief in an impersonal Mind.

The followers of biblical Christianity perhaps face their greatest challenge with assessing the beliefs of Unity because the vocabulary is so similar. Born-again Christians must keep asking the followers of Unity to define their terms; only then will it be seen how far Unity is from biblical Christianity.

The followers of Unity believe they have the truth, but they are only deceiving themselves and making God a liar. "If we say that we have no sin, we deceive ourselves, and the truth is not in us. . . . If we say that we have not sinned, we make Him [God] a liar, and His word is not in us" (1 John 1:8,10). Until the followers of Unity recognize the reality of sin and their need for a personal Savior, no amount of wisdom and mental enlightenment will be able to save them.

Summary

Name of Organization: Unity School of Christianity
Also Known As: Unity

Founders: Charles Fillmore (1854–1948)
Myrtle Fillmore (1845–1931)
Headquarters: Lees Summit, Missouri
Membership: U.S.: 31,000; Worldwide: About 1 million
Web Site: www.unityonline.org
Publications: *Unity* and *Daily Word*

What They Believe

Unity Followers: **Biblical Christians:**

Source of Authority

There is truth in all teachings. All people are free to find the truth for themselves. Believe in continuing revelation ("the continuing revelations of the Christ Presence").

The Bible is the sole authority for beliefs and practices. There is no inspired revelation for any person after the inspiration of the 66 books of the Bible.

The Trinity

Metaphysically, the Trinity refers to the mind, idea and expression, or thinker, thought and action. God is merely a principle, not a person.

The three Persons of the Godhead are one yet distinct, with each being co-equally and coeternally God. God is a divine person who has intellect, emotions and will, and supernatural ability.

Jesus Christ

Jesus Christ is one complete idea of perfect man and divine Mind. He was not God but was a man who possessed the Christ principle.

Jesus Christ is God and took on human form to die for the sins of the world. *Jesus* is the human name (meaning "Jehovah is salvation"), and *Christ* is the divine name (meaning "Messiah" or "Anointed").

Sin and Salvation

Evil does not exist. The spiritual man becomes equal with God when he overcomes the faculties of the body.

All people have sinned and fall short of the glory of God (Rom. 3:23). Mankind receives redemption by believing in Jesus Christ, but a redeemed person never becomes equal with God.

Hell

Hell is not a real place. Both heaven and hell are only states of mind, or conditions, which people experience as a direct outworking of their thoughts, beliefs, words and acts.

Hell is the future place of punishment for those who reject salvation through Christ.

Sickness

Humans do not inherit disease, sickness, ignorance or any mental limitation whatsoever. People should keep saying, "Pain, sickness, poverty, old age, death cannot master me, for they are not real."

Everyone is affected by sin, and death and disease are the result of sin (Rom. 5:12). Disease and death eventually affect each person no matter how much the person denies their reality or effect.

Reincarnation

Believe in reincarnation—that through a long process of rebirths mankind eventually reaches perfection and immortality.

The Bible nowhere teaches reincarnation; instead, "It is appointed for men to die once, but after this the judgment" (Heb. 9:27), not reincarnation.

Recommended Reading

Ankerberg, John, and Weldon, John. *Encyclopedia of Cults and New Religions.* Eugene, Ore.: Harvest House Publishers, 1999.

Boa, Kenneth. *Cults, World Religions & the Occult.* Wheaton, Ill.: Victor Books, 1990.

Gruss, Edmond C. *Cults and the Occult.* P&R Publishing, 1994.

Martin, Walter R. *The Kingdom of the Cults.* Minneapolis: Bethany House Publishers, 1965, 1977, 1985.

Mather, George A., and Nichols, Larry A. *Dictionary of Cults, Sects, Religions and the Occult.* Grand Rapids, Mich.: Zondervan Publishing House, 1993.

Mead, Frank S., Hill, Samuel S., and Atwood, Craig D. *Handbook of Denominations in the United States*, 12th ed. Nashville: Abingdon Press, 2005.

McDowell, Josh, and Stewart, Don. *Handbook of Today's Religions.* San Bernardino, Calif.: Here's Life Publishers, Inc., 1983.

ENDNOTES

[1] Frank S. Mead, Samuel S. Hill, and Craig D. Atwood, *Handbook of Denominations in the United States*, 12th ed. (Nashville: Abingdon Press, 2005), 366.

[2] James Dillet Freeman, *The Household of Faith* (Lees Summit, Mo.: Unity School of

Christianity, 1951), 42.

[3] Ibid.

[4] www.unityonline.org (formerly www.unityworldhq.org), Aug. 1997, and Mead, et al, 367.

[5] www.unityonline.org, Oct. 2005.

[6] "New Thought," *Encyclopaedia Britannica*, 1981, Vol. 13, 14.

[7] J. K. Van Baalen, *The Chaos of Cults* (Grand Rapids, Mich.: Wm. B. Eerdmans Publishing Company, 1962), 134.

[8] Josh McDowell and Don Stewart, *Handbook of Today's Religions* (San Bernardino, Calif.: Here's Life Publishers, Inc., 1983), 131.

[9] Walter R. Martin, *The Kingdom of the Cults* (Minneapolis: Bethany House Publishers, 1965, 1977, 1985), 280.

[10] John H. Gerstner, *The Theology of the Major Sects* (Grand Rapids, Mich.: Baker Book House, 1960), 63.

[11] www.unityonline.org, Aug. 1997.

[12] Marilyn Ferguson, *The Aquarian Conspiracy* (Los Angeles: J. P. Tarcher, 1980), 428.

[13] cited in Josh McDowell and Don Stewart, *Understanding the Cults* (San Bernardino, Calif.: Here's Life Publishers, Inc., 1982), 179.

[14] www.unityonline.org, Aug. 1997.

[15] Ibid.

[16] James Dillet Freeman, *What Is Unity?* (Lees Summit, Mo.: Unity School of Christianity, n.d.), 5, cited by McDowell and Stewart, *Handbook of Today's Religions*, 132.

[17] Charles Fillmore, *Christian Healing* (Kansas City, Mo.: Unity School of Christianity, 1922), 31.

[18] Ibid., 28.

[19] Ibid., 111.

[20] Charles Fillmore, *Prosperity* (Kansas City, Mo.: Unity School of Christianity, 1937), foreword.

[21] Fillmore, *Christian Healing*, 10.

[22] Charles Fillmore, *Keep a True Lent* (Lees Summit, Mo.: Unity School of Christianity, 1953), 14.

[23] Georgine Milmine, *The Life of Mary Baker G. Eddy and the History of Christian Science* (Grand Rapids, Mich.: Baker Book House, reprinted 1971), 331.

[24] Ibid.

[25] H. Emilie Cady, *Lessons in Truth* (Kansas City, Mo.: Unity School of Christianity, 1930), 6–7.

[26] *Metaphysical Bible Dictionary* (Lees Summit, Mo.: Unity School of Christianity, 1962), 150, cited by Martin, *The Kingdom of the Cults*, 280.

[27] www.unityonline.org, Aug. 1997.

[28] Freeman, *The Household of Faith*, 274.

[29] Fillmore, *Christian Healing*, 226.

What They Believe

[30] Elizabeth S. Turner, *What Unity Teaches*, 3, cited by Martin, *The Kingdom of the Cults*, 280.

[31] Fillmore, *Christian Healing*, 150, 250–251, cited by Martin, *The Kingdom of the Cults*, 81.

[32] Charles Fillmore, *Twelve Powers of Man* (Kansas City, Mo.: Unity School of Christianity, 1943), 163, cited by Martin, *The Kingdom of the Cults*, 281.

[33] Marcus Bach, *The Unity Way of Life* (Englewood Cliffs, N.J.: Prentice-Hall, Inc., 1962), 151.

[34] *Metaphysical Bible Dictionary*, 271.

[35] Cady, *Lessons in Truth*, 37.

[36] Fillmore, *Christian Healing*, 249.

[37] Unity Statement of Faith, Article 22.

CHAPTER SIXTEEN

The Way International

The word *cult* is not used in *What They Believe* because most people usually think of mind-control when they hear that term, and most of the groups evaluated in this book could not be accused of practicing mind-control, even though they teach doctrines contrary to biblical Christianity. Yet some people claim that's what is involved in The Way International.

"I can't reason with my daughter," a brokenhearted mother told me. "We can talk about our doctrinal differences for a while, but then my daughter becomes unreasonable and seems to mechanically recite what The Way has programmed into her."

This mother is not alone in her frustration with this group and its tactics. In an article in *Newsweek*, Peter Klebnikov wrote of The Way, "Former members tell of sexual abuse in the ranks, para-military training and food deprivation."[1]

Because The Way International doesn't release official membership numbers, it's difficult to ascertain the size of the group. It likely peaked at about 35,000 in the 1970s or mid-1980s[2] and is now between 10,000 and 20,000.[3]

The loving support of The Way's fellowship groups (called twigs) and their emphasis on Bible study are appealing to many believers. In fact, those who are disappointed with the fellowship and teaching in their local churches seem to be especially susceptible to this aggressive group.

The Way International advertises itself as a "Biblical research, teaching, and fellowship ministry."[4] However, the organization has tax-exempt status, ordained ministers and a heavy emphasis on doctrine. But the issue of whether or not The Way is a church is not as important as determining whether it is teaching biblical truth or false doctrine. Because those raised in the church are especially vulnerable to this group, every Christian should be aware of its activities and teachings.

BACKGROUND

The Way International was founded by Victor Paul Wierwille, who led the group until his retirement in 1982 and who remained actively involved in leadership until his death in 1985. He was born on the family farm near New Knoxville, Ohio, on December 31, 1916. This farm of more than 300 acres later became the international headquarters for what *The New York Times* described as Wierwille's "unorthodox ministry."[5]

Wierwille was raised in the Evangelical and Reformed Church (now known as the United Church of Christ). He received a bachelor's degree from the Mission House College and Seminary in Sheboygan, Wisconsin. He also studied at the University of Chicago and later received a Master of Theology degree from Princeton Theological Seminary. Wierwille also claimed to have taken every correspondence course offered by Moody Bible Institute, but it has no record of his completing any courses.[6]

Following graduation from Princeton in 1941, Wierwille was ordained into the ministry by the Evangelical and Reformed Church. For 16 years he pastored churches in northwestern Ohio. During this time he also began a weekly radio program and conducted Bible studies that developed into his Power for Abundant Living (PFAL) course (replaced by The Way of Abundance and Power classes).

Shortly after his ordination, Wierwille experienced a spiritual crisis. In his search for spiritual truth, he became discontented with theological writings and took several hundred volumes (some sources say as many as 3,000) from his library and burned them. He then began to formulate his own theology. Wierwille became openly opposed to the church and devoted increasing time to his Bible studies. In 1957 he resigned his pastorate, supposedly to devote all of his time to this teaching ministry. However, some sources indicate that his differences with the denomination had grown in severity and number until his departure was not entirely his choice.[7]

The date of the founding of The Way International is not easily established. Some researchers mark it from the time Wierwille resigned his church in Van Wert, Ohio, in 1957.[8] Others date the group's inception in 1968 with the beginning of the Jesus Movement.[9] However, the group's Web site says The Way International was founded in 1942, a date backed up by researcher James K. Walker on The Watchman Expositor Web site.[10] That's when Wierwille's radio program, *Vesper Chimes*, first aired in Lima, Ohio. Regardless of the exact date of inception, The Way International did not experience any significant growth until the late 1960s.

J. L. Williams, founder and executive director of a cult resource group known as the New Directions Evangelistic Association, believes the Jesus Movement provided Wierwille with a ready audience of those who had rejected the institutional church and were searching for spiritual reality. They were also biblically unprepared to detect theological errors.

The Way International is highly structured. Wierwille used the picture of a tree to designate the levels of the organization. At the base, or roots, of the organization was Wierwille himself. A board of directors now serves as the roots. (John Juedes points out that "technically, the group has only three members—the trustees who control all aspects of The Way International, Inc."[11]) The association of national bodies is considered to be the trunk. The limbs of the tree are the statewide units, which have many branches, or city organizations. At the heart of the organization are the home or campus groups known as twigs, which are made up of individual members called leaves.

The Way is strongly evangelistic. Much of their recruitment was done by their WOW (The Word Over the World) ambassadors. This program was discontinued in 1994 during The Way's Rock of Ages conference and was replaced by Disciples of The Way Outreach.[12]

The Way is involved in a number of other outreaches. It has its own publishing house, The American Christian Press, located at its headquarters in New Knoxville, Ohio. Here The Way publishes *The Way Magazine* and numerous books. In addition, until recently it held an annual spiritual music fest, called the Rock of Ages, and sponsors a number of summer camps. Each of these is designed to introduce people to The Way's "new" theology that primarily originated with Wierwille. But are these teachings really new, or are they simply old heresies that he resurrected? Does The Way really point the way to God?

BELIEFS

The Way International's beliefs are a strange mixture of many schools of theology. Most critics of Wierwille's theology would agree with the assessment of Joseph M. Hopkins, experienced evaluator of counterfeit religious groups: "Way doctrines combine forms of biblical literalism . . . evangelicalism . . . Calvinism . . . dispensationalism . . . and Pentecostalism."[13]

While on the surface The Way International may appear to be teaching biblical truth, a closer examination of the writings and teachings of Victor Paul Wierwille reveals many theological errors. Even though Wierwille died in 1985, it seems fair to call the teachings of The Way International "the teachings of Wierwille," because by and large those are the beliefs that are promoted and defended by the group today. Paramount among these is the group's denial of the Trinity, the deity of Christ and the personality of the Holy Spirit. The Way's methods of indoctrination and other practices also raise serious questions, but our concern here is theology, not methodology. Although followers may draw social benefits from it, a group cannot be considered distinctly Christian unless it holds to the teachings revealed in the Bible, the written Word of God. If it does not consider the Bible to be the final authority, the group is following only a man-made religion. The Bible's authority must be maintained, not only by the statements of the group but also by its practices.

LIKE MANY GROUPS, THE WAY INTERNATIONAL CLAIMS THAT THE BIBLE IS ITS FINAL AUTHORITY.

SOURCE OF AUTHORITY

Like many groups, The Way International claims that the Bible is its final authority. However, in practice, Wierwille's interpretation of the Bible is the ultimate authority. Like many other founders of false religions, Wierwille claimed special communication with God. He stated, "God spoke to me audibly, just like I'm talking to you now. He said he would teach me the word as it had not been known since the first century, if I would teach it to others."[14] Wierwille's claim of special revelation shows that he did not consider the Bible to be the complete and inspired Word of God.

Wierwille also believed the New Testament was first written in Aramaic and not in Greek. Such a view is contrary to accepted scholarship on the subject.[15] While Wierwille claimed to have studied Greek and other languages, Walter Martin, in *The New Cults*, says his school records show that he never took one course in Greek.[16]

Even though The Way does use the Bible, Wierwille's teachings take precedence. This was true up to the time of his death in 1985 and still appears true today.

The Rev. L. Craig Martindale assumed the presidency of The Way when Wierwille died. Watchers of The Way seemed to think that Martindale exercised tight control over the followers and was more demanding than Wierwille. During Martindale's presidency, Juedes wrote, "The Way is striving to further restrict access to its activities, purge anyone who questions current Way leadership, increase control, and consolidate."[17] Martindale was forced to resign in 2000 amid allegations of sexual misconduct.[18]

The current president is Rosalie F. Rivenbark. A former teacher at the elementary, high school and college levels, she also worked in a leadership capacity directly with Wierwille and Martindale for more than 25 years.

Despite these changes in leadership, the current theology of The Way is still Wierwille's theology. In the future, it will be interesting to see if anyone is allowed to remain in fellowship with The Way who differs significantly from the words of Wierwille, regardless of what the Word of God says.

During his life, Wierwille frequently stated, "The Word of God means what it says and says what it means." In commenting on this expression, J. L. Williams correctly concluded, "What he really means is this: 'The Word of God means what I say and says what I mean.'"[19] This view becomes evident as we examine Wierwille's teachings on crucial doctrines.

What They Believe

THE TRINITY

One of The Way's most fundamental beliefs is that God is not a trinity—that is, Wierwille's view of God was unitarian, not trinitarian. Referring to the orthodox view that the Father and Son are coeternal and coequal, Wierwille wrote, "That defines the doctrine of the trinity, and this I do not believe the Bible teaches."[20]

Wierwille dogmatically claimed that "there was no formal, established doctrine of the trinity until the fourth century" as a "fully documented historical fact."[21] He taught that the concept of the Trinity originated with paganism and was brought into Christianity by the Council of Nicea in A.D. 325. Jack Sparks, a minister and former professor of behavioral psychology, charged, "Wierwille simply hasn't done his homework on the subject. His scholarship in general is irresponsible, slipshod, and false."[22] Sparks decisively refutes Wierwille's claim and reveals his many errors about the Council of Nicea.[23]

While the word *Trinity* is not used in the Bible (even as other theological words are not, such as *theocracy* and *millennium*), we find abundant evidence that the Father, Son and Holy Spirit are one God, existing in three Persons. The fact that the Bible uses plural pronouns when referring to God is evidence enough (Gen. 1:26; 11:7). In addition, Jesus was recognized as God throughout the Bible, as is the Holy Spirit. One of the creeds widely used in Christendom is the Athanasian Creed. Concerning the Trinity, it states: "We worship one God in three persons and three persons in one God, neither confusing the persons nor dividing the substance." In accepting Wierwille's distorted view of the Trinity and of church history, followers of The Way have denied many key passages of Scripture and what has been accepted by orthodox Christianity for centuries.

THE FATHER

Wierwille taught that only the Father is designated as "God" in the Bible, thus denying the deity of Jesus Christ and the personality of the Holy Spirit. "With all my heart," Wierwille stated, "I believe the Bible teaches that (1) God is the Father of our Lord Jesus Christ, that (2) Jesus Christ is the Son of God and that (3) God is Holy and God is Spirit."[24]

On the surface Wierwille's statement seems to be in line with the Scriptures, because he used the terminology of the Bible. But as we'll see, his meaning was far different from the Bible's teachings and from the views held by orthodox Christianity.

JESUS CHRIST

Some leaders of counterfeit religious groups make you guess what they believe about Christ's deity, but not Wierwille. He plainly and boldly entitled one of his books, *Jesus Christ Is Not God*. Though he would say, "Jesus Christ is the Son of God,"[25] he interpreted the expression "Son of God" to mean that Jesus Christ is not God. Following this statement, he added, "In other words, I am saying that Jesus Christ is not God, but the Son of God."[26]

This denial of Christ's deity is at the heart of Wierwille's faulty theology that is still perpetuated by The Way International. To convince others of his views, Wierwille used Greek, Aramaic and church history—but not always in an intellectually honest manner. As we have seen, Wierwille misused church history. But what about his use of Greek?

WIERWILLE TAUGHT THAT JESUS DID NOT EXIST BEFORE HE WAS BORN TO MARY.

To those without a knowledge of the Greek language, Wierwille's interpretations of Scripture often appear to be correct. However, Greek students easily recognize his misuse of the language.

A prime example is the meaning of John 1:1: "In the beginning was the Word, and the Word was with God, and the Word was God." Wierwille's view that Jesus Christ is not God caused him to give this verse some unusual interpretations. By comparing verses 1 and 14, it is obvious that the "Word" refers to Jesus Christ. The Greek words, like the English words, are clear in their meaning. However, Wierwille could not accept John 1:1 as is, because he would then have to admit Jesus Christ was with God from the beginning, proving He is God. Since Wierwille taught that Jesus did not exist before He was born to

Mary, he was forced to deny the obvious interpretation of these verses. He stated, "Jesus Christ was not literally with God in the beginning."[27] So what then was his interpretation of John 1:1? "Jesus Christ was with God in His foreknowledge."[28] In this sense it could be said that everyone of us was "with God."

Paul used the same Greek preposition translated "with" in John 1:1 when he reminded the Thessalonians, "Do you not remember that when I was still with you I told you these things?" (2 Thess. 2:5). Paul's words are clear enough in meaning, and so are the apostle John's—unless you do not accept what the Scriptures say about the deity of Christ.

Orthodox Christianity maintains that Jesus Christ had to be both completely man and completely God in order to provide redemption for humanity by His death and resurrection. On the contrary, Wierwille taught, "*If Jesus Christ is God and not the Son of God, we have not yet been redeemed*"[29] (emphasis his). And the adherents of The Way strongly push this point.

Once I received a phone call from a "Wayer" who said, "To me it is blasphemy to say Jesus Christ is God." I responded, "To me it is blasphemy to say Jesus Christ is not God." With that he slammed down the receiver as if I had placed a curse on him. This was at the end of a long conversation in which he had used swear words. I told him I would not continue the conversation if he was going to use that kind of language. He justified it as being "like the Greek of the first century—crude and graphic." I told him I had taught New Testament Greek for many years and that I disagreed with him about that point. Again I stressed that if we couldn't talk without that kind of language, I wouldn't talk with him. That's when he made the comment about blasphemy and quickly hung up when I made mine.

When the Bible refers to Jesus as the "only begotten" Son of God, it is not referring to a process whereby God brought Him into existence. Instead, it refers to the special, or unique, relationship Jesus had with the Father.

Wierwille also used the Greek word translated "only begotten" (*monogenēs*) to teach that Christ did not exist before He was born: "Literally this word means 'only offspring' or 'only begotten.' The usage of this Greek word in the New Testament is *always* found in the context of one and only one offspring"[30] (emphasis mine).

The primary emphasis of this word, however, is not birth but special relationship. Hebrews 11:17 says Abraham "offered up Isaac, and he who had received the promises offered up his only begotten [*monogenēs*] son." On the basis of what Wierwille taught, we would assume that Isaac was the "one and only one offspring" Abraham had. This is not true. In fact, Isaac was not even Abraham's firstborn son. Ishmael was (Gen. 16:15–16). So when the Bible refers to Jesus as the "only begotten" Son of God, it is not referring to a process whereby God brought Him into existence. Instead, it refers to the special, or unique, relationship Jesus had with the Father.

Wierwille referred to Greek a great deal in establishing his views about who Jesus Christ is. However, in doing so he ignored many of the rules of Greek grammar—especially the one that clearly proves Jesus Christ is God. The rule is named after the man who observed its occurrence, Granville Sharp.

This rule relates to the use of the Greek article (the) and two nouns joined by the Greek word translated "and." Such expressions as "our great God and Savior Jesus Christ" (Titus 2:13) and "of our God and Savior Jesus Christ" (2 Pet. 1:1) fit the Granville Sharp rule. In both constructions in the Greek New Testament, the Greek article appears with "God" but not with "Savior." In such a construction, when the article appears with the first noun (God) but not with the second (Savior), then the second noun is only a further description of the first. Thus, these passages are saying that the Savior is God.

The Granville Sharp rule is commonly accepted by those knowledgeable in Greek. A. T. Robertson (1883–1934), who made a monumental contribution to our present-day understanding of Greek, fully endorsed this rule of Greek grammar and believed it was another proof that Jesus is God.[31]

But we don't have to depend on this rule alone for proof that Jesus Christ is God. The Bible itself makes this truth abundantly clear in such passages as Micah 5:2; Isaiah 7:14; 9:6–7; John 5:18; 8:58; 17:5; and Colossians 1:15–19.[32]

Wierwille's belief about Jesus Christ—the foundational block of his theological superstructure—must be rejected because it does not agree with the clear teaching of Scripture. Nor can it be defended from the Greek New Testament, which he cited so often.

What They Believe

No doctrine could be more important than deciding what one believes about Jesus Christ. And like the Jehovah's Witnesses, because The Way is off on this key doctrine, it hardly matters what else they believe. But they do have other non-orthodox beliefs.

THE HOLY SPIRIT

Wierwille's disturbing way of distorting what the Scriptures say about God is also seen by his denial of the deity and personality of the Holy Spirit. He taught that the Holy Spirit was not the third Person of the Godhead but was merely a characteristic of God. He also distinguished between Holy Spirit (capitalized) and holy spirit (lowercased).

The early Greek manuscripts were copied primarily in either all capitals or all lowercase. Wierwille used this to make a case for his twisted interpretation. He wrote, "When the word *pneuma* is translated "Spirit" with a capital S it is an interpretation rather than a translation, and as such is of no higher authority than the person or translator giving it."[33] While it is true that capitalization has been added by the translators, this does not give Wierwille the right to make his own rules and interpretations for capitalization.

Wierwille redefined the terms in order to deny the unique personality of the Holy Spirit. He reasoned that since God was holy and God was spirit, the term "Holy Spirit" was simply another descriptive name for God. Likewise, whenever the Bible speaks of the Holy Spirit as God's gift to man, Wierwille always made it lowercase. He taught that the "holy spirit" was not God in us but was rather "an inherent spiritual ability" or "power from on high."[34]

Because Wierwille denied the doctrine of the Trinity, he could not admit that the Holy Spirit is God. Therefore, he also had to deny that the Holy Spirit is a person. His views, of course, are directly opposed to those held by orthodox Christianity and those clearly stated in the Scriptures. The Bible reveals that the Holy Spirit does what only a person can do. He teaches (John 14:26), convicts (16:8), baptizes (1 Cor. 12:13), seals (Eph. 1:13) and fills, or controls (5:18). He also has the attributes of God.[35] Likewise, the evidence of the Scripture points to the fact that the Holy Spirit is the third Person of the Trinity—separate from the Father and the Son but still equal with them (Matt. 28:19; Luke 3:21–22; Acts 5:3–4).

SPEAKING IN TONGUES

Even though Wierwille did not believe that Jesus Christ is God or that the Holy Spirit is a distinct Person of the Godhead, he strongly believed in speaking in tongues. It is a major emphasis in Way theology and practice. In his book *The New, Dynamic Church*, Wierwille wrote a section entitled "A Christian's Power Base." The three chapters in this section are "Speaking in Tongues," "How to Speak in Tongues" and "Filled to Overflowing." This leaves little doubt about the significance Wierwille placed on speaking in tongues. Most everyone who believes speaking in tongues is for today is a strong believer in the deity of Christ and the Person of the Holy Spirit, but Wierwille believed in neither.

Wierwille stressed that every believer should speak in tongues. "Before you can tap any of God's resources you must know, first of all, what is available. You know speaking in tongues is available because the Word of God says all born-again believers have the holy spirit within them, which is the ability to speak in tongues."[36]

Notice Wierwille's use of "holy spirit." It is clear that he considered the indwelling of the Spirit to refer not to the presence of a person but of a power—namely speaking in tongues. According to him, the two are synonymous. Wierwille not only taught that *every* true believer should speak in tongues, but he believed it was a sign of salvation itself. "The only visible and audible proof that a man has been born again and filled with the gift from the Holy Spirit is *always* that he speaks in a tongue or tongues"[37] (emphasis his).

Wierwille's misuse of Greek in defending his predetermined theology is especially seen in this issue of gifts. To support his belief about speaking in tongues, he made a distinction between two Greek words that cannot be defended by Greek scholarship. The words are *dechomai* and *lambanō*. These words are synonyms and mean "take" or "receive." It is commonly held that *lambanō* means the same as *dechomai* except *dechomai* has the added element of welcoming, or gladly receiving. (I used to tell my Greek students that when I distribute a test, they *lambanō* it; but if I would pass out ten-dollar bills, they would *dechomai* them.)

Wierwille, on the other hand, defined *dechomai* as "receiving from God spiritually within oneself. This is subjective reception."[38] He defined *lambanō* as "receiving the gift into manifestation after having received it spiritually. This is an objective reception to the end of manifestation."[39]

A basic error of Wierwille regarding Greek is that he loaded the words with theological meaning, whereas in the first century these words were commonly used by unbelievers as well as believers. Only the context can tell what is referred to by "taking" or "receiving."

Wierwille used his novel meanings of these Greek words to teach that "whenever anyone had received salvation he also had received the gift from the Holy Spirit into manifestation."[40] In other words, anyone who is saved should manifest his salvation by speaking in tongues.

Making such a distinction between these Greek words to fit his theology may sound impressive to his followers who have not studied Greek. However, any serious student of the Word who checks the helps available on Greek words will discover that Wierwille's definitions cannot be supported.[41]

Wierwille was correct in teaching that every believer is indwelt by the Holy Spirit (Rom. 8:9; 1 Cor. 6:19). Likewise, speaking in tongues was a legitimate gift of the Spirit in the first century, although many people question its validity today. However, God's Word never teaches—as The Way does—that every believer should speak in tongues, nor is it ever made a requirement for salvation.

This is evident from Paul's words in 1 Corinthians 12. He asked, "Are all apostles? Are all prophets? Are all teachers? Are all workers of miracles? Do all have gifts of healings? Do all speak with tongues? Do all interpret?" (vv. 29–30). The answer to these seven questions is obvious in the Greek text. From his supposed knowledge of Greek, Wierwille should have known that the individual Greek word inserted in each question clearly indicated Paul expected a no answer to all seven questions. Not even in the first century, when few scholars doubt the legitimacy of speaking in tongues, was it right to insist that everyone should have this gift.

All of 1 Corinthians 12 speaks to this issue of not making one gift a requirement for all believers. Paul stressed again and again that the Holy Spirit gives a variety of gifts but that not everyone receives the same gift. He used the illustration of a body to show this diversity and the fact that each part is equally important (vv. 4–25). In addition,

Paul also warned against placing undue emphasis on speaking in tongues (1 Cor. 14). He gave strict instructions on the use of tongues and urged, "Let all things be done decently and in order" (v. 40). The Way has made speaking in tongues a requirement for salvation and fellowship. Clearly this is not what the Lord intended.

SOUL SLEEP

The Way International teaches that believers do not have a conscious existence after death until the resurrection. While this doctrine is not as crucial as others, such as the deity of Christ, it does demonstrate how Wierwille's teachings are not in the mainstream of orthodox Christianity.

Wierwille wrote, "No passage of Scripture teaches that there is conscious existence after death."[42] He added, "The teaching that when a person dies he immediately goes to God in heaven is one of the many doctrines of Satan and his fallen angels."[43]

> THE WAY INTER-NATIONAL TEACHES THAT BELIEVERS DO NOT HAVE A CONSCIOUS EXISTENCE AFTER DEATH UNTIL THE RESURRECTION.

The Scriptures teach, however, that even though a believer's body remains in the grave at death, his soul and spirit (the real person) immediately go to be with God. The apostle Paul saw no time lapse between his life in the body and his life with the Lord. "We are confident, yes, well pleased rather to be absent from the body and to be present with the Lord," he wrote (2 Cor. 5:8).

On another occasion Paul admitted he had "a desire to depart and be with Christ" (Phil. 1:23). However, he realized the believers in Philippi needed him, and so he was torn between the two. Paul's words give no indication that he thought he would remain in an unconscious state in the grave for an indefinite time before he would see Christ at the resurrection.

In addition, the Bible clearly states that when Christ comes for His Church, He will bring the believers who have died with Him so they can receive their bodies at the resurrection. "For if we believe that Jesus died and rose again," says 1 Thessalonians 4:14, "even so God will bring with Him those who sleep in Jesus." Where are these believers who have died before they are reunited with their bodies? They are "with Him." Once again, the biblical evidence reveals that Wierwille was teaching false doctrine.

CONCLUSION

Even though he died in 1985, the followers of Victor Paul Wierwille continue teaching his theological errors. Although they claim that the Bible is their final authority, the members of The Way are really following the words of Wierwille.

The history of The Way International serves as a warning to churches and believers today. As we have seen, any group can fall into false doctrine when it begins to stray from the Word of God. We must guard against making the same mistakes the followers of The Way have made.

First, a religious leader must make sure that his teachings are clear, easy to understand and biblically sound. A leader should point his followers to historically reliable sources so they can do their own research and call him into question if he has misused God's Word.

Likewise, those who are spiritually hungry should not blindly follow one person whose teachings they cannot understand. They should test every word they hear by the Scriptures to make sure that person is handling the truth responsibly.

The teachings of Wierwille also show us that the use of Greek and other biblical languages does not automatically result in accurate theology. Wierwille's mind-set against the Trinity, the deity of Christ and the personality of the Holy Spirit caused him to ignore the clear meanings of Greek words and to fabricate his own meanings in order to support his new emphasis of old heresies. In addition, Wierwille's twisting of the Scriptures shows us the danger of forming our own beliefs and then reinterpreting passages to fit them. We must allow the Scriptures to speak for themselves.

The experience of The Way also teaches us an important lesson about the sensational and "miraculous." Everything supernatural is not always from God. Therefore, anything that appears to be miraculous must always be tested by God's revelation.

As early as 1400 B.C., Moses warned the Israelites, "If there arises among you a prophet or a dreamer of dreams, and he gives you a sign or a wonder, and the sign or the wonder comes to pass, of which he spoke to you, saying, 'Let us go after other gods which you have not known, and let us serve them,' you shall not listen to the words of that prophet or that dreamer of dreams, for the LORD your God is testing you to know whether you love the LORD your God with all your heart and with all your soul" (Deut. 13:1–3). A miracle must always be tested by the message.

Even though the followers of The Way claim to know the way to God, we should not follow them because their teachings do not agree with God's written revelation. The Bible clearly states the only way to be saved is through faith in Jesus Christ (John 14:6). And The Way International has denied this faith.

Summary

Name of Organization: The Way International
Founder: Victor Paul Wierwille (1916–1985)
Headquarters: New Knoxville, Ohio
Membership (1998): Worldwide: 10,000–20,000
Web Site: www.theway.org
Publications: *The Way Magazine*

Jesus Christ Is Not God, by Victor Paul Wierwille

The Rise and Expansion of the Christian Church in the First Century, by former president L. Craig Martindale

What They Believe

Followers of The Way International: **Biblical Christians:**

Source of Authority

Followers of The Way International:	Biblical Christians:
Claim that the Bible is the final authority but follow interpretations of founder Victor Paul Wierwille. He claimed special revelation from God.	The Bible is the sole authority for beliefs and practices. They make no claim for inspired revelation to any person after inspiration of 66 books.

What They Believe

The Trinity

Deny biblical doctrine of the Trinity, claiming it is a pagan concept brought into Christianity.

The three Persons of the Godhead are one, yet distinct, with each being co-equally and coeternally God.

Jesus Christ

Jesus is the Son of God but He is not God. They change the meanings of common Greek words in John 1:1 that declare Jesus was with God. Say that "if Jesus Christ is God . . . we have not been redeemed."

Believe that Jesus Christ is God and reject fourth century view of Arius that Jesus Christ is not God. Say that John 1:1 and 1:14 clearly show that Jesus Christ was with God in eternity past and became man. Claim that if Jesus Christ were not fully God as well as fully man we have not been redeemed.

The Holy Spirit

Deny the deity and personality of the Holy Spirit. "Holy Spirit" is another name for God, but "holy spirit" refers to a spiritual ability.

The Holy Spirit is the third Person of the Trinity and as such is a divine person, not an ability or impersonal force.

Speaking in Tongues

Speaking in tongues is the only visible and audible proof that a person has been born again.

Even in the first century it was wrong to say all should speak in tongues (1 Cor. 12).

Soul Sleep

"No passage of Scripture teaches that there is conscious existence after death." Believers do not go to be with God at death.

Believe that Paul expected to be immediately in the presence of God after death (2 Cor. 5:8). Christ will bring "with Him" those who have placed faith in Him and who have died (1 Thess. 4:14), showing they have gone to be with God.

Recommended Reading

Ankerberg, John, and Weldon, John. *Encyclopedia of Cults and New Religions*. Eugene, Ore.: Harvest House Publishers, 1999.

Boa, Kenneth. *Cults, World Religions & the Occult*. Wheaton, Ill.: Victor Books, 1990.

Enroth, Ronald, & others. *A Guide to Cults & New Religions*. Downers Grove, Ill.: InterVarsity Press, 1983.

Martin, Walter. *The Kingdom of the Cults*. Minneapolis: Bethany House Publishers, 1985.

Mather, George A., and Nichols, Larry A. *Dictionary of Cults, Sects, Religions and the Occult*. Grand Rapids, Mich.: Zondervan Publishing House, 1993.

McDowell, Josh, and Stewart, Don. *Handbook of Today's Religions*. San Bernardino, Calif.: Here's Life Publishers, Inc., 1983.

ENDNOTES

[1] Peter Klebnikov, *Newsweek*, April 7, 1997, 48B.

[2] John P. Juedes, "A Special Report: Sweeping Changes in The Way International," *Christian Research Journal*, Summer 1996, 6.

[3] Religious Movements Web site, http://religiousmovements.lib.virginia.edu/nrms/way-intl.html, Nov. 1, 2005.

[4] "What Is the Way?," The Way International Web site, www.theway.org/info.htm, Nov. 1, 2005.

[5] *The New York Times*, May 23, 1985, D-25.

[6] For documentation see Walter R. Martin, ed., *The New Cults* (Ventura, Calif.: Regal Books, 1980), 37–39.

[7] J. L. Williams, *Victor Paul Wierwille and The Way International* (Chicago: Moody Press, 1979), 23–24.

[8] Irvine Robertson, *What the Cults Believe* (Chicago: Moody Press, 1983), 97.

[9] Williams, 26.

[10] "The Way, International," The Watchman Expositor Web site, www.watchman.org/profile/waypro.htm, Nov. 1, 2005.

[11] Juedes, "A Special Report: Sweeping Changes in The Way International," *Christian Research Journal*, Summer 1996, 44.

[12] Ibid., 6–7.

[13] Joseph M. Hopkins, "The Word and The Way According to Victor Wierwille," *Christianity Today*, Sept. 26, 1975, 42.

[14] Elena S. Whiteside, *The Way: Living in Love*, 2nd ed. (New Knoxville, Ohio: American Christian Press, 1974), 178, cited by Williams, *Victor Paul Wierwille and The Way International*, 21.

[15] For discussion see F. F. Bruce, *The Books and the Parchments*, rev. ed. (Old Tappan, N.J.: Fleming H. Revell Company, 1984) and Bruce M. Metzger, *The Text of the New Testament*, rev. ed. (New York: Oxford University Press, 1968).

[16] See Martin, *The New Cults*, 38.

[17] Juedes, "A Special Report: Sweeping Changes in The Way International," *Christian Research Journal*, Summer 1996, 44.

[18] "Watchman Fellowship's 2001 Index of Cults and Religions," The Watchman Expositor Web site, www.watchman.org/cat95.htm#Martindale, Nov. 2, 2005.

[19] Williams, 47.

[20] Victor Paul Wierwille, *Jesus Christ Is Not God* (New Knoxville, Ohio: American Christian Press, 1975), 5.

[21] Ibid., 13.

[22] Jack Sparks, *The Mindbenders* (Nashville: Thomas Nelson, Inc., Publishers, 1977), 191.

[23] Ibid., 191–192.

[24] Wierwille, *Jesus Christ Is Not God*, 5.

[25] Ibid.

[26] Ibid.

[27] Ibid.

[28] Ibid., 28.

[29] Ibid., 6.

[30] Ibid., 115.

[31] For documentation see A. T. Robertson, "The Greek Article and the Deity of Christ," in *The Minister and His Greek New Testament* (Grand Rapids, Mich.: Baker Book House, paperback ed., 1979), 61–68.

[32] For further explanation see Lewis Sperry Chafer, *Major Bible Themes*, rev. by John F. Walvoord (Grand Rapids, Mich.: Zondervan Publishing House, 1974), 52–55.

[33] Victor Paul Wierwille, *Receiving the Holy Spirit Today* (New Knoxville, Ohio: American Christian Press, 1972), 2.

[34] Ibid., 5.

[35] For documentation see Chafer, *Major Bible Themes*, 87–90.

[36] Victor Paul Wierwille, *The New, Dynamic Church* (New Knoxville, Ohio: American Christian Press, 1971), 115–116.

[37] Wierwille, *Receiving the Holy Spirit Today*, 148.

[38] Ibid., 260.

[39] Ibid.

[40] Ibid., 261.

[41] For documentation see *New International Dictionary of New Testament Theology*, Vol. 3 (Grand Rapids, Mich.: Zondervan Publishing House, 1978), 744–751 and *The Expanded Vine's Expository Dictionary of New Testament Words* (Minneapolis: Bethany House Publishers, 1984), 926–927.

[42] Victor Paul Wierwille, *Are the Dead Alive Now?* (Old Greenwich, Conn.: Devin-Adair Co., n.d.), 97, cited by Robert Passantino and Gretchen Passantino, *Answers to the Cultist at Your Door* (Eugene, Oreg.: Harvest House Publishers, 1981), 173.

[43] Ibid.

CHAPTER SEVENTEEN

How to Answer the Counterfeits

You answer the doorbell and find some members of another religious group trying to sell or give their literature to you. How do you react? Do you slam the door in their faces? Do you engage them in a conversation, comparing their beliefs with yours? Do you hand them some literature that explains your beliefs? Or do you stumble over your own words, trying to remember what you believe?

Relatively few Christians will have successful ministries of witnessing to members of spiritual counterfeits. In fact, many people who work with spiritual counterfeits do not encourage Christians in general to seek out adherents of other beliefs. For some Christians, the study of the counterfeits motivates them to better defend their faith; for others, it seems to produce endless confusion because they pay too much attention to the counterfeits and not enough to the genuine faith. For the most part, your time will be better invested if you become well anchored in the Word of God and have an effective ministry of teaching and outreach through your local church.

But even if you don't seek out members of other belief systems, you need to be able to defend your faith when they come knocking at your door. In addition to being able to defend specific doctrines of historical Christianity, you should keep several things in mind about the approach of counterfeit religions.

Never underestimate the importance of knowing the genuine as a help in being able to recognize a counterfeit. If you don't know what biblical Christianity believes, you will have difficulty recognizing those who differ from it.

Be sure that you are in a right relationship with God by having trusted Jesus Christ for your salvation. As you appreciate the grace He has showered upon you, your growing desire to study the Bible will result in a closer relationship with Him. You will grow in your knowledge of the Word of God as you study it for yourself and are involved in a local church where you hear consistent biblical teaching. In such a setting you also can demonstrate your faith by relating to others within the family of God, and being a part of an outreach to the community and the world. Then, as others approach you from counterfeit belief systems, you'll have a better idea of how you should respond and the questions you should ask them.

In your discussion of beliefs, keep the source of authority—the Bible—in central focus. When differing on a doctrine, no conclusion will be reached unless both parties agree on what will be accepted as the final word on the subject. Some groups who approach you will use the Bible merely as an attention-getter so they can entice you to talk about their teachings. Other groups will refer to it extensively.

Some groups will have a lot to say about the original languages of the Bible—Hebrew in the Old Testament (along with some Aramaic) and Greek in the New Testament. They will give you the impression that if you only knew the original languages, then surely you would agree with their theology.

What they neglect to tell you is that many of us who know the original languages—and even teach them at college and seminary levels—do not agree with the way they use the languages. And we absolutely do not think the original languages prove what some spiritual counterfeits claim they say. But what should a believer do who has never studied Hebrew or Greek?

You might ask the person at your door, "Does everyone who knows Greek (or Hebrew) agree with what you're saying about this Bible text?" If he answers yes, you should be wise enough to realize that is not true. You might say something like this: "My pastor has studied the original languages, but I know he doesn't agree with the doctrine you're presenting." If he answers no, then you can point out that the problem is basic theological assumptions rather than knowledge of the original languages.

Be assured that most English translations of the Bible effectively communicate what was in the Hebrew and Greek manuscripts. Knowing the original languages often gives fuller and richer meanings, but rarely will it yield different meanings. It is similar to watching a movie in color rather than in black and white. You notice additional details in color, but you're still watching the same show.

Realize also that many who appeal to the original languages have not studied these languages themselves. They are merely reciting what their superiors have told them. When you ask them other questions about Hebrew and Greek, they usually have no idea how to answer.

For instance, the appeal the Jehovah's Witnesses make to the Greek text of John 1:1 to "prove" that Jesus Christ is not God is not based on standard Greek grammars. Nor is it consistent with their own interpretations later in the same passage. This is a case where their theological view causes them to force the text to fit their teaching. The real problem is not what the Greek text says but what the Jehovah's Witnesses want it to say to match their beliefs (see Chapter Three for more details).

Although it is a group's particular system of beliefs that makes it a spiritual counterfeit, many people join these groups because of personal rather than doctrinal reasons. Warren Wiersbe, a well-known Bible teacher and author, says, "Many people join cults because of *psychology* and not *theology*. If you were to ask them what their group believes or teaches, they would have a hard time giving a good answer. Why? Because people who decide to join a cult often use their *heart* instead of their *head*"[1] (emphasis his).

Wiersbe believes that cult leaders know how to take advantage of people's psychological problems, such as insecurity, a desire for pat answers, repressed feelings, hostility, aggression and guilt feelings.

Others agree with Wiersbe. Robert and Gretchen Passantino say, "Our basic premise is quite simple: we believe, after almost 35 years in the field of cult apologetics, that people start and join cults because they have personal needs that aren't being met in traditional churches."[2] The Passantinos believe there are three main reasons why cults are born: "Faults within the church, wrong responses to world problems, and wrong motivations of people who become cult leaders or cult followers."[3]

It is sobering to realize that many of those who have begun deviant religious groups had a background in biblical Christianity. Evangelical churches and Christian families need to be careful not to foster a climate that makes people, especially young people, vulnerable to these groups. The Passantinos tell parents, "One of the best preventive measures to insure that your children do not join cults is to give them a Bible-based, Christ-centered home life that will prepare them to face all the problems of the world with a confident Christian commitment."[4]

Harold Busséll, a former dean at Gordon College, identifies attitudes in evangelicalism that can make people susceptible to sects. One of these is the attitude toward fellowship. He writes, "I often hear Christians saying, 'There is no real fellowship in my church. I wish we had fellowship like they did in the New Testament church.'"[5]

Busséll blasts this kind of thinking. "Our modern misunderstanding of fellowship is complicated by 'me-first' messages presented in the religious media, which picture the church as the cosmic supermarket, a consumerist field day. We come to God with our spiritual credit cards to receive, on demand, all the displayed benefits."[6]

Focusing on the apostle John's statements recorded in 1 John 1:1–4, Busséll states, "John points out that Christian fellowship is based on an orthodox understanding of the person and work of Jesus Christ. Out of our knowledge of Christ comes our joy."[7]

If people join counterfeit groups to meet some personal needs, they may find after joining that those needs aren't being met. Then a Christian, showing love and compassion, can help such a person see that his needs can only be met through the Person and work of the Lord Jesus Christ, as set forth in the Bible.

When approached by spiritual counterfeits, Christians must be able to defend what they believe. Crucial topics to concentrate on are source of authority, God, Jesus Christ, the Holy Spirit, sin, salvation and future life.

SOURCE OF AUTHORITY

When you discuss differing doctrinal views with an adherent of a counterfeit group, you need to establish what that group considers to be the final source of authority. Some groups emphatically claim to be Christian, but they do not follow the Bible alone as the final source of authority. In addition to the Bible, they may follow tradition or the teaching of church leaders. Or they may consider other books to be equal to, if not superior to, the Bible.

Even among those groups who accept the Bible alone as final authority, you can recognize a counterfeit religion if it accepts only one person, or a special group, as the only trustworthy interpreter of the Bible. Historical Christianity holds that the Bible can be read and interpreted by every believer. While it may be difficult to decide what is taught in a given passage, no particular person or group should be regarded as the only interpreter of the Word of God.

The key matter to establish when differing over doctrine is that the Bible—and the Bible alone—is the final source of authority. If you cannot agree on that, you won't be able to agree on the other doctrines you discuss.

GOD

Having established the Bible as the final authority, you need to define the terms being used. With some groups, it is important even to establish what is meant by the word *God*.

> BE SURE YOU UNDERSTAND WHAT OTHERS MEAN BY THE TERMINOLOGY THEY USE.

Those accustomed to thinking in terms of biblical Christianity assume the word *God* refers to the God of the Bible. Many religious groups in America (often influenced by Eastern religions), however, do not view God as a person but as an impersonal force. Such groups include Christian Science, the New Age Movement, Transcendental Meditation and Unity School of Christianity.

The Bible presents God as a person with intellect, emotions and will. He is greater than the universe, for He created it. God is Spirit (John 4:24). He is also all-powerful, is everywhere present, has all knowledge and is absolutely holy.

God is also a trinity; that is, three Persons—Father, Son and Holy Spirit—comprise the one Godhead. The Trinity of the Godhead has been accepted by historical Christianity since the second century, as reflected in the Apostles' Creed.

What They Believe

When many groups refer to "God," they are not thinking about the God who is precisely defined by the Bible and accepted by biblical Christianity. Be sure you understand what others mean by the terminology they use, or your discussion will not be beneficial to you or them because you'll be talking about different concepts.

JESUS CHRIST

The Person and work of Jesus Christ must be the focus of special attention when you talk about spiritual matters. Be suspicious of the theology of anyone who talks only about God and never mentions Jesus Christ.

Crucial to the discussion is whether or not an individual believes that Jesus Christ is God. Since early in the fourth century, historical Christianity has accepted that Jesus Christ is God. The first ecumenical council met in Nicea in 325 A.D. to consider the controversy over the deity of Christ. The Council of Nicea condemned as heresy the view that Christ was not God. Although the heresy continued to flourish for a while, by 381 "the question was officially settled by the church."[8]

If Jesus Christ were not God as well as man, He could not have provided for our salvation. He had to be man to die for our sins, but He had to be God for His death to pay the penalty for all of our sin.

Those who deny the deity of Jesus Christ, such as the Jehovah's Witnesses and The Way International, are free to believe what they wish, of course. But we should not mistake their views as being what the Bible teaches nor what historical Christianity has long believed.

The Bible teaches that Jesus Christ is God. John 1:1 says, "In the beginning was the Word, and the Word was with God, and the Word was God." Verse 14 makes it clear that "the Word" is referring to Christ. The Jews of Christ's day clearly understood that when He referred to God as His father, He was "making Himself equal with God" (5:18). That is why Jesus could say, "I and My Father are one" (10:30).

What a person believes about the Lord Jesus Christ is crucial. If you cannot agree with others on the Person of Christ, it is useless to discuss other topics, such as prophecy or social issues.

THE HOLY SPIRIT

Some groups, such as The Way International, not only deny that the Holy Spirit is a member of the Trinity, but they even deny that He is a person. The Unification Church goes so far as to make the Holy Spirit the female part of their concept of God.

The Bible, however, refers to the Holy Spirit as a person. He does things only a person can do. He convicts, guides, discloses things to come and glorifies Christ (John 16:7–15). He searches the depths of God and knows the thoughts of God (1 Cor. 2:10–11). It is also possible for the Holy Spirit to be grieved (Eph. 4:30). In addition, the Holy Spirit is called "God" (Acts 5:3–4). What He does, only God can do.

Macedonius, bishop of Constantinople from 341 to 360, denied the deity of the Holy Spirit (although he did not seem to deny His personhood). At the ecumenical council in Constantinople in 381, Macedonius' view was condemned. Historical Christianity believes in both the personhood and the deity of the Holy Spirit.

SIN

In defending the "faith which was once for all delivered to the saints" (Jude 1:3), it is important to be able to agree on mankind's basic problem. Are all guilty of sin or not? If the answer is yes, we must determine what can remove the condemnation of that sin. But if a group or person claims that sin does not exist, there will be no need to seek a remedy.

Groups such as Christian Science, Rosicrucians, Masons, Unity School of Christianity and the New Age Movement reject the biblical view of sin. Any "weaknesses" or "mistakes" can be overcome, they claim, through enlightenment rather than by a personal relationship to Jesus Christ. They constantly seek right thinking, not a relationship with an eternal Savior.

By using a concordance, it is easy to see how frequently the word *sin* is used in the Bible. In the New Testament alone, the noun for sin (*hamartia*) occurs 174 times and the verb (*hamartanō*) occurs 43 times. Those who reject the existence of sin clearly reject the teaching of the Bible.

What They Believe

The basic meaning of the word *sin* refers to a missing of the mark, and this is what mankind has done. Romans 3:23 says that all have sinned and come short of God's glory, or His standards. Romans 5:12 and 6:23 reveal that death results from sin. This includes spiritual death as well as physical death. All are under condemnation because of sin (John 3:18). Because of this, we have no hope apart from salvation, which God has provided.

SALVATION

Any group that claims to be religious will propose some means of improving mankind's condition—even if it is by self-reformation. The various counterfeit groups discussed in this book make it seem that there are many ways to achieve salvation. But all the proposed means can really be categorized into only two: One is a salvation by works; the other is salvation by grace through faith in the Lord Jesus Christ.

Counterfeit groups seem to offer many means to salvation because it's difficult to discern what is really being said by any one group. Salvation that is not by grace, however, is really a salvation by works (where you try to earn your salvation by doing certain things). Some counterfeit groups even speak of salvation by grace; but as you read their authoritative sources, it is evident that they add other requirements to faith in Christ for salvation.

It is a basic principle of life that a gift is not something you can earn. Whether referring to God's call of Israel, to salvation or to anything else, it is an accepted truism that "if by grace, then it is no longer of works; otherwise grace is no longer grace. But if it is of works, it is no longer grace; otherwise work is no longer work" (Rom. 11:6).

A gift, by its very nature, cannot be earned. When you present a gift to someone on a special occasion, it is understood that the gift does not have to be earned—you give it out of your good grace.

Salvation is a *gift* to those who place their trust in Jesus Christ. The only thing a person can do to receive that gift is to accept it by faith through placing trust in Jesus Christ. This act changes a person's eternal destiny from hell to heaven. But some people insist on working for their salvation. On one occasion, a crowd asked Jesus, "What shall we do, that we may work the works of God?" Jesus' answer was, "This is the work of God, that you believe in Him whom He sent" (John 6:28–29).

After some individuals in Ephesus had trusted in Jesus Christ as their Savior, Paul told them, "For by grace you have been saved through faith, and that not of yourselves; it is the gift of God, not of works, lest anyone should boast" (Eph. 2:8–9). The inspired writings of the apostle Paul reveal that if anything is added to faith in Christ as a requirement for salvation, the result is a salvation by works, which does not save.

Any person or group who says that in addition to believing in Jesus Christ you are required to do certain things for salvation is offering a salvation by works, not by grace. And a salvation by works is no salvation at all. "To him who does not work but believes on Him who justifies the ungodly, his faith is accounted for righteousness" (Rom. 4:5).

A person is to do good works *because* he is saved, not *to obtain* salvation. Paul told the Ephesians that their salvation was by grace through faith and not by works. Then he added, "For we are His workmanship, created in Christ Jesus for good works, which God prepared beforehand that we should walk in them" (Eph. 2:10).

Some believers in the first century wanted to make keeping the Old Testament Law a requirement for salvation, in addition to believing in Christ. But Paul said, "I do not set aside the grace of God; for if righteousness comes through the law, then Christ died in vain" (Gal. 2:21). What Paul said of the Old Testament Law could be said of any requirement that is added for salvation, such as water baptism or membership in a particular religious group.

Jesus Christ is the propitiation, or satisfaction, for all of our sins (1 John 2:1–2). All who trust in Him for salvation have forgiveness of sins and eternal life (John 1:12; Rom. 6:23; 1 John 2:2).

FUTURE LIFE

Ask the person at your door what happens to an individual after this life. Will he be resurrected or not? In the great resurrection chapter of the Bible (1 Cor. 15), Paul gave many reasons to establish the certainty of our future resurrection. He wrote, "If in this life only we have hope in Christ, we are of all men the most pitiable" (v. 19). Dallas

Seminary professor David Lowery, a professor of New Testament studies, comments on this verse: "If there were no Resurrection, the pagans would be right. The 'foolishness of the Cross' (1:18) would be just that, and men such as Paul and the apostles who had suffered for the gospel (4:9–13) could only be **pitied**. Those who lived for the pleasure of the moment would be right and the sacrifices of Christians would only be cruel, self-inflicted jokes (cf. 15:32)"[9] (emphasis his).

But there is a resurrection! Paul also wrote: "I tell you a mystery: We shall not all sleep, but we shall all be changed—in a moment, in the twinkling of an eye, at the last trumpet. For the trumpet will sound, and the dead will be raised incorruptible, and we shall be changed" (15:51–52).

> ONLY BELIEVING IN CHRIST CLEANSES A PERSON OF SIN AND DELIVERS HIM FROM ETERNAL CONDEMNATION.

Groups such as the New Age Movement, Rosicrucians, Transcendental Meditation and Unity School of Christianity teach reincarnation, not resurrection. This is similar to Hinduism, which teaches that through a cycle of rebirths a person will eventually achieve eternal bliss with the impersonal divine principle, or Brahman, the Ultimate Reality of Hinduism.

This belief of Eastern religions is not taught in the Bible nor accepted by historical Christianity. Instead of reincarnation, the Bible teaches that once death occurs, "after this the judgment" (Heb. 9:27). This judgment will be a time of reward for those who have trusted in Jesus Christ (1 Cor. 3:10–15), but a time of eternal condemnation for those who have not (Rev. 20:11–15).

Because the God-Man, Jesus Christ, fully paid the penalty of sin, anyone can be delivered from condemnation once for all by believing in Him for salvation. John 3:18 says, "He who believes in Him [Jesus Christ] is not condemned; but he who does not believe is condemned already, because he has not believed in the name of the only begotten Son of God."

Romans 8:1 declares, "There is therefore now no condemnation to those who are in Christ Jesus." Only believing in Christ—not reincarnation or good works—cleanses a person of sin and delivers him from eternal condemnation.

CONCLUSION

When you are approached by those who hold views differing from historic, or biblical, Christianity, it is important for you to remember that they may not know what their own group teaches. Groups such as the Masons and Mormons seem to have many adherents who do not know what the official teaching of their group actually is.

At first they will charge that you have not done your research well in studying their group. But if you have read what the leaders of these groups have written, you probably know more about the beliefs of the groups than many members themselves.

Be sure to present facts with kindness. The person who believes in Christ alone for salvation should exhibit the fruit of the Spirit (Gal. 5:22–23), even if he does not agree with another's viewpoint.

Be careful to define your terms as you talk with a follower of any religious group. Study the Bible well, and seek to use language in what was its normal, customary sense when it was written. One of the greatest difficulties in seeking to understand the teachings of groups such as the Masons, Rosicrucians and Christian Science is their use of language. The basis of understanding any language or terminology is that words are to be understood as they are normally and customarily used. This allows for figures of speech and metaphors, but they must be understood on the basis of normal use.

For example, when John the Baptist referred to Jesus Christ as the "The Lamb of God who takes away the sin of the world!" (John 1:29), he did not mean that Jesus was actually a lamb. He was using a figure of speech based on the normal, customary use of *lamb* in the Old Testament. The lamb was a sacrificial animal offered for the sins of the people. Jesus had now come to offer Himself as the perfect sacrifice to take away the sin of the people. So John's figure of speech had to be understood in the way the words were customarily used.

This is not so with Christian Science. The meaning of their terms has nothing to do with customary usage. This becomes glaringly evident when you glance at the glossary in *Science and Health*. Notice some words and the meanings they assign: "Death. An illusion, the lie of life in matter; the unreal and untrue"; "Miracle. That which is divinely natural, but must be learned humanly; a phenomenon of Science"; "Mother. God; divine and eternal Principle; Life, Truth, and Love"; "Resurrection. Spiritualization of thought; a new and higher idea of immortality, or spiritual existence; material belief yielding to spiritual understanding."[10]

But who decides that these terms mean what Mary Baker Eddy said? Terms of the Bible lose all historical significance with such an allegorical, metaphysical approach.

Do not expect to be able to open closed minds. Even the Lord does not force Himself on others against their wills (as is apparent because He lets people go against His moral will when they lie, steal, commit adultery and murder, for example). Present your position about the Bible and biblical Christianity positively. Stick to the main issues—source of authority, God (especially who Jesus Christ is), sin, salvation and future life. Don't get detoured to other topics that might be interesting but are secondary to these key doctrines. Add a personal testimony concerning the peace you have about meeting God face to face in the future.

Above all, pray that God will use the truth you quote from the Bible to speak to needy hearts. Pray that the people you talk to will know the joy of being delivered from all condemnation by believing in Jesus Christ for salvation. Remind yourself that others have been bound in these counterfeit groups but have trusted Christ as Savior when someone shared the Gospel with them, but don't be disappointed if you do not see immediate answers to your prayers. Think of those who have long prayed for the followers of Herbert W. Armstrong to see the light, and now the organization's leaders have turned to evangelicalism. Prayer changes people!

Then be ready to patiently stand beside and nurture those who come to Christ. They will be rejected by their former religious friends and will be in desperate need of friendship and spiritual support.

Sometimes members of counterfeit religions far outstrip evangelicals in their commitment to their cause. In the words of Warren Wiersbe: "The cults should challenge us to examine our own church ministries to see if we are really meeting the needs of people. It is important to

teach the Bible, but we must also give our members opportunities to serve, to perform difficult tasks and to make some sacrifices. People also need intimate fellowship that heals wounds, removes festering fears or hate and encourages people to be open and honest without fear of rejection. We need to say to people, 'We care!' and then prove it by our love and acceptance."[11]

The recommended reading that follows could be considered a mini library of anti-counterfeit religion books. Not all can be added to your library at once, of course, but the list will help you know what to look for in Christian bookstores. Also, be sure to make use of libraries and the InterLibrary Loan system as you search for sources to help you give a defense of what you believe.

God bless you as you seek to answer the counterfeits.

Recommended Reading

Adherents.com Web site, www.adherents.com.

Ankerberg Theological Research Institute Web site, www.ankerberg.org.

Ankerberg, John, and Weldon, John. *Cult Watch: What You Need to Know about Spiritual Deception.* Eugene, Ore.: Harvest House Publishers, 1991.

_____. *Encyclopedia of Cults and New Religions.* Eugene, Ore.: Harvest House Publishers, 1999.

Archer, Gleason. *Encyclopedia of Bible Difficulties.* Grand Rapids, Mich.: Zondervan Publishing House, 1982.

Bickel, Bruce, and Jantz, Stan. *World Religions & Cults 101: A Guide to Spiritual Beliefs.* Eugene, Ore.: Harvest House Publishers, 2002.

Boa, Kenneth. *Cults, World Religions & the Occult.* Wheaton, Ill.: Victor Books, 1995.

_____, and Moody, Larry. *I'm Glad You Asked: In-Depth Answers to Difficult Questions about Christianity.* ChariotVictor Publishing, 1994.

Cairns, Earle E. *Christianity through the Centuries.* Grand Rapids, Mich.: Zondervan Publishing House, 1981.

Carlson, Ron, and Decker, Ed. *Fast Facts on False Teachings.* Eugene, Ore.: Harvest House Publishers, 1994.

Christian Research Institute Web site, www.equip.org.

Enroth, Ronald, Ed. *A Guide to New Religious Movements.* Downers Grove, Ill.:

What They Believe

InterVarsity Press, 2005.

Geisler, Norman L., and Rhodes, Ron. *Correcting the Cults.* Grand Rapids, Mich.: Baker Books, 1997.

_____, and Howe, Thomas. *When Critics Ask.* Wheaton, Ill.: Victor Books, 1992.

_____, and Brooks, Ronald M. *When Skeptics Ask.* Wheaton, Ill.: Victor Books, 1990.

Gomes, Alan W. *Unmasking the Cults.* Grand Rapids, Mich.: Zondervan Publishing House, 1995.

Gospel Communications Web site (providing information and answers from many evangelical organizations), www.gospelcom.net.

Lewis, Gordon R. *Confronting the Cults.* Phillipsburg, N.J.: Presbyterian & Reformed Publishing Company, 1966.

Martin, Walter. *The Kingdom of the Cults.* Ravi Zacharias, gen. ed. Minneapolis: Bethany House Publishers, 2003.

Mather, George A., and Nichols, Larry A. *Dictionary of Cults, Sects, Religions and the Occult.* Grand Rapids, Mich.: Zondervan Publishing House, 1993.

McDowell, Josh, and Stewart, Don. *Handbook of Today's Religions.* San Bernardino, Calif.: Here's Life Publishers, Inc., 1983.

Mead, Frank S., Hill, Samuel S., and Atwood, Craig D. *Handbook of Denominations in the United States,* 12th ed. Nashville: Abingdon Press, 2005.

Rhodes, Ron. *The Challenge of the Cults and New Religions.* Grand Rapids, Mich.: Zondervan, 2001.

_____. *The Complete Book of Bible Answers: Answers to the Tough Questions.* Eugene, Ore.: Harvest House Publishers, 1997.

Robertson, Irvine. *What the Cults Believe.* Chicago: Moody Press, 1991.

Ryrie, Charles C. *Basic Theology.* Wheaton, Ill.: Victor Books, 1986.

ENDNOTES

[1] Warren W. Wiersbe, "The Psychology of the Cults," in *What They Believe: Discerning the Differences* (Lincoln, Neb.: Back to the Bible, 1985), 15.

[2] Robert Passantino and Gretchen Passantino, *Answers to the Cultist at Your Door* (Eugene, Ore.: Harvest House Publishers, 1981), 13.

[3] Ibid., 14.

[4] Ibid., 22.

[5] Harold L. Busséll, *Unholy Devotion: Why Cults Lure Christians* (Grand Rapids, Mich.: Zondervan Publishing House, 1983), 52.

[6] Ibid.

[7] Ibid., 53.

[8] "Arius," in *The Wycliffe Biographical Dictionary of the Church* (Chicago: Moody Press, 1982), 17.

[9] David K. Lowery, "1 Corinthians," in *The Bible Knowledge Commentary, New Testament Edition* (Wheaton, Ill.: Victor Books, 1983), 543.

[10] Mary Baker Eddy, *Science and Health with Key to the Scriptures* (Boston: Trustees Under the Will of Mary Baker G. Eddy, first published in 1875), 584, 591–593.

[11] Wiersbe, "The Psychology of the Cults," in *What They Believe*, 17.

Made in United States
Troutdale, OR
08/25/2023

12357941R00216